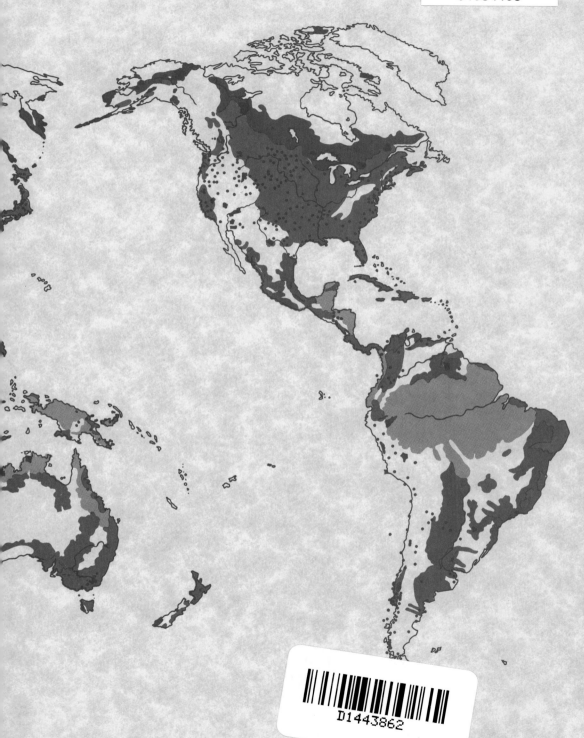

DATE DUE

ONLY ONE WORLD

OUR OWN TO MAKE
AND TO KEEP

GERARD PIEL

For the René Dubos Center

W. H. Freeman and Company
NEW YORK

Only One World: Our Own to Make and to Keep is the first book in The United Nations Publications *Vox populi* series.

The derivation of many of the illustrations from the pages of *Scientific American* is hereby acknowledged.

Library of Congress Cataloging-in-Publication Data

Piel, Gerard.
    Only one world—our own to make and to keep / Gerard Piel.
      p.   cm.
    Includes bibliographical references and index.
    ISBN 0-7167-2316-6
    1. Human ecology. 2. Economic development—social aspects.
  3. Environmental policy. 4. Demographic transition. 5. Basic needs.
  I. Title.
    HM206.P54 1992
    304.2—dc20   92-2867
                                                   CIP

PRINTED IN THE UNITED STATES OF AMERICA

1 2 3 4 5 6 7 8 9 VB 9 9 8 7 6 5 4 3 2

For
Sarah Harfield and Katherine Harfield
Chase Benjamin, Joshua Gerard, and Samuel Harriss

May their century
start a happier millennium

CONTENTS

FOREWORD

In this splendid book, Gerard Piel examines how natural and social systems have interacted to shape the course of human development. Across the broad sweep of history, he unravels some of the complex threads of cause and effect that link human behavior and its environmental consequences, documenting the essentially integrated nature of environment and development. He illustrates his arguments with a profusion of vivid and persuasive detail.

Conclusively, this book demonstrates that business as usual is simply not an option that we can entertain. The quality of future life on Earth will depend to a high degree on the size of the stable world population that is likely to be reached some time in the next century, and on the speed of the demographic transition in the preindustrial world. Key to this transition are the survival of infants and the consequent decline of birth rates. For this as well as for humanitarian reasons, the priority must be the eradication of poverty and the meeting of basic needs of the world's poorest people.

The description of how life has evolved on this Earth, the miracle of human existence, and the impact that the human species has had on the planet in its geologically momentary dominion are all described with a literary ease and elegance that almost disguises the wealth of scientific information that is imparted. Recognizing human development as the prerequisite of sustainable development, Mr. Piel examines basic human needs for food and energy and the capacity of the Earth's systems to provide for those needs.

Free from either environmental doom-mongering or techno-optimism, this book provides a balanced prescription for our sustainable future: a new partnership between the developing and the industrialized worlds. The people of the industrialized world will lead lives that are less resource-consumptive and polluting, and the people of developing countries will receive greater support in their attempts to achieve livelihoods that do not undermine or destroy the environment and the resource base on which their future livelihoods depend. This must entail considerably greater technological and financial assistance to enable the preindustrial countries to overcome their burdens of debt, poverty, and underdevelopment and to make the transition from dependence to interdependence. The key to success here is a quantum leap in the crucial investment in human development: education, training, and the capacity to manage the collective enterprises of industrialization. The special roles and advantages of regional organizations and cooperation are highlighted.

This book is a tour de force. As the founding father of the *Scientific American* we have known since May 1948, its author is the doyen of science writing. But his profound understanding of social systems—the paramount importance of democracy and a judicious balance between the workings of the free market and governmental intervention—and his superb handling of detail and of historical perspective make this much more than a scientific volume, and they add the insight and enlightenment of a truly wise and universal man.

This book will make a timely and invaluable contribution in illuminating the issues to be addressed by the Earth Summit in Rio de Janeiro in June 1992, and it will point the way to the new and more hopeful future that should emerge from Rio as we move toward the twenty-first century.

MAURICE F. STRONG
Secretary-General,
United Nations Conference on Environment and Development

ACKNOWLEDGMENTS

In framing the major theses of this book, I am indebted to René Dubos, Roger Revelle, and Gunnar Myrdal. To René, for his hopeful vision of humankind as steward of nature; to Roger, for his assurance that the forgiving Earth has yet more to give to stewardship; to Gunnar, for his comprehension of the circular, cumulative causation that describes the real world. It was my privilege to know each as my friend, at closer range as his editor, and, attentively, over many years, as his reader.

To authorities, who know more than I about each element in the picture I have attempted to assemble here, I am indebted for critical reading of my manuscript at various stages in its evolution. In alphabetical order, I tender special thanks to Noel Brown, Bernard T. G. Chidzero, Ruth and William Eblen, Pupul Jayakar, Arthur E. Goldschmidt, Genady Golubev, Sergei P. Kapitza, Philip Morrison, Thomas Odhiambo, James A. Perkins, Anthony Piel, David Pimentel, Jane Pratt, Edward Rubin, Harrison Salisbury, James R. Sheffield, Theodore Taylor, and Zhang Zhenbang. I am grateful to Maurice F. Strong for his kind words and for his encouragement to me in this enterprise from its beginning. None of these people are to be held accountable for errors with respect to matters in their purview. The responsibility for what is said here is mine.

To my colleagues at W. H. Freeman and Company, who undertook to get this book to press in time to herald the Earth Summit at Rio de Janeiro, I say thank you: to Linda Chaput, president and editor; to Gunder Hefta, my editor; to Jeremiah Lyons, my publisher; to Philip McCaffrey, ringmaster; to Alison Lew, book designer; to Andrew Kudlacik, electronic compositor; to Janet Hornberger, production director; to Paul Rohloff, production coordinator; to Bill Page, illustration coordinator; and to Karin Agosta, Laura Schalk, Richard Flagg, and others, who helped bring this book to your attention. To Alan Iselin, I am grateful for the artless art of the endpapers and illustrations.

Eleanor Jackson Piel has thought out loud with me and has read every edition of the manuscript; the perfections are hers and the imperfections mine.

25 December 1991
New York City   GERARD PIEL

ONLY ONE WORLD

1

BIOLOGY AND HUMANITY

The present half century has recast the human predicament. Toil and want are no longer necessary conditions of our existence. The industrial revolution that began only four centuries ago has lifted these afflictions from the lives of more than 1 billion of the world population of 5 billion.

These fortunate people are assured the survival of their first infants. Never before has such a large minority of the population had this assurance. It has brought them to demonstrate a capacity unique to human biology: procreation of the species is subject to control by the cerebral cortex. For love of their children and by the simple arithmetic that shows "the fewer, the more for each," these people have brought their fertility under rational restraint. The populations of the industrial countries are universally approaching zero growth.

The possibility that the same future may be within the reach of the rest of humankind who dwell in the preindustrial world—in the "poor," "underdeveloped," or "developing" countries—must now be considered. These people live in the age-old condition of want, not much relieved by their toil. Against high death rates, besetting especially their children under five years of age, they maintain high birth rates. The much bruited explosion of their population accounts for most of the doubling of the world population that has occurred in the present half century.

This population explosion may soon be seen, however, to have been a benign event. It is the consequence not of the fertility of these people but of the lengthening of their life expectancy. This is the consequence, in turn, of the beginning of their industrial revolution. With production of the means of subsistence increasing faster than their population growth, they have begun to experience improvement in their material circumstances. If that improvement can be continued and hastened, if the transformation of their existence by industrial revolution can be secured earlier rather than later, then humankind may bring its increase to a halt at a number that the planetary environment can sustain.

In fact, the rate of world population growth has been declining since 1970. The prospect that the world population may stabilize at some finite number—perhaps double the present number—by the end of the next century is real. That prospect must command the interest of everyone who rejoices in posterity.

People equipped with industrial technology use energy from sources external to their bodies to increase, apparently without limit, the yield that they secure from their resources. Thus, in the present half century, by the input of technology and of electrical energy incorporated in nitrogen fertilizer, they have more than doubled the world output of food. People have doubled the food supply before, of course, to meet earlier doublings of their numbers; they did so by extending the land under cultivation. This time, they multiplied the yield from the land. The principal increases were secured in the industrial countries, but the "green revolution" is spreading the technology worldwide.

With other industrial technologies, the people of the preindustrial countries can bring about the same catalytic reaction between energy and their abundant resources of other kinds. Industrial revolution can ensure, therefore, not only food sufficient to sustain their still growing populations but the rest of what is necessary to secure to them the survival of their first children. Among the necessities taken for granted by people fortunate enough to have their industrial revolutions behind them are potable water, sanitary disposal of their excrement, and a dwelling secure against the weather. The same lucky people know still other necessities: electric light to lengthen the day, retinues of large and small household appliances, personal mobility and the public services of communication and transportation, safety, medical care, and education. All of this comes from the value that these people add by technology to their resources, the same resources that are available in one combination or another in preindustrial countries.

Presently, for lack of industrial technology, the human and physical resources of those countries go underemployed and under-utilized. The plain remedy is transfer of the technology to them from the industrial countries. In fact, the transfer has begun, reaching the people most widely in public-health measures and education. Technology of more substantial kind has been installed in the building of railroads, highways, and port facilities to expedite the export to the industrial world of resources that people in the preindustrial world have not learned to use. Those resources have supplied and fueled the recent enormous expansion of the industrial economies. The technologies for the production of goods to meet the needs of the increasing population of the preindustrial countries and the necessary improvement in their material circumstances have moved more slow-ly. The early installation of these technologies, in time to secure stabilization of the world population at a smaller size in a nearer future, calls for massive transfer of economic assistance in the form, primarily, of the books, the tools, and the machines that embody the technologies.

The prospects for the transfer of such assistance are strongly conditioned by the long-standing relation between the rich and the poor. Ever since the beginning of civilization, people have organized their social institutions to secure the inequitable distribution of goods that were always, until recent times, in short supply. Now the inequity that divides humankind is international; people are inhabitants of rich nations or of poor nations. And the rich go on living at the expense of the poor.

From historic habit, nations make policy and people continue to root their morality in the assumption that there can never be enough to go around. The industrial revolution has confuted that assumption. If people will use industrial technology equitably and wisely, they may at last, in the words of Indira Gandhi, "make this only Earth a fit home for man."

INDUSTRIAL REVOLUTION

The people of Japan have shown best how a poor nation can become rich by industrial revolution. Their island arc has no resources but the people themselves, rainfall, and some arable land. All the rest, energy and raw materials, they must import. With mastery of industrial technology, also imported but now incorporating their own innovation, the Japanese in 1987 transformed their imports to $16,000 of product per capita. After all the value they added by technology—value added by manufacture, in the language of economics—the cost of the imports came to a mere 6 percent of their gross national

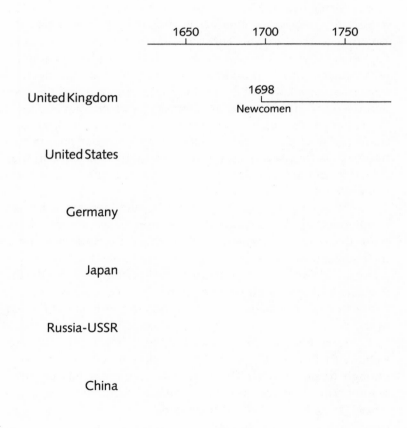

COURSE OF INDUSTRIAL REVOLUTION *run by six nations is plotted from starting to completion dates of at least symbolic kind. British revolution begins in 1700 with Newcomen steam engine and culminates in 1857 electoral reform laws. Bismarck creates the German welfare state in 1887. The U.S. revolution culminates*

product (GNP) of $2400 billion. They more than paid this cost with exports worth 10 percent of their GNP, a dividend from their value-added.

The industrial revolution has happened often enough in different countries under sufficiently different circumstances to suggest that people have begun to learn how to manage it. The prolonged agony of the first industrial revolution has not had to be endured

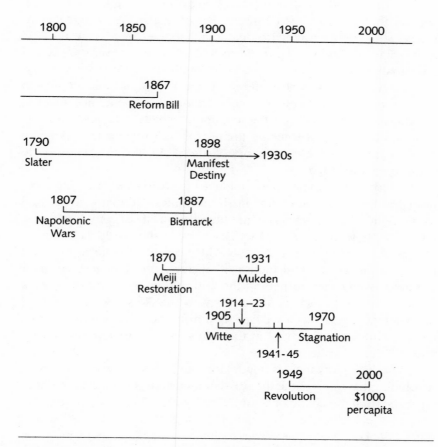

in Spanish-American war in 1898; its welfare state waits for creation by New Deal in 1930s. Japan asserts its industrialization by conquest of Manchuria in 1931. Political revolution and war interrupts the Russia-USSR industrial revolution. China projects $1000-per-capita income in A.D. 2000.

again. The British industrial revolution required no less than 150 years, if it may be dated somewhat arbitrarily from the demonstration of the first practical steam engine by Thomas Newcomen around 1700 to the founding of the welfare state by Benjamin Disraeli around the middle of the nineteenth century. The latter event signified the political arrival of the urban industrial working class and the moral recognition that there was beginning to be enough to go around. Along the way, industrial revolution had to wait on the invention of the first industrial technologies, proceeding as it proceeded.

The second revolution could borrow technology from the first. Samuel Slater, in truth, stole the design of Richard Arkwright's spinning machine to set up the first textile mill in the United States in 1793 at Providence, Rhode Island. From that symbolic event, the second industrial revolution ran its course through the nineteenth century. Considerable investment came in from Britain at midcentury to finance railroad building and to develop the continent's mineral resources. The wealth of the continent, chattel slavery, and the continuous supply of steerage immigrants (35 million from 1865 to 1915) permitted the installation of the U.S. welfare state to be postponed until 1936.

Succeeding revolutions, taking off from an ever enlarging technological base, ran the course in shorter times. Germany, awakened to nationhood by the Napoleonic humiliation of its petty kingdoms, arrived at its welfare state under Bismarck in the 1880s. Japan, from the Meiji restoration in 1870, took 50 years to emerge as a world power in the 1920s. Ridiculed as "imitators," the Japanese set their brightest young men to getting the educations necessary to ransack the accumulated stock of technology in the West. With its feudal order intact, Japan was a welfare state from the start. A mission from the Harvard Medical School in the 1870s found a lower infant-death rate in Tokyo than in Boston.

If due allowance is made for the years of war and social revolution that intervened, the Russian industrial revolution ran about 50 years, from the laying of Count Witte's trans-Siberian railroad at the turn of the century to the economic stagnation of the 1970s that started the collapse of the Soviet regime. The gigantic industrial plant was in full-blast operation, with no market to take away its product. If the Chinese make their deadline of 2000 A.D., they too will have accomplished their industrial revolution in 50 years. By rigorously enforced equality in the distribution of the rising product of their economy, they have already secured many human welfare objectives—including a rapidly declining birth rate—that other nations reached only at much higher incomes.

History attests, therefore, that a 50-year schedule for the industrial revolution of the preindustrial countries is not unreasonable. On that schedule, the revolution will increase individual well-being to a level that assures the survival of their first infants to all people in a world population increasing to 10 billion or less, or not much more. Multiplication of the present world product by four times would meet that objective. By the same multiple, in the present half century, the industrial nations increased their output to bring the first quarter of the world population to stabilize its numbers.

The satisfaction of this logistical requirement does not hang on some breakthrough in fundamental research. The technology is in hand. It is there, on the shelf; it is highly portable and becoming more so every day. Even steelmaking, the most heavy of industries, has acquired mobility. Direct, continuous casting of the solid product from the molten metal, made possible by electronic feedback control, has abolished the economies of gigantism. Ocean transport negates the comparative advantage of the possession of iron ore. Japanese steelmakers have lower raw-material costs than the U.S. steel industry. Any country with a deep harbor can make steel.

The resources are there. Industrial technology defines resources. The Chippewa had no use for the iron ore in the Mesabi Range when they hunted deer over that territory. The Chatanooga shale underlying the Appalachian states holds uranium with more potential energy available to present nuclear fuel cycles than the original supply of coal in that region.

It is now nearly 50 years since the urgency of the worldwide industrial revolution was proclaimed and written into the charter of the United Nations. The industrial nations then undertook to supply technical and economic assistance to the "underdeveloped countries." That promise, renewed on the initiative of the United States in the 1960s, remains unfulfilled. In this same half century, the world population doubled.

Industrial expansion as conducted during these years in the rich nations and rising desperation in the poor nations have now put in doubt the Earth's capacity to yield to the genius of industrial technology and the demands of the rising world population. The fires that generate the soaring output of industrial energy have suddenly begun to perturb the modulation of the Sun's radiation by the global atmosphere, threatening change in climate and sea level with prospectively calamitous consequences to both rich and poor. Fires set by ranchers and planters and by landless people to clear forests in the poor countries amplify this perturbation and lay the further threat of desertification to the existing pattern of world climate. In both the preindustrial and the industrial nations, unloving cultivation of the soil erodes its capacity, and the effluent of both poverty and abundance pollute the water in their different ways. Reduction of the diversity of life on the planet at last compels recognition of the dependence of human life on that diversity.

The human predicament is now defined, therefore, by two questions. It is whether common humanity will heal in time the mutual estrangement in which, for so long, some people have lived rich and most have died poor. At the same time, it is whether the understanding possessed by some few people will bring the rest soon enough to cherish the Earth as the only planet known to harbor life. The two perplexities are one: the Earth cannot long sustain the folly of affluence and the desperation of poverty it knows today.

THE ACCELERATION OF HISTORY

It cannot be said that people have been slow to comprehend the change, four centuries in the making, of their circumstances and prospects. The rate of change has proved, suddenly, to be exponential.

Not only did the doubling of the world population since 1950 bring the largest absolute increase in population, it came also in the shortest doubling time in history. As the doubling population more than doubled the production of food, it also doubled the tonnage of iron above ground and smelted more iron and steel than in all the centuries since the Bronze Age. For this and countless other purposes, people consumed two-thirds of all the coal, oil, and gas they have so far extracted from the Earth and nine-tenths of all the electrical energy they have generated in the 150 years since they mastered the electromagnetic force. Much of the primary fossil-fuel energy went to increase human mobility. More people are traveling farther and faster in all directions over the planet. The average annual distance per capita exceeds 10,000 kilometers—a quarter of the planet's circumference.

At the same time, the species was perfecting its command of the forces of nature and of the Earth's resources with the devices of solid-state electronics. This technology, its essential principles represented in the computer chip, is extending the reach of the human nervous system as the steam engine, in the preceding two centuries, amplified the strength of human muscle. To outer space, the Earth glows in the wavelengths of the electromagnetic spectrum radiated by the communication networks of the collective extended nervous system of humankind.

The ramification of solid-state electronics into every human activity is astonishing because this technology applies a science that, it is said, no one understands. The science of quantum electrodynamics mocks common sense. It suspends cause and effect; it puts the direction of time in question, and it denies the topology of the world within reach of the unaided human sensory apparatus. Yet the equations of quantum theory describe, with precision many places to the right of the decimal point, events out of reach of that apparatus and submit them to human purpose. Since 1950, its daughter technologies have stretched the range of human perception by many orders of magnitude.

The instruments of science now embrace 42 powers of 10, from 10^{25} meters down to 10^{-16} meter. The unimaginable 10^{25} meters make 1 billion light years, the distance that light travels all those years at 300,000 kilometers per second; this is the scale of cosmic megastructures, such as the recently perceived "Great Wall" of galactic clusters that reaches across one stretch of the universe. The incomprehensible 10^{-16} meter is one-trillionth of a micrometer (which is one-thousandth of a millimeter); this is the approximate diameter of an atomic particle. From the two extremes of dimension, observation is converging on the most ancient questions: of creation and of the nature of time and space, of matter and energy.

More consequentially, in the words of the physicist-philosopher Percy Bridgman, the new science has shown that the answers to such question are not to be found inside the human head but only by getting the thinking in there into accordance with what goes on in the world outside. Practice of this art has brought, in this same half century, new understanding in realms of more immediate bearing on human existence: the dynamics of the planet's interior that quakes the ground and moves the continents; the molecular anatomy and physiology of the living cell; the ascent of the human species from a line of tool-making primates.

It is the propensity for making tools that has now brought the entire planet into the custody of the human species. Largely from unanticipated consequences of the exercise of this evolutionary adaptation, people are beginning to learn the dimensions of their sudden new responsibility.

From new acquaintance with other planets in the solar system and better acquaintance with their own, people have come to know that Earth is uniquely enveloped in a biosphere. This is the web of life that interpenetrates and interconnects the air, water, and rock—the atmosphere, hydrosphere, and lithosphere—of the planet. In that web, human beings are discovering their interdependence with all other living things. Further, they are discovering, perhaps not too late, that their vaunted dominion over the Earth has put their existence in peril.

It is the nearly fourfold increase in the annual consumption of fossil fuels since 1950 that perturbs the global exchange of gases among the atmosphere, the hydrosphere, the lithosphere, and the interpenetrating, interconnecting biosphere. Furnaces and internal-combustion engines exhaust into the atmosphere 20 percent as much carbon, in the form of carbon dioxide, as is cycled by the two primary life processes: photosynthesis and respiration. The injection of nitrogen and its compounds into the air, water, and soil from the products of artificial nitrogen fixation, principally to make fertilizers, has increased to equal the turnover of nitrogen by the synthesis and breakdown of protein in living tissue. The contribution of sulfur and phosphorus from human activity exceeds the natural cycles of these elements. From the alimentary tracts of the growing human population and its cattle herds and from thousands of square kilometers of paddy fields comes 10 to 20 percent of the rising concentration of methane in the atmosphere. Entirely novel, manmade gaseous compounds, such as the chlorofluorocarbon refrigerants and spray-can propellants (the now notorious "CFCs"), start up hitherto unknown photochemical cycles of molecular breakdown and synthesis in the atmosphere. In consequence, there is in process an observed thinning of the high-altitude ozone barrier to the ultraviolet and shorter wavelengths of solar radiation.

Local air pollution, regional acid rainfall, apparent global warming, and the "hole" in the ozone layer all testify to the planetary reach of the industrial revolution. Taken together with noxious solid-waste landfills, toxic chemical dumps, the acidification of lakes, the contamination of groundwater, streams, and estuaries, the erosion of the soil on all continents, and the impoverishment of ecosystems invaded by human habitation, these offenses of the present and threats to the future have put "the environment" on the political agenda of every country in the world.

All of this is the price the world has been paying for the good fortune of the 25 percent of the population that lives in the industrial countries. They consume 75 percent of the now so vastly expanded world output of material wealth. For the first time, whole populations of nations are rich.

They are rich in the fundamental sense that, for them, the economic problem defined by Adam's first question after the Fall—"When do we eat?"—is solved. For them, toil is no longer their living and their life. Their work is done by machines in progressively workless economies. In the U.S. economy, the climax to which all are trending, less than 3 percent of the so-called labor force remains engaged in agriculture; less than 30 percent, in the production of goods. Their jobs employ their nervous systems in operating and tending the machines that are turning out goods for this "service economy" in more than twice the annual volume of 1950. All of the rest hold jobs at occupations that employ their nervous systems in relating to other people and to information and ideas rather than to things. From these occupations they are being displaced, however, by the same solid-state electronic devices that employ so many of them.

Technological disemployment has been absorbed up to now in the United States and other industrial countries, by resilient economic and social institutions. Shorter and fewer working days in the year and years of prolonged education and earlier retirement may be counted the principal product of automatic production. In the United States, nearly half of the rising generation goes on to some higher education; such opportunity is opening to the young throughout the industrial world. The value of this time eludes quantification; it is not reckoned in the gross national product. The values beyond economic value to be had from the exercise of human capacity liberated from the compulsions of getting a living defy imaginations presently bound to that task.

THE DEMOGRAPHIC TRANSITION

The change in the human condition in the industrial world is conclusively stated by its vital statistics. People live entire biological
lifetimes; life expectancy everywhere exceeds 70 years. This signifies
death rates fallen to 10 and less per thousand population. Birth rates,
having declined more slowly, now are intersecting death rates at the
same low numbers. Population growth has decelerated to less than 1
percent per annum and is declining throughout the industrial world;
in some countries, it has halted.

This quarter of the world population has made the
"demographic transition." Until 1600, from which the onset of the
industrial revolution may be dated, the life expectancy of the human
species was 25 years. Against high death rates, especially among their
infants, people resolutely maintained high birth rates. Since they lived
barely long enough to reproduce themselves, the growth of the
human population proceeded at a rate very near zero. Now the
population of the industrial world is approaching a population-
growth rate near zero once again, but at low death rates and low birth
rates [see illustration on page 101].

Thus it appears that the human species may escape the ter-
minal misery forecast for it by Thomas Malthus in 1798. His fateful
equation showed population increasing at the geometric rate—the
series 1, 2, 4, 8, 16, and so on—against arithmetic increase—the series
1, 2, 3, 4, 5, and so on—of the means of subsistence. At the fourth
doubling, as can be seen, the population has outgrown by three times
the fourfold increase in production. The propensity for making tools
was already revising the second term of Malthus's equation, however,
at the time he wrote it. In Great Britain, the production of the means
of subsistence was increasing faster than the population. Experience
since then has revised the first term; every population that has
enjoyed increase in the means of subsistence per capita has reduced
its fertility.

The family remains a Malthusian unit: with fewer to feed, there
is more for each. Moreover, children in industrial societies have
negative economic value. The money return on the cost of their
rearing and education rarely goes to the parents. As soon as the
survival of the first infants is assured, parents are ready to make the
intensely private decision to stop having children. In some families
today, wider considerations—of society, of the environment—are

coming into play in these decisions. The sample is large enough to encourage demographers to project a world population arriving at zero growth with the completion of its next doubling, which they have scheduled for the end of the twenty-first century. That doubling—the present doubling—is already proceeding at a slower rate than the last. From its all-time peak, at a little above 2 percent around 1970, the rate of population growth has been declining steadily.

Projection of a world population stabilized at around 10 billion rests, however, upon the assumption that the 75 percent of the world population inhabiting the preindustrial countries will follow the first 25 percent through the demographic transition. That vast majority has had small share in the surge of material abundance that began in 1950. From the doubling of the world output of food, they have had some improvement in their nutrition. Since 1970, however, the nutrition of the poorest has suffered actual decline. In the preindustrial world, the half century has seen the number of people living in misery increase to the largest in all time.

The setting of the existence of most of the world's poor is the traditional village. There are more than 2 million of these villages, with populations on the order of 1000. They are subsistence-farming settlements, with weak economic connection to the world outside. They are traditional in that the way of life there is close to that of the villages settled in the Old World agricultural revolution.

The technology by which most villagers subsist has improved little on the yields and comforts that made life in the first villages 10,000 years ago preferable to the migratory hunting-and-gathering way of life. Depending upon the resources of the local landscape, people dwell in grass, wattle, adobe, or mud huts and houses that they build with craft perfected by the founding ancestors. The villages, even today, retain their self-sufficiency in large part, the villagers fed and sheltered and, often, still clothed by the work of their own hands. There is little division of labor, except between that of men and women.

The poverty of village people is in part relative, by comparison with the new industrial world. It is also absolute, in that population growth in recent years has outrun the capacity of the traditional institutions and technology to sustain their existence.

In rising numbers, landless people in the preindustrial countries are making their way from the village into the new, strange environment of the city. Of the world's seven cities of more than 10 million population in 1980, four were in preindustrial countries; of the 23 cities of that size predicted for the year 2000, 17 will be in those countries [see table on page 293]. No city in the agricultural high civilizations of the past ever exceeded 500,000 in population. Owing primarily to the growth of the cities of the poor, more than half the world population will be urban in the year 2000. In the shantytowns that surround those cities on every continent, half or more of their populations live in shelters they have contrived for themselves. People live in these communities without any of the amenity afforded to the rest of the urban population by the infrastructure and public utilities of the city proper.

Vital statistics give, again, the plainest description of the human condition in the poor countries. The death rate of children under 5 years of age exceeds 100 per 1000 live births each year in the countries of Asia; more than 125 in Latin America; more than 150 in Africa. That compares to under-five mortality rates of 15 or less in the industrial countries. Infant mortality, death at birth, persists at correspondingly high rates in all the preindustrial countries. The uncertainty of the life of infants motivates childbearing at rates two to three times that prevailing in the industrial world. Accidents, complications, and infections attending childbirth become the largest cause of death among females during the childbearing years.

These death rates are the net, however, of considerable decline in all of them since 1950. Installation of the first rudiments of industrial civilization, literacy as well as sanitation and hygiene, has proved to be a potent public-health measure, in the cities especially. It has worked best for those more securely alive, above the age of five years, and brought rapid increase in their numbers, especially in the urban populations. Life expectancy has lengthened by more than a decade since 1950 throughout the preindustrial world: to more than 60 years in Latin America; to nearly 60 years in Asia; to nearly 50 years in Africa. In favor of hope for stabilization of the world population by the end of the twenty-first century, it can be said that the preindustrial world has entered the first phase of the demographic transition—that is, its death rates are falling.

The same statistics add up to population explosion. It was the more-than-doubling of the number of people in the preindustrial countries that doubled the world population. From 1.8 times the population of the industrial countries, the poor have multiplied to 3 times that population. This is the "population bomb." In truth, of course, a newborn in the traditional village lays less burden on the Earth's resources than, for example, an infant born in the United States, where the consumption of primary energy requires combustion of 14 metric tons of coal-equivalent fuels per capita per annum.

Poverty taxes the Earth, however, in its own insidious way. Fuel wood provides what little energy, external to their own metabolism, is available to most of the world's poor, and that means to most of the world population. Some 400 million villagers suffer a fuelwood shortage, a way of saying that they have burned up most or all of the trees, brush, and shrubbery in their countrysides. On the long-since deforested central plateau of India, the fuel is cattle dung. Deforestation proceeds more abruptly where the practice of slash-and-burn agriculture persists. For centuries, this practice of planting in soil fertilized by the ashes of the forest cover and then returning it to forest fallow yielded subsistence at the edges of the world's forests to people on all continents. Under pressure of the growing population, the slash-and-burn cycle now overtakes the regrowth of forest before it has restored the soil.

The straightaway clearing of land for cultivation and pasturage has obliterated most of the tropical dry forest around the world. Invasion of the tropical rain forest by lumbering, mining, ranching, and plantation enterprises, as well as by the landless poor, is destroying 6 to 7.5 million square kilometers of forest by fire each year. The falloff and cessation of the forest-regenerated rainfall and the exhaustion of the fragile soils bring extension of the deserts. In keeping with their share in the world economy, the preindustrial countries are contributing 25 percent of the human species' overload of carbon dioxide on the natural carbon cycle. To the rising anxiety of the industrial world, destruction of the tropical rain forest promises its own exacerbation of the threatened change in the global climate.

The industrial world has, of course, its own complicity in the abuse of resources that now threatens its well-being. That was made clear in 1949 by Arthur Goldschmidt, then chief of the electric power division of the U.S. Department of the Interior and thereafter a principal economic-development officer in the UN Secretariat. In an address to the American Academy of Arts and Sciences, he said: "The areas of the world that have been used merely as sources of raw materials, that have not been taken into partnership in the growth of world civilization through industrial and agricultural balance, are the areas where conservation practice has lagged most lamentably, and where the problems of population pressure upon resources are most evident."

TOOLMAKING AND HUMAN EVOLUTION

Everyone wants a world safer and happier than the present one. That humankind can choose its destiny is a proposition that follows from history—in particular, from the history of the present half century. It can be seen now that history has had a plot: the tool-making species has been making itself. The arrow of its history is the accumulation of objective knowledge. From age to age, as history went on repeating itself, that enterprise has pointed the direction of time. The human species that came to this present can choose the future.

The accumulation of objective knowledge began, the evidence suggests, about 3 million years ago in the Great Rift Valley of southern Africa. Stone tools have been found there in association with the fossil remains of 90-pound primates. At first, this tool-making advantage had to be conveyed to the next generation by genetic inheritance and Darwinian selection of individuals that possessed the constellation of genes for its expanding contribution to survival. Later in our biological evolution came a time when an innovation in toolmaking achieved by one generation could be conveyed to the next by the extragenetic procedure of teaching. The accumulation of objective knowledge then began to acclerate.

Those early toolmakers brought useful physical properties out of their materials by the way they fashioned them into tools. They learned that they could reliably expect to find the same properties demonstrated in another piece of the same material by working it in the same way. From their materials, they got truth as well as tools. This way of knowing is objective, in that different people get the same answer whenever and wherever they put the same question to the same test. It accumulates because each finding excites at least one new question, and the next finding incorporates the last. The accumulation of knowledge accelerates because most findings ask more than one question. The refinement and elaboration of the stone tools—the ones made from the only material that has lasted all this time—give us the primary record of the evolution of the great hemispheres of the brain.

The same record, spread across the African and Eurasian continents, testifies unambiguously to the acquisition of the faculty of speech and the organization of social order, necessarily bound by moral constraint, all before the emergence of *Homo sapiens*. The will and purpose of our forerunners went along with their anatomy and physiology into the making of us. Because their food-gathering and hunting took them into the geologically most active settings—lakeshores, riverbanks, and seacoasts—their bones are scarce. According to the careful estimate of the late Edward S. Deevey, a pioneer of the new science of ecology, some 36 billion of them must have come and gone through the 3000 millennia before *Homo sapiens* appeared in the fossil record. Deevey based that estimate in part on the inventory of stone tools; they are, as he observed, "the most common fossil of the Pleistocene."

The species *Homo sapiens,* born of this prolonged cultural revolution, was a relatively immediate biological success. In the first population explosion upon their appearance less than 3000 centuries ago [see illustration on page 101], people pioneered every frontier on Earth, from the Arctic almost all the way to the Antarctic, all of the continents and tiny islands in the vast Pacific Ocean. "Primitive," as applied to them, must be taken as a narrow term of art. Their speech, known from the few primitive communities not compromised by contact with the modern world, is as complex in grammar and syntax and as semantically rich as any in that outside world. Paintings on cave walls speak across 25,000 years to beholders today. Textiles from 15,000-year-old middens show that there is no primitive weaving. The precision and keenness of these peoples' observation and comprehension of the world around them is suggested by reports from botanists in Amazonia that the Indians there have use—in tools, shelter, clothing, food, drink, narcosis, medicine—for nearly every plant in their territory.

In keeping with the appellation "primitive," however, the life expectancy of these people did not exceed 25 years. They lived just long enough to beget and bear the next generation. At high death and birth rates, the increase in their numbers proceeded on the time scale of geology. According to Deevey, some 30 billion primitive people lived and died before the agricultural revolution that came at the beginning of history, about 100 centuries ago.

Their increasing sophistication in food-gathering and hunting made that revolution inevitable. Its inevitability is evidenced by its happening as an independent event at different times in three different places. Within the same tenth millennium before the present, people domesticated wheat in the "fertile crescent" of Asia Minor, and a different people domesticated rice in the wetlands of the Indochinese peninsula. Somewhat more recently, still other people in Mesoamerica domesticated maize and the potato, along with its nightshade cousins, the pepper and the tomato. In all three centers, the firing of clay made possible the storage of the harvest, and the domestication of animals provided an external source of biological energy as well as animal protein in the diet.

Again, in all three centers, the settling of people in the first villages brought on the same social revolution. In the words of the early nineteenth-century patrician Russian revolutionary Alexander Herzen, "Slavery was the beginning of civilization." The yield from agriculture freed a minority of the population from toil and want. They used their freedom to build cities, create high civilization, and make history. Hotter fire (evidence suggests that fire may be another pre–*Homo sapiens* tool) brought first copper, then iron into use and adorned the holders of power with gold and silver. On the Eurasian continent, the wheel speeded the settlement of ever wider frontiers and the diffusion of the new technologies from the places of their origin. The wheel also harnessed the energy of falling water. The sail, in its turn, harnessed the wind.

It is evident that the accumulation of objective knowledge, embodied in the technologies of civilization, was accelerating through this period of history. Increase in the product from human toil did not proceed fast enough, however, to make a difference in a human lifetime. Increase of the means of subsistence continued to lag behind increase of the population.

Under these circumstances, as succinctly explained by Bertrand de Jouvenel, "one man can gain wealth only by making use of another man's labor. . . . All ancient civilizations rested upon the inexplicit premise that the productivity of labor is constant." That arrangement worked well enough to secure the organization of continental empires around the red-walled forts and forbidden cities of China and India as early as 4000 years ago and, somewhat later, of the more open maritime empires of the Mediterranean basin.

The reduction in the amount of land required to support a family (from 2 to 5 square kilometers for hunting and food-gathering to 2 to 5 hectares under cultivation and pasturage, or a hundredth the land that supported hunter-gatherers) brought on the second population explosion. This was an explosion, however, on the biological time scale. In contrast with the present, ongoing explosion, it was near-zero population growth that proceeded in equilibrium with misery at high birth rates and high death rates. Deevey's calculations suggest that the number of people that ever lived in these 100 centuries was about 25 billion. By 1600, the world population had increased to about 500 million.

There was no doubt now about the biological success of the species. No animal of comparable size had appeared before on Earth in such numbers. In biology, the unit of success is the species; the individual counts only as the bearer of surviving genes. For all but a very few of the human individuals that lived during this stretch of history, life was as it was described by Thomas Hobbes: nasty, brutish, and short.

It is only recently that people have found it possible to aspire to another kind of success. This is a human, moral invention. The unit of success in industrial civilization is the individual, surviving and fulfilling his or her capacity and aspiration.

THE FIRST INDUSTRIAL REVOLUTION

Around 1600, the industrial revolution started in Europe. Why it started in Europe, then a backward peninsula of the Eurasian continent, is a question awaiting sustained investigation. The (by then) ancient civilizations of India and China and the younger Muslim empire, embracing Asia Minor and Africa north of the Sahara, were richer and technically more advanced. Akbar, the great Mogul emperor of India, was in possession of 10 times the wealth of Louis XIV and 40 times that of Elizabeth. European navigators had opened up the New World and circumnavigated the globe, drawn by visions of the wealth of the Indies and Cathay. But, in the century before, sailing the largest ships to put to sea until the age of steam and iron, Chinese navigators mapped the southern sky and went home to the Central Kingdom. Europeans were reaping improved harvests of wheat and had brought maize and the potato, from the New World, under cultivation. But the yield from the paddy fields of the East was higher.

Perhaps it is that European societies, from the times of the Graeco-Roman Mediterranean civilization, were more egalitarian. They had to be; the wine-dark sea made comrades of all who sailed it. Disparities of wealth and income were great, but not as extreme as in the empires of the East. The Acropolis at Athens presented modest splendor compared with that concealed behind red walls in the red forts of the Oriental despots, but it stood there for all to see. Elizabeth could rely on counsellors and captains less servile than Akbar's.

With more equal participation in the wealth and income of society, Europeans had longer life expectancy. The persistence of the individual beyond the age of 25 compelled respect for the individual. In the sixteenth century, Martin Luther had asserted the religious autonomy of the individual. In the seventeenth century, John Locke asserted the individual's political autonomy.

It had become possible, as a practical matter, for society to cherish the individual human being. The sanctity of life displaced the divinity that hedged a king. In history, the industrial and the democratic revolution have come forward together. Where one has preceded the other in more recent times, the other has always followed.

The onset of the industrial revolution was surely tripped by the rising confidence of people in individual human capacity. Copernicus, in 1543, took care to dedicate his sun-centered cosmology to Pope Paul III. Galileo, under house arrest following his condemnation for circulating the Copernican heresy, circumvented the Inquisition with the surreptitious publication, in 1638, of his unification of celestial and terrestrial mechanics. *Probabilitas*—true because susceptible of proof—was taking its place alongside *veritas*—truth revealed. Even before Galileo published, Francis Bacon could declare that this way of knowing held the power of "effecting all things possible." In 1687, Newton completed the unification of celestial and terrestrial mechanics.

Only half in jest, the late Lord Ritchie-Calder, science journalist and Labor peer, argued that the industrial revolution was the outcome of a conspiracy. He observed that the discussions of the Lunar Society, in mid-eighteenth-century Birmingham, went outside technological innovation, strictly defined. The likes of Erasmus Darwin, Matthew Boulton, James Watt, and William Small (who was introduced to the circle by Benjamin Franklin and had been the young Thomas Jefferson's professor of natural philosophy) could not help indulging in speculation on the prospective favorable social consequences of the introduction of steam power into "manufactures."

Traditional social arrangements had begun to serve the new purpose of building the plant and machinery of industrial revolution. In 1802, Humphry Davy, founder of electrochemistry and tutor of

Michael Faraday, was moved to declare: "The unequal division of property and labor, the difference of rank and condition amongst mankind, are the sources of power in civilized life, its moving causes and even its very soul." Investment in manufactures was proving to be an increasingly attractive alternative to expenditure on the ostentation that advertised the unequal division of wealth and income. The possession of wealth acquired new validation as the reward earned by the denial of present gratification, called "saving."

The capital invested in industrial revolution absorbed not alone the savings of those who had, however, but also saving by those who had not. Most of the capital was, in fact, accumulated by involuntary saving. As the Canadian economist B. S. Keirstead observed, "It is not possible to get people on the margin of subsistence to abstain voluntarily." The Enclosure Acts enacted by parliaments of landlords and merchants in eighteenth-century England provided not only pasture to grow wool for the new textile mills but also a work force of displaced, impoverished yeomen willing to accept work in the mills at sufficiently low wages. By the end of the century, the number of offenses against property that earned capital punishment in England increased to more than 200. The world forecast in the deliberations of the Lunar Society had to wait out the world described by Charles Dickens.

During the Irish potato famine in the 1840s, Thomas Malthus was brought, by the logic of his economics, to testify to a royal commission that the country would be better off without one million redundant Irishmen. The economic historian Asa Briggs dates the fission of learning into the arts and sciences to the recoil of the Romantic poets from Carboniferous Capitalism. The industrial revolution has a secret history that scholars have only begun to explore. In official history, the Luddites are derided as opponents of progress. As the economic historian E. P. Thompson showed in *The Making of the English Working Class*, they grasped the single economic weapon in their reach when they broke the looms.

To the accumulation of capital, the new worlds overseas made their own large contribution. The triangular trade in slaves, cotton and sugar, and textiles and rum generated investment capital in Boston and Charleston as well as in London. The despoliation of the princes of India by Robert Clive, denounced so eloquently by Thomas Babington Macaulay, was outdone in the devastation of the village textile economy of that still unhappy country by the steam-powered textile mills of Lancashire. The Treaty of Nanking, ending the Opium War in 1842, exacted the cession of Hong Kong to Britain and opened the ports of Amoy, Canton, Foochow, Ninghsien, and Shanghai to British residence and trade. Concessions in these and other cities of imperial China were granted thereafter to each of the nations that followed Britain into industrial revolution. At Berlin in 1885, the colonial powers parceled out to each other what was left of Africa and conceded portions of the continent to the newly united German nation, giving it, too, the status of empire.

At about this time, Japan's entry on the course of industrial revolution showed that the knack for industrial technology was not confined somehow, by race or culture, to the European peoples. For other non-European peoples, still waiting in line for their turn, Japan's success has another lesson. Japan escaped incorporation in the colonial system that exacted capital contributions from the rest of the world to the industrial revolutions of the West.

The industrial revolution of Russia started later than Japan's. Aborted by war and political revolution, it began again in the 1920s under a different mode of capital accumulation and culminated in time to break the back of Hitler's armies at Stalingrad in February 1943.

THE INDUSTRIAL WORLD ASCENDS

By 1950, the industrial world was in steep ascent from the world of traditional agriculture. Mechanical energy had long since displaced the biological energy of men and women and draft animals. People had ceased to be self-employed in digging their subsistence from the soil. They had moved into the cities and were employed by corporate enterprises using mechanical energy to make and distribute material goods in increasing volume and variety. A secure and comfortable setting had been prepared for their existence by the urban technologies developed in the nineteenth century. They willingly traded the independence of country people for the free time of urban employees. In each industrial country, as increase of production exceeded increase of population, entire populations enjoyed increase in physical well-being.

At the middle of the twentieth century, the third population explosion was completing its European phase. Since 1600, another 15 billion people had come and gone. The European peoples, who had been less than one-tenth of the world population of 500 million in 1600, were one-third of the 1950 population of 2.5 billion, having multiplied nearly 20 times and avalanched into the New World and Oceania. The rest of the world population had meanwhile multiplied by little more than three times.

Death rates had begun to fall steeply in Europe by 1800. Birth rates followed; so much more slowly, however, as to induce harsh measures of population-growth control. According to William L. Langer—the historian of Bismarck's diplomacy who became interested in secret history late in his career—infanticide, by abandonment, played as large a role as abortion in the cities of nineteenth-century Europe and America. The decline in birth rates was already overtaking the decline in death rates in 1950, when contraception in aesthetically acceptable modes became the general practice.

As the unprecedented economic expansion of this half century got under way, the diverse social institutions of the industrial nations were apparently working. Capital for the expansion came easily as a by-product of expanding production. Income distribution, reflecting the need for large numbers of people trained in diverse skills, became more egalitarian than ever before in such large societies. The share in the gross domestic product of people in the top 20 percent income group was less than 10 times the share of the bottom 20 percent in the United States as well as in the Soviet Union.

The majority of the people were not only enjoying increasing physical well-being but enjoying almost as much the anticipation of its further increase—by 50 percent, to 100 percent and more, in constant-value income, in their lifetimes. In the market economies, especially, whole new categories of experience were entering the measure of well-being: prolonged good health as well as longevity; possession of the next novel durable good; education; out-of-door activities; serious "culture" and mass entertainment; ease of communication; travel to distant places, and often a second home; a still more expansive future for the children. People in these societies who did not share fully in the rising abundance remained bound to them by the expectation that they might soon have their share also. Economic growth offset disparity in income because it brought new participants into the celebration. Resources were abundant, and air and water were still widely regarded as free goods.

It was at midcentury that the contrast between the transformed human condition in the industrial world and the traditional poverty of the agricultural-village world first entered political discourse. World War II and the nuclear weapons demonstrated at its end brought the industrial nations to attempt again to secure international political and economic order, in the first instance, among themselves.

In conference at Bretton Woods, New Hampshire, in 1944, they addressed the question of economic order. With the German army still in the field in the Soviet Union and the Japanese in control of the Pacific Archipelago and Southeast Asia, the alliance set the foundations at Bretton Woods for a postwar economic order. It was to be grounded on worldwide freedom of trade. Its keystones were the International Monetary Fund ("the IMF") and the International Bank for Reconstruction and Development ("the World Bank"). The IMF was to keep nations committed to free trade by loans that would tide them over deficits in their balance of trade. The World Bank was to finance the reconstruction of the warring industrial nations, but it was charged also to finance the economic development that would close the gap between the wealth of the industrial countries and the poverty of the rest.

Having failed meanwhile to establish an International Trade Organization, the alliance nations sought, in 1948, to secure the freedom of trade by negotiation of a General Agreement on Tariffs and Trade. Negotiation of that agreement continues under the acronym GATT. It has yet to breach the barriers to trade within the industrial world, and it has not touched the steeper barriers between it and the preindustrial world.

In San Francisco in 1945, with the war in the Pacific still proceeding, the industrial nations sought international political order in the creation of the United Nations. It was to be a peace-keeping forum with an executive Secretariat to give effect to its consensus. In the Security Council of the United Nations, they vowed to settle differences among themselves. In the Economic and Social Council, they promised to develop measures to assist the economic development of the "underdeveloped countries."

That term appears in a resolution adopted by the General Assembly in 1949, sitting then in temporary quarters at Lake Success, New York; Resolution 408(V) called for action to promote the economic development of those countries. They were "countries," not nations, because so much of the territory they occupied came under the jurisdiction of the Trusteeship Council, set up as receiver for the disbanding colonial empires of the industrial nations of Europe. The appellation "underdeveloped" acknowledged a moral compulsion sensed, in the industrial world, that measures should be taken to cure this undesirable condition.

A "Group of Experts" convened by General Assembly Resolution 408(V) estimated that the transfer of technology and capital from the rich countries at the rate of $19 billion per year would see the under-developed countries well on the way through industrial revolution by A.D. 2000. Financing would be supplied in part by the export earnings of the developing countries and low-cost loans from the industrial countries. In addition, the experts calculated, substantial aid in the form of outright gifts of financial and in-kind aid would be required. In the general opinion, economic and technical assistance would bridge the period of capital accumulation. Aid, in particular, would avert the coercion endured by people in the early phase, at least, of all past industrial revolutions. The coercion required to get savings out of a poor society has been likened by the economist J. K. Galbraith to "extracting blood from a stone." In his words, aid is, instead, "the process by which savings are transferred from countries where saving is comparatively unpainful to those where it is very painful."

As one of the measures proposed by Harry S Truman in Point IV of his inaugural address in 1949, aid to the underdeveloped countries found a resonant chord in U.S. public opinion. The vision of a postwar world concerted on the constructive enterprises of peace had not yet yielded to the acceptance of a world divided by the Cold War. On the precedent of the Marshall Plan, then firing up the recovery of Western Europe, the U.S. electorate was ready to help the underdeveloped countries through their industrial revolution.

Members of the world scientific community from every country volunteered their initiative in this great enterprise. With a grasp of technology and concern about resources (if not, at that time, "the environment") and population growth, they were stirred by the urgency of the enterprise. That concern was, incidentally, the emblematic distinction of the scientific culture argued by C. P. Snow in his controversy-setting essay on "the two cultures"; that the protests from the other culture betrayed no awareness of or interest in the human condition supported his minor premise: the humanists were lacking in humanity.

Drawing on the political capital accrued from their service in the war, the scientists equipped the UN with its technical agencies. John Boyd-Orr, a pediatrician who found that medicine could do little for his charges in the slums of Glasgow and had gone into the House of Commons early in the century, led the establishment of the Food and Agriculture Organization (FA0) and was its first director general. The psychiatrist Brock Chisholm brought his understanding of the difference between health and medicine to the constitution of the World Health Organization (WHO). The biologist Julian Huxley and the cosmic-ray physicist Pierre Auger took the lead in inventing the United Nations Educational, Scientific, and Cultural Organization (UNESCO) to bring science and technology, carried by books and teachers, into the village culture. These and the numerous other technical agencies have mobilized tens of thousands of scientists and engineers from every nation in the world for the cause, over the years, and have given the UN a presence in the villages as well as in the capitals of the preindustrial countries.

The consensus of the scientific community was expressed in the Rehovoth Declaration, which issued from an international conference on the role of science in economic development held in that Israeli town in 1960:

> There is no law of nature confining scientific and technological progress to the developed nations of the West. New nations do not have to tread long and tormented paths. They can skip the turbulent phases through which the Western industrial revolutions had to pass. Nor is there any need to pay the price in human suffering which Western man had to undergo across the centuries. . . . New states are more fortunate than were the older industrial countries, in that they have at their disposal both the promise of 20th-century science—and the conscience of 20th-century society.

Almost from the founding of the United Nations, however, the Security Council has occupied the foreground. The pragmatic UN charter recognized that effective international action on the world's besetting problems would require concert among the industrial world powers, especially between the two superpowers. In the absence of concert, it has been the work of the United Nations, voicing world anxiety in resolutions of the General Assembly, to keep the superpowers talking in the Security Council and in interminable rounds of arms control negotiations. The Economic and Social Council has meanwhile continued to hold out the promise not yet kept. As for the

Trusteeship Council, its jurisdiction has retreated to small fragments of the former world empires and to the shores of a few tiny Pacific islands that came under U.S. occupation in World War II.

THE PREINDUSTRIAL WORLD ARRIVES

In little more than a decade, the European colonies had taken seats in the General Assembly as sovereign states. The membership multiplied from the founding 51 to 159 by 1990. In the Assembly, the new states have agitated their right to the economic and technical assistance that twentieth-century society is supposed to have had on its conscience. They have been compelled to agitate there also for fairer terms of trade on their exports and imports than that conscience affords them.

The little that they have got by way of economic and technical assistance through UN agencies is the best that they have got. Flows in those channels have averaged less than 15 percent of the total flow of assistance and investment from the industrial to the traditional world. The multilateral flows have brought, however, the largest and longest-term boost toward economic development and promise still more. They have brought, to begin with, industrial technology in its most portable forms: teachers, books, sanitation, and medicine. If, in some countries, there has been little other progress to report, almost all have seen increase in their human capital. That is measured by the spread of literacy and by decline in death and birth rates.

Aerial photographic surveys at the instance of the UN Development Program (UNDP) have equipped nation after nation with detailed topographic maps such as the United States required more than a century to secure (from the Lewis and Clark expedition to the complete set of 10-foot-contour-interval, 1:24,000-scale maps published by the U.S. Geological Survey). The technologies of aerial prospecting have similarly inventoried soil, forest, and mineral resources, adding 40 million acres to the forest reserves of Mexico, for example, and locating a lode of 10 billion tons of 60 percent iron ore in Chile. Even as military rampage disrupted the social order and landscape of Cambodia, Laos, and Vietnam, preliminary mapping and drilling prepared the Mekong Valley for the rational management of the floods of its great river. The tilapia—Peter's fish in the Sea of Galilee—now supplies much needed protein from aquaculture ponds on every continent. Fossil water of Pleistocene vintage from aquifers under the Sahara and the Arabian Peninsula irrigates new farmlands there (at least for as long as those nonrecharging aquifers hold out). Smallpox has been eradicated, and a start has been made on controlling the parasitic diseases that interdict agricultural development and ravage so many lives in the river valleys of Africa and Asia.

Especially as the Cold War set in, governments of the industrial states preferred to by-pass the multilateral channels and to extend economic assistance directly to recipients of their own choosing. The much larger bilateral flows have been going in big lumps to projects with high political or military motivation in the satellites of the superpowers and the former colonies of the European industrial countries. Where the outlays have been large enough (as in U.S. economic and military assistance to Taiwan and South Korea) and the circumstances favorable enough (as with Japanese commercial investment in those two countries), they have ignited actual economic development. Most of the time, however, no matter how big the expenditure, the effect on development has been nugatory or negative (as in Egypt, by the Soviet Union and the United States in turn). Popular disillusion from such experience with economic assistance—and official disappointment, just as often, in what it bought politically—has put "foreign aid" at the bottom of the priority list in the politics of the United States and most other industrial countries.

Starting as a trickle and then surpassing government outlays, investment by transnational corporations and lending by banks have established the closest economic links between the industrial and traditional worlds. The flow of private funds has been even more narrowly directed, however, than the flow of official funds. More than 60 percent went to six preindustrial economies—Argentina, Brazil, Mexico, South Korea, Malaysia, and Singapore—with less than 10 percent of the population of the preindustrial world. Yet the little that was shared by the rest—the less than 40 percent that went to the countries with more than 90 percent of that population—established their closest links to the world economy as well.

The transnational corporations, another innovation of the present half century, constitute an entirely new kind of world-bestriding sovereignty. Only four preindustrial economies had a gross national product (GNP) in 1985 larger than the turnover of the biggest transnational that year (see table on page 247). One-third of the 159 members of the United Nations in 1989 were smaller, by that comparison, than the smallest of the 350 largest transnationals.

Investments by transnational corporations have tended to run between the "home" country of their domicile and its former colonies and from the United States to Latin America and the Philippines. Their plantations, mines, and branch plants typically do a third or more of their host country's production but employ less than 5 percent of the local labor force. Beyond the jobs their presence generates in the cities, they have exerted small secondary developmental effect. They conduct more than a third of the trade between the two worlds. Nearly half of that goes as internal transactions in the privacy of the companies' books. As will be seen at closer range in Chapter 6, the economic links they establish attach enclaves of affluence in the cities of the poor nations more closely to the corporate home countries than to the hinterlands of their own countries.

Bank loans mounted to a flood in the late 1970s. The banks in the oil-importing countries, especially in the United States, had to find someplace to put the petrodollars deposited with them by the oil exporters. In Latin America, they found ready borrowers. According to a World Bank study, however, the inflow of this credit to that continent was just about offset by flight of private capital to havens in the United States and Europe.

The surge in demand on the world's resources in the industrial countries has given the principal thrust to the economic growth, if not to the economic development, of the underdeveloped countries over these years. During the 1950s and 1960s, the preindustrial world grew at an even faster rate, at a higher percentage from its smaller base, than the industrial world. It did so in the face of steady decline in the prices of its commodity exports—except for petroleum in the corner briefly held by the Organization of Petroleum Exporting Countries (OPEC)—and the inexorable rise in the prices of its manufactured imports. With decline in the rate of growth of the industrial economies beginning around 1975, all but a few of the preindustrial countries lost headway and the poorest have suffered actual decline in their gross domestic product. The bank loans and the austerity measures urged and pressed upon them by their creditors now stifle halting measures of recovery.

The present half century has seen, therefore, not the narrowing of the gap between the rich nations and the poor expected at the founding of the United Nations but the widening of that gap. This ominous development can be measured quantitatively in the increasing volume per capita of the gross planetary product going to the people of the rich nations. It can be seen in the immeasurable qualitative difference in the circumstances and expectation of life between the peoples of the rich nations and those of the poor nations. It has cruel expression in the weakness of the ties between the two worlds, which the current stagnation of the world economy has weakened even more.

As with Thomas Malthus's redundant Irishmen, the industrial world could get on quite comfortably without the rest. Except for petroleum, which it will have to learn to do without when the petroleum is gone, the industrial world has substitutes for everything it imports from the preindustrial world. The substitutes—polyethelene fiber in place of jute, for example—give it the ultimate bargaining chip in negotiating terms of trade with the poor nations. Weak as they are, the ties that exist lock the parties in an interdependence that is inimical to the economic interests of both.

In 1976, as president of the World Bank, Robert S. McNamara had to confront the failure of the "international community to assist [the preindustrial countries] in the development task." In his report to the board of governors, he deplored a world inhabited by "severely deprived human beings struggling to survive in a set of squalid and degraded circumstances almost beyond the power of our sophisticated imaginations and privileged circumstances to conceive."

In their unhappy mutual embrace, the rich and poor nations have been doing injury to the biosphere. Inequity within and between nations has now placed that glorious system in jeopardy. Increase in the concentration of carbon dioxide in the atmosphere may have been detected in time for the rich nations to develop alternatives to fossil fuels—including even, possibly, the more efficient use of energy, which seems the least expensive alternative. Without alternative means of subsistence, however, landless families will continue to invade the tropical rain forests with axe and fire. There might not be enough time for a technological or other fix. Nature does not always proceed on smooth trend lines. The global warming trend (if indeed there proves to be one) need not lie upon the line plotted by the measured increase of the concentration of carbon dioxide in the atmosphere. As earthquakes and hurricanes demonstrate, proceedings in nature run to surprise and catastrophe as well.

The first protests and warnings from nature have served to remind rich nations and poor that they share the same planet. At the UN Conference on the Human Environment at Stockholm in 1972, spokesmen for the poor nations were inclined at first to denounce the whole proceeding as a rich-nation subterfuge: they were being told to forgo development that might disturb the environment for the rich. The location of the headquarters of the UN Environment Program in Nairobi and the enlistment of the intellectual leadership of the poor countries in the cause of environmental protection has now turned the argument around. The report of the World Commission on Environment and Development to the UN General Assembly in October 1989 has set the agenda for a second UN conference on the environment, this time on environment and development. The UN Conference on Environment and Development (UNCED), to convene in Rio de Janeiro in June 1992, will explore, for wider public understanding, the fusion of the two realms of concern—for nature and for humanity.

Public opinion in the rich countries has understandably been readier to respond to environmental concerns; in the United States, the Superfund toxic-waste dump is just down the road at the right. In facing threats to the environment on the global scale, at least, people in the rich countries will now be compelled to face the corresponding issues of economic development. A global perspective on their own life ways may encourage them also to face the cost to their fellow human beings, as well as to the environment, of the industrial world's extravagance in energy consumption and in the manufacture of solid waste. Development might then begin to climb from its low point on the priority scale toward the place occupied by environment, even in the domestic politics of the United States.

ECONOMIC COMPULSION FOR ECONOMIC ASSISTANCE

There is now to be entertained, in fact, the prospect that economic compulsion in the coming decade may bring the industrial nations together in concerted economic and technical assistance to the under-developed nations on a scale approaching the need. The prospect is brought into view by the sudden collapse of the centralized political regimes in Eastern Europe. The Cold War has come therewith to an equally abrupt end. With concert among the industrial world powers—recognized in the pragmatic UN Charter as the essential precondition—the enormous technical competence of humankind may be mobilized to accelerate industrial revolution in the prein-dustrial world.

The magnitude of the enterprise has grown, of course, over the decades lost to the Cold War. What the Group of Experts estimated at $19 billion a year in 1951 must now be reckoned at least one order of magnitude larger, at $100 billion and more. That reckoning is made easier by comparison with the $1000 billion the industrial nations have been spending each year on their arms race. The economic compulsions that have, on both sides, spurred the arms race remain. They will find happier satisfaction for all concerned in promoting economic development.

The Communist regime in the Soviet Union had long outlasted its success in the accumulation of capital. By 1980, the Soviet Union and the nations in its Comecon economic union were generating 24 percent of the world's total value added by manufacture (MVA, or value-added)—compared with the 27 percent share of the Western European countries, the 21 percent share of the United States, and Japan's 10 percent. Moreover, they had increased their share by 60 percent since 1963 (see illustration on facing page). The Comecon bloc could be said to be as fully industrialized as the West. In 1984, the Soviet Union produced 154 million tons of steel—more, by 70 million tons, than the output that year in the United States. Its total industrial output was second only to that of the United States. As closer acquaintance has recently shown, however, the industrial installation in the Soviet Union and Eastern Europe presents a mixed picture, many of the plants being obsolete and few of them respectful of environmental concerns.

The Communist regimes were embarrassingly incapable of securing to their peoples the benefits of their success in industrial revolution. Imaginations, such as they were, in the industrial ministries in Moscow and the other Comecon capitals could not begin to conjure up the nooks and crannies in consumer preferences and in intermediate manufacture and distribution into which market processes would naturally carry the country's now ample supplies of primary materials. This was their economic compulsion for the manufacture of armaments.

Nor did the Soviet Union succeed in getting food to the country's households. Soviet agriculture was set back decades by the extermination of the peasantry in the 1930s and then by the pseudo-science of Stalin's agricultural wizard, Trofim Lysenko. By a kind of misplaced concreteness, tractors dominated Soviet farm policy; genetics and fertilizer came late to its field-crop lands. Yet those lands

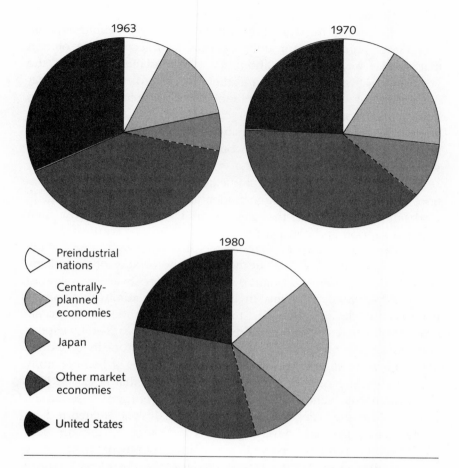

PROGRESS IN INDUSTRIALIZATION *from 1963 to 1980 increased the share of pre-industrial countries in world MVA (manufacturing value-added) from 8 to 14 percent and share of centrally planned economies from 15 to 23 percent. As world MVA more than doubled, share of industrial market economies shrank to 63 percent.*

were producing more wheat than the United States in the 1980s. It was the loss of product between field and market that compelled the Soviet Union to import wheat from the United States.

After growing at annual rates approaching 10 percent through the first decades after World War II, the Soviet economy wallowed into the doldrums in the mid-1970s.

In carrying through the country's industrial revolution, the
Communist regime had proudly sponsored an accessory revolution
that was bound to bring about its own downfall. It cured the
population's historic illiteracy and then proceeded to bring a higher
percentage of the rising generations through secondary and into
higher education than any other country but the United States. A
higher percentage of its university graduates have scientific and
technical educations. Men and women who have learned that—as
was said best by Gunnar Myrdal, a social scientist—"Facts kick!" have
acquired habits of mind resistant to external authority. A new generation was ready to take charge under the leadership of Mikhail S.
Gorbachev. Thereupon, the regimes in Eastern Europe lost their
external support and collapsed.

These developments have come at a propitious time for the
other party to the Cold War. In the 1970s, the capture of the pricing
of petroleum by OPEC brought the prolonged postwar expansion of
the world economy to a halt. In 1973, the Nixon administration was
compelled to devalue the dollar that had underpinned the economic
order established at Bretton Woods. The United States thereby capitu-
lated to an ascendant Japan and an emerging European economic
community the sharing, on not yet resolved terms, of its hegemony
over the world economy. Now the "rearmament" that began in 1980
has brought insolvency to the current accounts of the U.S. economy,
redressed by the sale of assets. The Federal deficits incurred by
military procurement have sustained a sluggish growth and
moderated recurring recession, in accordance with the prescription of
J. M. Keynes. The world's largest creditor has become its largest
debtor.

The manufacturing output of the United States, stimulated by
military procurement and including it, has increased by 64 percent
over 1970. Increasingly workless technology has created no net new
blue-collar jobs, however, and no more than a million new white-collar jobs in industry. Blue-collar jobs have been lost to the U.S. labor
force also with the farming out of work by transnational corporations
to low-paid workers in the preindustrial countries. The unemployment throttle for noninflationary growth has been raised to 5 percent
and above despite the creation, since 1970, of some 30 million new
jobs.

The trouble is that 23 million of the new jobs are in the
category that the manpower-economist Eli Ginsberg calls "lousy"—

that is, low-paying, nontenure, high-turnover jobs in the consumer-service industries, at least two of which are needed to keep a household above the poverty line (see illustration on page 36). During 1991, the average income of the U.S. household, discounted by inflation, climbed from its level in 1972 to its level in 1973. In consequence, the percentage of the population seeking jobs is much larger than in years past.

Distribution of wealth and income has become correspondingly less equitable in the United States. From 5.4 percent in 1970, the share in the country's total household income of the bottom 20 percent income group—including income transfers—declined by 24 percent to 4.2 percent in 1986. Those percentiles, along with contributions from the two 20 percent income groups above, went to push the share of the top 20 percent from 40.9 to 46.1 percent of the total household income.

Statistics of this kind produce statistics of another kind: in the incidence of crimes of violence in the population; in the drug epidemic (crack cocaine is the fastest way out of Harlem, as gin was from nineteenth-century Birmingham); in the sudden ubiquity of beggars and homeless people. Toward a deepening of such social pathology in the future, 25 percent of the children under 18 are growing up in poverty, most of them in single-parent (female) households. The *de*-redistribution of wealth has been carried further in the decay of the public-sector infrastructure, all the way from public services (such as education) in the central cities to potholes in the interstate highways.

Along with domestic public works, a substantial commitment to outlays for economic development overseas commends itself as alternative to the military budget in maintaining the public deficit that sustains consumption. Most of the expenditure would, like military-procurement outlays, stay in the domestic economy. Abroad, the expenditure would create markets for the country's exports. Spent in domestic "peacetime" industries, the money would generate half again as much direct employment, none of it in the "lousy" category. Along with its countercyclical effect, Federal deficit incurred by domestic and overseas development expenditures would reverse the increase in the disparity among U.S. income groups.

Such a commitment, grounded on the same economic compulsion, was commended to the industrial nations by Eduard Schevardnadze, then foreign minister of the Soviet Union. In October

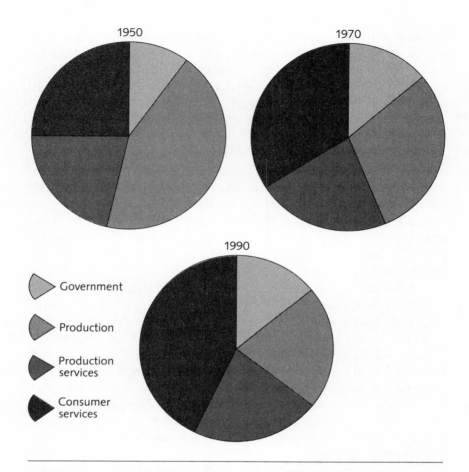

STRUCTURE OF U.S. LABOR FORCE, *from 1950 to 1990, shows effect of mechaniza-*
tion on blue-collar production jobs and recent export of those jobs to low-wage
countries. Nearly half of labor force now finds jobs in lower-paid consumer ser-
vices. Jobs in the services are also being mechanized by computers and
peripheral gear.

1989, to the Foreign Policy Association in New York City, he declared:

> Right before our eyes, the world is sliding into a deep depres-
> sion. The debt of the Third World countries, the interest they
> have to pay and the pace of their economic development—are
> these not signs of an impending catastrophe? . . . Radical, bold

steps are needed, a kind of New Deal, a transition to a policy that would draw the developing countries into the scientific, technological, and information revolution.

The proposal excited no great response from the United States under the administration of Ronald Reagan. Each of the industrial countries has its own economic and political compulsions in favor of such an enterprise, however, analogous to those welling up in the United States. In England, France, and Germany, those compulsions are already framing measures for assisting the countries of Eastern Europe through their uncertain reconstruction as market economies.

To consider whether and how the planet can accommodate a population of 10 billion in such comfort and security as to incline people to halt its growth has become more than a sentimental or academic exercise. Some hard questions are now really worth asking. Contemplation of what appears be a future favored by the economics and politics of the international community compels their asking. Antecedent questions about the feasibilty of this Faustian vision must be met before people can commit themselves to working for it. Whether that future can be chosen is a question antecedent to the choosing of it.

To Welcome 5 Billion More

No one, in 1950, planned for the requirements of a population doubling to 5 billion today. The present doubling to 10 billion involves larger absolute numbers. To welcome 5 billion more people between now and A.D. 2100 into the already threatened biosphere calls for estimating if not planning. The requirements of a population of 10 billion may be estimated from what is needed now to sustain a population of 5 billion.

Assuming that thirst will be met by adequate supplies of potable water—most of the world's households are still a kilometer or more distant from their water sources—the first need is food. The late Roger Revelle, who started the measurement of atmospheric carbon dioxide that grounds concern about world climate change, once undertook the necessary estimating. For this service, Revelle, an oceanographer, was prepared by field experience in the salt-poisoned farmland of Pakistan and by his direction of population studies at Harvard University.

Revelle began with the annual consumption by the world's present population of 2.8 billion metric tons of plant tissue—as food or, indirectly, as animal feed. That includes 0.4 billion tons of waste and supplies about half a ton per capita for consumption, supporting the world average intake of 2600 kilocalories (colloquially referred to as "calories") per capita per day. The one-quarter of the population in the industrial countries eats 1 billion tons, more than one-third, of the net after waste. That gives them 800 kilograms per capita per year, which yields 10,000 kilocalories per capita per day in primary plant tissue. They feed 0.7 billion tons, two-thirds of it, to animals first to derive more than 1000 kilocalories per day in the protein of meat, dairy, and poultry products. The rest of their average 3000 kilocalories per day they get direct from the balance of 0.3 billion tons left over in primary plant tissue.

The other three-quarters of the world population gets by on the 1.4 billion tons of the net after waste. This gives them about 370 kilograms per capita, or an average 4600 kilocalories per day in primary plant tissue. They get most of their calories direct from that tissue, consuming 0.9 billion tons of cereals. They feed the balance of 0.5 billion tons to animals and get about 200 kilocalories per day in protein. Maldistribution of this barely adequate supply of food presses a population of 1 billion, mostly children, below the adequate-nutrition line.

To put the 10 billion population in A.D. 2100 on the rich world's diet would require 10 billion tons of primary plant tissue per year. This might afflict everyone, however, with the ills the rich world attributes to its excessive intake of animal tissue. Adjusting the protein intake downward to 700 kilocalories per day, Revelle calculated that the population of 10 billion would do well on 7.3 billion tons of primary plant tissue per year, with no malnutrition. On yields from established technology applied to the world's farmland, Revelle found the carrying capacity to be 2.5 times that requirement.

No change in world climate, such as might result from increase in the concentration of carbon dioxide in the atmosphere, was reckoned in these calculations. "Established technology," furthermore, implied measures to reduce soil erosion, presently the most serious threat to the long-term food supply. To eliminate the malnutrition that afflicts people everywhere will require fairer distribution than at present. The international distribution system must be responsive, as well, to the vagaries of weather and crop yields, if famines, such as those that afflicted Africa in the 1980s, are to be averted.

The next need is for energy, including the inputs required by agricultural technology to multiply the yield from solar energy. The U.S. consumer enjoys energy equivalent to the burning of 14 tons of coal per year. Multiplied by 10 billion people, that standard of energy consumption would, if supplied by coal alone, be 42 times present coal production and would put a 50-year horizon on world coal reserves. The corresponding input of carbon dioxide into the atmosphere would, doubtless, also serve as the conclusive experiment in climate change.

The rest of the industrial world gets along very well on the coal-equivalent energy of 5 tons per capita. To put 10 billion people on that standard would require a fivefold increase in the world's present output of energy from all sources. That more modest standard would also multiply by five the mechanical energy available to people in the poor countries; not many have any mechanical energy available to them today.

This requirement lays a more manageable demand on fossil-fuel reserves. Most of the 50 billion tons of coal-equivalence must be met, however, from primary sources other than fossil fuels; the biosphere could not survive such increase of the injection of carbon dioxide into the atmosphere. Alternative sources of primary energy in the necessary abundance are there, as will be seen in Chapter 4. It is a question for technology, and it may be the biggest one there is.

To put technology to work takes materials. This is still the Iron Age. Even the U.S. economy continues to produce some 80 million tons of steel each year. What counts increasingly in steel production is the tonnage of iron above ground. Except for a momentary rise in the consumption of new iron ore occasioned by the favored basic oxygen process, the steel economy is approaching steady-state recycling of its scrap. The United States has 5 billion tons of iron above ground, 20 tons per capita. The rest of the industrial world has 10 tons per capita. To bring a population of 10 billion to the 10-ton standard will require a fivefold increase in the world's present above-ground total. A doubling, over the course of the next century, of the world iron-ore reduction capacity of 750 million tons would meet that need and would sustain the recycling of the iron above ground to meet demand.

Is there iron in the ground? If there is not enough ore containing 60 percent iron oxide, there is 10 times as much ore with 10 percent less iron oxide. It is then a question of energy again.

Something more than a Domesday Book census of the population and inventory of resources is required. Resources are not static but are a variable function of technology. The biosphere is a dynamic, evolving system. Human activities must be seen as one set of variables in that system. They change it, not always for the bad. Thus, people may enlarge the reach of the biosphere into the lithosphere by improving the extraction of iron. They are on the verge of bringing more energy into the biosphere from outside its own store of fossil fuel.

For the long term, into the next century and the centuries beyond, the human population must organize its activities to secure what one study has called "sustainable development of the biosphere." That 1987 study came, appropriately enough, from a joint venture of U.S. and Soviet academicians established in the Cold War detente of the late 1960s and early 1970s. At the International Institute for Applied Systems Analysis at Laxenburg, Austria, all through the more recent freeze-down, scientists from around the world have been learning to put the power of mathematical analysis, so hugely amplified by electronic computation, to work on questions neglected hitherto because their scope and time-scale put them out of reach of intellectual enterprise.

As people comprehend the ways in which their activities degrade the biosphere, they are learning, at the same time, how to direct their efforts to its development. They may yet make real the vision of V. I. Vernadsky, the Russian naturalist of the early years of this century, who first conceived the notion of the biosphere. He saw the biosphere interpenetrated with what he called the noosphere. The root *noos,* like *bios,* is from ancient Greek; it signifies "mind" or "thought." In Vernadsky's vision, the human presence, generated and sustained by the biosphere, would sustain the biosphere in turn.

It is too early in history to celebrate that event. The unequal division of labor and property, so pragmatically celebrated by Humphry Davy, now puts the biosphere in peril. It has also outlived what contribution it can make to securing people's comfort and safety. The human condition, in which only a quarter of the population has been relieved of toil and want, cannot long endure. The liberation must proceed to its completion, if the biosphere is to sustain the human presence.

What has principally made the difference between the rich and the poor nations is the availability of mechanical energy. The wider availability of mechanical energy is the equally principal requirement to be met if that difference is to be narrowed. During the present half century, the generation of energy from fossil fuels has overtaken agriculture as the hugest human perturbation of the biosphere. Whether favored by the discount rate or not, highest priority must be given to development of alternative energy technologies. The best alternative—to spread solar-energy collectors in imitation of the green leaves that power the biosphere—appears to be also the most feasible technically. This would constitute the supreme demonstration of sustainable development of the biosphere.

The founding technology of civilization is agriculture. By its extension into the planet's forest cover—clearing away an estimated half of the original cover—by draining the wetlands, and by irrigating the arid lands, this technology fostered the growth of the population to 2.5 billion by 1950. The doubling of the population since then was supported not by an increase in the land under cultivation but by an increase in the yield from the land. Intensive cultivation, based upon understanding of plant physiology, has more than doubled the world average yield per hectare. Henceforth, this is the only way the food supply can be increased.

On land under cultivation by the best practice of modern agricultural technology, the yield is five times the average. A population larger than predicted by any Malthusian nightmare—the 25 billion, for example, of the Revelle carrying capacity—could be fed. The new agricultural technology is extravagant of energy, multiplying the input per hectare many times over the expenditure of biological energy by which traditional agriculture secured its yields. The harsh impact of this input on the ecology of the soils must be ameliorated soon, if there is to be long-term development of the biosphere.

Where and how people live is, tautologically, what makes life worth living. The city dwellers of Western industrial civilization brought with them to the city their memory of the past. That is set out most eloquently in the words of the economic historian R. H. Tawney: "Whatever the future may contain, the past has shown no more excellent social order than that in which the mass of the people were masters of the holdings which they plowed and of the tools with which they worked and could boast: 'It is a quietness in a man's mind to live upon his own and know his heir certain.'"

After the end of World War II, Americans abandoned the city for the suburbs in larger numbers from year to year, and now they are leaving the suburbs for the exurbs. The prospect of 10 billion dwellers in single-family detached houses spread out on the world landscape conjures up a pollution more irreversible than the perturbation of the biosphere by fossil-fuel gases. It may be that landless refugees fleeing the overcrowded countryside of the poor world, with hope and a vision of the future and no regrets about the past, have a better approach to the urban existence to which the world population is committed.

Development of the biosphere implies concurrent human development. The industrial revolution is a social revolution. It has tranformed human existence: the self-employed, self-sufficient village farmer has become the urban employee engaged in intricately organized corporate enterprise. The ongoing revolution now invites less than the full human capacity of most of the people engaged. The industrial economy produces its abundance employing fewer and fewer members of the population. Technology has disengaged production from work. No industrial economy has found its way through the ensuing crisis in values.

The old values are embedded and expressed in the concern to keep people employed. The concern, however, is not to get things produced but to get them consumed. How to disengage consumption from work? As things now stand, people must have jobs, even in a workless economy, if they are to qualify as consumers.

The most superficial survey of the built and the natural environment of the wealthiest country in the world shows that a great deal of work goes undone. What is more, work that contributes most to society and its future—the advancement of human understanding and the education of the next generation—goes underpaid. The work that goes undone and underpaid requires political, not market, demand to get it done and properly rewarded. New values, yet to be evolved and incorporated in the political and economic process, must validate and motivate this work for the enrichment of industrial society beyond its material abundance.

Whatever the distress suffered by the fortunate 25 percent who face this value crisis, there is no discouraging the 75 percent now in poverty from wanting to face, if necessary, the same dilemmas. Industrial revolution, having happened more than once, has been rehearsed often enough to make its next enactments less cruel and costly. By economic assistance from the rich nations, an experiment yet to be tried, it may be possible to spare the 3.75 billion living poor, their children, and their grandchildren—a prospective total of 10 billion people—the coercion endured by those who preceded them into industrial revolution.

To secure the environment and the necessary development will require moral revolutions. The exploiter of nature must become steward; the exploiter of man must join the human family. The interest rate must incorporate an inverse discount on investment that averts irreversible consequences flowing 50 years hence from the short-term choice, made today. Goods of necessity for which demand is finite, even at 10 billion population, can be had from the Earth's resources. Satisfaction in reward of other kinds must displace the hankering after goods of status for which demand is infinite.

An extended future for the human species demands the will and action of people of good will. Good purposes and policy are essential, but it takes the cherished individual to realize them. Individuals owe it to the world to try. Individuals who have done and are doing so today in rising numbers give confidence to the hope for the necessary moral revolutions [see "Nongovernmental Organizations and Private Voluntary Organizatiions," page 347].

That there were real people there all the time in the Soviet Union and Eastern Europe, those people themselves triumphantly demonstrated in the tumultuous years of l989, 1990, and 1991. In the West as well, individuals have been giving a good account of themselves. The concern for the environment that brought the establishment of environmental-protection agencies in every Western industrial country did not originate in political and industrial bureaucracies. Less celebrated are the thousands of individuals who have found ways, from where they live and with what they have, to make contributions to economic development.

The moral compulsions of scarcity are inverted by the obsolescence of toil and want. One individual cannot profit today at the expense of others; the amenity of that one individual is diminished by the impoverishment of the community (as de-redistribution of income has recently impoverished the United States). The individual can profit now only by enrichment of the community. That is work that can engage the will and energy of everyone.

2

THE BIOSPHERE

The solid-state electronic navigators have now visited all but one of the eight other planets that orbit the Sun. Nearer to the solar inferno, the other terrestrial planets wear the same barren landscape as the Moon on which men have stood. Craters, cratered by craters, testify to the freezing of planetary cores a billion years ago. Out beyond the orbit of Mars, four cold midget stars, the great Jovian planets, reflect the light of the now distant Sun, still hot enough to stir slow, age-long storms in their gassy depths. There is no sign of life out there.

At the face of the Earth, 90 million miles away, the Sun beams radiant energy with a power of 173 trillion watts, and a solar wind blusters high energy particles. Life as we know it on Earth today could not exist in the glare of this star were it not for the presence of life on this planet. Living organisms themselves established and today maintain on this one planet the physical conditions in which the energy of sunlight is transformed to the energy of life.

High in the blue sky that distinguishes the Earth, molecules of oxygen and ozone absorb and scatter the ultraviolet and shorter wavelengths of solar radiation that are inimical to life. Lower in the atmosphere, carbon dioxide and a couple of other trace gases modulate the reradiation from the Earth of the solar radiation, but on wavelengths on the long-wave side of the visible spectrum. This "greenhouse effect" keeps the surface temperature within the narrow range in which water occupies the liquid state [see illustration on pages 52 and 53]. In its thin outer reaches and in its denser inner

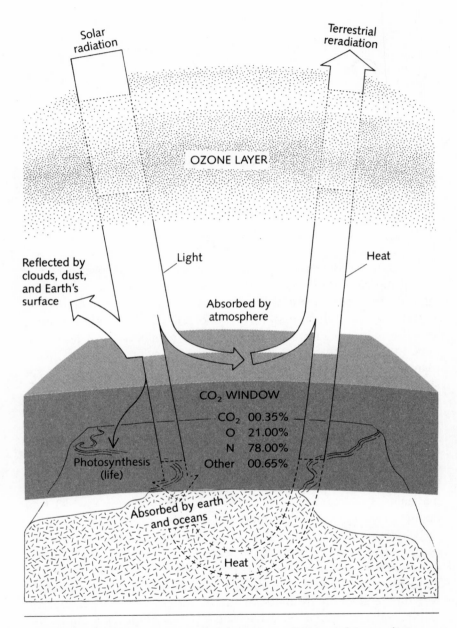

OZONE LAYER AND CO_2 WINDOW *modulate solar radiation and its reradiation from the Earth to optimize environment for life on Earth. Ozone layer absorbs lethal high-energy short-wave radiation. CO_2 window absorbs long waves in reradiated solar energy; this "greenhouse effect" regulates Earth temperature.*

depths, the atmosphere absorbs and scatters high energy particles from the solar wind and from more distant starting places in the universe. Life processes generate this life-sustaining and life-protecting steady-state mixture of gases in the atmosphere (see illustration on opposite page).

The oldest known sedimentary rock, laid down in the first billion of the planet's 4.5 billion years, holds evidence of the presence of living cells. That early start argues for the inevitability of life in the circumstances afforded by the Earth.

The planet is the right distance from the Sun, not too close nor too distant to be either too hot or too cold. It is the right size—that is, it has sufficient mass—to keep its iron-nickel core in the molten state. That, too, keeps the planet at the right temperature. Cooling of the interior from the high temperature the planet reached in its gravitational collapse is slowed also by heat from the decay of radioactive elements in the core and in the rocky mantle between the core and the crust. Convective turnover in the viscous boiling of the molten core sets up a magnetic field around the Earth that deflects the solar wind high above the atmosphere [see illustration on page 61]. Similar convection cells in the mantle bring new rock up into the ocean floor and rearrange the layout of the continental plates. Between the mountain building that attends this activity and the weathering of the continents by the Earth's more recent atmospheres, craters from the early sweep-up of solar-system debris by the planet's gravitational field were obliterated long ago. The Earth remains, in sum, geologically alive.

The mass of the planet also sets a high enough escape velocity (11.7 kilometers per second) to minimize the loss of the light elements—hydrogen, carbon, nitrogen, and oxygen—of which living tissue is principally made. Nitrogen and oxygen are the principal constituents of the atmosphere. Hydrogen and oxygen, of course, combine as water (H_2O). The water, along with atmospheric gases, came from chemical bonds in the crystal structure of the rock. "Juvenile" water and gases continue to be released today in volcanic eruptions that bring molten rock from the depths to the surface. Life got started here, apparently, just as soon as the range of temperatures on the planet's surface allowed water to stay in the liquid state.

It is the improbability of the conditions afforded by the Earth, not the improbability of life, that made life an apparently unique event in the solar system. The probability of this event elsewhere in the universe is supported, however, by numbers large enough to permit the conditions necessary for it to occur. The Sun is a member of a class of stars numbering in the hundreds of millions among the several billion stars in our galaxy, the Milky Way. Among the several billion galaxies in the observable universe, the Milky Way is a member of an equally common class of spiral galaxies. Planetary systems must be common enough, therefore, for another star like the Sun to shine, at the right distance away, on another planet like the Earth. The existence of the Earth suggests that the probability is no smaller than one in several hundred million that such another planet exists or has existed somewhere in the universe, even in the Milky Way. The probabilities support the possibility of life, therefore, elsewhere in the universe.

Life on Earth has come abruptly under the trusteeship of human beings. The improbability of this event exceeds statement in astronomical numbers. It is an event, moreover, that introduces factors transcending chance. People have demonstrated capacity to acquire objective knowledge and to act in rational accordance with it. Long before circumstances urged the wisdom of the inquiry, they were asking how life began. In their new trusteeship of the planet, it is essential for them to know how life got started here and how it came to occupy and envelop the Earth. Having had a beginning and a history, that envelope of life, the biosphere, has no assured permanence. The presence of increasing numbers of human beings in the system strongly conditions its future.

THE ORIGIN OF LIFE

While water was essential for the event, life could not have begun in the Earth's present atmosphere. Whatever the composition of the atmosphere then, it had no oxygen. That element's avidity for combination with others would take it quickly out of the present atmosphere if the massive turnover of atmospheric gasses conducted by the biosphere did not, as will be seen, constantly restore it. From various considerations, including what is known about the thick (Venus) and thin (Mars) atmospheres of other planets, it is thought that the Earth's atmosphere at this early time was composed of methane (a compound of one carbon and four hydrogen atoms, CH_4) and ammonia (one nitrogen and three hydrogens, NH_3), plus carbon dioxide (familiar as CO_2) in much higher concentration than now. This apparently thin atmosphere offered little insulation from the ultraviolet radiation and the x rays and gamma rays in the solar radiation, or even from the solar wind.

In laboratory glassware, the exposure of such a mixture of water vapor and gases to such fierce radiation has brought about the synthesis of small organic molecules. Their essential ingredients are carbon, hydrogen, and oxygen, and often nitrogen as well. They are called "organic" because compounds of this kind were first understood, by the chemists who resolved their composition in the nineteenth century, to be products of life processes. Organic chemists soon learned, however, to synthesize them. The subsequent discovery of these compounds in carbon-laden meteorites has led some workers to speculate that life on Earth was seeded by such meteorites. Be that as it may, among the small organic molecules synthesized from models of the ancient atmosphere, investigators have identified the simple piece-parts, the "monomers," that link together repetitively in the long-chain molecules, "polymers," that conduct life processes in the living cell.

That the double helix of the DNA (deoxyribonucleic acid) polymer encodes the plan of the living cell and conducts its replication is now popular science. Proteins have similarly wide recognition as the polymers that conduct life processes in the cell. What they do is supply energy to speed up chemical reactions between atom and atom, atom and molecule, and molecule and molecule that would without them proceed much too slowly. Proteins, having the basic helical structure, also give the cell structure. How the monomers found in sooty meteorites and in laboratory glassware got lined up in these remarkable polymers breaks down into questions that keep a great many clever biochemists busy. One alluring possibility is that highly ordered crystals of silicon in compound with aluminum and other metals and with oxygen and hydrogen, forming the clays on the bottom of the early seas, provided templates on which the monomers lined up and linked up into polymers. The sequences that had the right properties took off from there. How such molecules came to assemble in the living cell presents another whole class of dazzling questions.

Biochemists have reason to be confident that answers can be had. Isolated from the living cell, protein and DNA molecules exhibit spontaneously the chemical reactivities that, orchestrated in the cell, make the cell a living organism. What is more, evidence from geology establishes that such molecules became associated in living cells in the last 100 million years or so of the first billion years of Earth history. This prebiotic, chemical phase of evolution did not even take much time.

It took a much longer time for evolution to proceed from the first living cells to the genesis of multicelled organisms. That process occupied most of the history of the Earth, nearly 3 billion years, on into the last, or present, billion. On this long history, the fossil record is largely silent. The paleontology of the cell must consult the array of living organisms.

Cells that must be very much like early descendants of the first can be found in airless environments today, in marshes and ocean-bottom oozes, in the rumen of cattle (where they perform the useful service of digesting cellulose, the most abundant organic molecule), in the hindguts of termites, and in the lower intestines of human beings. Their metabolism turns over very well without oxygen and proceeds on various plans. Some anaerobic metabolisms have been harnessed industrially in familiar fermentation processes, producing, for example, methane as a potential automotive fuel to extend petroleum supplies.

The first living cells had to get their nourishment from the organic molecules compounded in the primordial broth by the photosynthetic action of the raw sunlight. Solar energy captured in the bonding of one of these molecules became available upon breakdown of the molecule to sustain the next biochemical reaction in the cell. In the metabolism of this manna from the Sun, the cells engaged sulfur. This element, similar to oxygen in chemical avidity, is not nearly so abundant. Being also less avid, however, it was more available. Life was confined to narrow niches, to waters where sustenance was available and the organisms were sheltered from the energetic short-wave radiation that supplied their sustenance.

During the Earth's second billion years, living cells acquired a new competence. Certain cells evolved pigments to absorb the smaller packets of energy carried by longer waves in the visible spectrum of sunlight; with that energy they manufactured their own organic molecules from inorganic elements. To carbon dioxide (CO_2) they attached hydrogen, at first from hydrogen sulfide (H_2S), to form the primary organic molecule (CH_2O), returning sulfur to the cycle as a by-product. Photosynthesis gave its practitioners a huge advantage.

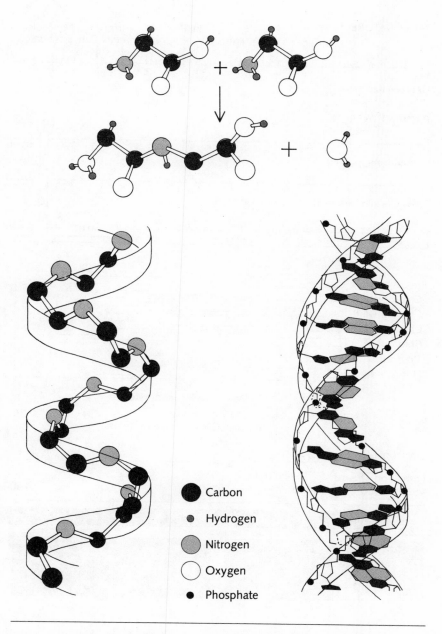

Carbon

Hydrogen

Nitrogen

Oxygen

Phosphate

ORIGIN OF LIFE *was induced by action of sunlight on elements in air and water, producing simple compounds like the amino acid glycine, at top. Such "monomers" link up to form "polymers" structured in the irreducibly simple helix of proteins (left) and the double helices of DNA, which self-replicates and encodes protein recipes.*

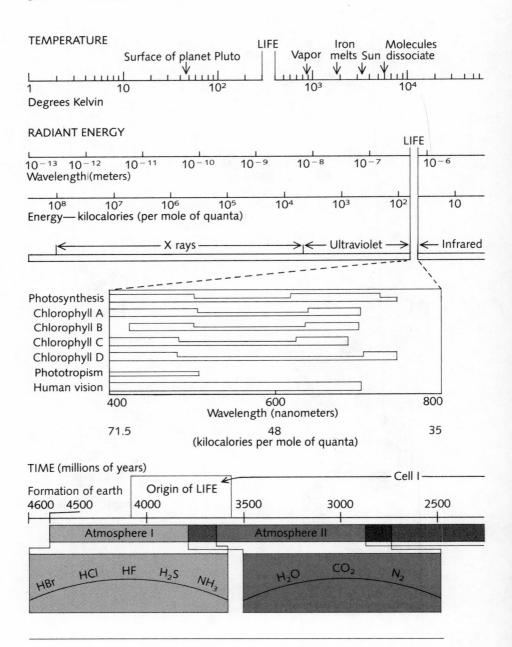

TEMPERATURE

| | LIFE | Iron | Molecules |
Surface of planet Pluto | | Vapor | melts Sun | dissociate |

1   10 10^2 10^3 10^4
Degrees Kelvin

RADIANT ENERGY

LIFE

10^{-13} 10^{-12} 10^{-11} 10^{-10} 10^{-9} 10^{-8} 10^{-7} 10^{-6}
Wavelength (meters)

10^8 10^7 10^6 10^5 10^4 10^3 10^2 10
Energy— kilocalories (per mole of quanta)

←———————— X rays ————————→ ← Ultraviolet → ← Infrared

Photosynthesis
Chlorophyll A
Chlorophyll B
Chlorophyll C
Chlorophyll D
Phototropism
Human vision

400   600   800
Wavelength (nanometers)

71.5   48   35
(kilocalories per mole of quanta)

TIME (millions of years)

Formation of earth   Origin of LIFE   — Cell I —
4600   4500   4000   3500   3000   2500

Atmosphere I   Atmosphere II

HBr   HCl   HF H_2S NH_3 H_2O CO_2 N_2

NARROW NICHE OF LIFE *embraces a mere 100 degrees Kelvin in the 10^9-degree temperature range of the universe (line at top) and a bare octave of wavelengths in the radiant-energy spectrum (second and fourth lines) that activate human vision, photosynthesis, and cell motion (phototropism). The time line of Earth*

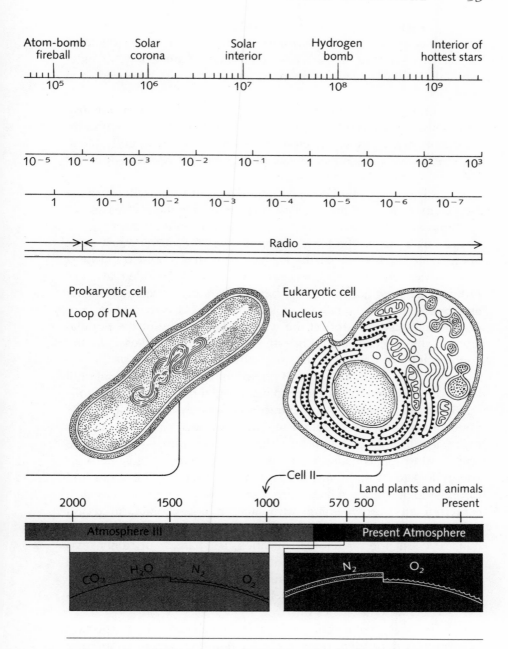

history plots major events in evolution. Primitive cells appeared in the first billion years. Appearance of nucleated cells (at right) after nearly 3 billion years was followed by the abrupt arrival of multicelled organisms. Evolution of life drove the evolution of the atmosphere.

These "autotrophs"—self-nourishers—could live in waters depleted or barren of organic matter. The acquisition of autonomy, of independence of the immediate environment, is a trend to be observed in evolution.

Alongside the autotrophs lived practitioners of the primitive metabolism. They continued to depend upon the Sun to synthesize their nutrients. To these "heterotrophs"—by others nourished—life in association with the novel autotrophs brought a readier supply of sulfur to support their metabolism.

A later photosynthesis split hydrogen from water. Because the oxygen by-product of this reaction was a poison to themselves and all contemporary life, these cells could manage it only by trapping the oxygen with iron in the form of iron oxides. With water much more abundant than hydrogen sulfide, however, they could populate a much wider territory. Their success is witnessed by banded layers of sedimentary rock laid down 2.8 billion years ago, alternately richer and poorer in concentrations of iron oxides. The variation in concentration is taken to reflect the waxing and waning of the populations of these cells and hence the increase and decrease in the concentration of oxygen in the atmosphere.

The success of this kind of photosynthesis remained local until some cells evolved the capacity to use oxygen in their metabolism— that is, in the breakdown and extraction of energy from molecules of nourishment. Oxygen metabolism—with so much oxygen in the air today, it is called aerobic metabolism—reverses photosynthesis. The "combustion" or oxidation of the nutrient molecules yields the solar energy locked in them and releases, as by-products, the water and carbon dioxide from which they were made. Aerobic metabolism conferred an overwhelming advantage; it is reckoned, in round numbers, to be 16 times as efficient as anaerobic metabolism. (In human cells, the anaerobic metabolism charges up only two molecules of ATP, the energy carrier in the cell, with the metabolism of each molecule of glucose; the aerobic cycle charges up 38 of them. The jogger feels the difference between the two metabolisms when the "second wind" switches on.)

The photosynthesizing autotrophs, which had been supporting heterotrophs dependent upon them for nutrients, began supporting heterotrophs dependent upon them also for oxygen, just as plants sustain the animal kingdom today. The oxygen-metabolizing heterotrophs recompensed their benefactors, of course, by regenerating water and carbon dioxide, the raw materials of photosynthesis, just as the animal kingdom repays the plant world today.

Soon after this development, the rising presence of oxygen in the atmosphere was recorded in the secondary oxidation of the banded formations and the presence of iron oxide in "red beds" all around the globe, dating back nearly 2 billion years. Life processes were then releasing oxygen into the atmosphere at a rate that maintained its presence there at 1 percent of its present concentration. At the top of the atmosphere, where high energy radiation from the sun is absorbed in the breakdown of ozone (O_3) to (O_2) and (O), enough oxygen was arriving to establish an effective ozone screen against that radiation. Vast new territory, the entire water surface of the Earth, was thereby opened to occupation by living cells. The phytoplankton, the layer of photosynthesizing organisms that sustains life in the ocean today, came into being.

Evolution had meanwhile been assembling a new kind of cell. In the primitive cells that had carried life through its first 2 billion years, the DNA molecules that encode genetic information were dispersed in the cell substance; this is the case with bacteria today. In the new, more omnicompetent cell, the correspondingly more elaborate genetic apparatus was contained within a membrane inside the cell, giving the cell a "nucleus." The modern "eukaryote," or nucleated cell, has many other organelles, some contained in their own membranes and several with their own auxiliary genetic apparatus [see illustration on page 53].

THE FIRST ECOSYSTEMS

To the genesis of this development in the Precambrian era—meaning all of the 4 billion years prior to the appearance of multicelled organisms—the fossil record holds one large clue. The oldest sample of sedimentary rock, 3.5 billion years old and located in Australia, bears some of the oldest fossils. The rock contains "stromatolites," large mats of cells—photosynthesizers similar to the blue-green bacteria known today—that chained together in colonies. Colonial algae still grow stromatolite mats in shallow ocean waters today.

In the primordial broth from which the fossil stromatolites date, colonial association must have given the single-celled organisms significant advantage in exploiting concentrations of nutrients and in the recycling by some cells of nutrients incompletely metabolized by others. Later on, it is easy to imagine, such communities began to include members specialized in one or another metabolic function. Each new niche-filling organism itself proferred a niche to the next. Together, they formed the first ecosystems, communities of mutual dependence and support.

In these communities, cells that had acquired the knack of photosynthesis supplied, in the by-products of their metabolism, nourishment to cells that lacked the capacity. Symbiotic association of this kind may have led more than once to the fusion of associates in a single cell. Thus the cell of the green leaf may owe its chromophore—the organelle that, stacked in the chloroplasts of the green leaf, conducts the trapping of solar energy in photosynthesis— to the fusion of a photosynthesizing cell with a less competent partner. Significantly, the chromophore is one of the organelles enclosed in its own membrane and bearing its own DNA. Aerobic metabolism, or respiration, is conducted by another organelle, the mitochondrion, which has its own membrane and DNA. Its presence in all plant and animal cells may be owing also to the fusion, after long association, of an efficient metabolizer with other cells.

Symbiotic associations that may represent evolution continuing in the same mode have been found today in many nooks and crannies of nature—notably by Lynn Margulis, who is a most per- suasive proponent of the hypothesis. The root hairs of legumes, for example, engulf rod-shaped *Rhizobium* bacteria, which fix nitrogen from the air and go on doing so inside the nodule they form with root-hair cells. Coral polyps have similarly intimate associations with carbon-fixing (that is, photosynthesizing) algae. Lichens, seemingly single organisms, are fusions of fungi with photosynthesizing algae; the partners in some species of lichens can also live independently where the environment is favorable.

About a billion years ago, cells with nuclei, capacitated for efficient capture and utilization of solar energy, began to associate in the elaboration of multicelled organisms. The generation of new forms of life thereupon went into high acceleration. A unique treasure of fossils of soft-bodied organisms discovered in the Rocky Mountains of British Columbia—the so-called Burgess shale fossils—testifies to an exuberance of invention. All the rich diversity of the later fossil record and of life forms today seems but a small sampling from the experiments fossilized there.

From the original diversity of basic anatomy in the Burgess

shale and the inscrutable criteria of the selection from it, the Harvard paleontologist Stephen J. Gould concludes that evolution might have adorned the Earth with an assemblage of organisms entirely different from the one we know—and it might not have produced *Homo sapiens* to wonder at them. On the same ground, he rejects the possibility that the evolution of life elsewhere in the universe might ever produce a species resembling the human.

By the time the Burgess shale organisms were trapped in the ooze, about 650 million years ago, the concentration of oxygen in the atmosphere had reached as much as 10 percent of the present concentration. In a regenerative exchange, the increase in oxygen was accompanied by an increase in the capacity to utilize it. Soon the first land plants, along with the first insects—air-breathing, land-going descendants of the enormously successful marine arthropods, animals with external skeletons, like those of lobsters and crabs— were colonizing the continents. The basic plan of the vertebrates that later went ashore—for example, the central nervous system, the bilateral symmetry, the four limbs, the head and jaw, and so on—had also been worked out under water.

The activity of the biosphere through Earth history to this point may be seen in the marks it left in the planet's crust, in the lithosphere. In more recent geological eras, photosynthesis laid down, in the fossil fuels, a tonnage of carbon exceeding by more than 50 times the carbon contained in the biomass—the total mass of all living things—today. Long before multicelled organisms appeared, however, single-celled photosynthesizers and their dependents laid down a much larger quantity of carbon. Samples of their work can be seen in sea-floor sediments now stranded on the continents. Their existence is part of the landscape, in the calcium carbonate of the white cliffs of Dover, for example, or the oil in the Rocky Mountain shales. All told, the biosphere returned an estimated 20,000,000 billion tons of carbon to the lithosphere in this period.

Events in the lithosphere played their role in the evolution of life in turn. The breakup of the supercontinent Pangaea, beginning about 200 million years ago, and the drifting of its daughter continents brought a larger percentage of the Earth's total landmass into the tropical and temperate zones, exposed more of the land to moderation by oceanic climates, and vastly increased the length of the shorelines [see illustration on page 71]. All of these developments went to multiply the number and diversity of geographic niches open to colonization by life and thereby to invite the diversification of multicellular and single-celled organisms and their communities.

The reptiles put in their appearance in those times. Lording it over the biosphere for more than 100 million years, they evolved to produce the largest land animals that ever lived. Life on land must have been easier in those days. Reptile metabolism operates at about the same temperature as the mammalian, but it depends upon externally supplied warmth to get it up to speed. With that warmth and abundant vegetation reliably supplied, the dinosaurs could devote their intake of nourishment to getting bigger. Size was an advantage; the huge mass of the tissue of the *Barosaurus*—the biggest land animal ever—retained vital heat, both externally supplied and internally generated by its metabolism. The trend in saurian evolution toward large mass argues against recent effort to show them to have been, like the mammals and birds descended from them, "warm blooded."

Events in the lithosphere also tested the resilience of the biosphere. Outbreaks of vulcanism that attended the rifting and collision of continents brought sudden periods of cooling, caused by the veiling of the skies by volcanic dust and gases. The carbon dioxide injected into the atmosphere would later on bring longer periods of climatic warming. The biosphere also survived sudden catastrophic climatic changes that attended the impacts of large meteorites. One of these events, recorded by a thin stratum of iridium-rich rock found at many sites around the globe, is implicated in the relatively abrupt extinction of the dinosaurs (and a great many other life forms) at the end of the Cretaceous period, 70 million years ago.

The largest excursions in world temperature and climate, to which tectonic processes may have contributed, attended the five great ice ages of more recent times. These are attributed principally to triggering by periodic coincidences in the inclination of the Earth's axis and variation in the planet's maximum distance from the Sun in the millions of trips it has made on its elliptical orbit around the Sun since multicelled organisms arrived.

By about 50 million years ago, life processes completed the transformation of the atmosphere to its present mixture of oxygen at 21 percent and nitrogen at 78 percent. In the remaining 1 percent, carbon dioxide, at 0.3 percent, is the most abundant of the trace gases. There was now sufficient oxygen to sustain the high rates of metabolism that keep the bodies of birds and mammals at temperatures around 37 degrees Celsius. Because that metabolism consumes the major portion of a mammal's nutrition, land mammals cannot get as big as dinosaurs. Floating in the ocean, on the other hand, mammalian metabolism has produced, in the great blue whale, the largest animal that has ever lived.

Relatively few species of reptiles remain today. They are confined to territories where external warmth is reliably supplied and adapted by behavior to seek it. Independence of environmental temperature constitutes the most important advance in the trend toward autonomy until the development of the human cerebral cortex.

Not far above the 21 percent concentration of oxygen maintained by the biosphere, the chemical avidity of oxygen can ignite spontaneous combustion in plant tissue and, at a somewhat higher concentration, in mammalian tissue. The biosphere keeps the concentration at the critical percentage by not fully understood feedback loops in its chemical cycles, including, apparently, the output of methane from all its sources.

THE BIOSPHERE ENVELOPS THE PLANET

The biosphere had now also completed its envelopment of the planet. The bottom of the biosphere may be said to be located in the deepest oceanic trenches. There, 10,000 meters down, detritus of marine life tens of millions of years old lies buried under successively younger depositions. This material has been carried on the sea floor from the midocean rift, whence the upwelling of new rock has pushed the sea floor outward toward the continents on either side. In the oceanic trench, this portion of the biosphere is approaching reincorporation into the lithosphere, as subduction of the sea floor carries it under the continental plate [see illustration on page 73]. After tens of millions years more, it may return to the biosphere in the dust and vapor of volcanic eruption.

The top of the biosphere may be located in the ozone layer in the stratosphere, at 30,000 to 50,000 meters, supplied with oxygen by transpiration from the leaves of plants, or only somewhat less extremely in the aeolian heights of the Himalayas, where a last few algae catch the sunlight. The major mass of living tissue in the biosphere is contained between the sea floor on the continental shelf, at perhaps 1000 meters down, and the land at the tree line, 3000 meters up. On a sphere one meter in diameter, this would be less than 0.1 millimeter thick, about as thick as a single page of this book.

The biomass, the total mass of living tissue in the biosphere, has a dry weight (that is, minus the water it contains in transit, as green grass before it dries to hay) of 1200 to 1800 billion (1.2 to 1.8 × 10^{12}) tons. These are large numbers on the human scale, but they are, of course, a tiny fraction—1 billionth (10^{-9})—of the mass of the Earth. The tininess of that fraction supplies an inverse measure of the enormous potency of life processes in Earth history.

These estimates of the biomass do not include organic matter outside of living tissue, in the soil and the sea-bottom ooze. Essentially all of the mass is plants, plant tissue; in a word, phytomass. The rest of all other kinds of living things make up such a negligible portion of the whole—less than 1 percent—that that they may be neglected entirely in reckonings at this scale. This fraction includes, in addition to animals, the three remaining kingdoms of life: bacteria (but only the heterotrophic species, the autotrophic or photosynthesizing bacteria being counted loosely in the phytomass), protists (eukaryotic cells, like the amoeba and the plasmodium of malaria), and fungi. They constitute a major fraction of the less than 1 percent that is not plant life. The 5 billion human beings and all the furred, feathered, and finned creatures that occupy the foreground of their consciousness (and attract 100 times as many visitors to zoos as to botanical gardens) make up the rest.

By weight, the biomass is *nearly* 99 percent air and water, atmosphere and hydrosphere. By volume, the biomass is *more than* 99 percent air and water. The slight change in percentage is accounted for by hydrogen. The lightest of the atoms, it is only 6.5 percent of the mass of 1800 billion tons, but it accounts for nearly half the population of atoms in the assembly. Carbon and oxygen, the two other constituents of air and water, make up nearly 93.5 percent of the mass and almost all the other half of the atoms.

The greatest tonnage and volume of tissue, by far, is in cellulose, the fiber that makes the paper this sentence is printed on. Cellulose is a polymer of sugar (or carbohydrate) monomers composed of carbon, hydrogen, and oxygen. Incorporation of nitrogen, from the air, makes the proteins in the biomass.

To the four elements from the atmosphere and hydrosphere, the lithosphere, the rock and soil, contributes no more than a pinch; 1.2 percent by weight. It is an essential pinch. Sulfur cross links adjacent chains in folded long protein molecules and holds them in

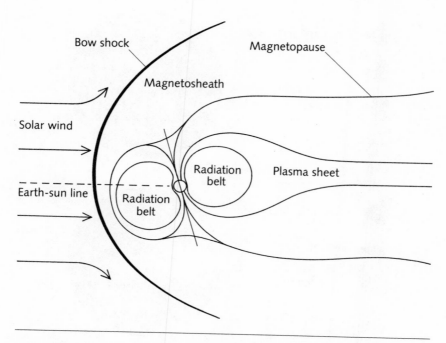

EARTH'S MAGNETIC FIELD, *the biosphere's "first line of defense," deflects the lethal solar wind of charged particles. The bow shock wave deflects some particles electromechanically. Other particles are trapped in the radiation belt around the equator and then stream downwind from the Earth in the plasma sheet.*

DEPTH OF THE BIOSPHERE *enveloping Earth, with its radius of 8700 kilometers, is proportional to the thickness of the line inscribing the arc above, a segment of a circle with a radius of 1 meter. This is the 4000-meter depth (from 1000 meters below sea level to 3000 meters above) that contains 95 percent of the biomass.*

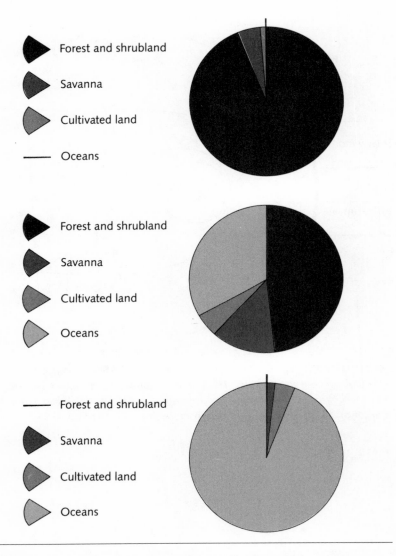

THE BIOMASS, *the dry weight of the living tissue in the biosphere, is contained mostly in forests and shrublands (top). Forests also generate most of the annual production of new biomass (middle). With its huge productivity (bottom), the tiny oceanic biomass generates second largest annual tonnage of biomass.*

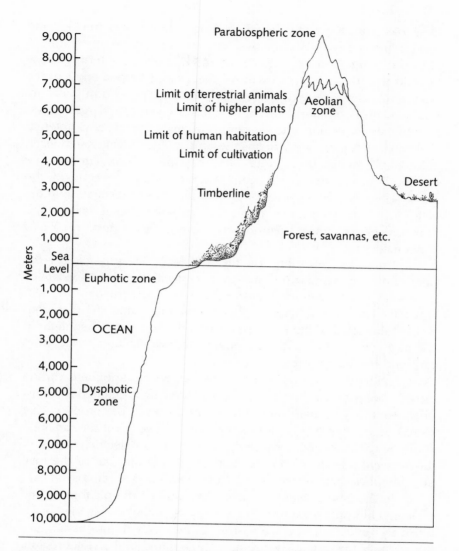

BIOSPHERE IN CROSS SECTION *reaches, in principle, from the abyss, where some forms of life exist without sunlight, to high mountain peaks, where single-cell forms persist. Nearly all the biomass lies in reach of sunlight, from about 1000 meters below sea level to the tree line, about 3000 meters above sea level.*

their biochemically active configuration. Phosphorus in ATP and related molecules picks up and delivers energy in the form of electrical charges from reaction to reaction. In electrical terms, it may be said that these molecules move the charges superconductively, with zero resistance and energy loss. Sodium, potassium, calcium, and sometimes lithium come in to transfer electrical charges across membranes. Calcium and silicon harden external and internal skeletons. A single atom of magnesium in the interstices of each chlorophyll molecule activates the capture of sunlight in the chromophore of the green leaf. Iron atoms in the coils of the hemoglobin molecule deliver oxygen to the sites of respiration in the cells of all vertebrates and in those of a few invertebrates as well. The biomass and its human offspring are more gas than dust; to air and water most of it returns.

Thus, the anatomy of the biomass. Its physiology—the photosynthetic manufacture of organic molecules and the oxidative–metabolic breakdown of them—secures its perpetuation by self-renewal. The photosynthetic phytomass—the plant life that constitutes almost all of the biomass—captures the energy of sunlight in chemical bonds and uses this energy to manufacture tissue from carbon dioxide and water.

Absorption and reflection by ozone, water vapor, and carbon dioxide bring down the wattage at which sunlight enters the atmosphere to a flux of 1000 watts per square meter at the ground. That would be enough to light a bulb of that wattage, if all the radiation could be collected and converted, without loss, to electricity. Most of this wattage goes to warm the ground and the air. Out of the total flux, the phytomass utilizes a tiny 1 percent to power photosynthesis.

In the green plants that make up most of the phytomass, the pigment chlorophyll captures the energy of sunlight. This pigment is tuned to wavelengths in two narrow bands, each about one-tenth of the width of the visible spectrum, in the red and in the violet region. With creditable efficiency, it traps about 10 percent of the energy carried by those wavelengths. Photosynthesis uses the energy with high efficiency: four light quanta to detach the two hydrogen atoms from the water molecule. It is the breaking of the avid oxygen-to-hydrogen bonds in H_2O that requires the input of external energy. Via a downhill reaction, the energy is stored in the bonds of CH_2O, with carbon dioxide supplying the carbon. The energy is available thereafter for the synthesis of the many larger and more complex molecules in the tissue of the biomass. Thus, with the energy of sunlight, the phytomass makes new tissue atom by atom.

In a forest, the surface that the phytomass arrays to intercept the sunlight is no more than 5 leaves deep. In the ocean, if all the photosynthesizing organisms in the illuminated depth under a square meter of surface were arrayed at the surface, they would make a layer less than a millimeter thick. Through these same surfaces, in the processes driven by solar energy, the phytomass inhales carbon dioxide and exhales oxygen and water vapor.

For all its delicacy, the manufacture of biomass proceeds on a titanic scale. Each year, the phytomass manufactures new tissue equal to 10 percent of its mass, 120 to 180 billion tons, in rough balance with the mass of tissue recycled by the metabolism of the heterotrophs to the atmosphere and hydrosphere. The 40 percent of the solar energy that warms the air and the ground helps the phytomass to pump water from the ground: 2000 tons of water for the production of 5 tons, dry weight, of tissue in which 3 tons of water is fixed. Worldwide, to produce the annual 10 percent of the lower bound of its estimated total mass, the biomass pumps 60,000 cubic kilometers of water through its tissues, and it turns over the entire hydrosphere in the chemical bonds of its tissues every 15 million years. It releases the oxygen from the water to the atmosphere. From the atmosphere, it draws 8 million cubic kilometers of air, fixing about 60 billion tons of carbon from carbon dioxide with hydrogen from the water. It turns over all of the atmospheric carbon in photosynthesis in about a century and, in the manufacture of the morsel of protein, all of the atmospheric nitrogen every 100,000 years. To carry on this immense operation, the phytomass uses, in its own metabolism, about half of the solar energy it captures and also half of the oxygen it frees from the hydrosphere.

The entire new production of plant tissue, except in years when the phytomass is increasing, goes into the metabolism of the tiny heterotrophic fraction of the biomass. In metabolizing the plant tissue, the heterotrophs engage the atmospheric oxygen supplied by the phytomass to break down the year's production back to the water and carbon dioxide from which it was made. The return of the starting materials to the atmosphere and hydrosphere, in turn, fuels the life processes of the autotrophic phytomass.

The two planetary cycles of photosynthesis and aerobic metabolism in the biomass not only secure renewal of the biomass but also secure the steady-state mixture of gases in the atmosphere. Thereby, these life processes mediate the inflow and outflow of solar energy through the system; they screen out lethal radiation, and they keep the temperature of the planet in the narrow range compatible with life.

In this perspective, the biosphere itself—and indeed the entire Earth enveloped in its biosphere—may be thought of as a living organism. The Gaia hypothesis, put forward by the British ecologist J. E. Lovelock, develops this metaphor in detail that illuminates what is known about the planet and its biosphere and suggests new lines of research into the feedback loops that tie the system together. Some of Lovelock's readers have improved upon the hypothesis and placed Gaia on the altar of a naturist cult. That must be respected as a measure, at least, of the immense importance of the well-being of Gaia to the infinitesimal fraction of her total mass that is the human population.

Ecology, the study of the mutual relations among organisms and between them and their physical setting—the biosphere and its ecosystems—is the newest discipline in the life sciences. It is still engaged in assembling its intellectual apparatus. Necessarily, the emerging method runs counter to the method that brought the momentous advances in human understanding over the past four centuries. Objective knowledge is the product of analysis: the disassembly of the whole in order to comprehend the part. The challenge now is to put the parts back together.

One observer of this intellectual crisis was Warren Weaver. During the 1930s and 1940s, Weaver deployed the modest funds available from the Rockefeller Foundation for the support of science. His grants—to scientists who were bringing tools from the physical sciences to bear upon questions of life—accelerated by at least a decade the arrival of molecular biology. Among his grantees were 17 winners, later on, of the Nobel Prize for their contributions to that field. From his strategic perspective, Weaver described the crisis this way: In Newtonian mechanics, science comprehended the realm of ordered simplicity; in nineteenth-century statistical mechanics, the realm of disordered simplicity; in twentieth-century quantum electrodynamics, the realm of disordered complexity; and now, in questions of life, science confronts the realm of ordered complexity.

To put the parts back together, ecology must call upon all of the disciplines that have so decisively placed the parts at human command; it must do so to bring wisdom into the exercise of that command. Remarkably, the task seems to be feasible. In the nick of time, to cope with the complexity it must comprehend, human intelligence has equipped itself with the megabyte power of the computer.

In every ecosystem, human understanding is challenged by the same fundamental strategy of life. Unlike human economies, ecosystems never proceed as if energy, air, water, and soil were infinite. In a finite world, the strategy of life is to make the most of what is at hand.

MAXIMIZING YIELD FROM ENERGY

An ecosystem, over time and up to its "climax," maximizes the capture and retention of solar energy in an increasing volume of biomass by constant increase in the diversity of the plant life. In a closed forest, for example, plants intercept the light at the canopy, then in the middle storeys, and finally at the ground, the different plants being adapted to make the most of what light each receives. As the captured energy flows to the heterotrophs, their numbers and diversity increase in step. Food chains organize, lengthen, and interweave in every direction. Herbivores, the most numerous heterotrophs, derive their nourishment directly from the autotrophic plant life. They are prey to carnivores, as are carnivores I to carnivores II. There are omnivores as well, of course, most notably the human.

For all living things there await, at last, the detritivores—small invertebrates (such as slugs and snails), fungi, bacteria, and some protists. Some detritivores, of course, nourish other life forms before they arrive at the same end. Fungi and bacteria conduct the final work of disassembling organic matter, deriving their sustenance from the last turnover of a quantum of energy first caught from sunlight in a photosynthesizing pigment. In the anaerobic atmosphere of the humus, the bog and the oceanic ooze, some operate on metabolic cycles that would have worked well in the primordial broth and may actually have originated there.

The soluble minerals thus salvaged return through the soil to the roots of plants or go downstream in the run-off. The energy flow may also, of course, short-circuit from autotrophs directly to detritivores. This is the case with the flinty tissue of *Phragmites australis,* the tall feather-tipped marsh grass or ditch reed; only certain detritivores can disassemble it.

From link to link in the food chain, from node to node in the web of the ecosystem, the stream of material and energy narrows. The general rule is that at each link, the volume of tissue diminishes to one-tenth. The nine-tenths consumed at each stage sustains the much higher rate of metabolism in the heterotrophs; that 90 percent compares to the 50 percent of the solar energy consumed in the generation of the starting plant tissue. This explains how it is that the negligible mass of the heterotrophs in the total biomass turns over one-tenth of that total each year.

Of the total turnover, nearly half is conducted by the forest ecosystems and nearly half of that in the tropical rain forests. Another 20 percent goes on in the savannas, grasslands, marshes, and cultivated lands on the continents. That leaves a third of the work to be done in the seas, which cover two-thirds of the Earth's surface. The annual turnover per unit area of these three sectors of the biomass ranks in the same order: the tropical forests produce from 1 to 3.5 kilograms of organic matter, dry weight, per square meter per year; the temperate-zone forests, 0.6 to 2.5 kilograms; the savannas and grasslands, 0.2 to 2 kilograms; and the oceans, from 0.02 to 0.4 kilograms over their vast pelagic reaches and 0.2 to 0.6 kilograms on the continental shelves.

The productivity of the three sectors runs inversely, however, to their mass. In the forests, holding more than 90 percent of the biomass, the huge annual turnover comes to less than 5 percent of their mass. It is apparent that a great portion of the total biomass is locked up in cellulose and lignin in the tree trunks, branches, and twigs that spread the leaves and connect them to the roots through the thin layers of active cells under the bark. If the production of biomass by the forests were credited to the small fraction of active tissue in their total mass, their product would be a very much higher percentage of that mass. It is difficult, however, to think of how the active tissue could array its solar-energy-collecting surface without manufacturing tree trunks, branches, and twigs as well as leaves.

The productivity of the rest of the continental biomass, which is to say almost all the rest of the entire biomass, amounts to 30 percent, with a productivity as high as 65 percent on the cultivated land. To produce its third of the total turnover, the thinly dispersed marine biomass, less than 0.5 percent of the total, turns over its entire substance nearly 15 times. Productivity per gram of tissue is highest by a great margin, therefore, in the original habitat of life. To achieve such turnover, it is apparent, requires assiduity on the part of the heterotrophs as well as the autotrophs.

Diversification of the heterotrophs in every habitat matches the diversification of plant life, providing diners on almost every part of almost every plant: borers at the roots, aphids tapping juices from the tender leaves and shoots, worms in the fruit. The diversification works both ways: heterotrophs, performing such services for the plant world as pollination (by bees and bats) and seed transport (by birds and small mammals), extend its range and open new niches. As in the primordial broth where it all started, each niche filler presents itself as a niche to be filled; moles get the borers; ants milk the aphids, birds find the worms.

It was doubtless in the primordial broth, where the presence of nourishment was accidental if there were any nourishment at all, that life was first held to the rule of parsimony that so distinguishes the ecosystems it has created. The rule has its paradoxical expression in the seemingly profligate splendor of those ecosystems. At closer range, ecology is learning to tease its way into the webs of chains, cross-links and feedback loops that hold the organisms together in systems of mutual sustenance that waste none or very few of the photons they catch in their chloroplasts.

In the tropical rain forests, where evolution of the ecosystems has proceeded for tens of millions of years, diversification has fashioned the tightest and most intricate of these webs. Taxonomists, who carry on the work begun in Eden of giving the plants and animals their names, estimate that 90 percent of the species there remain to be identified. The number of species per hectare being at maximum requires conversely that the number of members of a given species per hectare be at minimum. This makes not only for intricacy but for stability of the system. Parasites are constrained to be symbiotic rather than lethal. With the nearest specimen of the species of a dead host on the other side of the next hectare, the lethal parasite dies with its host and cannot break loose in an epidemic.

For this stability, nature, as always, exacts a price. To maintain genetic diversity within a species sufficient to continue its evolution requires, it has been estimated, a minimum breeding population of 500. Such a population in the tropics occupies a much larger territory than in, say, temperate-zone ecosystems, where healthy specimens of a species are closer neighbors. In regions of the world increasingly occupied by humans, the need for large territory necessarily places a species of plant or animal in peril.

Many species of plants and animals—perhaps tens of thousands—survive now only in "island" ecosystems confined and threatened by human occupation and exploitation of the continent around them. The existence of a smaller number of highly desirable species, the dense hardwoods of the rain forests, is threatened by the export trade and the debt-imposed need for foreign exchange.

Tropical forests stand in another peril. In Africa and South America, they stand on continental shields that were last plowed by glaciers 200 and more millions of years ago. With Antarctica and the Indian subcontinent, they then formed the continent of Gondwanaland, located in the higher latitudes of the Southern Hemisphere. The subcrustal forces of plate tectonics disrupted that continent, and continental drift brought its fragments to their present locations in the middle, equatorial latitudes. After all those millennia of weathering, the last soluble minerals from the lithosphere are turning over in the tissues of the forests and in the litter on their floors. A fallen leaf comes under instant colonization by fungi, and recycling of the minerals back into living tissue proceeds in hours and days, rather than months and years.

Most notably in the rain forests of Africa, Latin America, and Indonesia, these perils are advancing from potential to immediate. The shrinking of the perimeters of the forests by human invasion threatens biodiversity at a distance from the part of the forest that is actually destroyed by fire and human habitation. At the sites of invasion, clearing of the forest by cutting and fire exposes the soil to the leaching away of the last soluble minerals; after a few rainy seasons, the soil is barren, some ancient lateritic soils hardening to a kind of concrete.

Amazonia, in particular, has resisted efforts to establish monoculture plantations. The Para rubber tree, *Hevea brasiliensis,* lives at its natural spacing in the Amazon forest with many indigenous fungi. Rubber plantations attempted there early in the century were wiped out by one or more of them. Seeds from Amazonia established the rubber plantations in the southwest Pacific archipelago, where the trees are safely isolated from those fungi.

In temperate-zone ecosystems, each of these variables changes in sign; advantages become disadvantages, and vice versa. The much younger forests have fewer species. With fewer species per hectare, species members can grow closer together, and a breeding population occupies a smaller territory. Growing closer together, on the

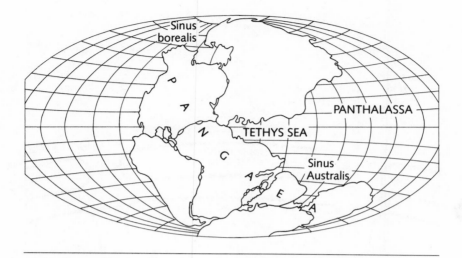

SUPERCONTINENT OF PANGAEA, *reconstructed from shoreline fit of present continents, from direction of magnetic field frozen in rocks, and from recent trends in continental drift, existed about 200 million years ago. Most of the landmass, cold and arid in high latitudes and far from the ocean, was not hospitable to life.*

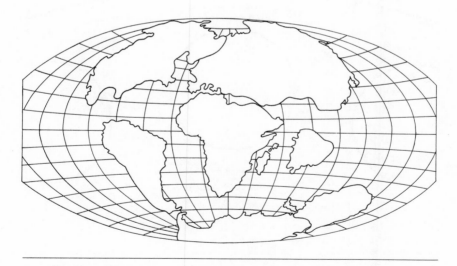

BREAKUP OF PANGAEA *by continental drift (see next two pages) extended the shoreline and brought ocean closer to continental interiors. Resulting increase in the number and diversity of niches favorable to life excited proliferation of species. Continents appear as of 135 million years ago, in the "age of reptiles."*

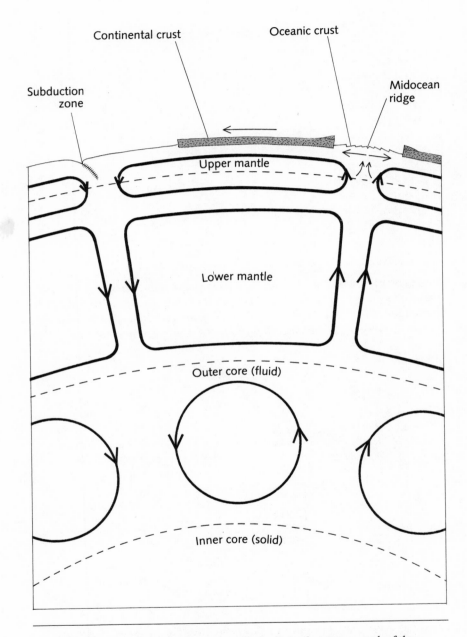

CONTINENTAL DRIFT *is caused by convection cells in the viscous rock of the mantle. Heat stored in the Earth's interior at its formation and generated by decay of radioactive elements drives this slow "boiling." Horizontal motion in upper mantle moves the continents; vertical motion rifts the ocean floor.*

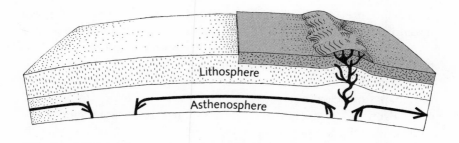

RIFTING OF A CONTINENT *occurs when convection cell or cells in mantle rock be-come active beneath it. The lighter continental "raft" rides on top of the litho-sphere crust. Volcanic upwelling of the rock of the viscous mantle, in this case from two convection cells, fractures and weakens the continental crust.*

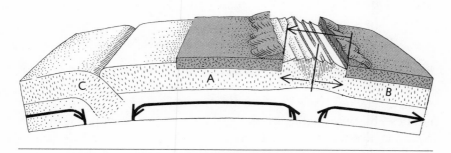

THINNER CRUST *of sea floor appears between fragments of the rifted continent. Upwelling of mantle into crust exerts horizontal force that pushes continental fragments A and B away from one another in the continental drift now under way. Drift is promoted by horizontal forces in mantle convection cells below.*

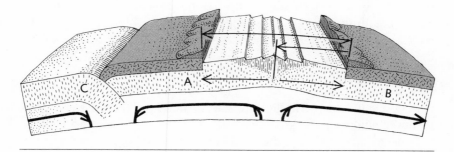

SEA-FLOOR SPREADING *continues on either side of midocean rifted ridge formed by upwelling mantle. Addition of rock to crust and widening of ocean is compen-sated by subduction of the sea floor (C) under far edge of the crustal plate on which drifting continent rides. Subduction is promoted by convection cell at left.*

other hand, they are susceptible to epidemics and outbreaks of insect predators. Standing on soil glaciated 10 times in the Pleistocene, the last time only 20,000 years ago, and receiving more hours of sunlight in their growing season, these forests are more robust. They can be brought under plantation, and they make good recovery from fire, infestation, and clearing.

Even so, temperate-zone ecosystems are losing diversity to careless exploitation or simply to encroaching human habitation. It is said that a species is as safe as its habitat. The spotted owl, reduced to an estimated 2000 breeding pairs, is menaced by the continued reduction of its habitat, the closed-canopy evergreen forest of Oregon and Washington. The chestnut blight and Dutch elm disease have eliminated American chestnut and American elm from habitat long ago yielded to humans in the country's northeast.

HUMAN BEHAVIOR BRINGS UNCERTAINTY

For 3.5 billion years, the future of the biosphere hung on the constancy of sunlight. From now on, it turns on human behavior. Human activities have assumed the biosphere's own orders of magnitude. That is declared by the reckoning that the population of 5 billion is diverting to its sustenance and other purposes nearly half of the annual turnover of the biomass.

In arriving at this estimate, ecologists Robert H. Whittaker and Gene E. Likens reckoned that the output from the 3 percent of the Earth's surface that is under cultivation equals 10 percent of the biomass turnover from year to year. That is evidence of the high productivity of modern agriculture. To the pasturing of cattle, people shunt the entire turnover on the savannas and grasslands of the world, another 10 percent—which, on the food-chain rule, yields 1 percent to human nutrition. To this 20 percent must next be added some percentage of the one-third of the biomass turnover that proceeds in the ocean. The yield from the world's fisheries had flattened at around 60 million tons and had stayed flat for some years when Whittaker and Likens made their estimate. They were inclined to consign 100 percent of the oceanic turnover to human exploitation. The fishery yield has since then exceeded 100 million tons, and it continues to rise; aquaculture may, in the future, increase the product and productivity of the nearshore ocean waters. To agree that humankind has appropriated two-thirds the oceanic turnover would seem prudent enough. That brings the total of the turnover diverted by human uses to 40 percent; conservatively, in round numbers, "nearly half."

To welcome another 5 billion people to this planet calls for diversion, at higher efficiency, of a still larger portion of the turnover of the biomass and, ultimately, enlargement (or restoration) of the size of the biomass. That means improvement on the 10 percent of the total that agriculture now secures from the 3 percent of the land under cultivation and some extension of cultivation to new land. Aquaculture may similarly improve yields from the ocean. The margins are so narrow that every such measure necessarily engages the integrity of the whole biosphere.

In a very short time, people must learn a great deal more about the planetary ecosystem and find the will to act rationally upon what they learn. The Geosphere–Biosphere Program launched by the International Council of Scientific Unions in 1990 has begun surveillance of the effects of human activity on the biosphere, which must never let up. From this study will come the first indicators of current, ongoing change in the mass and diversity of the biosphere; they must take their place alongside the gross national product (GNP), the consumer price index, and like economic indicators in the management of the world's economies.

Of course, the biosphere has felt the presence of humankind for many thousands of years. Long before the agricultural revolution, manmade fire opened up forests for hunting. In the extinction of the large mammals of the North American and Eurasian continents, Stone Age hunters are prime suspects. There is no question about human complicity in major losses of mass and diversity from the biosphere since the agricultural revolution.

As of 1850, extension of arable land had cleared 600 million square kilometers of the world forest. The next century brought the clearing of 850 million square kilometers more. Half of the original forest has now, therefore, been cleared. That must be acknowledged as a substantial reduction of the biomass: by perhaps a third of what it was at the beginning of history, with more than half of that reduction in the last century and a half.

Deforestation places future production of biomass at risk as well. The clear-cutting of trees in the highlands exposes the slopes to erosion and the downstream lands to flooding by run-off no longer retained by the forest. Replacement of a forest with cultivated fields downstream increases the rate of erosion (for soluble minerals leach even from the soil of a mature, closed forest) by 100 to 1000 times. The breaking of a grassland sod accelerates the process there by 20 to 200 times.

Recently, the use of a radioisotope of the light metal beryllium, with a half-life of 1.5 million years, has provided a sensitive measure of the rate of soil erosion from nine of the world's principal watersheds. This isotope arises from high-energy nuclear reactions induced in the upper atmosphere at a constant rate by the solar wind and cosmic rays. It is deposited in the soil as the rains wash it out of the atmosphere. In the outwashed soil in the sediments on the bottom of estuaries and on the continental shelves, the concentration of the isotope provides a measure of the rate of erosion and outwash; its long half-life permits the establishment of a historical record from cores taken from the sediments. In all nine watersheds, the loss of soil was proceeding faster than biogeochemical processes could replace it upstream—by a factor of 1.2 in the Susquehanna watershed, by a factor of 14 in the immense territory drained by the Yellow River in China, by a factor of 24 in the Narmada Valley in India.

The sites of the most ancient civilizations present the most hard-used and impoverished landscapes in the world today. There is little doubt that unwitting and reckless despoiling of the environment played its role in the decline of great agricultural civilizations; it has its part today, for sure, in world poverty. Deforestation of the uplands and flood and erosion downstream brought the denudation of the Greek landscape deplored by Plato 2300 years ago and advertised in travel folders today. By the same process, by the little day-to-day decisions and actions of people making their living, that landscape has come to ring the entire Mediterranean. Today there is little anywhere to suggest the self-sufficiency in grain and in the olive and grape that flourished in Classical times all around the shores of the sea. That the land can be made to produce again has been well demonstrated, however, in Israel and Morocco.

In China, the flourishing of civilization under the Han dynasty, from the seventh through ninth centuries A.D., completed the deforestation of the loess plateau between the Great Wall and arid prairies of Mongolia. The Yellow River is so named from those times. The loess plateau was laid down by winds bearing finely divided dust particles from the deserts of inner Asia. Upon its deforestation, erosion began to deliver the cubic meter of silt that the Yellow River picks up today in each cubic meter of water at the worst sites of erosion as it flows southward along the plateau. Downstream, on its eastward course across the flat paddy fields of North China to the China Sea, calamitous flooding became annual as the deposition of loess silt raised the riverbed above the level of the land, today all the way to the Yangtze River on the south and to the Jehol mountains bordering Manchuria on the north.

In five centuries to 1850, with the river spilling out of its raised bed on to a new course from year to year, its delta wandered 400 kilometers from south to north along the coast of the China Sea. Since 1850, heroic labor and vigilant engineering has confined its course— visible in satellite photographs as the only straight line of its 500-kilometer length on the Earth's surface—and has held the migration of its delta to 40 kilometers of coastline. The "curse of the sons of Han" still hangs over China; for the "suspended" river now flows to the sea at an average height of 8 meters above the habitations of 250 million people.

No greater discount has been laid on the future than by the opening up of the last 850 million square kilometers of farmland. Big institutional decisions opened the way for little individual ones. In the United States, they ignored the terrain and laid the rectangular grid of section lines on the North American prairie and then infiltrated it with the capillary networks of railroad track that once took the wheat to market.

The plow that broke the plains north of the Ohio and west of the Mississippi rivers invaded a 10,000-year-old ecosystem. The diversity of grasses and flowering plants that grew there has vanished. Botanists have managed to collect survivors of the various species in botanical gardens, notably in the arboretum of the University of Wisconsin, but the community is gone. The bison and pronghorn antelope that it supported survive, but not in the ecosystem that made them and that they made in their transcontinental migrations. The invasion of the prairie involved as well the draining of vast stretches of wetlands in the basins of the Mississippi and its tributaries. Reduction of the wetlands to one-third of their original reach had continental consequences in the reduction of the populations of migrating waterfowl and shore birds. Their narrowed and broken midcontinental flyway is now jealously defended by duck hunters.

Gone too—to build the Mississippi delta out into the Gulf—is half of the 6 feet of topsoil accumulated in those 10,000 years. Dust storms in 1936 blew out large stretches west of the 20-inch annual rainfall line, along the hundredth meridian, where the broken sod no longer held in dry years.

The prairie remains nonetheless one of the country's richest resources, for the present, one of its few export-income earners. Under cultivation, its yield of edible seed is comparable to the total production of dry matter per square meter of the natural ecosystem. The big agribusiness decisions now being made about its future are not reassuring. Laser-navigated tractors plow furrows across section lines that once defined the economic units of farmland. Over many stretches, they have plowed through the shelter belts that were planted to hold the soil after the dust storms of 1936. The long distance between feedlot and cornfield makes it more economical to flush millions of tons of manure into the rivers of the Mississippi watershed. Chemically driven plant growth has polluted the soil and ground water with nitrates. Exhaustion, in only 30 years, of the fossil waters of the Oglala aquifer (under the states of Colorado, Nebraska, Kansas, Oklahoma, and Arkansas) is exposing low-rainfall land again to dust storms.

Invasion of forest and grasslands hitherto untouched, in Africa, South Asia, and South America, has been under way since the middle of this century. Deforestation is proceeding in these regions at the rate of 6 to 7.5 million square kilometers per year. In some places, in Africa and South Asia, people had subsisted by slash-and-burn agriculture in reasonable symbiosis with the forest. Now population pressure has shortened and halted the cycle; the land stays cleared and declines in productivity. Persistence of the slash-and-burn practice by the indigenous populations accounts for 35 percent of the deforestation of Amazonia, 50 percent of the damage in South and Southeast Asia, and 70 percent in Africa. Landless new settlers, clearing or simply burning the forests to open the land to cultivation, do most of the rest of the damage in Asia and Africa.

In Latin America, the damage done by the landless is outdone by large-scale enterprises still convinced that the fragile abundance of the forest promises productive land for cultivation. While the land will not yield after being cleared and placed under monoculture, individual settlers and small enterprises are learning that the forest itself may be cultivated. Ethnobotanical studies conducted by the Institute of Economic Botany at the New York Botanical Garden show that managing the forest for its yield of fruits and other edibles and latex for the manufacture of rubber can produce twice and three times as much value as harvesting it for lumber or clearing it for pasture. Manmade miniecosystems of compatible fruit trees and crop plants are being fitted into the forest with increasing success as experience is gained.

In Brazil, the little decisions have been facilitated by big decisions, sponsored even by the World Bank, to run highways into the Amazon rain forest. Meteorologists close to that scene fear abrupt escalation of the consequences: half the rainfall on upstream Amazonia is water regenerated by transpiration from the forest downstream, closer to the Atlantic; deforestation could stop that rainfall, with reduction of the river flow, further shrinking of the forest, and curtailment of rainfall, in a reverse regenerative cycle, to terminate in the creation of a New World Sahara.

REDUCTION OF THE DIVERSITY OF LIFE

The extension of agriculture has most often meant reduction of the diversity of the natural landscape. The community of plants that were there must give way to the monoculture of plants bred, planted, and harvested for human sustenance. The native community of heterotrophs must go as well. The California condor, its too-wide range occupied by human settlement and activity, is confined now to aviaries; with less than a breeding population, its evolutionary history is closed. The Andean condor faces the same future. Small isolates, like Miss Furbish's lousewort and the desert pupfish, must disappear more often without a name. Nameless also are the uncounted species of bacteria extinguished in deforested soils and in soils abused by careless cultivation.

Extinction and its threat can also be merely incidental to other developments. The raptors, carnivores II at the top of the food chain, were nearly exterminated in the northeastern United States by DDT concentrated in the tissues of their prey. In New England, the cutting of green hay for the silo made two harvests possible. The harvest scheduled for the season in which the bobolink, meadowlark, and whip-poor-will normally attempt to raise young drove these ground-nesting birds out of much of the countryside. Confined now largely to abandoned meadows in northern Vermont and New Hampshire, these birds are further confined by the growth there of succession forest.

Where the ecosystem is not simply cleared out, its diversity may be reduced by a practice called "high-grading." The first trees to go from the forest of New England after the English settlers arrived were the tallest white pines, which, marked by the king's broad arrow, were harvested for ship masts. Then, for two centuries, the forests yielded saw timber to build the white-clapboard towns and the farmhouses and barns that are cannibalized today for 18-inch white-pine boards. Now the lumber companies and the peckerwood sawmills are taking out the third- and fourth-growth pulpwood; having exhausted the softwoods, cellulose technology has adapted to hardwoods and to the pulping, in some mills, of bark, branches, and leaves.

From the tropical rain forests of Amazonia and the Antilles, the treasure hunters are shipping the dense hardwood of teak and mahogany to nouveau riche industrial economies. To the new mass markets across the Pacific, in countries deforested by high agricultural civilization, avarice under Federal subsidy is rafting the tall timber of the Alaska panhandle. A similar procedure in the fisheries has exhausted the populations of once favored and familiar fish and brought formerly scorned species to the table.

Reduction in the mass of an ecosystem and reduction in its diversity go together. In a succinct summary by George Woodwell, the overall effect is to disrupt the structure of the ecosystem, shortening the food chains and favoring: "(1) populations of small, hardy plants, (2) small-bodied herbivores that reproduce rapidly and (3) the food chains of decay. The loss of structure implies loss of 'regulation'; the simplified communities are subject to rapid changes in the density of these smaller, more rapidly reproducing organisms that have been released from their normal controls." This is the all-too-familiar picture of the land along the highways and in the weedy meadows and woodlots of exurbia in the United States.

Such mournful prospect is not fated to attend human habitation. René Dubos, who was much persuaded to this view, often quoted the words of Rabindranath Tagore on his first visit to Europe. Coming from landscapes exhausted long ago by the extravagance and poverty of traditional agricultural civilization, Tagore wrote: "In the course of a railway journey across Europe from Brindisi to Calais, I watched with keen delight and wonder that continent flowing with richness under the age-long attention of her chivalrous lover, western humanity . . . the heroic love-adventure of the West, the active wooing of the Earth."

Again, Henry R. Luce, his American publicist's pride in the wilderness of the Sierra and the Rockies humbled by a panorama of Austrian Alps, asked his Austrian companion, "Raimund, why are those mountains so beautiful?" He was not prepared for the answer: "Because they are inhabited!"

That is nonetheless the case. Great tracts of land, held in one piece for centuries under feudal and then in successor-public ownership, show how the biosphere can be cherished. Managed forests, with flora and fauna both cultivated, produce timber and game. Truck gardens, vineyards and mountain meadows, in the ownership and occupation by generations of one family, become a way of life. The historical circumstances cannot be re-created, but such ecosystems can inspire the will to replicate them.

In the U.S. Northwest, several large lumber companies manage their own forestlands on 50-year (and even longer) harvest cycles. One can wish that they would show the same foresight in their operations in the national forests or that the Forest Service would compel it. The thin-stemmed succession forest growing on the woodlots and abandoned farmlands of the Northeast cries out for restoration and management. Even that landscape is demonstrating the recuperative power of the biosphere in the temperate zone. In Massachusetts and Connecticut, taking over from the last discouraged dairy farmers, second-home city folk are thrilled by signs of the return of the wild turkey, the coyote, and the black bear to their woods. They are still too squeamish to countenance the measures necessary to keep the deer population under control and in good health. Meanwhile, closer to town, suburban trees and lawns have created a sufficiently persuasive similacrum of the forest–meadow margin, but with one for every dwelling, to bring the populations of many songbirds to their all-time high. Those populations are reflecting, however, the shrinkage of their winter ranges in the Caribbean, Central America, and northern South America.

The present rate of extinction of plant and animal species is comparable to that of the catastrophe that extinguished the dinosaurs and marked the Cretaceous–Tertiary boundary. By one count, 211 species of mammals, marsupials, and birds have vanished since 1600; 81 species, since 1900. Most of these were island isolates. Now, however, extinction proceeds on the continents. Destruction of the tropical rain forests brings the extinction of plant species at the rate of 20 to 100 a year, according to one estimate, with other credible estimates running as high as 1000 per year. Fragmentation of the large ranges required to sustain tropical communities of animals and plants isolates them in ecological islands in which they are threatened with extinction en masse. As the ecologists O. H. Frankel and M. E. Soulé have observed, ". . . the stability of ecosystems (particularly in the tropics) may be sensitive to the presence of a relatively small fraction of the species [present], particularly large mammals, certain insects and birds, and certain key plants. The extinction of any of these . . . could precipitate a cascade of extinctions in ecologically linked [series]."

The International Union for the Conservation of Nature reckons 20,000 species as endangered: 1000 vertebrates, 6000 insects in Europe alone, and about 10 percent of the named species of plants. For many large animals and plants, the future is foreclosed. Of the 291 rare or endangered mammals, 162 survive only in zoos. No more than 30 have been bred there with success that holds hope of their return to nature. Captivity has reduced the genetic and behavioral fitness of these animals.

The population of Przewalski's horse—the last wild horse, native to the deserts on the inner Asian frontier of China and now confined to the world's zoos—approaches 500 breeding pairs. They are the progeny, however, of the last three stallions and seven mares taken from the highland Gobi desert. The surviving gene pool is narrower than that of the wild herd that contributed, it is thought, to the stamina on short rations exhibited by the Mongol ponies of Genghis Khan. In arriving earlier at sexual maturity and in loss of seasonal breeding rhythm, the zoo horses exhibit the primary symptoms of domestication.

Frankel and Soule observe: "There is simply no way that evolution in large plants and animals can keep up with the rate [at which] man is modifying the planet's surface." No farmer, they add, would bet on the survival of a White Leghorn in a hedgerow.

The present half century has made meaningless the notion of wilderness. The entire planet has come into the custody of humankind. China has announced its intention to create in the Qian Tang region on its arid northern frontier a "rare animal garden" larger than the Yukon and the Arctic national wildlife refuges in Alaska, hitherto the world's largest. Otherwise, it appears, the last nature reserves large enough to contain significant ecosystems have already been established. According to the International Union for the Conservation of Nature, less than 1 million square kilometers has been set aside for refuges; only 24 refuges exceed 10,000 square kilometers.

The largest refuges in the contiguous 48 states of the United States were dedicated from the public domain in response to the conservation movement led by Theodore Roosevelt and Gifford Pinchot in the first quarter of this century. In Africa, 15 percent of the total world refuge area, divided among many smaller refuges, cannot contain the communities of large mammalian herbivores (especially the ungulates) and their predators in any continuation of their evolutionary interdependence. All of the members of some species are confined to a single refuge. In India, the confinement of the 1100 surviving Indian rhinoceroses (single-horned) to two refuges does not secure survival of the minimum breeding population against the outbreak of some epidemic disease. The best the current conservation movement can do is to fight the poaching on the big reserves that supplies, for example, ivory to the world market and to corral small parcels of land that can help keep agreeable large animals, such as deer and wild turkeys, in circulation in exurbia.

The need for regions of protected wilderness goes beyond the assuaging of nostalgia and guilt to the highly practical purpose of securing the future nutrition of the human species. In the industrial world, people get their primary nutrition from no more than 10 plant species (including those processed through animal metabolism), and the standard recipes call on less than 100. These are the select few from an estimated 1000 species that have been in wide cultivation since the time of the agricultural revolution. The principal reduction of variety has come during the past 150 years, with the industrialization of agriculture and lengthening of the distribution chain from farm to market. The plants in this narrowed selection are cultivated on an ever narrowing genetic base, with fewer and fewer primary strains contributing to the profitable hybrid lines.

The hybrid strains of maize, or "corn," most notably, and several other grains have a single maternal ancestry. It is the egg cell, not the stripped-down sperm cell, that contributes the mitochondria, the respiratory organelles of the eukaryotic cell, to the next generation. A fungal disease affecting the mitochondria can wipe out an entire crop and, conceivably, even the entire strain of the crop plant.

The wild ancestors of maize and wheat have been identified. Conceivably, the wild plants have more than one maternal line. In any case, they can contribute other genes for heightened resistance to diseases or for improved tolerance of extremes of temperature and moisture in the cultivated strains. The establishment of refuges in which their survival can be protected constitutes an essential measure in the maintenance of the genetic diversity of these vital plants.

In the tropical wilds, where the native people consume such a great variety of the indigenous flora, economic botanists are identifying attractive prospective additions to the cuisine of the outside world. Amaranth, "the cereal of the Aztecs," is already emerging as the first innovation in the "cereal" nutrition of the industrial world in hundreds of years, the first ever from a plant not in the grass family. Some tampering with its genes has brought the yield of seed above the economic threshold of the market.

FOSSIL FUELS PERTURB THE BIOSPHERE

Until 1950, the human species had disturbed the biosphere principally by clearing the forests to harness the energy of sunlight, at first on the local scale, then on the regional scale and, lately, with converging regional disturbances, on the global scale. Now, harnessing the energy of fire, the species has set disturbances going that suddenly compromise the entire biosphere.

The burning of fossil fuels upsets the equilibrium of concentration of the atmospheric gases by which the biosphere filters and modulates, at each end of the visible spectrum, the pitiless energy of the Sun. From furnaces and combustion chambers, carbon, in a volume equal to 20 percent of the turnover of carbon in the biosphere, goes to increase the concentration of carbon dioxide in the long-wavelength window through which the planet reradiates solar energy.

Oxides of nitrogen from the same sources find their way into the stratosphere and, there, into catalytic interference with the photochemistry that maintains the ozone shield against the high-energy ultraviolet and solar radiation of shorter wavelengths. Methane takes similar effect in the ozone layer; its concentration in the atmosphere, normally sustained by the metabolism of anaerobic bacteria, is increased by the work of such bacteria in the alimentary systems of the world's growing cattle population and of the growing human population as well. The ingenuity of chemists, taming the reactivity of chlorine and fluorine in the fashioning of the chlorofluorocarbons (CFCs), has turned that reactivity loose in the ozone layer. On local and regional (if not yet global) scale, the burning of fossil fuels is pumping oxides of sulfur and nitrogen into the atmosphere, overriding the natural cycles of those elements and bringing acid rains that damage the works of man and nature alike.

There is no doubt about the increase in the rate of injection of carbon dioxide into the atmosphere from the fourfold multiplication of the consumption of fossil fuels since 1950. Nor is there any doubt about the resulting increase in the concentration of this gas in the atmosphere, which serves its critically important function at a "normal" concentration around 0.033 percent. The longest record, kept since the early 1960s by the observatory established by Roger Revelle at Mauna Loa in Hawaii, showed a two-decade increase of 9 percent in the atmospheric concentration of carbon dioxide—raising it to 0.036 percent. This is about half the increase that should have accumulated from the estimated injection of carbon dioxide from the increasing combustion of fossil fuels during that time. To roughly that extent, increase in the volume of photosynthesis on land and at sea is thought to have absorbed extra carbon in plant tissue and in ocean sediments.

The Hungarian agronomist Istvan Szabolcs offers the reassuring calculation that photosynthesis on the 200 to 400 million hectares projected for addition to the world's irrigated lands will more than double the tonnage of carbon fixed each year on agricultural lands. G. E. Likens points out, however, that not much of the carbon fixed by agricultural plants remains in storage as it does in the forest biomass.

Nor is there any doubt that increase in the carbon dioxide concentration has the effect of opaquing the long-wavelength window. This is the "greenhouse effect," already served by the normal concentration; a doubling of the concentration would dangerously magnify the effect. Such an increase is practically guaranteed by the projected fourfold or fivefold increase in mechanical energy that must necessarily attend the industrialization of the preindustrial countries, should that huge increase in energy be supplied by fossil fuels. One responsible estimate says that the resulting increase in the world temperature would range from 1 to 10 degrees Celsius; another says from 1.5 to 4.5 degrees Celsius.

About the consequences there is less certainty. An increase in the temperature, even on the low side of these estimates, could result in the remaking of the world map—in the time scale of a human lifetime rather than that of geology. Small increases in the mean temperature are accompanied by large swings in the extreme temperatures. Melting of any substantial part of the Antarctic and Greenland ice caps would raise the sea level by several meters, inundating the centers of civilization along with the habitations of the world's poorest people. In Bangladesh, even now, high tides attending monsoon storms regularly inundate the villages of the large portion of the country's population that lives in the broad delta of the Brahmaputra River. The warming would move the climate belts northward, with unpredictable consequences for world food production. Increasing cloud cover attending an increase in rainfall might then, in turn, reverse the warming and trigger a glaciation.

While there is no certainty about any of this, the consensus is that civilization is engaged already in an experiment with climate change on a global scale. Changes in climate and sea level set in motion by changes in the concentrations of atmospheric gases could move on nonlinear trajectories, perhaps reaching points of catastrophic acceleration. The geologic record shows that the biosphere has survived large excursions in the concentration of carbon dioxide in its atmosphere, attended at the extremes by flooding or the glaciation of vast reaches of the Earth's land area. There is nothing in history, however, to suggest that civilizations have ever possessed such hardiness. Against enormous economic and political inertia, it will be necessary to develop, at the earliest date, sources of primary energy alternative to fossil fuels.

The now widespread concern about the integrity of the ozone layer has its origins in the debate over the proposed Federal financing of a supersonic passenger aircraft (known as the Supersonic Transport, or SST) in the early 1960s. From a fleet of these aircraft in the stratosphere, it was feared, exhaust gases—including, especially, oxides of nitrogen—would find their way into the ozone layer. It had been shown that oxides of nitrogen lay a special threat because they destroy ozone catalytically. With molecules of the nitrogen oxides being regenerated in each reaction to engage in the next one, a few of them do great damage up there. Short of taking the biosphere back to its genesis 4.5 billion years ago, as might be the consequence of eliminating the ozone layer, the thinning of it risks such health hazards as skin cancers and blindness (not limited to the human species) and such threats to the entire system as the derangement of photosynthesis. The publicizing of these fears plus the unnerving nuisance of sonic booms proved sufficient to kill the SST, a project that did not have a large public following of its own. Public opinion was thus sensitized and ready to respond to the first word that chlorofluorocarbon compounds, the CFCs, might work similar harm.

ENVIRONMENT: ECONOMICS AND POLITICS

What followed is instructive on the question of when and how environmental considerations may prove effective in the contention of economic and political interests that shapes public policy. It is necessary to declare, preliminarily, that the photochemistry of the stratosphere is a subject of great complication and almost equal uncertainty. Direct observation and laboratory experiment encounter enormous difficulties. Most of what is thought to be known rests upon knowledge of chemistry that is secure enough but can be observed at work only in computer models of the sunlit upper atmosphere. Advanced models put 50 different chemical species through 150 different reaction cycles, with variation in stratospheric winds and solar radiation as additional variables. Studies of CFCs contend with chemical compounds and cycles of reaction not encountered in natural processes.

CFCs played a critical role in the separation of uranium isotopes for the making of the first nuclear weapons. They found their way into many domestic uses in the decades that followed. In the Teflon linings of frying pans and chemical drums, they approach the performance of the universal container dreamt of by the alchemist. As Freon refrigerants, they maximize the yield from electric power in air-conditioning systems. Freon, until recently, was more familiar in aerosol propellants.

CFCs became implicated in damage to the ozone layer by the accident of being chosen as the target in a test of new instrumentation designed to detect concentrations of substances as low as 50 parts per trillion. The test not only showed the instrumentation working to specification but produced indications that the durable CFC molecules were accumulating in the lower atmosphere. This prompted speculation that CFCs might be finding their way into the upper atmosphere. There, it was feared, they might not prove so durable under ultraviolet and more energetic radiation from the Sun.

A study published in 1975 stirred public opinion with the

prediction that the release of CFC propellant from aerosol cans, at the rate of release then common, might destroy 20 percent of the ozone layer. Without much more to go on, a Federal task force and a committee of the National Academy of Sciences concurred in the finding of "legitimate cause for concern." Thereupon, the appropriate Federal agencies, anticipated in their action by at least one responsive purveyor of household aerosols (S. C. Johnson & Son), suspended all "nonessential uses" of CFCs. In the language of the Food and Drug Administration, it was "a negligible benefit measured against possible catastrophic risk."

Similar action by governments of other industrial countries still left the major portion of the world inventory of CFCs in uses of presumably larger benefit—in automobile air-conditioning systems, for example. Increase in those uses soon offset the reduction of release to the atmosphere secured by banning CFCs from aerosols. They did not come under attack until a decade later. In 1988, observations of the wintertime ozone layer over Antarctica showed a pronounced thinning above the pole, speedily touted by the press as the "hole in the ozone layer." Observation in succeeding years confirmed the appearance of the hole over Antarctica and a thinning of the layer in lower latitudes. This was enough to bring seven major industrial nations to the framing and signing, in 1989, of the historic Montreal convention on the ozone layer. They agreed to reduce the use of CFCs to one half in the following decade while seeking substitutes to permit elimination of the whole family from use, if possible, by that time. The originator and principal manufacturer of CFCs, the Du Pont Company, immediately announced its own commitment to the convention and the earlier phasing out of the materials from its product line.

The Montreal convention is historic because it represents the first time that governments have taken such an action on the strength of theory, well-established as the modeling of high-altitude photochemistry may be, and inference, there being no proof that CFCs have been eroding the ozone layer. In truth, a great many other species of chemicals are known to be at work up there. They cannot be so easily removed from the picture. In consequence, it may be suspected, no Montreal conventions are being drafted to eliminate them.

The greatest obstacles would be faced in any attempt to reduce the release of the nitrogen oxides and methane, the one issuing from combustion of any sort, but especially internal-combustion engines, and the other from metabolisms widely practiced in the heterotrophic portion of the biomass. What is more, these ubiquitous compounds have other long-established roles in the biosphere. Methane is said to function in the feedback loop that keeps the concentration of oxygen at 21 percent; it is not known how much is enough. The nitrogen oxides increase the concentration of ozone in lower altitudes. They do so noxiously at street level. By increasing the concentration of ozone in the altitudes of subsonic air transport, however, their action may partially offset depletion of the ozone layer proper, in the stratosphere. That does not cure another effect of ozone depletion up there. Absorption of solar energy by the ozone layer heats the stratosphere. Lowering the temperature of the stratosphere could grossly affect the coupling of its winds to the troposphere below, the scene of the world's weather, with unpredictable effects on climate.

Offsetting these anxieties, the biosphere—or perhaps Gaia herself—holds out the possibility that increase in atmospheric carbon dioxide may increase stratospheric ozone. The likely better strategy, however, is not to stretch the resilience of the biosphere—or the patience of Gaia—by increasing the injection of carbon dioxide into the atmosphere.

For action that may be necessary in the future, the experience with the hazards of CFCs must be taken as a finger exercise. There was a comparatively small economic interest at stake; the few enterprises that held it demonstrated commendable social responsibility. Other hazards are more likely to involve bigger economic interest with many more stakeholders, more essential consumer necessity and less ready alternative satisfaction for it. Against these hazards, it may be difficult to organize political action, even with better data supporting more conclusive argument.

THE CASE OF ACID RAIN

Such is the case of acid rain. In addition to carbon dioxide, the burning of fossil fuels delivers oxides of nitrogen and sulfur into the atmosphere. Processed by sunlight and dissolved in raindrops, these become, respectively, nitrous and sulfurous acids. They are the more active ingredients of the familiar urban air pollution that blackened the white cathedrals and eats the finer details of public monuments. The blighting of vegetation and the irritation of people's eyes downwind from the smokestacks brought the remedy of taller smoke-stacks. They dissolve the combustion products in larger volumes of air and send them downwind over larger and more distant stretches of the landscape. Taller stacks promoted air pollution from local to regional.

The falling and the effects of acid rain on regional ecosystems were first established in North America in 1972 by F. H. Bormann, N. M. Johnson, and G. E. Likens. On the pH scale of alkalinity–acidity, distilled water measures pH 7—that is, neutral. Vinegar has pH 2.3—that is, acidic. The scale measures the concentration of hydrogen ions, expressed as its negative logarithm. The smaller number, there-fore, stands for higher concentration of the H^+ ions, which give an acid its reactivity. Inside, the human body tolerates a pH range of 3 to 8; outside, a somewhat wider range. A pH of 6 is near the lower bound for a trout. On the upper slopes of the White Mountains in New Hampshire, Likens and his colleagues measured rains at pH 2.8, near that of vinegar. In the Adirondacks, they found lake water at pH 5 and lower.

On Mt. Washington, the evergreens, especially, look sick. In the Adirondacks, 20 percent of the lakes are acidified above trout tolerance. Where local geology neutralizes the rain, lakes and streams may continue to harbor life. Most of the time, over most of the territory of the northeastern states, the rain falls at a pH ranging from 4.2 to 4.0. The debilitation of the evergreens on the upper slopes of the White, Green, and Adirondack mountains and the acidification of Adirondack lakes offer the closest approximation to a smoking gun, so far.

Acid rain goes beyond regional to international status. Ontario and Quebec, like the northeastern states, are downwind from the U.S. industrial Rust Belt heartland of Pennsylvania, Ohio, Indiana, and Illinois. Acid rain there is mean return to Canada of the crystal cold-front air that sweeps into the United States from the western provinces. Scandinavia complains of being downwind from Birming-ham and Manchester. Downwind from the Saar and the Ruhr in-dustrial centers are the Black and other forests of Europe. There, the sickening and dying trees, evergreens especially, have caused the Germans to speak of *Waldsterben,* forest death.

The cause–effect chain is difficult to establish, even between *Waldsterben* and the chimneys in the Saar and Ruhr districts. Acid rain does not overtly and obviously destroy vegetation. At the established pH-sensitivity of bacteria in the soil, however, it cannot fail to derange the ecosystem that processes the litter for return to the phytomass. Because so little was known about the normal ecosystem before acid rain, the changes can only be surmised. Acid rain leaches from the lithospheric grains in the soil many more elements than neutral rain, including metals not ordinarily active in plant physiology. Studies have pinpointed aluminum as a significant poison. The principal effect of the disruption of the soil ecosytem, however, is to deprive the plant community of nutrients.

The effects of acid rain are cumulative. Botanists and ecologists remark a reduced vitality in the northeastern woodlands of the United States, a heightened susceptibility to blights among various species of trees and slower recovery from outbreaks of such insects as the gypsy moth. In this scene, however, they cannot surely distinguish acid-rain effects from secular swings in the severity of winter, say, or in inches of rainfall. It will take time for the effects to develop and become more distinguishable. The trends may not, however, proceed linearly over time and, at some point, might swing abruptly to surprise, as with *Waldsterben* in Germany.

In the United States, the indicated countermeasures—cleaner fuels, and filters and scrubbers in the stacks—await enforcement of the 1990 amendments to the Clean Air Act of 1970. The considerable economic interest against them has its thumb firm on the political scale. Behind the Rust Belt power plants and factories stands a large constituency enlisted by monthly utility bills and weekly paychecks. There is no smoking gun and not even a corpus delicti, except for the acidified lakes.

As to the expenditures necessary to restore the lakes, David Stockman, chief budget officer of the Reagan administration, did a cost/benefit analysis that came out at $6,000 to $10,000 per trout. George Bush, who found it expedient to run for president as the "environment" candidate, nonetheless set a 50 percent reduction in the emission of the sulfur oxides as the objective of the amendments to the Clean Air Act.

Whatever the debate about acid rain and its consequences, official studies have established the easier connection between ground-level ozone and injury to vegetation and to human respiratory tracts. This may promote action as well on the other culprit, the nitrogen oxides. In addition to acidifying raindrops, they engage in photochemical reactions with oxygen to produce ozone. The major volume of this pollutant issues from 160 million motor-vehicle tail pipes. Enforcement of the Clean Air Act has here another powerful economic interest to contend with.

The "environment" holds a strong place in American political priorities. When mobilized, its constituency can carry the day against interests not ordinarily responsive to public opinion. It is an unusual constituency in that its members draw motivation from public and long-range concerns as well as selfish interest. In the establishment in 1971 of the Environmental Protection Agency in the Federal government—and then in every state government—and with the promise of the environment president to lift the agency to cabinet level, this social movement has run successfully against the 20-year trend to withdraw the Federal government from civil life.

Some of the most noisome offenses against the environment and public amenity have been cleaned up. Possibly the greatest progress has been made against water pollution. Paper company executives take pride in serving the effluent of their mills in the water glasses on their luncheon tables. The anadromous shad and salmon are running from the Atlantic again in the rivers of the northeastern states of the United States.

A measure of the long lead that technological innovation has held over social invention is presented by the problem of the toxic waste dump. On the Environmental Protection Agency list are 27,000 toxic waste dumps marked for cleanup at an estimated average cost of $25 million at each site. The product of these two numbers comes to about one-third the assets deployed by the 500 largest U.S. industrial enterprises. Protection of ground waters across the country must also reckon with numberless buried fuel tanks of households, shopping malls, and filling stations; taint from these sources has made the bottling of spring water a growth industry.

Technological innovation may still be lengthening its lead. To the number of different organic chemical compounds currently marketed—a low estimate says 40,000; a high estimate, 70,000—the chemical industry adds a conservatively estimated 1000 new compounds each year. In 1940, the industry shipped 10 million pounds of these chemicals. In 1980, it was shipping 80 compounds in volume exceeding 100 million pounds each and 100 billion pounds in all, a 10,000-fold increase.

Much of this increase in poundage is accounted for by the tonnage of plastics. By volume, if not by weight, plastic materials bulk larger in the U.S. economy than steel. After one stop in the kitchen, a significant fraction of the output of plastics makes a large and imperishable contribution to the country's accumulation of solid waste.

Pesticides and other biologically active products now come under regulations approximating the strictness of those applied to pharmaceuticals; it was the bitter hindsight of the experience with DDT that brought this innovation in policy. Consumers never hear of most new compounds. They are reagents in manufacturing processes such as those that make dubious neighbors of "clean" high-technology industries in the outer suburbs. Their regulation comes under the jurisdiction of occupational health and safety agencies.

Corporations in the United States and Europe that have lost markets to environmental regulation have made up for those losses with the continued sale abroad of products banned at home. Attempts by U.S. legislators to regulate such trade include requiring approval of the product at its destination or at least the giving of notice there of its status at home; some sales can be stopped by U.S. agencies. Preindustrial countries have been protesting double standards that permit sales to them of products banned in the domicile of the manufacturer; yet they continue, in ignorance or desperation, to use such products as DDT. On the list of their grievances is another mode of pollution export practiced by some transnational corporations: the failure to observe abroad the occupational health and safety practices enforced by law at home and even the establishment of plants abroad expressly to make products illegal at home.

THE DISCOUNTED FUTURE

The economic calculus motivates the same behavior that made deserts of the Mediterranean lands. The peasant got the tree and, centuries later, the goat ate the last blade of grass. In modern parlance, the calculus internalizes benefits and externalizes costs. On the manufacture of solid waste, the packaging industry makes its profit now. On the disposal of it, the taxpayer pays later to open up new landfills.

The market, reconciler of contending interests and objectifier of value, cannot see farther than the discounted future. The higher the interest rate, the nearer is that future. Against the always ready calculation of the interest rate, the political forum must be convened. There, as well, present optimum return holds plainer visibility than the countervalue of long-range future potential benefit. People only live once, and even the 70-plus years of present expectation are fleeting. In the contest over who gets the electricity and who gets the pollution, now and not in the future, it is also to the political forum rather than the market that contenders must repair. For these two functions, self-governing people have yet to perfect their political institutions.

A Bush administration spokesman has improved on David Stockman's cost/benefit analysis with the estimate that eliminating acid rain would soak up the military budget. A more reliable calculation, employing the Leontief input/output model of the economy maintained by the Environmental Protection Agency, shows that management of all the major forms of pollution should cost no more than 4 percent of the GNP. That would create more jobs than equal military expenditure does now and still leave enough for a post–Cold War military budget of, say, 2 percent of the GNP.

The environmental protection agencies, now chartered in most countries, hold principal historic significance as laboratories for fashioning ways to quantify long-range future potential benefit and bring it into the political and economic calculus. One now established instrument is the environmental impact statement. Its preparation in the siting of a major public or private installation in the countryside compels acknowledgement and measurement of hitherto blithely externalized costs, future as well as present, and their assessment against present benefit.

In 16 of the 24 member countries of the Organization for Economic Cooperation and Development (OECD), the principal market economies, recurrent "state of the environment" reports are mandated. The format of the U.S. report takes up questions under industry and "problem" headings and has room for global isssues. Canada has been divided into "15 terrestrial ecozones and four aquatic ecosystems" that ignore political boundaries for the purpose of reporting on "interrelationships between environmental conditions and socio-economic activities." A decent regard for the environment is becoming well established in the political forum.

The environmental impact of public works provided the first occasion for the admission of public opinion to the shaping of public policy in the Soviet Union. In the days when Lenin was extolling Communism as "Socialism plus electrification," engineers were challenged to come forward with revolutionary enterprises. The "Project of the Century" then went on the state agenda. It was to divert the northward-flowing rivers of Russia and Siberia southward to the arid back slopes of the Himalayan highlands and to replenish the increasingly saline Caspian Sea, from which irrigation was beginning to steal the waters of the Volga. Abroad, it was derided as the project to "make the Ob flow Don." Work actually began on a canal to carry water from the sub-Arctic Dvina River to the upper watershed of the Volga. Early in 1985, before *glasnost* had entered political parlance, the Central Committee issued a decree calling the whole project off.

The decree cited "public opinion" as a source of wise counsel. The opinion was shaped by poets and scientists. They decried, respectively, the arrogance of the enterprise and the possible destabilization of the climate of Siberia and wider reaches of the Northern Hemisphere by evaporation of the temperature-stabilizing Arctic permafrost as the result of the cessation or reduction of its natural recharge by the rivers.

For international action on global environmental questions, the world scientific community has been establishing the method for securing the necessary objective knowledge. In 1957–58, the International Geophysical Year assembled the first synoptic picture of the grand-scale machinery of climate and weather, of the circulation of the ocean and atmosphere and the exchange of energy between them. Some tens of thousands of scientists from 70 nations participated in this 18-month enterprise. It set the model for the many such undertakings that followed: the International Year of the Quiet Sun, the Upper Mantle Program, the International Magnetospheric Study, the Global Atmospheric Research Program, the International Biological Program, the Man in the Biosphere Program, the International Hydrological Decade, and the International Decade of Ocean Exploration. All this work has laid the foundation for the International Geosphere–Biosphere program that now continuously monitors the principal atmospheric and hydrologic cycles and such processes as soil erosion and the burning of forests in which human activity is implicated.

One consequence of these enterprises is the present dedication of Antarctica to the long-range future potential benefit of humankind under a treaty that hangs on the good faith of nations that formerly claimed territory on the continent. Another is the Law of the Sea, which was supposed to secure the conservation and development of the sea and the sea floor to the same end. That treaty did manage to secure those abyssal stretches of the floor not brought into the new 250-mile national economic-interest zones by the progress achieved in deep-water technology while negotiation of the treaty dragged on. Despite concessions made to its negotiators, the United States has failed to ratify the treaty.

When the Stockholm Conference on the Human Environment convened in 1972, 26 nations had established environmental protection agencies. By 1982, 144 nations had done so. Necessarily, because the poor nations so outnumber the rich, this meant that the environment had become an active concern of the intellectual leadership of the new nations. It is they who established the identity of the questions of environmental protection and economic development.

At the "second Stockholm Conference," the UN Conference on Environment and Development (UNCED) to be held in Rio de Janeiro in 1992, the fusion of these two concerns will come most clearly into focus under the heading of energy. The stifling of the respiration of the biomass and the perturbing of the biosphere's transaction with the Sun cannot be permitted to continue with the prospective quadrupling in the next century of the fourfold increase in the consumption of fossil fuels since 1950.

In the present crisis, there is blame enough to go around. The world market has no mechanism for establishing the true scarcity value of the dwindling petroleum reserve. From the attempt to charge a proper Ricardian rent ("that portion of the product of the earth which is paid to the landlord . . ."), the Organization of Petroleum Exporting Countries was long since driven by competition from high-cost fields brought back into production, especially in the United States, by the high OPEC price and by the greed and many-cornered political antipathies of its members. In consequence, there is no economic incentive to develop environmentally safe alternative energy sources for the voracious consumers of petroleum before geology establishes that scarcity price. The dependence of the U.S. energy economy on imported oil now exceeds the 40 percent at which the Arab export boycott of 1974 put the nation in panic. China has committed its onrushing development effort to coal that is loaded with sulfur. India has the resources to do the same. Development elsewhere will be at the mercy of the inevitable inflation in the price of oil.

No commodities or capital market reckons the future potential benefit of alternatives yet to be developed at any price near the future potential necessity. Nor have environmental activists, in foreclosing the development of nuclear power in the United States and almost everywhere else except France, given due weight to the more certain hazard posed by increase of carbon dioxide in the atmosphere. The political stampede away from nuclear energy has gone to increase the opaquing of the infrared window of the planetary greenhouse.

The planetary catastrophe invited by continued increase in the combustion of fossil fuels compels re-examination of the nuclear alternative. Progress in mastery of the photoelectric effect brings solar power into early economic contention, meaning as soon as circumstances exact the true price of energy. So urgent is the situation, as long as the concentration of carbon dioxide in the atmosphere continues to rise, that even the free-lunch alternatives—wind, tide, geothermy, and the rest—must be re-examined. By the time the UNCED conference convenes, the world may be ready to respond to rational counsel. That will mean stretching the time horizon of public investment in research and development beyond that by which the members of the world's business and political communities now live.

3

THE HUMAN CONDITION

Under natural selection, all but a very few species of plants and animals have evolved profligate modes of reproduction. Trees shed quantities of pollen that can be counted as a measurable constituent of the atmosphere. A pollen count of 1000 in the air of New York City means 1000 grains of pollen per cubic meter of air, probably many miles downwind from the forest or meadow where it was shed. The tasseled tree flowers spread a springtime litter on the ground. In the life cycle of the Atlantic salmon, the 20,000 eggs deposited by the average female yield 2000 fry; 300 parr drift downstream; 90 smolt reach the ocean; and only 3 grilse return to the natal river.

A plotting of the population of any such species by its numbers at each stage of metamorphosis or appropriate age interval produces the same geometric figure: a pyramid. With the youngest cohort in huge numbers at the base, the numbers in each age cohort above diminish rapidly, and a tiny fraction of the starting number survives to reproductive age at the peak [see illustration on page 102]. The mature adult is the survivor of selection that requires extravagant expenditure of life. In the biosphere, of course, each life goes to sustain another.

Until most recent times, this evolutionary pyramid plotted the age-cohort structure of the human population. That was the human condition.

Against unsparing selection, the species evolved the prolongation of the growth and dependency of its infants. This biological adaptation allowed the embryonic development of the cerebral cortex to come to completion under social stimulus outside the womb. Natural selection had to be for sheer biological vigor at birth, therefore, and through the first five years. If a woman survived six pregnancies, death took two infants at birth and nearly always two more before the age of 5, permitting no more than an imperceptible increase in the population. Selection and survival after five years must, of course, have related also to capacities unique to the elaborated cortex.

The natural-selection population pyramid is still approximated by the plot of the age-cohort pyramid that describes the condition of 75 percent of the world population today. In the plot for Nigeria in 1985 [see illustration on page 102], the panel for the age cohort of 0 to 4 years at the base represents the survivors of birth and of the infection and trauma that kill, before their fifth birthday, 174 out of every 1000 children born each year. Visual inspection of the pyramid suggests that the three youngest cohorts constitute half of the population. In fact, the median age of the population is 15. Nearly all the other half of the population is numbered in the cohorts under 50. Life expectancy at birth in Nigeria had reached 51 years in 1985; in reflection of the high death rate among children under 5 years of age, the life expectancy of the population at 10 years of age was higher: 53 years. These expectancies represent considerable improvement on the life expectancy of Nigerians in 1950, which was less than 40 years.

Nigeria has entered the first phase of the demographic transition. With death rates declining faster than birth rates, the population has also progressed from near-zero growth at high death rates and high birth rates into the phase of rapid growth, and even "explosion," that must, apparently, attend the transition. The rate of increase will decline as the population enters the second phase of the transition and birth rates fall.

Given the median age of 15, however, half the population has its childbearing years still ahead. The population pyramid forecast for Nigeria in 2020 [see illustration on page 102], when the 1985 0-to-4-year age cohort will be 35 to 39 years old, shows how the lengthening of life expectancy accelerates the growth of the population to the much deplored "explosion" rate. The 0-to-4-year age cohort of 2020 is nearly double the size of that cohort in 1985. They are the offspring, however, of a fertility rate that has been reduced by more than half. The 0-to-4-year age cohort of 2020 is bigger because, to begin with,

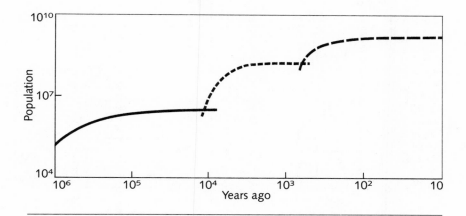

POPULATION "EXPLOSIONS" *attended each revolution in technology: the toolmaking revolution that started human evolution from primates 3 million years ago; the agricultural revolution, 10 millennia ago; and the industrial revolution that began less than 500 years ago. Time and population scales are logarithmic.*

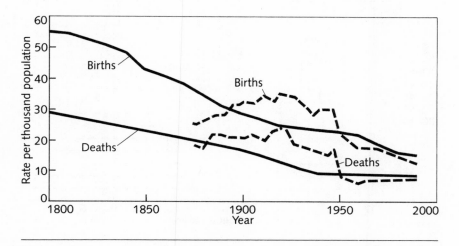

APPROACHING ZERO GROWTH, *the populations of the United States (solid line) and Japan are completing the demographic transition as their death and birth rates converge at almost the same low level. Each population grew rapidly in the period of widest spread between its birth rate and its death rate.*

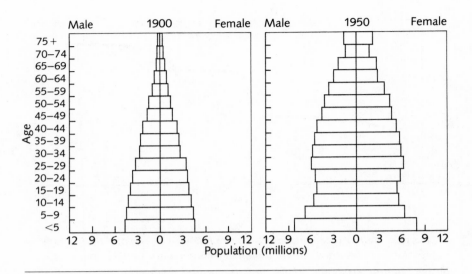

U.S. POPULATION GROWTH *from 1900 to 1950 (above) and then from 1985 to 2015 (opposite) is attended by change in the age (on vertical axis) and sex (numbers of males and females in each age cohort on horizontal axis) structure of the population. With birth rate in constant decline, growth comes mostly by*

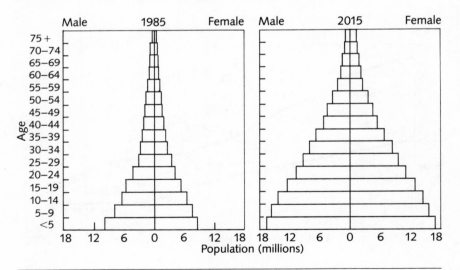

NIGERIAN POPULATION EXPLOSION, *from 100 million in 1985 to 137 million in 2015, reflects lengthening life expectancy with larger numbers in all age groups above 30–34. The number of females in that age group increases fourfold; with lower birth rate, the number of 0–4 infants increases only twofold.*

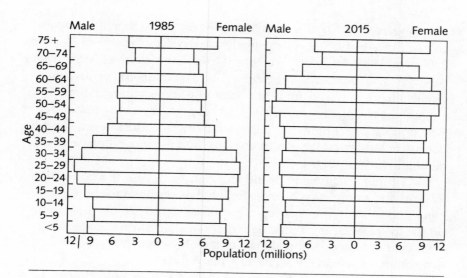

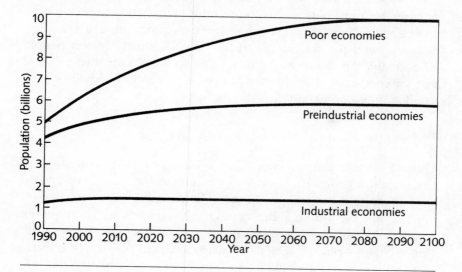

immigration and lengthening life expectancy and so by increase in the number of older people in the population from one plot to the next. In consequence, population goes on increasing, even after arrival at zero-growth birth rate in 1980s. The most rapidly growing age cohort is the "75+."

WORLD POPULATION AT A.D. 2100, *it may be hoped, will not exceed 10 or 11 billion. Industrial countries, at zero growth in A.D. 2000, will contribute 1.5 billion. Preindustrial countries that stabilize first, notably China and India, will have 4.5 billion. The present poorest 1 billion will increase to 5 billion.*

the number of women in the 35-to-39-year age cohort (the 0-to-4-year-old girls in 1985) is nearly quadruple the size of the 35-to-39-year cohort of 1985; 86 percent of the 0-to-4-year cohort of 1985 have survived. The number of Nigerian infants has doubled because more women have survived to bear them. Life expectancy at birth has lengthened to 63 years and exceeds life expectancy at 10 years of age. The population continues to grow rapidly, therefore, even as the decline in fertility rate marks its entrance into the second phase of the demographic transition.

Further lengthening of the life span will cause the population to grow for a time even after its fertility has declined to the replacement rate—that is, the "net reproduction rate" of 1, at which women, on the average, bear a single daughter. This growth will come solely from the realization by individuals of their life expectancy as the next generation comes on the scene to replace them.

The structure and dynamics of the Nigerian population may be taken to describe the condition and the prospects of the world's poorest billion people. These people and the nearly 3 billion others who live in the preindustrial countries are indubitably alive, if not all in the best of health. They are bound to procreate and to increase in number. No power at human command is authorized to remove or to reduce their presence; none can forbid their procreation. Their numbers are fated to increase. What the more fortunate billion people who inhabit the industrial countries can do is help them to arrive at that improvement in the human condition at which they will be glad to bring their population growth to a halt.

DEMOGRAPHIC TRANSITION COMPLETED

Those fortunate people—more than a billion of them, consituting a numerically significant minority of the human species—have arrived at or are approaching the replacement fertility rate. They are completing the passage through the demographic transition. The age–sex structure of the population of an industrial nation—in this case the United States—plots a very different geometrical figure [see illustrations on pages 102 and 103]. The 0-to-4-year age cohort of the U.S. population in 1985 counts nearly all the infants born in each year, 988 out of 1000. The width of this panel relative to those for the cohorts above reflects the near cessation of population growth by natural increase. In the wider panels for the 20-to-24-year through the

30-to-34-year cohorts are counted the infants of the postwar baby boom, babies "banked" during the years of World War II. The median age of the population, at 33 years, is closer to the end than to the beginning of the childbearing years. Among the industrial nations, there are several in Europe with median ages two or three years older. The variation in the size of successive cohorts declares that procreation has come under voluntary control; the country's net reproduction rate in 1985 was less than 1; to be exact, it was 0.904. Completing the demographic transition, the U.S. population is approaching zero growth at low death rates and low birth rates.

The shorter life expectancy of men—71.2 years in 1985, compared with 78.2 for women—which is attributed to greater exposure to trauma and stress, is evident in panels for the older cohorts. The width of the panels for the 60-to-69-year cohorts is still more than half that of the base, and the number of people 75 or older exceeds that of the 70-to-74-year cohort. Everyone in the industrial world who enjoys good health expects to live out the biological life span of the human species. The continuation of population growth by the lengthening of life expectancy can be seen in the still larger size of the elderly cohorts forecast for the United States in 2020 [see illustration on page 103]. Growth even from that benign trend must cease as life expectancy arrives at the apparent biological limit.

While the struggle for existence pre-empted and shortened the lifetimes of most of the people ever born, some few people enjoyed wealth and longer life. They did so at the expense of the shorter-lived poor. The arrangement worked, as Alexander Herzen observed, only as long as the chatelaine did not ask how it was that all her comforts were provided, and as long as the serf did not ask why the product of his toil went to the enjoyment of others.

Now the world population is divided into rich and poor nations. The well-being of the 25 percent who live in the industrial nations was won and is maintained in part at the expense of the 75 percent in the preindustrial world. That arrangement is turning out to be not only absurd—as the chatelaine and the serf, when they asked, discovered theirs to be—but, further, an increasing menace to the survival of the human species.

The internationalization of inequity is absurd because it is not compelled by any scarcity of physical resources—and absurd again because the stock of objective knowledge that commands the Earth's resources, going back to the first stone tool, is the common heritage of all humankind. It is a menace because the poverty of the 75 percent amplifies the destruction that the rich have been wreaking on the biosphere. However the industrial nations may now succeed in reducing the destruction they do, it must continue to be amplified by the rising numbers and desperation of the poor.

Neither party to the self-destruction of the species can extricate itself from this impasse without the help of the other. The industrial nations cannot escape the danger to their existence laid by increase in the population and in the cost of poverty to the biosphere except by sharing with the preindustrial nations the science and technology that brought their own liberation from poverty. The poor nations cannot escape without that help. Because objective knowledge does not diminish but, on the contrary, increases by its sharing, the help can proceed at no cost to the rich. Help is not the right word for the transaction, in any case, because the poor have their right in the common heritage. The impasse, if not common humanity, compels humankind to seek its reunification as a single species.

The division of the species was well under way when Thomas Malthus attempted what was probably the first estimate of the world population. The population growth that he deplored and that John Stuart Mill called the "dynamics of political economy" was, in fact, an explosion. The European population—better termed the population of Europeans, because they were already spilling onto other continents—was growing at a rate that must have been close to 3 percent per year. Their increase to an estimated 250 million in 1800 from 50 million in 1600 requires an average annual growth rate over that time in excess of 2 percent. Offsetting the loss of population to the Thirty Years' War and the starvation and epidemics that attended it in the seventeenth century, the growth rate must have exceeded 3 percent in the eighteenth century. The growth came, of course, by return to normalcy and then by increase in life expectancy—to more than 40 years in England by 1800—and not by some freak of procreative prowess.

If humankind had ever had a similar surge of increase in its numbers, it is lost in the absence of demographic records. The rest of the world population in the early nineteenth century was still increasing at rates not much above zero, with the prevailing life expectancy at 25 years.

What made possible the geometric increase of population was, it is now clear, the parallel and equally unprecedented geometric increase in production of the means of subsistence. In 1919, in his paper "The Rule of Phase Applied in History," the historian Henry Adams undertook to quantify the quickening of the industrial revolution. "The acceleration of the 17th century was rapid, and that of the 18th was startling," he wrote. "The acceleration even became measurable, for it took the form of utilizing heat as force, through the steam engine, and this addition of power was measurable in the coal output." His reckonings and the curves he plotted from them followed "the old, familiar law of squares"; they swung upward

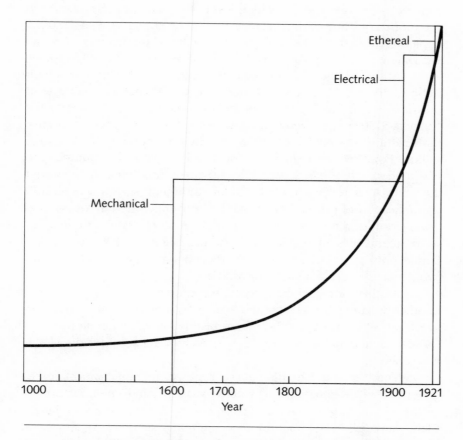

ACCELERATION *of history plotted by Henry Adams from estimates of rising consumption of energy and rate of invention. Short span of "electrical" age compared to "mechanical" age bespeaks the acceleration. Brevity of the "ethereal" age expressed Adams's despair of technology. Baseline is logarithmic.*

geometrically even from his logarithmic baseline [see illustration on page 107].

Statistical series do not exist to measure the change in the condition of individual existence that attended the breakaway of the European peoples from the rest of humankind. Life for most people in traditional agricultural civilization was not monetized. From his study of the question, Simon Kuznets, the Harvard University economist (who established "gross national product" accounting in the 1930s), concluded that people in all centers of civilization from antiquity until the middle of the nineteenth century had about the same average "income," meaning level of subsistence. He calculated the monetary value of that average subsistence to have been $150 per capita, reckoned in 1960 dollars. That is about the average income-equivalent of the population of the village people in the world today.

At the middle of the nineteenth century, the Europeans in their habitats around the world had increased to 300 million, their rate of increase in decline from its eighteenth-century peak. Accepting the Kuznets $150 as the average income of the Europeans, the economist Surhendra Patel puts the output of their economies then at $45 billion. By 1960, the Europeans had nearly tripled their numbers, to 850 million. They had meanwhile, however, multiplied their output 20 times, to a recorded $930 billion. Arithmetic shows a sevenfold multiplication of output per capita. Concurrently, the rate of population growth declined in all the industrial countries. Patel observes that John Stuart Mill's "dynamics of political economy"—his cause–effect connection of population growth to economic growth—had been broken at the very time he proposed it.

At that time, in fact, economic growth had acquired quite another dynamic. It was impelled by acceleration of the accumulation of objective knowledge. The recent history of the generation, transformation, and use of energy even suggests an acceleration of the acceleration.

Thus, in the late nineteenth century, the mechanical force, governed by the equations of Isaac Newton, began to be transformed to the electromagnetic force, governed by the equations of James Clerk Maxwell. The continuously spinning steam turbine of Sir Charles Algernon Parsons replaced the back-and-forth reciprocal steam engine of James Watt. Electrical conductors, replacing leather belts and pulleys, put electrical motors at the elbows or in the hands of production workers. Heinrich Hertz, in the course of experiments carried out between 1885 and 1889, extended the electromagnetic spectrum by demonstrating the existence of radio waves out beyond infrared radiation on the long-wave side of the visible spectrum. Wilhelm Roentgen, in 1895, demonstrated in turn the existence of x rays out beyond the ultraviolet on the short-wave side. At the turn of the twentieth century, Max Planck and Albert Einstein established the quantum nature of radiant energy, and P. A. M. Dirac, Wolfgang Pauli, and Werner Heisenberg, in the 1920s, wrote the equations of quantum electrodynamics. Solid-state electronics is now employing quantum effects to supply the sensory organs, the central nervous systems, and the motor ganglions of automatic production. In the 1950s, the Einstein equivalence of energy and matter, demonstrated for the nuclear strong force by Lord Rutherford during World War II, began to displace combustion of fossil fuels as a source of primary energy.

The sevenfold multiplication of the output of the industrial world has multiplied four more times since 1950. In parallel, its population growth has now come close to halting.

The industrial revolution must be recognized, therefore, as an abrupt and very recent change in the human condition. Such change cannot be comprehended in exclusively quantitative economic terms. The revolution—the multidimensional social, cultural, and political transformation of human existence—transcends industrial technology as well.

The living beneficiaries of the first industrial revolutions, in what has called itself the "free world," have dim memory of the event in their histories and small record of its human cost. In the dismay and distaste they feel for the regimes under which the revolution has more recently proceeded, however, they might find some measure of the price paid (or exacted) by their ancestors. The agony of the revolution was surely more prolonged in its earlier events.

History shows that the economic discipline required to induce capital formation by sufficiently large populations from sufficiently adequate resources was imposed by the political invention of the nation-state. In the dense cultural diversity of the European peninsula, this invention involved four centuries of nation-building wars that culminated in the paroxysms of the two world wars of the twentieth century. The reckless commitment of resources to the fighting of those wars induced some of the principal advances in technology and in the building of the infrastructures of the Western industrial nations.

The nuclear weapons that terminated World War II—and have consumed so much human capacity and material wealth in their perfection in the course of the Cold War since—have now made the nation-state obsolete. It is well known that the nation-state can no longer secure the safety of its citizens. The industrial revolution has made obsolete the political invention that sponsored it. In the anarchy of their jealous sovereignties and with thermonuclear weapons in their arsenals, the continued existence of nation-states surely threatens the life of civilization, perhaps the life of the human species, and even the web of life in the biosphere. Mutual assured destruction of the superpowers has indeed secured the longest period of peace among industrial states since the end of the Napoleonic wars. The breakup of the Soviet Union, with the possible parcelling out of its weapons to independent republics, and the proliferation of nuclear weapons into the arsenals of smaller states (and prospectively into the hands of tyrants or terrorists), sets a finite term, however, on security imputed to the possession of a nuclear arsenal.

THE ECONOMIC PROBLEM SOLVED

In the three decades of steep economic growth that followed World War II, the industrial nations fared differently, depending upon the time of their entry into industrial revolution and the rate of their progress through it. For all the differences in history, tradition, and ideology that distinguish them from one another, they have been proceeding in the same direction. From their different starting points, they have each accomplished a fourfold to fivefold multiplication of output per capita. They are all converging in a common industrial world culture.

The United States, in the lead on the basis of income per capita until the present decade, remains the model to which all trend. In the short memory of this country, its present popularization of abundance is taken as given. Only the older generation recalls Franklin D. Roosevelt exclaiming, in his second inaugural address in 1937, "I see one-third of a nation ill-housed, ill-clad and ill-nourished!" In fact, the investigation by the Bureau of Home Economics of the U.S. Department of Agriculture that grounded this statement had found two-thirds of the nation in such deprivation. (According to Harold Ickes, his Secretary of the Interior, Roosevelt thought two-thirds too depressing for the occasion and rounded it down to one-third.)

Now the fourfold multiplication of the country's real product, with no more than marginal changes in the distribution of income, has lifted the middle third into middle-class affluence. It has reduced poverty to the estate of less than one-third of the nation. The U.S. gross national product (GNP) per capita has been exceeded by that of Switzerland, Japan, and Norway. Other European countries, notably Sweden, Denmark, Finland, and Germany, are approaching it, with more equitable income distribution and no such poverty as the U.S. public tolerates in its midst.

For the vast majority of the population of the industrial world, therefore, and prospectively for the entire population—with the remaining barriers being institutional rather than physical—the economic problem has been solved. In bringing about this change in the human condition, the industrial revolution has mechanized work, taking it off human backs and out of human hands.

Toil had to go along with want. That is the only way the economic problem could be solved for a population exceeding a billion people. People could not do the work that had to be done. The 150 kilowatt-hours that is the accepted man-year energy-equivalent could not accomplish the extraction, transportation, and processing of the titanic volume of resources. That required the megawatt power of the dynamo and the displacement of manpower by mechanical horsepower.

By 1987, the mechanization of work had reduced U.S. employment in the production of goods—in agriculture and the other extractive industries, in manufacturing and construction—to just under 30 percent of the labor force. If "production" be limited to the blue-collar functions, the number engaged in making things falls closer to 20 percent. On the factory floor, moreover, it is the nervous system, not the musculature, of the worker that is engaged in monitoring the performance of the machinery of automatic production. The increasing number of professional and technical personnel on the industrial payroll, whose function is to bring that machinery to the production line, has raised employment off the factory floor to one-third of the total. Decline in blue-collar employment in the United States has been steepened in recent years by the importation from preindustrial countries of underpaid labor incorporated into textiles, electronic circuits, and other products sent abroad for the labor-intensive phase of their manufacture by transnational corporations.

Origin of Gross National Product by Sector

| | PORTION OF GNP (%) | | | | | | | |
| | AGRICULTURE | | MANUFAC- TURING | | TOTAL INDUSTRY | | SERVICES | |
COUNTRY	1965	1988	1965	1988	1965	1988	1965	1988
United States	3	2	28	22	38	33	59	65
Japan	9	3	32	29	43	41	48	57
Germany (FRG)	4	2	40	44	53	51	43	47
China	44	32	31	33	39	46	17	21
India	44	32	16	19	22	30	34	38
South Korea	38	11	18	32	25	43	37	46
Thailand	32	17	14	24	23	35	45	48
Philippines	26	23	20	25	28	34	46	44
Saudi Arabia	8	8	9	8	60	43	31	50
Nigeria	54	34	6	18	13	36	33	30
Kenya	35	31	11	12	18	20	47	49
Argentina	17	13	33	31	42	44	42	44
Brazil	19	9	26	29	33	43	48	49
Costa Rica	24	18			23	28	53	54

INDUSTRIALIZATION REDUCES CONTRIBUTION *of agriculture to GNP relative to that of industry, even though output of agriculture remains substantial. In later phase of development, contribution of services increases relative to industry. In low preindustrial GNPs, services underemploy big percentage of labor force.*

If it be reckoned that the biggest enterprises produce 75 percent of the output, as the 500 largest U.S. manufacturing corporations do, then less than 15 percent of the labor force produces the goods. Transportation, communication, and public utilities employ another 7 percent; the production of the energy that makes it all possible engages many fewer people than the supply of food.

Of the remaining 70 percent of jobs in the economy, perhaps one-third—in government, in the not-for-profit sector, in finance and other business services—challenge their holders with managerial and professional and technical responsibilities. The rest, nearly half of all the jobs in the economy, are in the trade-and-distribution and consumer-services industries that move the goods and facilitate their use and consumption.

These are the "lousy" jobs that have employed 8 out of 10 of the 30 million young men and women who entered the labor force since 1970. They account for most of the part-time jobs that employed 17 percent of the jobholders in 1987 and the jobs that 6 percent held two or more of (these percentages being up from 15 and 5 percent, respectively, in 1970). The widening penumbra of uncertain employment blurs the line between employment and unemployment and between "participation" in the labor force and withdrawal from it.

Such is the "opportunity" that the workless economy offers to the majority of the recruits to its labor force. From the high reported rate of participation in the labor force, it is apparent that many people want, or need, jobs.

The "creation" of jobs, conversely, gives political incumbents and business spokesmen occasion for self-congratulation. On neither side—neither the creator's nor the seeker's—is the concern for the production of goods. It is, rather, the consumption of goods that motivates the seeking and creating. Until society invents some alternative institution, the economic function of the job is to qualify the consumer with purchasing power, to make human need effective as economic demand. The people's capacity to consume—need made effective by paychecks—employs less than the country's capacity to produce, however, and fewer than all of the potential consumers.

For many young citizens of the United States, in their first jobs and establishing their own households, the American Dream lies in their country's past, not in their future. Evidently, the industrial market economies have not yet solved the problem of distribution to everyone's satisfaction.

The economic problem that the industrial revolution has solved is that of producing the goods. J. M. Keynes defined it as ". . . the struggle for subsistence, always . . . hitherto the primary, most pressing problem of the human race—not only of the human race, but of the whole biological kingdom from the beginnings of life in its most primitive forms." Confronting the possibility that the economic problem, so defined, might not be "the permanent problem of the human race," Keynes asked: "Must we not expect a general nervous breakdown?"

Evidence is strong that the nervous breakdown is under way. The institutions and values that scarcity and want imposed—work, thrift, property—have begun to lose their sanction. Thus, disjoined from production, work is a job that certifies a consumer with a paycheck.

Saving was long ago disjoined from investment in new productive capacity by the write-up of the consumer's price to cover depreciation and the otherwise retained earnings that have been building and rebuilding the country's industrial plant since before the middle of the century. In recent years, the managements of the biggest industrial enterprises have been putting these funds to other uses. The binge of merger, acquisition, and junk-bond buyout that closed the 1980s confounded equity with debt. The swapping of paper for paper had become more lucrative than the swapping of goods. The stock exchange, in the metaphor of the Cambridge University economist Joan Robinson, has dropped its "saving for investment" fig leaf.

Thrift has been disjoined from consumption as well. At $3000 billion, the debt incurred by U.S. consumers equals their country's much deplored national debt. The installment plan makes ownership of chattel property ambiguous. Title in real property is qualified by mortgage debt and by the public interest in what owners do with their real estate in this ever more crowded world.

Whatever the state of their health, the institutions and values devised to distribute goods in short supply fail to secure distribution of the goods that the industrial revolution produces in such generous actual or potential supply. The problem is, of course, a new one; the success at producion is recent. On the topic of distribution, the science of economics has never had much to say. As Robert Heilbroner observed, it talks of capital and labor, but it does not mention Park Avenue and the Bronx.

Pragmatic politics has created in each market economy its welfare state. In the United States, the New Deal and the Great Society established social-security "entitlements" and welfare income transfers that today pre-empt 45 percent of the Federal budget and equal 10 percent of the GNP. All of the market economies resort to public deficit to maintain consumption against downturns in the business cycle. Since 1980, the United States, under administrations that profess abhorrence of the idea, has been relying upon annual public deficits to keep its economy running in place.

A system of values governing the distribution of goods comparable to that for their production remains to be distilled from experience still in the future. Workless technology and increase in the concentration of wealth and income in the United States during the

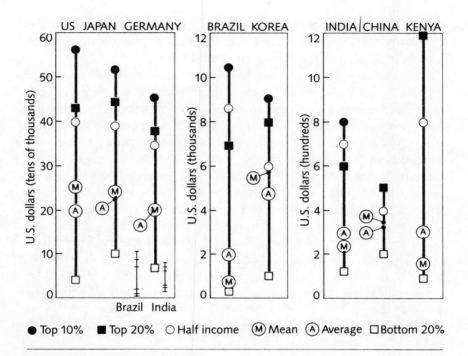

INCOME DISTRIBUTION *betrays international and national inequity. Markers on vertical lines indicate average income at each point—e.g., open circle is average income of minority that receives half of a nation's income. Inequity is so extreme in preindustrial countries that mean income is often below average income.*

1980s have pressed such value questions to the fore. The bottom 20 percent of the population earned 1.1 percent of the money income of households in 1986, while the top 20 percent kept 50.3 percent after taxes. Cash and noncash transfers from taxes paid by other households raised the share of the bottom 20 percent to 4.2 percent (and raised the share of the next 20 percent from 8.4 percent to 10.4 percent), bringing the share in household income of the top 20 percent down to 46.1 percent of the redistributed total but with no reduction of the absolute share they kept after taxes.

Poverty, the estate of a minority of the population, is plainly a social arrangement not attributable to lack of resources. The presence of a permanent underclass, made apparent by beggary, homelessness, and a rising crime rate, reflects inadequacy in the welfare measures authorized to offset the inequity in the distribution of income and a lag in the invocation even of these.

Such arrangements compromise the satisfactions of the middle income groups above the poverty line. For "affordable housing," good schools, and nice neighborhoods, the majority of families are hard pressed, and many are deprived. These essentials—along with upkeep of the built and the natural public domain, public transportation, the enhancement of human capital, and the advancement of human understanding by the education and research establishment—require political as well as market choices. Taxes are decried, however, as subtraction from the income that the citizenry jealously commits to purchase of the durable and less durable goods pressed upon them by the marketing genius of American industry. Unmindful, perhaps, that not one-third but two-thirds of the nation were so recently ill-clad and ill-nourished as well as ill-housed, the middle one-third income group casts its lot with the top one-third and votes against taxes. The certification of consumers by the jobs now generated by market demand and authorized by the electorate does not create all the jobs that need doing.

The sudden change in the human condition has drawn a vacuum elsewhere in the system of received values. The end of population growth has brought the extinction of the three-generation household and the extended-kinship family. Thus far, the two-child, two-job progenitive family has proved unstable. Divorce now breaks up half of these institutions; 20 percent of households with children under 18 are headed by a single, female parent—nearly 30 percent of the Hispanic and 50 percent of the African-American households, in the prevailing racial–ethnic stratification, are headed by single females. Those percentages embrace most of the 25 percent of the nation's children growing up in households with incomes under the official poverty line.

Moreover, it appears that the two-child family—necessarily the norm in a zero-population-growth society—is an inadequate institution for the socialization of the young. It proves especially inadequate where parents have weak control of their own destinies. Studies of the ecology of child development in the United States by the social psychologist Uri Bronfenbrenner show most children in minimal contact outside of school with adults, including their own parents. They are immersed in peer-group activity notable for its alienation from the adult community.

Anomie and preoccupation with the isolated self recur as a central themes of U.S. popular culture. That they find resonance in every other industrial country suggests that the solving of the economic problem brings on these quandaries everywhere. The answer to the simplifying question of survival asks a host of new questions for which there are no ready answers.

INDUSTRIAL REVOLUTION BY PLAN

The division of the industrial world by the Cold War has concealed the progress of the centrally planned economy of the Soviet Union into the same set of quandaries. In isolation from world trade, the Communist regime went on with the building of the country's heavy-industry infrastructure protected from competition by longer-established industries outside. The people—under severe political discipline, assured of shelter and sustenance, and waiting in long queues for access to goods widely available in other industrial countries—continued patiently to render their involuntary contribution to capital formation. Between 1950 and 1975, the steel industry of the USSR expanded its capacity from 50 million to 200 million tons. The generation of electrical energy increased from 300 billion kilowatt-hours in 1950 to 1600 billion kilowatt-hours in 1985, or 6000 kilowatt-hours per capita, in that respect equal to Japan. Pioneering the resources of Siberia under scientific leadership from the Akademgorodok at Novosibirsk, the Soviet Union became the world's largest producer of oil and incidentally broke (and then joined) the industrial- and gem-diamond monopoly held by British, U.S., and South African mining companies.

If only on the testimony of the U.S. Department of Defense, the industrial development of the USSR proceeded to formidable successes in high technology. The industrial installation that is now to enter the world market carries, however, serious deficiencies from its centrally managed past. In general, the heavy industrial plant consumes excessive quantities of raw materials and energy per unit of output and at high cost to the environment in the process. The electric-power industry operates at the 1960 rate of efficiency of other industrial countries. The steel industry counts, in its 200-million ton capacity, plants that rolled steel for World War II as well as those equipped with the latest continuous-casting technology. The end-product industries have had the armed forces as their primary customer and have low capacity for the production of domestic products, even of the obsolete designs they have offered Soviet consumers.

The centralized management of the Soviet industrial revolution achieved, beyond doubt, its greatest success in the necessary and concomitant urbanization of the population. Between the two wars, the Soviet Union had built nearly a thousand new cities. Their planning turned on a nuclear module of about 10,000 people housed in multifamily apartment buildings. Along with the modest (by European and American standards, minimal) apartments, the module provided the requisite number of classrooms (elementary and secondary), food stores and other consumer services, clinics, public places, and gardens. The land, having no value in a socialist economy, afforded generous green space around and between the modular centers in the new cities. The clustering of modules determined, in turn, the provision of hospital facilities, fire and police stations, sanitation services, and so on, up to the organization of the city government itself.

In keeping with the collective ethos, the financing, peopling, and management of the dwelling places was often the responsibility of the employing factory, government agency, university, or scientific institute. These collectives also organized, as material progress permitted, the provision of vacation spas and country places, the essential *dachas,* for their members. Middle management and blue-collar workers enjoyed approximately the same square footage of dwelling space. By most accounts, these arrangements have been agreeable to the citizenry. Most of them and their parents do not remember any better. If they did not enjoy freedom of speech, they did, as the late Paul Baran (who held simultaneous professorships in economics at Stanford University and the State University of Moscow) observed, have some control over "the unimportant questions": the education of their children, their health care, how they spent their holidays, and the administration of justice at the pettier levels of antisocial behavior.

The penetration of Soviet culture by rock music and blue jeans from the United States provided a measure of the country's progress in the resettling of its population in the cities, and the concomitant breakdown of its extended kinship families, the engagement of women in the economy outside the home, and all the rest of the social transformations of industrial revolution. In the comprehensive survey of modern Soviet society assembled by Basile Kerblay, the reader finds, that country's urban population increased from 33 percent of the total population in 1940 to 60 percent in 1970; the average number of persons per household was 3.7 in 1970, compared with 7 persons a century ago. By 1970, 86 percent of women of working age had income-earning jobs; 78 percent of households had two employed members, and the natural rate of population increase declined to 0.8 percent from 1.3 percent in 1940. At a GNP per capita of only 25 percent of that of the United States, but more equitably distributed, the people of the Slavic republics of the Soviet Union have now nearly completed their passage through the demographic transition.

To its own internal preindustrial countries, the associated Muslim republics of Central Asia with populations totalling 50 million in 1970, the Soviet Union brought industrial development by the strategy of ruralizing technology. Leaving traditional ways of life and modes of subsistence largely undisturbed, this strategy introduced the most portable elements of industrialization, such as electric power, literacy, and penicillin to those peoples. Its success is expressed in a population explosion that was to have made the Russians a minority of the Soviet Union and by the emergence now of those republics as sovereign nations.

The failure of the Soviet system to connect its heavy industrial plant to comparable light industries and to satisfy the consumer demand it had capacitated with purchasing power brought on its own kind of nervous breakdown. The horrors of World War II fresh in memory and at the end of patience with bureaucratic dictatorship, the people demanded at last the fruits that were owing to three generations of sacrifice. A sounding of their values and attitudes, now that they are to be consulted on questions of public policy, will surely yield the same profile as that found in Poland by the sociologist Stefan Nowak in his remarkable, generation-long surveillance, by periodic opinion polling, of the yearnings of his countrymen.

Those yearnings erupted into public consciousness as the agenda of the Solidarity rebellion of 1980–1981. They are only now being shaped into a political program, as the Solidarity leadership takes over the governance of Poland. With small, even random, differences among people identified by age, income group, occupation, years of education, place of residence, and prior class identity, Nowak's studies showed strong consensus on a set of basic principles. The Polish people wanted, above all, "equality of opportunity regardless of social origin" and "assurance of a proper standard of living for all citizens." Less unanimously, with warmer conviction among the young, they wanted "freedom of speech; conditions under which differing views can be freely expressed" and "influence of all citizens on the way society is governed." Few were in favor of "approximately equal incomes for all citizens," "nationalized industry," or "a large measure of independence for various experts and specialists." So few favored "strong apparatus of central power deciding all important issues" or "limitation of freedom of action for adversaries of the political system" that the Polish people can be said to have been almost unanimously against such propositions and, to that degree, alienated from the governing regime. Consistently, in polls taken from 1958 to 1978, Polish college students favored "unlimited freedom of enterprise" in handicrafts, small-scale trade, and small industrial enterprises, and they strongly opposed free enterprise in wholesale trade, foreign trade, large landholding, and medium and heavy industry. Rejecting identification as "Marxist," they hoped to see the world "move toward some form of socialism."

There is nothing in the Polish agenda strange to the values of U.S. citizenship except, of course, the Polish students' qualified commitment to socialism. In the market economies of Europe a poll would show the same values embraced. It would, moreover, find Western Europeans not nearly as skittish about socialism as people in the United States, in reflection of the stronger sentiment in favor of economic democracy prevailing in those older and more homogeneous societies. There and in Eastern Europe and the Soviet Union, people recoil from the economic insecurity accepted in U.S. free-enterprise ideology even as they celebrate the dismantling of their centralized economic directorates. In sum, it appears that the common experience of life in the industrial world brings people of all nations—differing as they may in prior histories and ways of life—together in the sharing of a common set of decencies and hopes.

The collapse of the authoritarian governments of the Soviet Union and its East European bloc opens the way to the unification of the industrial world. That may take longer than the recovery of Western Europe under Marshall Plan financing, however, and the outcome remains uncertain. The economies of Eastern Europe have some memory and experience of the market process, but their industrial plant comes into the world market 25 years behind the state of the art. In Eastern Europe, as in the disintegrating Soviet Union, the evaporation of central authority has let old national antipathies and ethnic prejudices erupt to the surface, diverting social energies away from urgent economic questions. Hitherto assured of economic security, the people of the Soviet Union draw back from the market incentives of insecurity and differential reward. The breakdown of the centralized machinery of distribution, meanwhile, heightens their new insecurity about what was once assured, and it could well lead on to disruption of the fragile public order.

For the present, at least, Western Europeans have embraced the prospective unification of the industrial world more warmly than Americans, and they are moving more sympathetically to help their neighbors find their way into the world economy. The Japanese as well, with export outposts firmly established in Western Europe, are moving ahead of their U.S. competitors to establish bases in Eastern Europe.

The reconciliation of the industrial world, even if it is proceeding uncertainly, opens the way to the promotion of industrial revolution in the preindustrial world. Nearly a half century of delay and even outright obstruction of this urgent task by the superpower rivalry recedes into the past. The concerted effort now possible will present new occasions for cooperative enterprise among the industrial countries that can lift them out of the economic doldrums in which they have been becalmed since the middle of the 1970s. A return to work on the original economic problem—this time, the elimination of want in a population of 3.75 billion people that will increase over the next century to more than 8 billion [see illustration on page 103]—will give the people of the industrial world a respite, furthermore, from contention with the quandaries brought on by their own liberation from want.

THE PREINDUSTRIAL WORLD

 Want is the one thing that the peoples of the preindustrial world have in common. Otherwise, few generalizations can be made about 130 different countries that have been diverging from their common background in traditional agricultural civilization as they have been finding their separate ways to industrial revolution. Except for China in its isolation from the world economy, they have been impelled on that course by aggres-

sive intrusion from the industrial world in search of resources to support its fourfold economic growth since 1950.

In principle, the export of their resources, along with some financing and assistance from the industrial nations, should have brought them the means to purchase the technology they require for the ignition of their own industrial revolutions. In the event, the export of their resources yielded little because they have received less and less in return for them—except, of course, for the petroleum exported by a few of them. The extraction and export of their resources did bring a flush of income to their cities and some development of infrastructure in the building of rail and port facilities. Until 1975, in fact, the intrusion from the industrial world brought significant economic growth to most of the preindustrial countries, to many at a faster rate than that of the industrial world. Economic growth even exceeded population growth and brought an increase in average income per capita in many countries.

For the vast majority of their people, income per capita, so essential to the thought process of economics, is meaningless. The disparity of distribution of income and wealth in these countries, far more extreme than in the industrial countries, leaves little for the people at the bottom of the income scale. They are self-employed in the daily struggle to get enough to eat—that is, in contention with the original economic problem.

About the human condition in the preindustrial world certain other general statements can be made. Nearly 70 percent of the population lives in villages, except in Latin America, where 70 percent of the population is urban. Except in China, they have seen little or no improvement in the supply to them of food and other necessities. In the last decade, African villagers have suffered an actual decline in consumption.

The biggest change in the lives of these peoples has been the population explosion that attends the first phase of the demographic transition. Such improvement in nutrition as they have experienced— the consequence of increase in food production ahead of population growth—and hygiene and immunization campaigns conducted by field workers trained by the World Health Organization have brought prolongation of lives, albeit in want, and the countrysides have been filling up. Infant mortality remains high in the poorest countries, however, and the fertility rate remains high with it. The poorest people in Africa and in some Latin American countries have fed themselves by extending the land under cultivation at primitive rates of productivity. That has taken them onto marginal lands and has started new rounds of deforestation and desertification. Migration of the landless into the cities has relocated their poverty to the shantytowns that surround those cities.

The measured and reported economic growth of the preindustrial countries has been largely in the cities, engendered by their traffic with the world outside. Such growth has increased the inequality in the distribution of wealth and income and created in many countries dual economies, one incorporated in the world market and the other subsisting in the countryside. The great exception to this generalization is, of course, China; there the distribution of income has had the narrowest spread between the top and the bottom income groups.

NEWLY INDUSTRIALIZING COUNTRIES

 From the preindustrial world, it can be said, four countries are crossing over to the industrial: South Korea, Taiwan, Hong Kong, and Singapore. Their early success brought the international bookkeepers to add, to the "developed" and the "underdeveloped," a third category: "newly industrializing" countries. They share this category with three Latin American countries—Argentina, Brazil, and Mexico.

The four "Asiatic tigers" are celebrated as exemplars of the market and the buoyant dynamics it lends to economic growth. In South Korea, Taiwan, and Singapore, in fact, authoritarian governments under strong lifetime leaders brought the installation of modern private-enterprise economies under state subsidy and protection. South Korea and Taiwan drew economic stimulus from substantial official development assistance (with a strong military component) from the United States following the Korean War and in the course of the Vietnam War. The Hong Kong city-state is dominated by the centralized power of a small financial oligarchy.

At the outset, the principal export of the four countries was low-wage labor—incorporated in textiles and in components of electronic devices sent to them from industrial countries, especially Japan and the United States, for sewing and assembly. South Korea and Taiwan have since climbed the value-added-by-manufacture ladder, with increasingly integrated industrial systems based on strong heavy-industry infrastructures. Manufactures—including automobiles, in the case of South Korea—keep their export income growing. While Hong Kong and Singapore continue to thrive as entrepôts for labor-intensive work on round-trip shipments of raw materials and components from industrial countries, they are developing indigenous light industries and are becoming important world financial centers.

Average income per capita exceeds $2500 per year in South Korea and Taiwan, and income distribution has become more equitable as their national incomes have grown. The percolation of material well-being into all income groups reflects itself in the decline of birth rates as well as death rates. In Hong Kong and Singapore, inequity in the distribution of income confines to the top income groups the advantages implied by average incomes exceeding $5000. All four countries have nonetheless entered the second phase of the demographic transition.

Six Preindustrial Regions

 It is useful to consider the 126 other preindustrial countries as clustered in six geographical and even ecological regions. Not all of them embrace an economically viable resource base or ecosystem. The existence of many sovereign states, especially in Africa, perpetuates a thoughtless joke of history or a cruel one played by their departing imperial patrons. The future for such states lies plainly in economic and prospectively political alliance, and perhaps ultimately in unification with neighbors in the same fix. That is the sense of considering them together in their regions.

More than half the population of the preindustrial world—more than half of the poor people in the world—lives in Asia, in lands hard used by ancient civilizations north and south of the Himalayas. China has pioneered its own course into industrialization. Its impending success, despite all the excesses of its revolutionary course, compels consideration of China's way as a model for economic development elsewhere in the preindustrial world. The condition and prospects of the Chinese fifth of the world population weighs heavily in any reckoning of the ultimate size of that population.

On the other side of the Himalayas, the six nations of the Indian subcontinent hold another fifth of the world population and share problems and prospects in common. They are clustered in world statistics as "South Asia." The population of India, now the second most populous country in the world, is bound to exceed that of China when the two countries have made their way through the demographic transition to zero growth. The size of the ultimate world population hangs just as critically on the industrialization of India as on the progress of China.

A third region of countries with common interests embraces Southeast Asia and the Southwest Pacific Archipelago. Population here is approaching 400 million and is crowding the land frontier in some countries. Resources are rich, however, and include the huge flow of the Irawaddy and the Mekong rivers, oil in Indonesia, and the rain forests of the archipelago. Economic development on the Indochinese Peninsula hangs on the termination at last of the war that has ravaged the countryside in Vietnam, Laos, and Kampuchea ever since the Japanese invasion in 1942. Economic development has been proceeding in Thailand, which stood apart from the war, and in Malaysia and Indonesia in step with the increasing economic interest in the region taken by Japan. The Greater East Asia Co-Prosperity Sphere, which was the object of Japanese military aggression half a century ago, may now be assembled by the arts of peace and may embrace the entire peninsula, the archipelago, and the Philippines as well.

Another case of preindustrial economies struggling to develop on the site of ancient civilization is presented by the "Arab nation." The population of nearly 200 million, in 17 nations on the Arabian Peninsula and the eastern and southern shores of the Mediterranean, has no land frontier but what it can restore from the hard usage of history. The naked landscape—long since deforested, agriculturally mined out, and barely sustaining its population of goats—can be restored. This has been demonstrated by a few centers of irrigation that draw upon fossil waters in nonrenewing Pleistocene aquifers in the Sahara and on the Arabian Peninsula—and even more convincingly by the Jews in Israel, cast out of the Arab nation by their Semitic cousins. The export of oil, even at the prices set by OPEC, yielded little capital for investment at home. In their contention with one another, the Arab states have started no development enterprises they can celebrate.

Black Africa, east and south of the Sahara, presents contrasts on all dimensions with China, India, and Islam. The 500 million pastoral and subsistence-farming (and even preagricultural) peoples of Africa are just beginning to acquire an indigenous intelligentsia capable of articulating their interests to the world outside. Their development will be facilitated by a large land frontier—much of the best of it infested by the agents and vectors of devastating parasitic diseases—and rich mineral resources that are supporting the growth of the industrial world. With population increase (at more than 2.5 percent) overwhelming the first halting steps to development, 26 of the world's 40 poorest nations are African.

To Latin America, Spain and Portugal transplanted their traditional agricultural civilization, incorporating in the populations of some of the 21 nations the native Indians and black slaves from Africa. The 400 million people of these urban, cosmopolitan nations have indigenous business and intellectual leadership capable of leading them into industrial revolution. While Argentina, Brazil, and Mexico are classified as "newly industrializing countries," that description is belied by the decline of their growth to stagnation during the past decade. The extreme inequality of distribution of wealth and income has excluded most of the population of these and other Latin American countries from any share in what economic growth they have attained. In their poverty, the people maintain a rate of population growth that is second only to that of the black Africans. For their ultimate escape from want, the continent of South America has land frontier and resources to support an integrated community of industrial nations.

The term "Third World" has been hitherto in vogue to assemble, under one "free world" heading, the countries that have been incorporated in the world market economy and to exclude consideration of China (and Vietnam and Cuba). The exclusion of China has suppressed what could have been useful comparisons with India—comparison of the approaches of the two countries to development and of their progress since they achieved their respective liberations.

Both countries are the sites of prolonged attempt at civilization. Their populations are in explosion from the large numbers to which they grew, at the universal near-zero rate, over 4 millennia of recorded history. Their ecosystems have been badly used; restoration of their forests and soils is the urgent, still unachieved, precondition to their development. They have no land frontier except what they may develop by irrigation; they each have the mineral and energy resources of a subcontinent; they each inherit, in their respective Mandarin and Brahmin intelligentsias, a resource of literacy; their industrial revolutions will compel their recognition as world powers in the next century.

China presents, of course, the model for the driving of economic development from the center and according to plan. In isolation from the world economy, the revolutionary government secured the rapid accumulation of the huge capital required from the people—the world's biggest population of desperately poor people—by holding them under harsh political discipline. With their morale sustained by strict rationing of equal shares in the little there was to go around, the people could be persuaded that "the small betterment of today must be subordinated to the big betterment of tomorrow." The country now possesses a substantial heavy industrial plant. The persisting concentration of power at the center, however, still bars China from open participation in the world economy.

Commanding no such coercive power, the unrevolutionary government of India could extract little capital from the world's second biggest population of desperately poor people. Instead, it turned to the wealth accumulated at the top of India's feudal society and to the considerable turnover of income in the transactions of the country's urban market economy with the world economy. Taxes and a virtual state monopoly on foreign trade granted by the country's democratically elected parliament, supplemented by economic assistance from abroad, put a modest flow of capital in reach of the executive power. By central planning and state ownership, the government put this capital into the building of a heavy industrial plant ahead of market demand for its products. Equipped now with an industrial plant less than half the size of that built by China, India has set the foundations for self-sustained economic growth.

INDUSTRIAL REVOLUTION IN CHINA

 China was still occupied by the Japanese, parcelled out in the fiefs of warlords only weakly federated to the Kuomintang government in retreat at Chungking, and coming under control of the Red Army in the northwest, when it was accorded anticipatory status as a world power by the award of a permanent seat on the Security Council of the United Nations. The Kuomintang government first occupied that seat, but it did so from exile on the island of Formosa from 1949 until 1971. By that time, the

success of the Chinese revolution could no longer be denied. In those few years, one quarter of the world population had moved on from long-arrested development in agricultural civilization into industrial revolution. Today, 20 years later, China is crossing the threshhold into the industrial world and achieving status as a world power in fact. The country's passage through industrial revolution promises to be the most rapid in history.

The success of the révolution must be attributed in no small part to the homogeneity of the Chinese people. On a subcontinent the size of the continental United States, nearly a billion people speak the same language and share the same 5000-year history of high civilization. This is in contrast to the diversity of language, history, and culture in Europe west of the Urals. Further, in contrast to other preindustrial countries awaiting industrial revolution, China had a large cosmopolitan urban population, a source of leadership in the minor nobility of the Mandarin civil service, a substantial cadre of Western-educated intellectuals, and an urban middle class of moneylenders and merchants well acquainted with the world market economy. By no means did all of those people follow the Kuomintang to Formosa. It was to them that Mao Zedong addressed his injunction: "Serve the people!" Under firmly imposed economic and social equality, the political revolution entrained the old order in industrial revolution.

The people to be served were the villagers. It was no doubt lucky for the course of the Chinese revolution that its urban intellectual leaders had had to share the hard life of the peasants in the impoverished landscape of the loess plateau in the great, 2000-kilometer-long northern bend of the Yellow River. They had brought with them there also a deep antipathy (dating back to Stalin's implication in the Kuomintang massacre of the Chinese Communists in 1927) to Soviet ways. Within a few years after the Japanese withdrawal, the revolution was in possession of the countryside and the cities were isolated.

The revolution in the villages was not bloodless. Landowners and moneylenders were lynched by their fellow villagers, however, not by troops sent out from the cities. Stalin's troops had massacred muzhiks and kulaks alike, and the word *mir,* in its meaning of village, was erased from the Soviet vocabulary. The Chinese revolution preserved the village and the communal institutions the people had maintained against the landowners. Around these it nucleated the collectivization of agriculture. Shrewd allocation of incentives within the communes and the maintenance of economic equity elicited the enterprise desired.

The villagers compelled the regime to back off its promotion of such extremes of collectivism as communal cooking, dining, and child rearing. As J. K. Galbraith, with his doctorate in agricultural economics, has observed: "The farmer has it within his powers, when working for others or for the state, to work at the minimum rather than the maximum, and the difference between the two is enormous." The Chinese farmer did, however, embrace the new technology supplied from the center and proceeded to produce the agricultural surplus that made possible the formation of capital for industrial revolution.

Increase in the production of food proceeded steadily (except in 1959) with the increase in the population, which was in the course of doubling from an estimated 475 million in 1950. In 1959, a bad farming season in southern China and the distractions of Mao's "great leap forward," which enlisted 90 million villagers in such industrial enterprises as the building of back-yard blast furnaces, brought on a famine in which as many as 20 million people may have perished. Responding to economic incentive and not much to slogans, the Chinese farmers increased output in the traditional way, by extension of the land under cultivation from 90 million to 100 million hectares. With capital input from the center, they increased the land under irrigation from 30 million hectares in 1950 to 45 million in 1985. The largest increase came, however, as all increase must come in the future: from increase in the yield per hectare and per each man-hour of labor-intensive cultivation. The input of energy per hectare, principally in the form of fertilizer, is estimated to have multiplied 100 times over the input of the biological energy of the farmer, equipped with mattock and sickle. Per hectare, the yield increased more than threefold, from 1200 kilograms of rice in 1950 to 3850 kilograms in 1985.

Scientists at the International Rice Research Institute in Manila were astonished to discover some of their high-yielding strains under wide cultivation in the paddy fields of China before they had been released from laboratory development. While the escape of those strains from the laboratory has not been explained, their speedy acceptance in China testifies to the readiness of Chinese farmers to respond to economic opportunity. Planted to those strains, what

Arthur Goldschmidt calls the "cruelest crop" better repays the backs that bend to reach fingers to transplant each stalk separately in the course of cultivation. The total production of grains multiplied more than three times, from 100 million metric tons in 1950 to 350 million metric tons in 1985. Calories available at the table per capita per day increased from less than 2000 to more than 2500, with a doubling of the protein fraction.

China continues to import food and is one of the larger food importers. At the same time, its "food-import dependency ratio" (that is, the ratio of its own food production to its food imports) is one of the lowest. The suspicion is that China imports low-cost wheat (and even accepts it in grants of aid) to replace rice that it exports at higher prices to other preindustrial countries.

The decades of revolution are the first in China's history without calamitous flooding by its two great rivers. Baskets carried on heads moved the first millions of cubic meters of earth that have confined the downstream stretch of the silt-laden Yellow River to the "suspended" bed on which it flows for 500 kilometers across the North China Plain, laid down by its sediments, to the sea. Heavy earth-moving gear maintains the levees now until longer-term solutions can be found. High dams on the river's far upstream stretch, the first on the river, generate electric power, irrigate thousands of hectares of new farmland in that arid country, and control release of flood water to the downstream stretch. The first bridges across the Yangtse River in the south were built early in the revolution. Its enormous flow, draining the northern slopes of the Himalayas, supplied water to the major portion of the 15 million hectares brought under irrigation and for the first time began to generate electric power.

The build-up of agricultural production also required repair of the hard use and abuse of China's land by its long human occupation. Afforestation had an early place in the mass campaigns to which the exhortations of Chairman Mao called the people. Restoration of forests on the highlands has served the well-recognized purpose of reducing erosion and conserving the rains. On the loess plateau, deforested 500 years ago, afforestation has a major place in the effort to reduce the silt burden of the Yellow River. The truly revolutionary innovation in afforestation has been the planting of four to six rows of trees on both sides of country highways; the paddy fields are enclosed, in effect, by linear forests. The favored fast-growing tree species serve another purpose; Chinese villagers have no fuel-wood shortage.

To feed the urban populations, the agricultural surplus produced by science and economic incentive was lifted as efficiently as in the most ruthless years of the old regime. With more noblesse oblige, the revolution recompensed the villages by the ruralization of technology as soon as there was some to spare. The capital input from the countryside has now been further repaid by the privatization of agriculture.

The capital formed by this strategy was human capital. Within remarkably few years, the well-fed population had become a healthy population. In the city and in the communes, "barefoot doctors" trained in the rudiments of hygiene, first aid, and the administration of antibiotics conducted a successful practice of preventive and curative medicine. Important health measures went beyond medicine. Schistosomiasis, a disease caused by snail-borne parasites, has been all but eliminated from cultivated land simply by moving earth: by filling snail-infested irrigation ditches and digging new ditches. The greatest health measure remains, of course, the improvement in the nutrition of the population.

The accumulation of human capital has been further multiplied by the most successful mass-literacy campaign and school-building enterprise in the preindustrial world. By 1985, illiteracy was down to 35 percent of the population. At least 75 percent of the children of China, a subpopulation larger than the whole population of the United States, was in elementary or secondary school. A formidable 2 percent of the college-age cohort, a big number in a population of a billion, was in higher education, and more engineers and scientists were in training than in the United States.

With the resources of a subcontinental nation available to the work of such people, China was able to undertake industrial revolution in self-reliant isolation from the world economy. It maintained that isolation, in revolutionary recoil from memories of the foreign concessions, through the building of its industrial infrastructure and its self-sufficiency in heavy industry. A railroad construction campaign extended the network to bring the product of newly opened coal and iron mines to the country's first steel industry, now built to a capacity of more than 50 million tons. Energy production increased from the equivalent of less than 100 million tons of coal in 1950 to nearly 900 million tons today; installed electrical generating capacity is nearly 100 megawatts, compared with the negligible installations serving a few cities in 1950. Light industry was devolved to new towns and the larger agricultural communes, with firm barriers set against migration of the population into the big cities. "Nonfactory" small-scale and cottage industry employs 20 million Chinese and produces a quarter of the country's manufactures.

China lost no time in qualifying as a nuclear power. Chinese physicists educated in the Soviet Union as well as in the United States made the nuclear warheads—successfully testing a thermonuclear warhead as early as 1964—and equipped them with intercontinental ballistic delivery vehicles as well.

It is well that China has acquired nuclear technology. The projected continued increase in the material well-being of the people implies at least a fourfold multiplication of the consumption of energy per capita in the next half century. That would bring the energy consumption per capita up to a little less than a third of that of U.S. citizens. The total energy consumption of China would then, how-ever, exceed that of the United States, which vents one-quarter of the human input of carbon dioxide into the atmosphere. With relatively small petroleum resources and with the end of the age of petroleum in sight, in any case, the Chinese are presently committed to securing that energy from their coal. Since Chinese coal is notoriously high in sulfur, the international community will want to encourage China to develop alternative primary energy sources.

As its industrial revolution advanced to the installation of higher technologies in the late 1960s, China was compelled to reduce its isolation. The United States then still stubbornly recognized Taiwan as China. It was to Japan and West Germany that China turned first for installation of control technology and equipment in its oil refineries and petrochemical plants. Upon the U.S. capitulation to reality, with the Nixon–Kissinger kowtow to Mao and Zhou Enlai in 1972, China was secure enough in its heavy industrial base to hasten the development of consumer industries by inviting joint ventures and foreign investment.

The progress of China's industrial revolution can be most easily seen in the country's vital statistics. The prevailing life expectancy of 70 years, infant mortality at 30 per thousand live births, and maternal mortality reduced to 44 per 100,000 deliveries take China out of the class of preindustrial countries. As in other countries that have entered into industrial revolution, Chinese parents have had the satisfaction of seeing their children grow taller than themselves. In Nanking, where such records had been better kept when it served as the Kuomintang capital, a study conducted in 1936 provided a base for comparsion with a study made in 1975, which showed postrevolutionary boys and girls at age 18 to be 15 centimeters taller and 7.5 kilograms heavier.

Still contributing 13 million more people to the world population each year, the rate of China's population growth has declined from 2 percent in 1960 to 1.3 percent. With a net reproduction rate not far above 1, China is approaching zero population growth at a lower standard of living than any nation that has preceded it into industrial revolution. It is able to do so because its average income, today at $300 per capita, is closer to its modal income—the income of most of the population—than that of any other large country in the world. The sense of economic equity abroad among the people still motivates willingness to submit to orders from the center. Such morale has made it possible for the national government to promote population control by draconian measures—the "rationing" of pregnancies among families in urban and rural communes and, lately, by the decree of one-child families.

Revolutionary unity has come under stress, however, with the opening of China to the world over the last two decades and the invocation of market incentives in the cause of economic development. The student protest that brought on the brutal repression in Tiananmen Square and the present retreat of the leadership into authoritarianism and isolation from the outside world had a double agenda. The cry was for economic as well as political democracy. Facing salaried employment in industry or the civil service, the students were protesting not only authoritarian government but also the conspicuous consumption of millionaires in the privatized agricultural system. This was not the objective for which Mao had summoned them for service to the people. Widening disparity in income distribution will make decree of the one-child family and like population control measures a good deal more difficult to enforce.

If, nonetheless, the decline now indicated brings the rate of population growth of the Chinese fifth of the world population below 1 percent in A.D. 2000, 40 percent of the world population will then have arrived at, or be closely approaching, zero growth. The chances that the world population may stop growing at the end of the twenty-first century will thereafter turn upon the progress into industrial revolution of the other 2.75 billion people now living in the preindustrial world—upon the progress, especially, of the next fifth of the world population, the billion people on the southern side of the Himalayas.

INDUSTRIAL REVOLUTION IN INDIA

 Never home to a single ethnic and language community, the Indian subcontinent was divided in 1947, with the encouragement of the departing British raj, by its Hindu and Muslim communities, forming the nations of India and Pakistan. In 1971, East Pakistan seceded from the exploitive West Pakistan (now known simply as Pakistan) to become the nation of Bangladesh. The people of these three nations, along with the Himalayan states of Nepal and Bhutan and the island state of Sri Lanka, share much the same condition of existence, evidenced by a rate of population growth that is close to 2 percent and is the net of high birth and death rates. The total population of the subcontinent, already exceeding that of China, is growing by 18.5 million each year. Pakistan, governed alternately by military dictatorship and landowner oligarchy, has found no certain course of development, despite heavy military subsidy by the United States. Bangladesh is the largest of the 40 poorest countries. The prospect for reduction of the rate of growth of this fifth of the present world population depends, therefore, upon the industrial revolution getting under way in India, where, in any case, 800 million of these people live.

The Indian nation is itself insecurely united, divided on many lines of ethnic, religious, linguistic, and even persisting tribal identity. Its Muslim minority of nearly 100 million is almost as big as the population of either Pakistan or Bangladesh. The important Sikh minority professes its own monotheistic fighting faith. The Hindu 65 percent of the population is divided into numerous language communities. Some shed blood to reverse the adoption in 1964 of Hindi, spoken by 30 percent of the people, as the national language. To bring peace and unity, the government of India undertook, in 1967, to publish its documents in each of the 13 languages spoken by more than 10 million Indians—including English, the nation's lingua franca.

In their division and poverty, the Indians do not live lives of quiet desperation: in almost any village at almost any time, issues incomprehensible to outsiders will bring on arson, mayhem, murder, and massacre. The nonviolence of Mahatma Gandhi drove out the British, but it did not heal his country. Gandhi was assassinated by a Hindu, who blamed him for the division of the subcontinent.

The famous caste system of Hindu India perpetuates the tribes and clans of preagricultural times. There are four hierarchical "castes" but, more important, there are 10,000 caste communities. Averaging 50,000 members today, these are extended-kinship families that have maintained their boundaries by marriage within the clan since prehistoric times. The British biologist J. B. S. Haldane, who spent his last years in India, never failed to find markers of genetic segregation in the castes whose members' blood sera he examined. (He identified three communities afflicted with the sickle-cell trait, which appears also in the African-American population of the United States. The trait confers some resistance to malaria, but it devastates the circulatory system when it is inherited from both parents.)

In each of the 575,000 villages of India, the ten or more castes present give each person a secure identity shared with other members of the same caste in whatever village they live. A member can rely upon the caste as a mutual aid society. In caste communities whose members had been sleeping on the sidewalks of Calcutta since the beginning of the twentieth century, the anthropologist Nirmal Kumar Bose could find not more than one marriage in 1000 outside the caste.

The four-layer ranking of the caste communities largely fixes the power and economic structure of the Indian village. Landownership tends to be concentrated in upper castes, and the trades tend to be practiced by persons in the middle castes, which function, in this sense, as guilds. Segregated on the edge of every village is the community of people without caste, the outcast 20 percent of the Indian population. To these "untouchables" Mahatma Gandhi attempted to give a caste identity; he called them *Harijans,* meaning the "chosen ones" of the deity Vishnu.

To caste and village, the Indian holds deeper fealty than to the remote entity of the Indian nation, in the reverse of the identity felt by citizens of modern industrial nations. Not all the villages are accessible by jeep. Such is their number and inaccessibility that the government of India has no census of its population. For monitoring trends, it relies upon sample surveys conducted in accordance with standards and procedures devised by the Indian Statistical Institute at

Calcutta and its founder P. C. Mahalanobis, a statistician of international standing and Fellow of the Royal Society of London.

Politically, the warp and woof of village and caste give Indian society an unyielding texture, especially as compared with a typical Western industrial democracy. There populations are better likened to a Maxwellian gas of identical particles, instantly responsive to change in pressure and temperature. Caste set the ideal foundation for agricultural civilization; it confers identity upon the poorest and most humble—except for the Harijans. Village India does not provide a responsive environment for revolution, but it may better contain the aftermath of industrial revolution.

Under the British, the superstructure of Indian society—the landed nobility, the civil service, the urban merchant and money people, and the indigenous intelligentsia—came to know the world outside. Early in the nineteenth century, the Bengali Raja Mohan Roy founded a new secular Hindu sect and caste community; his Brahma Simaj was committed to bringing European science and technology into India, along with the corresponding European social and political ideas. In the twentieth century, counting among its members such figures as Rabindranath Tagore, Jawaharlal Nehru, and the several Indian scientists elected to the Royal Society of London, the Brahma Simaj supplied the principal intellectual leadership to the Indian independence movement. The opening of India to the world received another thrust with the building of the dynastic trading and manufacturing empires of the Tata, Birla, Sarabhai, and other families.

In 1931, the independence movement came into the open; the declaration of the All-India Congress committed Muslims and Hindus alike to seek the liberation of India as a political and economic democracy, with social ownership of natural resources, key industries, transportation, communication, and foreign trade. To the Congress, the wave of popular rebellion excited by Gandhi among the urban poor, and even in the villages, brought the support of a mass movement. The sometimes brutal response of the British to provocation by Gandhian nonviolent civil disobedience united the entire country, except the relic princes, against them. The British, accordingly, traded Empire for Commonwealth. By the Indian Independence Act of 1947, Parliament created the independent Dominion of India (along with the independent dominion of Pakistan) and Great Britain withdrew from the government of the country.

It was thus a political revolution very different from the social revolution of China that launched India's industrial revolution. At liberation in 1947, there was no disposition to push for the social ownership called for in 1931. Nehru's quite unrevolutionary "socialist pattern" of development had the acceptance even of the business community. It supplied a sufficient agenda for a government that had less than 10 percent (even today, only 12 percent) of the GNP of the country at its disposal. In Jeffersonian spirit, from his upper-middle-class background, Nehru called for

> (1) Improvement of the position of the poor and socially disadvantaged; (2) rapid industrialization based on investment in heavy industry and expansion of the public sector; (3) central planning and government control over the economy through, in many areas, substitution of administrative controls for market forces of supply and demand; (4) a pragmatic and flexible approach to India's problems, and (5) democracy.

This itemization did not relegate democracy to last priority but, rather, set Nehru's limit on the exercise of state power in seeking economic objectives.

For the task of capital formation, the Indian village was not nearly as ready as the Chinese. The cities of colonial India, incorporated in the imperial British economy (in those days effectively the world-trade economy), were much dependent on imported food. It is not only that the subsistence agriculture of the Indian village yielded little for sale outside; market channels and transportation lines linking villages to cities were correspondingly weak. The independence of the modern state of India required that its cities be fed by its villages. To bring the villages (home to 75 percent of the population) into the new national economy, the government of India had to promote the flow of capital into the villages, not, as in China, out of them. That was the meaning of item (1) on the Nehru agenda. Item (2) called for the necessary industrial revolution.

To amplify its own modest capacity for capital formation, India looked, literally, to "the conscience of mankind." The first Indian five-year plans netted their capital requirement against the foreign-trade surplus and domestic-investment capacity and entered the remainder as economic assistance to be supplied by the industrial world. Year after year, the shortfall from the plans equalled the shortfall from external assistance, in evidence of the sophistication of Indian planning.

Ahead of economic assistance thus calculated, in the first years after liberation, India had need for plain charity. Failing monsoon seasons and bad crops brought hunger to the villages, to add to the demand from the urban population for food from abroad. Fortunately, the farm lobby in the United States secured the enactment of Public Law 480 in 1956. The unburdening, under this legislation, of farm surpluses held by the U.S. government saved India from famine.

As provided in P.L. 480, the shipments set up an account in rupees that was to be expended on economic development. Expenditures from the account, made in grain, went to feed Indian workers. As the workers' wiry, stunted bodies swarmed over highway-, railroad-, and dam-construction sites, the food energy in the grain became infrastructure for India's industrial revolution.

India fared less happily with the United States in its needs for economic and technical assistance of a higher order. In 1962, it became the turn of the United States to supply the hardware for a steel plant to be built at Bokaro, after West Germany and the Soviet Union had delivered their steel plants. Bokaro had been designed around U.S. technology by M. N. Dastur, a Calcutta engineer who had done his apprenticeship in the U.S. steel industry. Preoccupied with the Cold War, the Kennedy White House was glad to cite a review of the Bokaro plans by experts borrowed from the United States Steel Corporation. They had found, in effect, that steel could not be made in India. The Bokaro plant was built years later by the Soviet Union from designs around Soviet hardware.

In U.S. politics, in any case, economic assistance to India or any other preindustrial country was losing the romantic priority it held in the first postwar years. It could not compete with the pressure on the Federal budget laid by military expenditures, for which the Kennedy administration secured two 25 percent increases during its first year in office. With particular respect to India, the disposition in Washington was soured by the acerb and haughty baiting of the conscience of the industrial world by Krishna Menon, India's permanent representative to the United Nations.

On its side, concerned by mounting debt taken on in place of aid, India turned to the strategy of self-reliance. The five-year plans emphasized the replacement of imports by domestic manufactures and frugally secured a positive exchange balance for the import of capital goods. As Nehru's chief planning counsellor, P. C. Mahalanobis calculated that spending $2 billion or $3 billion to build a fertilizer plant could obviate spending $30 billion a year on imported wheat. Even though the free-trade doctrine of comparative advantage dictated the importation of cheaper U.S. wheat or fertilizer, this calculation was endorsed by George Woods, head of the World Bank and one of several U.S. bankers radicalized by that service.

With foreign trade under rigorous control of the planners, India was, for many years, one of the most solvent of the preindustrial countries. Its foreign debt was 19 percent of its GNP in 1988, and its debt-service payments were a manageable 25 percent of its export income. Since then, policies intended to speed development by giving a larger role to the private sector have increased those percentages closer to 25 and 30 percent, respectively, and the country's balance of payments has turned negative.

Under government ownership, and on the Soviet and Chinese model, India put its largest investments first into heavy industry and the industrial infrastructure—into steel production and the machine-building industries, into development of its mines, and into the transportation and electrical-power systems. By 1985, the Indian steel industry had reached a demonstrated capacity of 11 million tons. Primary energy production had passed the equivalent of 180 million tons of coal, and installed electrical generating capacity exceeded 50 megawatts. In state-owned electrochemical plants, India produces most of the 40 kilograms per hectare of nitrogen fertilizer that is spread on its croplands each year.

Development of light industries under private ownership is encouraged by state-subsidized industrial parks, with the manufacture of bicycles, for example, favored for the training of workers in basic skills. Nonfactory industry is as important to the Indian economy as to the Chinese; in 1961, it employed 11 million in "household" manufacturing establishments and another 4 million in "nonregistered" small factories. To bring in higher technologies, the government licenses joint ventures with foreign enterprises. It does so under regulations that compel purchase of increasing percentages of material and components within the country and the downstream sale, where appropriate, of components and parts to Indian manufacturers of final products. By these measures, the government has succeeded in stimulating secondary development.

India did not subscribe to the Non-Proliferation Treaty, intended to inhibit the spread of nuclear weapons to new national arsenals. Government-financed nuclear research in the Tata Institute at Trombay, near Bombay, was to have nurtured a nuclear-power industry. Under the leadership of Homi Bhabha, an imperious graduate of the Cavendish Laboratory at Cambridge University, the Indian physicists did make a nuclear "device," demonstrated in an underground test in 1974. Presently, the expansion of energy production relies upon the country's abundant low-grade coals. India reserves most of its small petroleum production for export and the foreign exchange it earns at the price levels secured by its Arab neighbors. Fulfillment of India's hopes for development portends another United States–sized contribution to the concentration of carbon dioxide in the atmosphere and the acidification of rain. India's neighbors, too, will want to encourage her in the development of alternative sources of primary energy.

Industrial investment went, from the beginning, to increase the productivity of the country's agriculture. Later plans recognized the need for direct intervention in the villages. Two great campaigns of rural development sent thousands of experts from the cities for the first time into the villages. They brought the new technologies of agriculture, sanitation, and medicine; they organized producer and marketing cooperatives and sought to establish in village councils, the "panchyati," the rudiments of democratic self-government.

The new agricultural technology, at least, took root. Between 1960 and 1970, results became visible in increases in total output averaging 1 percent per annum. When high-yielding seed varieties came from the laboratories in the 1970s, the annual increase in output went to 2.5 percent. In the state of Punjab, with the "Puritan ethic" of the Sikhs to amplify the input from the laboratories, the annual increase went to 5 percent. By 1985, India had tripled its annual output of grain—to more than 160 million tons, from 55 million tons in 1950. A doubling of the yield per hectare, from 700 to 1500 kilograms, accounts for most of this achievement. That yield is less than half of China's yield per hectare, however, and less than one-quarter of Japan's.

The unfavorable comparison does not reflect upon the Indian farmer. It betrays, rather, chronic shortfall in the planned production of fertilizer and in the building of the dams and reservoirs to conserve the seasonal monsoon rains for irrigation of the land through the nine-month dry season. With water, the land can yield two and even three crops per year. To feed its growing population, India has 170 million hectares of arable land, nearly twice that of China. Of the 100 million irrigable hectares, only 40 million have been brought under irrigation. For the present, the Indian industrial revolution has made the country self-sufficient in food supply and, for the first time, secure against famine. With food production increasing faster than population, kilocalories available per capita have increased from a wasting 1700 to an adequate 2500 per day.

Meanwhile, the central government has been addressing the more intractable institutional obstacles that stand in the way of agricultural development and the delivery of its output to market. The poorest 45 percent of the farmers, typically working less than one hectare, hold only 1.3 percent of the land and must be reckoned as subsisting, if they are doing well, with not much to sell. Another 45 percent of the farmers work holdings of less than 5 hectares, accounting for almost half of all the land. They can be counted as producers for the market, along with the remaining 10 percent who own the other half of the land in holdings of 5 to 50 and more hectares and work it with sharecroppers and hired hands. As may be imagined, new technology and irrigation water reach the bigger holdings first and are monopolized there. Incentive for conservation and enhancement of the land is lost, however, somewhere between the landlord and the tenant farmer.

The technology of the Green Revolution works as well on small as on large holdings, and it responds to the more intensive effort of the smaller farmer. This advantage is lost to continued rural population growth and the fractionation of small holdings to smaller ones. Between 1960 and 1980, holdings of less than 5 hectares increased from 87 percent to 91 percent of all holdings. Population pressure in the countryside drives small farmers onto marginal land, and it drives increasing numbers of landless people from the land. While there are more prosperous villagers than ever before, the number of the impoverished has grown faster, along with the number of hectares classified as barren.

The central and state governments maintain strong efforts against these untoward trends. Substantial soil reclamation and afforestation projects are conducted along with efforts to capture more of the monsoon rains for year-round cropping of the land.

The "substitution of administrative controls" has had equally qualified success against market forces in the traditional distribution system that give the smallest producers and the poorest consumers the worst deal. The small farmer, often a sharecropper, must give up so much to landlord, moneylender, and middleman that he sees little return from his labor. The income trickle in the villages is up, not down.

To improve the farmer's share and keep prices low to the consumer, the Indian government has tried stratagems all along the line, from price-fixing, to credit controls, to forced procurement from hoarding middlemen, to grain banks, to "fair-price" shops, to subsidy of farmer cooperatives. If any of them work, they do not do so for long against the manipulation of market forces by the village oligarchy.

Poverty remains the lot of the overwhelming percentage of the Indian people. Simple long division of the GNP by the 800 million population gives a GNP per capita of $270, not far below the $300 of China. Distribution of income and wealth in India places this average income high above the median. That makes for quite different kinds of existence at the top and bottom of the scale. It is not that the distribution is so unfair; India compares favorably with just about all the other preindustrial countries. Not counted in the monetary income, moreover, is the nonmonetized product of labor and land, which constitutes most of the "income" of the very poorest. India is the home of 300 million of the world's poorest people. It can boast, on the other hand, that the number of its very rich exceeds that of France.

In the country's vital statistics, poverty is expressed in a life expectancy still below 60 years and an infant mortality rate of nearly 100 per 1000 live births. With the rate of population growth declining, presently just below 1.8 percent, India is nonetheless entering the second phase of the demogaphic transition.

The Indian government long ago set population control as a national objective and has conducted family-planning programs on a large scale. Effective public response must await considerable reduction in the infant mortality rate, especially in the villages, where it runs above the national average. It requires as much motivation to practice contraception in a mud hut as to practice abstinence from intercourse. Indian couples blessed with two or more children are known to practice abstinence in accordance with the *karma,* the life-plan of their Hindu faith. That villagers will respond to assured survival of their infants is evidenced in Punjab, where the increasing agricultural prosperity of the past decade has been attended by concomitant reduction in the birth rate.

Industrial revolution thus far has made India a dual economy. Modern industrial urban India is the eleventh ranking market economy and the second largest, after Brazil, in the preindustrial world. It does not, however, embrace much more than the 30 percent of the population that produces 60 or 70 percent of the GNP and receives a like percentage of the country's total income. To the operations of this economy, the poorest villagers of traditional India, the bottom half of the population that receives less than a quarter of the total income, are as redundant as those starving Irishmen.

The rising output of agriculture has brought to the village elite a prosperity of their own. The holders of economic and political power in the villages receive 45 percent of the village income and enjoy incomes 5, 10, and 20 times the rural average. They now make the strategic political link between the village and the city of the dual economy.

Like so many other countries at this juncture in history, India is undergoing change in leadership and direction. Though a "soft government," in the language of Gunnar Myrdal, the government of India, under the leadership of the Congress party and the Nehru dynasty, valiantly pushed the industrial development of the country ahead of impulse from the market in order to improve "the position of the poor and the socially disadvantaged." The resulting surge in agricultural production has brought the state governments under the increasingly independent control of the newly prosperous village elite. In alliance with urban business leadership, they have come to dominate the Congress party and have given divisive new power to Hindu fundamentalism. The assassination of Rajiv Gandhi leaves the progressive elements in Indian society without a commanding symbol at the center of power. Whether the new leadership that must now emerge will be disposed to push development ahead of market forces—to brake the turning of the circles of cumulative causation that immures traditional India in its poverty—is one of the biggest questions the present now puts to the future.

Whatever the future brings, it is plain that no amount of industrialization will employ the increasing number of landless poor. Sound economics, whether dictated by plan or by market, will equip India with state-of-the-art workless industrial technology for competition in the world economy. Concern about employment of the hordes of landless people comes already from the need to qualify them as consumers, not for what they might contribute to the GNP.

It may be that, as Mahatma Gandhi urged, the village and its way of life have a place in industrial civilization. India has not seen the implosion of population into its big cities so dismayingly evident in other preindustrial countries. Families of the landless stay in their villages, supported for years at a time by fathers and brothers employed at casual labor in the cities and abroad.

In addition to labor and now, of course, food, Indian villages export handicrafts of all kinds, the kind from one village to the next depending upon which of the guild castes is in residence. Hand-spun as well as hand-woven textiles; pearls and precious and semiprecious stones worked and mounted in jewelry and costume jewelry; carvings in wood, stone, and (until recently) ivory; and inlaid stonework show up alongside petroleum on India's export bill of lading. Such products have growing markets, and they give pleasure in the making as well as in possession and use. With the ruralization of technology, starting with electric power and penicillin, villagers in India may have the best of industrial revolution.

GREATER EAST ASIA CO-PROSPERITY SPHERE

For the nearly 450 million diverse people of Southeast Asia and the Southwest Pacific Archipelago, the modern era began with the conquest and occupation of their countries by Japan in World War II. At the end of the war, the British, the French, and the Dutch, their imperial spell broken, were compelled to yield their colonies to independence. In any forecast of the eventual size of the world population, these peoples are a volatile factor. Their numbers are increasing at rates higher than 2 percent per annum, and some countries may increase in number at a still more rapid rate before their economic development brings down their rate of growth.

The region has yet to see an end to the war and its aftershocks. Upon their release from the British Commonwealth, the people of Burma (now Myanmar, population 40 million) endured a period of warlord anarchy and then partial occupation of their country by Kuomintang forces in retreat from southwest China. Strongly isolationist dictatorships have since kept the country out of the world economy. A monsoon climate, ample land, and significant mineral resources are there to support industrial revolution when it begins. Meanwhile, with infant mortality at more than 60 per 1000 live births, the 40 million Burmese are increasing at an annual rate higher than 2 percent.

For the three revolutionary Indochinese states—Laos, 4 million population; Kampuchea, 8 million population, and Vietnam, 65 million population—the war that began against the French upon the departure of the Japanese continues even today. The withdrawal of the United States from Vietnam in 1975 left the incidentally collapsed state of Kampuchea at the mercy of the Khmer Rouge party and the dictator Pol Pot. Their mad scheme for "ruralization" of the country brought death to 2 million Kampucheans. The presence of the Khmer Rouge in the provisional coalition government, set up this year under presidency of the country's former monarch, Prince Sihanouk, keeps the future of Kampuchea and its neighbors in doubt. Development of the wealth brought by the semiannual flood of the Mekong River, which these three states share with the independent kingdom of Thailand, remains accordingly stalled. Work on the Mekong Valley plan has continued under UN sponsorship all through all the disorder of war and revolution; it will be ready to harness the melting snows from the Himalayas and the monsoon rains when civil order has been restored. Population growth continues at close to 2.5 percent per annum.

On the western side of the Mekong River, meanwhile, Thailand—54 million population—has moved on into the early stages of industrial revolution, first under heavy military investment from the United States and now under commercial investment from Japan.

The new nations of Malaysia, 17 million population, and Indonesia, 175 million population, dividing the British and Dutch East Indies, have been approaching the ignition of self-sustained economic development, with Malaysia in the lead. Their development is favored by natural resources and by their proximity to the voracious market of Japan. Exports—of oil and plantation products and, in the case of Malaysia, manufactured goods—equal 25 percent of the GNP of Indonesia and fully half that of Malaysia. With their principal trading partner, Japan, they have been developing labor-intensive light manufacturing industries. Malaysia offsets its imports from Japan by its exports to the United States, its largest customer; in this respect, like South Korea, Malaysia represents an extension of Japanese economic power. In pressing their development, both countries have assumed relatively immense overseas debt: equal to 65 percent of the GNP of Malaysia and 45 percent of the GNP of Indonesia, despite that country's substantial revenue from its nationalized oil resources.

Malaysia's fast entrance into the world economy has brought its average GNP per capita to $850. The improvement in the people's circumstances is reflected in the decline of infant mortality from 88 to 28 per 1000 live births and the concurrent decline in the rate of population growth from nearly 3 percent to just under 2 percent per annum between 1965 and 1990. Indonesia, growing more slowly, has reached an average GNP per capita of $450. Its infant mortality rate stood at 84 per 1000 live births in 1988; its population growth rate, still above 2 percent. As may be assumed, inequality of income distribution in both countries keeps infant and child mortality rates (and so the fertility rate) high in the overwhelmingly larger bottom-income groups.

To the north and out of this engagement in world trade is the Republic of the Philippines, nurseling of the United States. Rich in soil and mineral resources, the islands became a colony of Spain in the sixteenth century. That history is reflected today in the extreme disparity of distribution of income and wealth, much as in the former colonies of Spain and Portugal in Latin America. The GNP of $33 billion is about the same as that of Malaysia, and the population, at 55 million, is nearly four times as large. Arithmetic discloses a relatively advanced average GNP per capita of $600. Given the feudal disparity of income distribution, however, most Filipinos live in deep poverty. With foreign trade at about 20 percent of the GNP, the country's overseas debt, principally to the United States, comes to half of its GNP, and payments on the debt come to 25 percent of the country's export income. The future of the Philippines may lie, the shifting direction of its trade suggests, in the Japanese economic sphere.

THE ARAB NATION?

 As the disparity in the availability of mechanical energy makes the principal difference between the rich and poor nations, so petroleum is the one resource that confers power in the trade between the two worlds. There is no substitute for the fluidity of oil and the mobility got from its burning. By an accident of geology, the biggest pool of oil outside the Soviet

Union is in the possession of the Arab nation. The worldwide search for new oil fields has found them in other preindustrial countries, most recently and most notably in Nigeria and Indonesia. Of all commodities, oil moves on the high seas in hugest volume and value. The Arab kings did not comprehend the value of their oil until their princes, attending Cornell University and the London School of Economics, saw that their ultimate customers were paying more in taxes at the gas pump than for gasoline. The renegotiation of the price of oil thereupon changed the world economy. It did not much change the condition of existence of the Arab people, however.

There are 17 Arab nations—18, if one counts their Semitic siblings in Israel. The Arab nation is divided by many other comparably hate-filled antagonisms: between Christians and Muslims; between the princely states (some owing their existence to customers who created them to legitimize the extraction of the oil) and the revolutionary states; between Muslim fundamentalists and the free-lance intellectuals supplied to all the states by Egypt, Lebanon, and homeless Palestine, and between rich and poor at extremes unknown in other nations. Arab nations have the richest GNPs per capita in the preindustrial world; the figures for 1985 show the United Arab Emirates at $19,000, Qatar at $16,000, Bahrein at $12,000, Kuwait at $11,000, Saudi Arabia and Oman at $8000, and even Libya at $7000. At the other extreme is the recently united Yemen, at the foot of the Arabian peninsula, with only $400 per capita.

It goes without saying that most Arabs, in rich and poor nations alike, live in poverty. Vital statistics betray the disparity of income distribution. In the tiny populations of the United Arab Emirates, Qatar, Bahrein, and Kuwait, infant mortality runs at the creditable rate of 32 per 1000 live births or less. In Saudi Arabia, it is 54; in Oman, 100; in Libya, 82; in Yemen, 120. Life expectancy follows a corresponding pattern. In reflection of the status of women as well as of the prevailing poverty, the growth rate of the 200 million Arab population exceeds 3 percent.

The landscape of Asia Minor and the shores of the Mediterranean Sea are the worse for 5000 and more years of high agricultural civilization. It responds nonetheless to water, as has been demonstrated so conclusively by the Israelis. From their agricultural research center at Volcani has come the "more crop for the drop" technology that harnesses the microphysics of the soil and of the root-hair cells of plants to convey the water from the drip-irrigation emitter directly to the root, with little water in storage to evaporate from the soil. Employing this technology and frugally recharging its aquifers, Israel boasts of using 110 percent of its water. Along with Israeli desalting technology, which supplies water from the Red Sea and the Persian Gulf to the Arab kingdoms, Israeli arid-land irrigation is helping to revive Arab agriculture.

The economic development of Israel demonstrates the effectiveness of generous financial assistance in economic development, which the country has received from the U.S. Jewish community as well as the U.S. government. But the movement of Israeli technology against the gradient of enmity demonstrates forcefully the economic sense of technical assistance.

Oil was, of course, the resource that might have financed the economic development of the Arab nation. The price increase from $5 per barrel to $34 was an earthquake in the world economy. It set off inflation and recession in the rich countries. It brought preindustrial economies to their knees. To the credit of the oil princes, they made some redress, by way of grants of petrodollars to economic assistance of the poorer preindustrial countries. The price increase brought little change, however, in the life of the fellaheen Arab.

Feudal regimes give the people no claim on national resources. Princely accounting makes weak distinction between the national income and the privy purse. Not all the princes are as conscientious as the emir of Kuwait, who published his intention to divide the revenue three ways: one-third for the household, one-third for investment overseas, and one-third for the public benefit. In other kingdoms and emirates, in less equitable division, it has gone to personal extravagance, assets abroad, and token development projects at home.

Among the so-called revolutionary states, Iraq was by far the largest producer of oil; in the aftermath of its invasion of Kuwait, its oil shipments are limited by UN sanction. Besides making war with the country's oil revenues, Saddam Hussein had put them into the building of the infrastructure of an industrial economy. With the peak of petroleum production in sight, export of the principal resource of the Arab nation has yet to ignite industrial revolution.

THE PLIGHT OF SUB-SAHARAN AFRICA

 Africa south of the Sahara holds one of the Earth's last frontiers open to human habitation and economic development. Its population density of 18 per square kilometer compares to 100 in Asia as a whole, 110 in China, 231 in India, and 685 in Bangladesh. The extent of frontier open to agriculture must be discounted, however, for deserts, for rain forests threatened by the invasion of fortune hunters and of the desperate poor, and for the savannas that sustain the dwindling diversity of the continent's large-mammal fauna. It must be discounted principally for the paucity of biologically essential elements in much of its ancient soil, not glaciated since the continent of Gondwana began to break up 200 million years ago and before the continental shield of Africa drifted into its present place on the world map [see illustration on page 71]. Nonetheless, in the 10 million square kilometers of alluvial soil in its river valleys and not yet surveyed reaches of soil in which essential elements have been renewed by volcanic fallout, there is land to feed the growing population. The continent's celebrated mineral wealth, long exploited for markets overseas, is still largely there to support Africa's own industrial development.

In principle, Africa now belongs to the Africans. The founding of the state of Namibia in March 1990 brought the last colonial territory under native government. It remains for South Africa to accede to the right of its black majority to join its electorate on equal terms with the members of the white oligarchy. That vision conjures up another: South Africa, with its fully developed industrial system, might thereafter lead its sister nations on to industrial revolution. Both visions appear tragically remote.

The boundaries of the 41 sub-Saharan states bear no relation to provinces of nature, nor to endowment with resources, nor to culture. They are the pieces of the jigsaw puzzle drawn, many of the lines with a straightedge, at the Berlin Conference in 1885 to admit the newly united Germany to the club of empire. The boundaries of the new states overlie the boundaries of the former colonies—some of them mere administrative units of those colonies. Of the 41 states, 30 have populations of less than 10 million; 19, of less than 5 million; 6, of less than 1 million. Only the biggest states embrace within their boundaries the population and resources to achieve self-sustained growth. Only in the second generation of their leadership are they developing the human resources to interface with the world outside and manage industrial development.

Independence came, not without bloodshed, to the African colonies and protectorates of Britain, France, and Belgium in the early 1960s. Unrest rising everywhere throughout the 1950s and guerilla warfare in the Belgian Congo and in the British holdings in East Africa had made the maintenance of empire as unpleasant as it was unnecessary. School teachers, physicians, and clerks, constituting the native intelligentsia that led the independence movements, now found themselves taking charge of their countries. Some of them—notably Julius Nyerere in Tanzania, Sekou Toure in Guinea, Kenneth David Kaunda in Zambia, and Leopold Senghor in Senegal—were still in charge in 1990. These fathers of their countries did not all plan to remain in office for life. Urging their countrymen on to political and economic democracy, they have learned that this ideal must await industrial revolution. Without the needed help from the industrial world, they find themselves heading one-party governments.

In most of the new countries south of the Sahara, however, leadership was seized by soldiers and policemen at the outset, as in Congo (formerly French Congo) in 1960 and Nigeria in 1963, or in coups d'état displacing the intelligentsia, as in Ghana in 1966. The legitimacy of their rule derives from the colonial governments that employed and trained them. The departing colonials installed such leadership where they found it necessary to secure their economic interests. Thus, the Belgians encouraged Colonel Sese Seko Mobutu in his rescue of Zaire (formerly Belgian Congo) and the Katanga copper mines from the suspect socialism of Patrice Lumumba in 1961. Dag Hammarsjkold, Secretary General of the United Nations, was an incidental fatal casualty of this episode. General Mobutu was still holding on as chief of state against rising popular discontent in 1991.

Considerable bloodshed attended the liberation of the colonies held by Portugal; Angola and Mozambique did not achieve their liberation until 1975. In Rhodesia, the British settlers tried to emulate the Boers of South Africa, even to the point of withdrawing from the British Commonwealth in order to continue their fight against the black majority. Only in 1981 did Rhodesia become Zimbabwe under the presidency of Robert Mugabe.

In place of development, the first half century of liberation has brought Africa not only wars of liberation but intertribal warfare; uncounted military coups d'état; at all times 5 to 10 million displaced persons; the brutal marauding of Idi Amin; the opera bouffe coronation of Emperor Bokassa of the Central African Empire (now the Central African Republic), and lately the still-to-be-sanctified World's Largest Basilica, modeled on St. Peter's in Rome and one-third larger, at Abidjan in the Cote d'Ivoire by which the world is to remember the presidency-for-life of Felix Houphouet-Boigny.

To the bloodshed and disorder, industrial nations have supplied instigation and weapons. The superpowers also sponsored violence quite directly, only thinly disguised by their proxies, as in the case of the Kantanga copper mines; in the still fulminating skirmishes and rebellions in Sudan and in and between Somalia and Ethiopia, and in the prolonged struggle that detached Southwest Africa from South Africa and created the new state of Namibia. In all the "frontier states" around the border of South Africa, from Angola on the Atlantic to Mozambique on the Indian Ocean, that country's mercenary hoodlum forces have destabilized the governments and terrorized the villages.

The poverty of Africa has brought strong men—as it did Robert McNamara, in his valedictory as president of the World Bank—to tears. In the 20 poorest states, the mortality of children under 5 years of age runs more than 300 per 1000 live births. It runs more than 200, or just under that number, in all the others. Since 1984, a sine wave of famine, affecting states with populations totalling 150 million, has perturbed these averages, with 30 million people suffering chronic malnutrition and 5 million children dying in the worst years. The work, as well as the sorrow, falls to the women, who do the primitive farming. While life expectancy has lengthened by a decade since 1950, the people have no assurance of the survival of their children.

The rate of population growth of the 41 sub-Saharan states, with populations totalling 400 million, averages more than 3 percent per year. Adding Sudan, Somalia, and Ethiopia, nations that share the same prospects, the total population to be reckoned with here comes to 500 million. With half the population of the Indian sub-continent, this region is making a nearly equal addition of 18 million people to the world population each year. By A.D. 2000 its population will inescapably total 700 million. With most of the African populations at that time increasing at rates above 2 percent, the ongoing population explosion will have its primary locus in Africa.

The African frontier is overdue for action—by indigenous initiative and external assistance—on development. The site of poverty is still the village, although the urban population is growing faster than that on any other continent. The primitive farming technology cannot feed the exploding population. Its traditional institutional supports are giving way to the incorporation of the village in the national economy. African farming was the cooperative working by the extended-kinship family of its communal land. Now communal holdings are yielding to private ownership. Land distribution, at the outset, has been fair: 95 percent of the farmers work holdings of 5 hectares or less, and 80 percent of the land is in such holdings.

In the 1970s, with increasing numbers of farmers cultivating more land, the African states saw annual increases in output averaging 3 percent. But only 20 states, with populations totalling 100 million, saw increases in output per capita. Since 1980, output per capita has been in decline everywhere. To feed their growing urban populations, the bigger trading states have had to increase their food imports since 1970 from $1 billion to $10 billion, from 13 percent to 20 percent of their total import bill, in deficit by $4 billion for the year 1985.

Food is important in the exports of most African states. For the 25 poorest, it is the only source of foreign exchange. The state buys cheap from the farmer and attempts to sell dear to the world market, most of the time against a declining trend in prices. Austerity measures, imposed by creditors holding the debt that burdens every country, squeeze the farmer's price still lower. Low technology and low prices drive farming to more extensive and destructive cultivation of marginal land. The worst harmed is the land of states that have borders on the Sahara. There, drought in recent years joined economics in obliterating the boundary between the Sahara and the arid-land farming region known as the Sahel. "Sahelization" has become a synonym for desertification.

Recurrent famine since 1984 has periodically excited world charity and brought food relief. What is needed is the technology that underfinanced UN agencies have been developing and bringing in too slowly. It may be that concern for the environment will compel recognition of the need for technology transfer on an emergency but sustained and grand scale. For at least the duration of such emergency, also, the appropriate international financial authorities might entertain relaxation of the austerity measures they are imposing on these poverty-stricken states in the name of solvency.

It was a treasure hunt—for diamonds, gold, and copper—that brought sub-Saharan Africa into the world economy in the late nineteenth century. The export of minerals, including now especially oil, maintains the principal connection between the region and the world outside. Minerals constituted half of the total exports from the region in 1970 and three-quarters in 1985, with oil bulking largest in the fourfold multiplication of the total. The exporters of oil and of ores or their metals are the dozen most prosperous (or least poor) nations and, of course, the ones best known to the industrial world: Angola, Nigeria, Zaire, Zambia, Zimbabwe.

Extraction of the resources employs a miniscule fraction of the labor force available in each country. The principal contribution of the resources to development has been to that part of the infrastructure that moves them most expeditiously out of the country. Claims on the resources for contribution to development beyond are not pressed hard by the governments of the nations because none, except oil, carry much compulsion. The governments are better known, in general, for keeping the law and order that facilitates the export operations.

The connection to the world outside in every African country does not reach inward much beyond the small urban enclave of persons employed by the exporting industries and the civil service of the national government. In the national capital—the only city in most countries—the incomes of these people excite enterprise in the usual array of consumer services. This much economic activity and the necessary public utilities sustain in some cities the beginnings of light manufacturing industries.

Now, in increasing numbers, the cities of Africa are attracting landless country people, displaced by crowding in the countryside or by the failure of the land. In many countries, the shantytowns are fast outgrowing the cities. The informal economy of bartered services and goods in these communities, with a small cash inflow from lower-end services to the formal economy of the city proper, is estimated in some countries to be equal, if the ferment of activity could be monetized, to the formal economy. Here is evidence that under-development in Africa cannot be laid to the people's lack of enterprise or failure to respond to economic incentive.

To finance what venture has gone into development and, sadly, the extravagances to which some national elites have been seduced, the nations of sub-Saharan Africa have accumulated external long-term debt equal to 40 percent of their combined GNP. Debt service lays a burden of 25 percent on export income. For 27 countries, the debt exceeds 50 percent of GNP; for 11 of these, it exceeds 100 percent of GNP.

The African debt, as a 10 percent share in the total debt of the poor nations to the rich, exceeds the African 8 percent share of the GNP of the poor countries. This might suggest that the new African nations have had their share of credit. Their 500 million population represents, however, a full 13 percent of the total population of the poor nations. The depth of African poverty, suggested by its 8 percent share of the combined GNP of the preindustrial nations, raises the African problem to something more like 20 percent of the total effort that must be summoned to bring world population growth to zero. The measures of austerity being urged and imposed on the African nations by the international credit authorities has put the industrialization of Africa on hold.

UNDERDEVELOPMENT IN LATIN AMERICA

 Latin America, with a population density of 19 persons per square kilometer, holds another frontier region open to the future. The 21 million square kilometers reach 90 degrees of latitude from the northern subtropics to the southern subantarctic. They present some of the Earth's most glorious landscapes, offer mineral treasure still undiscovered, and spread fertile soils for cultivation. From the great Cordillera that runs the region's length on the Pacific side, abundant rivers flow east to the Atlantic. The basin of the 4000-mile Amazon bears half of the planet's rain forest, a quarter of the total forest cover.

Latin America is rich as well in human resources. Many of its predominantly urban populations live in cities older than any in North America. The people proudly assert their right to freedom as citizens of the democracies which are proclaimed in the constitutions of all the Latin American countries. They are well acquainted with the mechanical trades of industrial civilization. A high percentage have higher education. If undersupplied with technologists, the lively intelligentsias are well trained in law and political economy.

How can it be, then, that the nations of Latin America are home to nearly 100 million of the world's poorest people? Poverty is, in fact, the lot of all but a few of the 400 million total population of the region. The underdevelopment of Latin America offers insight into the role of social institutions in the making and perpetuating of poverty because that is the only factor that can be charged in the plight of the people. The countries are not poor; the people are poor.

Latin American societies carry into our time the inequalities in the human condition that made possible the building of high civilization in preindustrial times. They reflect the history, very different from that of North America, of the conquest and settlement by Europeans of this vast region of the New World.

The two nations of Western Europe that are the last to have entered the industrial age conquered and settled Latin America. Spain and Portugal went on to the high seas ahead of the Netherlands and England. The soldiers and priests of their landed aristocracies overwhelmed the native high civilizations they found in America, in too early a stage of development to stand up to steel and gunpowder. They installed, in place of the Aztec and Inca feudal order, the plantations and ranches of their own feudal order, not the homesteads of North America.

This heritage is recognizable first in the cities of the cosmopolitan nations of Latin America today. As at home in the Old World, the Latin settlers built their cities to be centers for ostentation of power and wealth and for cultivation of the arts, not for commerce and manufacturing. With their great public spaces framed by cathedrals, palaces, and garrisons, they are Madrid and Lisbon, not Boston or Philadelphia. If surrounded now by crowded, market-economy real estate development, the past remains, cherished at the center of the cities.

The consequences of this heritage surrounds the old cities a second time today. Squatter settlements hold populations as large as in the cities proper and growing faster.

Inequality in Latin America begins with the most unequal land-distribution system in the world. Typically, except in the unstable small countries of Central America, fewer than 10 percent of the landholders own 98 percent of the land in *latifundios* of more than 50 hectares. These estates, some of them vast, merit designation by their Spanish name as the unique institutions that they are; the land, held for social status, is typically underutilized, with cattle pastured on hectares better planted to crops. On the remaining 2 percent of the land, in parcels of less than 5 hectares, the 20 to 30 percent of the population that is rural is self-employed in extracting subsistence from the soil, which, needless to say, is the soil that was left over.

The 70 percent of the poor who are not on the land are in the cities, in the reverse of the ratio in other preindustrial countries. Half or more of this population lives in the squatter settlements. Until recently, the squatter populations were increasing from within; now they are increasing by implosion of the landless from the countryside.

Inequality in the distribution of wealth produces corresponding inequality in the distribution of income. More than half of the income goes to the top 20 percent income groups: 52 percent in Argentina, 58 percent in Mexico, 62 percent in Brazil; 68 percent in Bolivia and Colombia. These percentages compare with 50 percent in the United States, skewed upward from 41 percent after the ten years of the Reagan-Bush administration of the U.S. economy. The top 5 percent enjoy average incomes 15 times the average income of the bottom 40 percent in Argentina, 22 times in Bolivia and Mexico, 25 times in Brazil, 44 times in Colombia—compared, again, with 12 times in the Reagan-Bush United States.

The rich in Latin America get their wealth in the main from the sale overseas of their countries' resources. The products of agriculture, food and raw materials, and minerals and oil constitute 70 percent of the exports. In recent years, except for oil, these exports have gone to market against deteriorating terms of trade. This has been of more consequence to the rich than to the poor; exports employ no more than a small minority of the labor force. The poor are more troubled by the chronic disorder of the domestic economies, by inflation in two digits. That is of less consequence to the rich; they have hard currency to buy their country's currency at any price.

Products of the *latifundios* make up 15 percent of the exports of the region, but they are 66 percent of Argentina's exports, 90 percent of Paraguay's, and 70 percent of the exports of the small Central American republics. Except for the pinch of lithosphere in the plant and animal tissue of these exports, the resources exported are, of course, renewable. Typically, however, the economic arrangements with the peons and tenant farmers do not encourage conserving agricultural practices. The *latifundistas* themselves are given to speculative response to market opportunities. In Central America, the dry tropical forest gave way to pasture in the last few decades to produce cheap beef for the fast-food market in North America. On more than one market impulse from abroad—rubber, sugar, pulp— the rain forest of the Amazon has been invaded by plantations that could not be supported by the fragile soil. For the *latifundios,* workers are always available at low wages, cushioned by fall-back to subsistence on their own small landholdings. To feed their urban populations, most Latin American countries depend, to a greater or lesser extent, on food imports.

The enforcement of these economic arrangements is visible in the layout of every provincial town. In miniature replica of the *zocalo* in the capital, the church stands at the head of the central square, the city hall on one side, and the garrison on the other. In some countries, the poor have fled to the woods. In the Sierra Madre in Cuba in the 1950s, the revolutionary junta found tens of thousands of people not counted in the census, living a feral existence in the forest. The landless invade the Amazon forest. The guerillas of the Shining Path have been at large in the Andes of Peru and Colombia for more than a decade. They have begun to complicate the cultivation of coca in the backwoods of Colombia and Peru for the *hidalgos* of the international drug economy.

Exports of minerals (presently 10 percent of the value of exports) and oil (presently 50 percent), both subject to large swings in the market, represent real depletion of nonrenewable resources. Principally from the Andean countries, Chile, Peru and Bolivia, the ores of nonferrous metals may be said to be exported on the spot, because so little of their value remains in the country. The extraction of minerals employs less than 5 percent of the labor force; no more than 20 percent of the value of the minerals is spent in local currency.

Oil has been for some years a bonanza for Mexico (60 percent of the country's exports, up from 4 percent in 1970), Venezuela (91 percent, down from 94 percent in 1970), Ecuador (70 percent, up from 1 percent in 1970) and Bolivia (56 percent, up from 4 percent in 1970). All of these countries are beneficiaries of the price rise secured in the early 1970s by the Arab oil exporters. The Arabs were indebted in turn, however, to Mexico and Venezuela. They were the first countries to demonstrate the unique economic leverage of oil in world commerce.

Mexico emerged in the 1920s, under development by U.S. oil companies, as the world's second oil-producing nation after the United States. A dispute over wages, undiplomatically managed, erupted into such popular resentment that, in 1938, President Lázaro Cárdenas was able to win acclaim by nationalizing the Mexican oil fields. The entry of Pemex (the Mexican state-owned producer, refiner, and marketer of oil) into the world market brought a boycott of Mexico by the big oil companies, then evolving to the transnational sovereignties that they are today.

To replace Mexico, the U.S. and British oil companies brought the oil resources of Venezuela under forced-draft development. They were able to do so in the benign shelter of the dictatorship of Juan Vicente Gómez. The social unrest that attends economic upswings rather than downswings brought the displacement of Gomez by the elected government of Rómulo Gallegos. In the wartime seller's market, Gallegos was able to compel the oil companies to accept, short of nationalization, first a 50–50, and then a 60–40, split on the profit from the oil. In 1976, under cover of the OPEC reorganization of the world market, Venezuela nationalized its oil resources. Between 1970 and 1985, Venezuela and Mexico, from a great new field, saw their oil revenues soar from less than $0.5 billion to $3 billion and $15 billion, respectively.

The income from exports that accrues to individuals in Latin America goes to expenditure on private luxury on a scale commensurate with their status in international society, where many are better known than at home, and into assets securely located in industrial countries. These people are chary of investment at home, as is suggested by the capital flight that balanced the inflow of petrodollar bank loans in the 1980s. That debt now inhibits development in all the larger Latin American economies, but especially the biggest, those of Argentina, Brazil, and Mexico.

The portion of export income accruing to governments goes, after attrition by corruption, to public investment principally in the infrastructure that expedites the flow of exports that produces it. In Venezuela, oil revenues transformed Caracas from a provincial capital to a show-case city of modern architecture and technology. To their credit, the governments of some Latin American countries, notably Argentina, Brazil, Mexico, and Venezuela, have also deployed substantial sums from export income and loans from abroad to investment in industry.

Argentina, Brazil, and Mexico saw vigorous industrial growth during World War II. Preoccupation of their biggest supplier, the United States, with warfare made it possible for them to substitute their own manufactures for imports. The three countries made a start on installation of heavy industry, including steel. Venezuela, financed by oil exports, joined them in planned industrialization during the postwar years. Economic growth slowed down in Argentina after 1975; Brazil, Mexico, and Venezuela managed to sustain their momentum into the 1980s. All are now becalmed by the debt they assumed in the boom years.

Export-financed affluence in the cities of Latin America has attracted foreign direct investment in the countries' urban markets. The branch plants of transnational consumer-product corporations do not, however, set off secondary development. For the skilled labor, raw materials, and intermediate products they require, they look to sources at home. The centers of affluence in the cities tend to develop closer economic ties to the country to which the exports go than to their own hinterland.

This much growth has improved the lot of people in the formal economies of the cities of Latin America. It has gone substantially unnoted in the lives of inhabitants of the shantytowns and the countrysides. Even the "newly industrializing" countries have entrained no more than a minority of their populations in industrial revolution.

The maintenance of a stable environment for exports underlies the alternation between elected government and military dictatorship that characterizes Latin American politics. In Venezuela, in recent times, the cycle went first from Gómez to Gallegos; it went back, in 1948, to dictatorship under Marcos Pérez Jiménez and then, in 1958, to elected government. In Chile, at the turn of the century, President José Balmaceda attempted to capture a portion of the income from nitrate exports for public purposes and was overthrown by coup d'état, a precedent for the disposal in 1974 of Salvador Allende, whose successor, Augusto Pinochet, is only now going off stage. These exchanges of power invariably attract the interest and sometimes the intervention of the United States, the principal export customer and economic partner of the Latin American oligarchies. The revolutionary governments of Cuba and Nicaragua won little more than the exclusion of their countries from the hemispheric trading system.

To and from the United States move one-third of the exports and one-third of the imports of Latin America. U.S. transnational corporations conduct 40 percent of Latin America's trade with the rest of the world. U.S. banks hold 80 percent of the Latin American debt of $400 billion, which has multiplied sixfold since 1970. Nearly half of the total debt of the preindustrial world, this burden is equal also to half of the GNP of Latin America; service of the debt equals 30 percent of the region's exports. The bulk of the debt was incurred by Argentina, Brazil, and Mexico; on their exports, it lays a toll of 64 percent, 35 percent, and 38 percent, respectively. Since 1979, the net financial flow for the three countries has been outward to a total of $30 billion and to a total of $50 billion for the entire region.

The economic picture finds plain translation in vital statistics. The Latin American countries with two-thirds of the region's population of 400 million have life expectancies of 65 years or less and infant mortality rates of more than 40 per 1000 live births. The rate of population growth exceeds 3 percent in countries with 100 million of the total population and 2 percent in countries with more than 300 million of that population. At A.D. 2000, the Latin American population will total 520 million, and present trends indicate that 100 million of the total will still be increasing by more than 2 percent per year, a rate that will double that number in a generation.

POOR NATIONS AND RICH NATIONS

At the end of the fourth century of industrial revolution it must be admitted that one quarter of the world population, principally in Asia, Africa, and Latin America, lives in such poverty that they cannot be sure of the survival of their children. Beset by that cruelest of uncertainties, these people maintain traditional fertility rates. They have nonetheless entered the first phase of the demographic transition; their lengthening life expectancy keeps this quarter of the population growing at rates in excess of 2 percent per year.

About half of the world population, principally in Asia, has seen measurable and more or less continuous improvement in their material circumstances over the past four decades. In the expectation that life will be still better for their children, they are beginning to practice fertility control. The rate of increase of this half of the population, now entering the second phase of the demographic transition, has declined below 2 percent per year. The decline proceeds on a slope that may well carry average annual growth of this half of the world population down to 1 percent or less by the end of this century.

From the lives of the remaining quarter of the world population, industrial revolution has eliminated toil and want. Their approach to, and arrival at, a population growth rate of zero holds out the same possibility to all of humankind. Realization of that possibility in the next half century depends in many ways upon what these fortunate people may feel disposed to do about it.

4

ENERGY

Biological energy—from life processes in the bodies of human beings and domestic animals—does the work of sustaining human life in the preindustrial nations of the world. Food is the fuel for generating the energy that gets the work done. Fuel wood, for 2 billion village people, supplies substantially all of the energy available to them external to their bodies. It cooks their food and warms their homes, but it does none of their work. Until the most recent times, food and fuel wood were the principal sources of energy for all humankind.

In this perspective, the rich industrial nations can be seen as the first in which energy from sources other than mammalian metabolism does the daily work. Principally from the fossil fuels, these people draw energy from inanimate sources in constantly increasing multiples of the biological energy of their bodies. To supply the food that sustains their existence, they expend less than 20 percent of the total expenditure of energy that gets their work done. They expend the rest of it, much of it wastefully, to enjoy a comfortable indoor environment, increased mobility, and dimensions of experience unknown to village people.

Early in the history of agricultural civilization, people engaged falling water to turn millstones and the wind to do the work of oarsmen. The water wheel and the sail exchange motion in one direction for motion in another. (The windmill was a much later, twelfth-century European invention; its rapid adoption across the continent from the Atlantic to the Black Sea constituted a kind of rehearsal for the age of steam.)

It was an entirely different kind of energy exchange that started industrial civilization. The steam engine transformed the energy of heat to the energy of motion.

James Watt invented the term horsepower to describe the superhuman power of his steam engine to do work. In his honor, the term is now interchangeable with "watt," especially for electrical energy and power (746 watts = 1 horsepower). Power, as distinguished from energy, is the rate at which a machine does work; in the case of an electrical generator, it is expressed in kilowatts (kW) or megawatts (mW). Energy is the total output of work, expressed for a given machine as the product of its power multiplied by the time it took to do the work (for example, kilowatt-hours, kWh).

After Watt, people learned to transform the energy of heat not only into motion but into electricity, and then into radiant energy, and then into chemical bonds, and back again and across the circle from one form of energy to another at will. By the middle of this century, energy-transforming machines had taken over the toil of human beings in the industrial countries. These machines summon enormous power to do work. They lift and move, hammer and squeeze things in masses, with forces and at velocities that no number of people and beasts could together manage.

With a command of energy on this scale, people have been making materials that enlarge and diversify their command and use of such energy. Thus, to increase the working temperature of gas turbines, and so the efficiency with which they transform heat to motion, they make the turbine buckets of a ceramic reinforced by single-crystal inorganic whiskers or fibers. These "composite" materials retain tensile strength at high temperature better than any metal against the immense centrifugal force exerted by the spinning of the turbine.

Employing another class of ceramic, the semiconductors, people have learned to make energy and information interchangeable. For this purpose, they employ power measured in tiny, nerve-impulse units of microwatts and fractions of microwatts. Information in this form controls gigantic flows of energy, in the electric drives of rolling mills, for example, and in the navigation of aircraft. Machines that interchange energy and information are now doing the work of human nervous systems as well as of human muscles.

The preindustrial difference between the rich and the poor was the possession of slaves by the rich to do their work and their bidding. Today the line between the rich and the poor nations is drawn most clearly by the command of energy from inanimate sources. The people of the United States once consumed a third and more of the world output of energy; with other people joining them in their estate, they still consume one-quarter of the annual output. From all the different primary sources—coal, petroleum, natural gas, falling water and nuclear fission—expressed in the common denominator of the energy evolved from the burning of a ton of coal, they consume the energy-equivalent of 2.3 billion tons of coal each year. That is nearly 14 tons of coal per capita.

If, as is the convention, a man-year of physical labor is the energy-equivalent of 150 kilowatt-hours, then the work of 200 in-animate-energy slaves (what the prophet of technology R. Buck-minster Fuller called "inanislaves") answers the needs of each man, woman, and child in the United States in the course of a year. Of these, 70 are electrical, called up by the flick of a switch. Some 45 do their work in the extractive and manufacturing industries; 25 heat and cool indoor spaces, and 56 do the work of transportation.

The power plant—consisting of the "prime movers" that convert the primary energy of heat or wind or falling water to the desired mechanical form—is extravagantly overbuilt. That is because U.S. citizens put such a high premium on the mobility afforded by the generous availability of energy. The total capacity of this power plant is 33.3 billion horsepower; of this total, 31.5 billion, or 95 percent, is in internal-combustion engines. Those engines put 126 horses at the disposal of each man, woman, and child in the country (and one horsepower is equal to 10 inanislave-power!). Because the people of the United States keep that power pent up at the curb 96 percent of the time, they get only 5.6 horsepower-years of energy per capita out of their huge investment in their internal-combustion power plant to do the work of transportation. They gladly pay that price for mobility, a dimension of experience about which the world's 2 billion villagers are just beginning to learn.

From the minuscule balance of 1.8 billion horsepower in their power plant (a mere 7 horses per capita), the U.S. population gets a great deal more work. Most of this power is installed in the turbine-generator sets in the country's electrical power stations. Measured in watts instead of horsepower, as is the custom, those generators have

Sources and Uses of Primary Energy
in the United States, 1988

| | ENERGY SOURCES (TRILLIONS OF BTU* | | | | | |
| | END USES | | | | | |
ENERGY SOURCES	RESIDEN-TIAL, COM-MERCIAL	INDUSTRIAL	TRANSPOR-TATION	GENERA-TION OF ELECTRICITY	TOTAL (BTU)	TOTAL (%)
Coal	177	2,797	—	15,850	18,824	23.6
Natural gas	7,540	7,778	561	2,719	18,598	23.2
Petroleum	2,700	8,443	21,255	1,561	33,959	42.5
Other	—	72	—	8,497	8,569	10.7
Total (Btu)	10,417	19,090	21,816	28,627	79,950	
Total (%)	13	24	27.2	35.8		100
Electricity distributed	5,727	3,016	12	[8,755]		30.6
Primary energy losses	12,998	6,846	28	[19,872]		69.4
Total (Btu)	29,142	28,952	21,856	[28,627]	79,950	
Total (%)	36	27.5	36.5			100

*Btu: British thermal unit is the quantity of heat-energy required to raise the temperature of 1 pound of water 1 degree Fahrenheit. Fossil-fuel steam electric power generators convert approximately 10,000 Btu to 1 kilowatt-hour.

ENERGY IN FLUID FORM—*petroleum, natural gas and electricity—satisfies all end uses except those met by the 2974 trillion Btu supplied by coal directly to industrial and residential-commercial uses. One-third of primary energy goes to generating electricity, and more than two-thirds of that is lost in the process.*

a total power of 718 million kilowatts. Spinning 24 hours a day, they generate more than 2500 billion kilowatt-hours in a year. That is more than 10,000 kilowatt-hours per capita. Translated back into horsepower, that comes to just about 7 horsepower-years per capita, more work than they get from their internal-combustion engines.

Energy—as available as air and water in industrial societies—has been taken, until very recently, to be a free good. That impression was affirmed by the steady reduction of the expenditure of heat (and so of fuel) to generate a kilowatt (a constant increase of nearly 4 percent per annum in the efficiency of central-power-station generators) that was prolonged to 1960. Not even the flattening of that curve, as the performance of the prime movers approached the theoretical limit, dampened the outlook. The oncoming of that inevitable event was discounted by reduction of the cost of fuel.

As coal had displaced fuel wood in the middle of the nineteenth century, the liquid fuels—petroleum and natural gas—displaced coal in the middle of the twentieth century. Along with the fluidity that expedites their delivery to the market and facilitates their use, oil and gas carry nearly twice as much energy per ton as coal does.

Furthermore, the combustion of these "clean" fuels arouses less environmental concern. Liquid fuels go mainly to increase the concentration of carbon dioxide in the atmosphere. The higher temperature of their combustion heightens ozone concentration in the street-level air and contributes oxides of nitrogen to acid rain, but the fallout of these pollutants is local. The burning of coal, a "dirty" fuel, injects nearly twice as much carbon dioxide into the atmosphere per kilowatt-hour of primary heat energy transformed, acidifies the rain with oxides of sulfur as well as oxides of nitrogen, and darkens the sky and the cityscape with sooty particulates.

ENERGY ECSTASY

The price of the liquid fuels, based on the cost of prospecting and extraction, was held down by the opening up of rich new oil fields. The richest and the cheapest fields, in the Arabian Peninsula and the mainland of East Asia, came on stream in the 1950s. Along with falling relative price, the increasing fluidity and convenience of energy in this primal form went to seize industrial civilization in an ecstasy of energy consumption.

Neither the price nor the soaring demand curve suggested that the supply of these fuels is finite. Energy consumption in the industrial world has multiplied nearly fourfold since 1950, and consumption per capita has doubled. Owing to the more convenient form of the liquid fuels, consumption has increased nearly sixfold. Petroleum and natural gas began to supply more than half the primary heat energy consumed in the United States in 1950, and it supplied nearly 80 percent of the much larger quantity of primary energy the country consumed in 1960.

A steadily increasing percentage of the primary energy went

to the generation of electricity. This is energy in its most fluid and most convenient form. In the United States, the portion of the heat energy transformed to electricity increased from 10 percent in 1950 to more than a third of the doubled consumption of primary energy in 1987. From the burning of fuel in the power stations, only 35 percent of the primary heat energy is transformed to the convenience of electricity; 65 percent of it goes up the stack. The cheapness and convenience of the liquid fuels and the still greater convenience of electrical energy made that waste of fuel energy worthwhile. Worldwide, the consumption of electricity multiplied 10 times from the 855 billion kilowatt-hours consumed in 1950 to more than 8 trillion kilowatt-hours—8 terawatt-hours—in 1985, with corresponding increase in the expenditure of primary fuel energy that goes up the stack.

Energy abundance had impact on all aspects of everyday life in the industrial countries. In the United States, the newly prosperous middle third of the population reversed a 150-year-long migration and began, at midcentury, to abandon the cities. With their newfound mobility, they sought to return to the country. What they had when they all settled there was, of course, sprawling suburbs.

They were encouraged to this resettlement by public policy that committed the country to personal, as distinguished from public, transportation. In the last major Federal public-works legislation in 1953, the U.S. Congress authorized the building of the interstate highway system that has now remade the map of the country. What formerly were 25 separate cities, each of more than 100,000 population, from Boston to Washington, D.C., are now a single conurbation, their suburbs overlapping, 450 miles long and 30 to 100 miles wide. A half dozen such conurbations hold two-thirds of the U.S. population. St. Louis, Missouri, once a city that stood on the Mississippi River, now spreads out west of the river around a triangle, 20 miles on a side, drawn by three interstate highways.

The heating of the new homes in the United States, which was never by coal, went from oil to gas. Railroads, though converted from coal-fired steam to diesel locomotives, could not serve the population thus resettled and yielded the transport of freight to the tractor-trailer on the new highways. Those tractors, in fulfillment of the law of cumulative causation, now intimidate other traffic on the highways, drawing two and three trailers as big as railway freight cars.

For their single-family dwelling in the suburbs, the people of the United States, and Canada as well, pay bigger heating and transportation bills and a higher percentage of their energy budget than any other people in the world. In the number and diversity of appliances, which increased the number of electric motors in the average North American household from 6 in 1950 to the present 15, their European contemporaries are overtaking them.

For industry, electricity priced in bulk at a few cents per kilowatt-hour became a powerfully attractive and innovative factor of production. The force exerted through a rolling mill by the electric motors that drive them today can be seen in the great slabs of steel plate in the Verrazano Bridge, compared with the spider web of steel shapes in the Eiffel Tower or the Brooklyn Bridge. Electric furnaces have been displacing fuel-fired furnaces in the steel and other metal-lurgical industries. Similarly, electrochemical processes have been displacing direct fuel-energy processing in the chemical industry.

With some reason, therefore, utilities-industry economists postulated a cause–effect relation between energy consumption per capita and GNP per capita. Demand for energy was held to be inelastic—that is, not sensitive to price and especially insensitive to increase in price. Demand, in effect, was infinite. It is difficult to find an economic forecast made before 1970 that did not project the continued doubling of the consumption of electrical energy at 25-year intervals indefinitely into the future [see illustration on page 168].

Given the mortal ration of real time allotted to each human being, such extrapolations are rarely carried forward more than a decade or two. They do not reach the absurdity that awaits beyond. Doubling of the output of electrical energy every decade from where it stood in 1970 would supply a world population of 10 billion people with 20 times the electrical energy per capita presently at the disposal of the citizens of the United States. For each of the 10 billion people, that would be 1400 electrical inanislaves.

Implicit in such projections of demand, even those short of the absurd, was the premise that the supply of energy is infinite as well. The market process itself works to give that impression. The market sets the price of oil, as it does that of other commodities and products, by the costs incurred by the highest-cost producer. It has no way of calibrating scarcity value except to the extent that the costs of discovery and extraction, in the case of oil, reflect the depletion of the resource in a competing region and cause its price to rise.

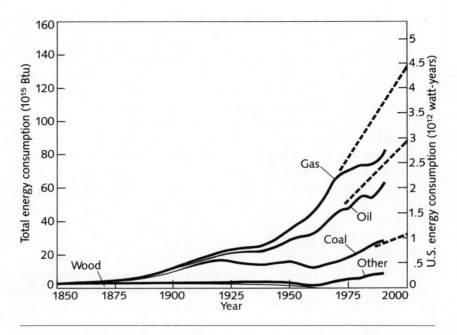

ENERGY-CONSUMPTION FORECAST *published in 1971 showed consumption increasing at 3 percent yearly (broken lines), doubling in 25 years, on assumption that demand was insensitive to price. Tripling and then doubling of oil price by OPEC brought actual consumption (solid lines) 25 percent below forecast.*

By 1963, the number of "new field" wildcat wells drilled in the United States to bring in a producing new field had climbed to 65, compared with 26 in 1945. The number of barrels of oil surfaced per foot of well drilled declined from 276 in 1938, when the great East Texas field came on stream, to 35 barrels per foot as early as 1970. The increasing scarcity of oil in the United States gave domestic producers higher costs. In competition with lower-cost producers overseas, however, they could scarcely add a surcharge for scarcity.

In the case of diamonds, the surcharge for scarcity over and above the cost of production is imposed by monopoly, in abrogation of the market process. In the case of oil, it must be admitted, there was also some distortion of the market process by the oligopoly of the half dozen companies that set the price paid to oil producers before 1973. It was a distortion, however, that concealed the scarcity of oil and understated its true value in use.

The industrial world thereby blinded itself to the fact that the commitment of its energy consumption to liquid fuels had made it dependent upon the preindustrial world for supply of the very essence of what makes the difference between the two kinds of human existence in the two worlds. Prior ages in the evolution of the biosphere had laid down more than 60 percent of the world's petroleum in what is now the preindustrial world, most of it in the region of the Persian Gulf.

Among the industrial countries, only the Soviet Union had its own supply of oil. Japan on its volcanic islands, lifted not long ago from within the Earth's crust into the biosphere, was almost totally dependent upon imported fuel. By 1970, the countries of Western Europe, with abundant coal, were deriving as much as two-thirds of their energy from imported oil. The United States, formerly the world's principal producer and exporter of oil, had passed the peak of its production. The country was now the largest importer, suddenly dependent upon overseas suppliers for more than 40 percent of its supply of oil.

The dependence of the life of the industrial world upon the resources of the preindustrial world is measured by the increasing flow of oil on the high seas. Now the hugest commodity in international trade, crude oil is one-eighth of the value and one-third of the tonnage. The daily flow of oil from the preindustrial countries into the ports of the industrial countries mounted from 2 million barrels in 1950 to 18 million barrels in 1985. Into U.S. ports, the flow increased from 250,000 barrels to 3.2 million barrels a day.

Along with the expansion of the world tanker fleet from around 2500 vessels in service in 1950 to more than 5000 came inflation of the size of tankers. Naval architects, in Japan especially, stretched the limits of steel structure to build 300,000-ton wallowing lakes of oil, too big to make passage through the Suez Canal but big enough to pay dividends on the journey made 15,000 kilometers longer by the detour around Cape Horn. From 25,000 to 30,000 tons in 1950, the average size of tankers approached 100,000 tons in 1980.

The 600 to 750 million barrels of oil at sea at all times presents a new hazard to the global environment. A score of tankers are lost on the reefs and at sea each year; less than 10 percent of the vessels lost, they account for—they spill—more than half the tonnage lost. Tankers afloat take their toll as well. They make their deadhead voyages ballasted with sea water, and they pump this oil-polluted water out at sea as they approach the loading ports. Other ships make the same contribution from emptied fuel bunkers that have been filled with sea water to keep their water lines at water level.

In addition to fouling the beaches and tarring the seabirds, it appears that the traffic in oil is polluting the ocean itself. To sample the microscopic "neuston," the biota of the ocean's top millimeter, research vessels tow arrays of fine-meshed nets. They have found no stretch of ocean where the crucial top millimeter—site of the all-important exchanges of oxygen and carbon dioxide between hydrosphere and atmosphere and window to the 70 percent of the solar radiation that drives one-third of the energy turnover in the biosphere—is not veiled by microbits of tar. In some waters, this tar has seeped from near-surface oilfields in the continental shelves. There is no doubt about the origin of most of it, especially that found on the broad pelagic reaches of the ocean. Such pollution must be reducing the rate of photosynthesis in the ocean and its contribution to the turnover of gases in the atmosphere.

With steady increase in the footage of drilling required to bring in a well and with lower yield per well, the United States became the highest-cost producer for the world market. Its costs ran more than 10 times that (10 cents) which brought a barrel of oil up from the sands of the Arabian Peninsula. On the U.S. cost, the oil companies set the world price.

ENTER OPEC

To keep the lion's share of that 'phantom cost' in the price they paid for Arabian oil on their own side of the transaction, the companies presented a solid front to the oil princes. At the outset, in 1948, the oil companies secured an 82/18 split in their favor. In 1960, the oil-producing countries organized their famous cartel, the Organization of Petroleum Exporting Countries (OPEC). With that solid phalanx at the table, the parties were more evenly matched. The split of the phantom cost went to 50/50 and, in 1970, to 30/70 in favor of the OPEC members.

To the OPEC members, it was by then apparent that the world market price set by their customers bore no relation to the true scarcity value of petroleum and not even to its present value to those customers. At the pump, as any oil exporter could see, the consumer in the United States was paying in taxes more than 3.5 times the producer's share of the price of a barrel of oil and, in Europe, as much as more than twice that markup. The oil-exporting countries of the preindustrial world were rendering an entirely unintentional economic subsidy to the industrial countries that had promised to come to their assistance. In addition to the emirates and kingdoms of the Arabian Peninsula, the membership of OPEC included such indubitably poor countries as Iraq, Iran, Libya, Algeria, Nigeria, and Indonesia.

In 1973, seizing the crisis mounted by the Arab embargo on the shipment of oil to the United States and other countries siding with Israel in the Yom Kippur war, OPEC took over the pricing of oil to the world market. The first OPEC price, at $17 a barrel, made a fivefold improvement on the companies' price. For the first time, oil appeared to its ultimate consumers as possibly a scarce resource.

Throughout the industrial world, the demand for energy developed sudden elasticity. In the United States, ending a prolonged increase at the rate of 3 percent per annum, the total consumption of energy topped off and, by 1975, had fallen 5 percent. Individual as well as industrial consumers contributed to this fall in consumption. Drivers who had queued for gasoline in 1973 were simply driving less. Householders switched out lights, turned down thermostats, and put up storm windows. Industry began charging energy costs to operating departments instead of to overhead. For the longer term, Congress set miles-per-gallon goals for the auto industry and hung energy-efficiency labels on electrical appliances. Conservationists, antinuclear activists and "small is beautiful" partisans had a new justification for picketing nuclear power plants under construction and for opposing even the siting of new fossil-fuel plants.

Economic recession in the United States and in Europe made its contribution also to the slackening of demand. It is estimated that the market economies in the industrial world lost more than $1 trillion in production as they adjusted to the new cost of energy.

The economic consequences in the preindustrial world went far beyond recession. Except for the coal-burning economies of China and India, the urban centers of economic growth in the poor countries (other than the oil exporters) were dependent on imported petroleum. Decline in commodity prices had already shrunk what positive balance some had developed in their foreign exchange. The new world price of oil drove all into the red or deeper into it.

Conscience-money economic assistance from the Arabian oil states and the recycling of petrodollars in the form of loans from the banks in the oil-importing countries kept the preindustrial countries supplied with fuel and maintained growth in some of them into the late 1970s. Under the mounting debt, economic growth then slowed, halted, and even reversed in most of them. Hardest hit were the poorest states, especially in sub-Saharan Africa. Under the present burden of debt, economic development remains almost everywhere at a standstill.

In 1973, a chastened United States was ready to be lectured to by spokesmen for the oil-producing countries. Jihangir Amuzegar, chief of the Iranian economic mission in Washington, D.C., wrote in the quarterly *Foreign Affairs* in July of that year:

> By keeping the Mideast oil price deliberately below its true scarcity value . . . the industrial world inadvertently perpetrated four hoaxes on itself and on its unborn generations. . . . [It] (a). discouraged oil producers from searching for new sources of supply; (b) helped hold down prices of substitutes (e.g., coal gas and hydroelectricity) and likewise dampened their development prospects despite their huge reserves; (c) stifled and/or delayed research in the development of more efficient technology for the economical use of energy; and, above all, (d) contributed to an inexcusably reckless waste and inefficient use of world premium fuels.

Under the presidency of Jimmy Carter, with his engineering degree from the U.S. Naval Academy, the newly created Department of Energy in 1978 undertook development, in accordance with item (b) of the Amuzegar agenda, of coal gasification processes and even sponsored research in nondepleting energy sources, such as the sun and wind. With recovery from recession, the consumption of oil by the industrial economies started upward again, but on a somewhat flatter trajectory.

The new world price of oil was affirmed by the ultimately stubborn demand, and the stage was set for the second oil shock. That came with the revolution in Iran and the disruption of deliveries from that major producer. OPEC members seized the disarray in the market in 1980 to double the world price they had set in 1973—to $34 a barrel.

Against this price, a renewed elasticity in demand carried the consumption of oil back to its 1973 level and even lower for two or three years. The $34 price, however, brought new and old high-cost producers on stream—item (a) on the Amuzegar agenda—and the market was glutted as early as 1982. Demoralization in the OPEC ranks, hastened by the fractiousness of the revolutionary Muslim government of Iran, broke the price.

Happy to accept credit for solving the energy problem, the Reagan administration terminated the Carter research into alternative energy sources. By 1985, demand for oil in the industrial world was back at the 1973 level and climbing once more. It has been climbing, however, at about half the pre-1973 rate. This more modest trajectory was maintained even with decline in the world price, for a time, under the first price set by OPEC. That and the fact that consumption of energy in the industrial world remains about one-third below the volume to which increase from 1973 on the classical trajectory would have carried it constitute the measure of the lesson learned thus far. It is a lesson well learned, however, because inflation by 1987 had discounted the increased price back to pre-1973, pre-OPEC prices.

In the United States, coal is supplying an increasing percentage of the primary energy—a larger percentage, again, than petroleum. Its consumption is principally in electric-power stations and industrial furnaces that have been converted from oil and gas. The disquiet this stirs in the community is reflected by the 1990 amendments to Federal clean-air legislation that mandate heavy investment for filters and scrubbers in the smokestacks.

For petroleum (still, together with natural gas, supplying more than half the primary heat energy) the country has returned to its former vulnerable dependence upon imports. U.S. imports reached pre-OPEC volume again in 1986 and now supply not 40 percent but 50 percent of the oil consumed.

In the energy metabolism of the Western European economies, the situation is very much the same: coal there is doing increasing damage to the environment, and oil consumption, increasing past the 1973 volume, has made them the more vulnerable to their suppliers. The economies in the former Soviet Union and its Eastern European bloc are beginning to contend with the environmental consequences of their reliance upon coal and to reckon with the reliability and duration of the supply of oil and gas from Siberian wells. Japan remains, as ever, 100 percent dependent upon imports.

The preindustrial oil-importing countries live at the mercy of the world market. The market is open again, for the present. At some future crisis, it is subject to closure and resumption of oligopolistic negotiation between oil exporters and the industrial economies. The interests of third parties will be quite incidental to their transactions.

Estimates of the world's initial supply of recoverable petroleum range from 1350 billion to 2100 billion barrels. For all practical purposes, the date of that initial supply may be set at 1950; until then, the pool had hardly been tapped. At the present rate of consumption, around 30 billion barrels a year, it will be gone in less than a century. This simple arithmetic fits the more careful plot of the production and consumption of petroleum made in the 1960s by M. King Hubbert, principal fuels geologist of the U.S. Geological Survey. The age of petroleum would last about 200 years, he showed, from the running in of Drake's well in 1885 in Pennsylvania until the last barrel goes into a museum in 2075. In the years of the production of the first 10 percent and the last 10 percent, as can be seen, petroleum makes a negligible contribution to the world's energy supply [see illustration page 176].

END OF THE PETROLEUM AGE

Of interest is the timing of the production of the middle 80 percent. As the world is now witnessing, Hubbert's cycle showed 80 percent of the initial supply produced in a 60- to 65-year period, starting in 1965 or 1970, rising to a maximum in the present decade, and terminating between 2025 and 2030. Assuming that the world was endowed with an initial supply of natural gas equivalent in energy content, its production can be visualized as moving in parallel with the petroleum cycle but lagging behind it, perhaps by a decade.

The petroleum age, shorter than a human lifetime, is plainly approaching its end. That must set an early date, perhaps within this decade, for the termination of energy ecstasy. Reckoning only the taxes collected on the oil they imported, the industrial countries have enjoyed, for 25 years, a subsidy on the order of $50 billion per year from the oil-exporting preindustrial countries. If the $17 or the $34 price approximates the value-in-use or the scarcity value of that transfusion of energy, that subsidy is doubled or quadrupled. The total exceeds by far the flow of official economic assistance in the other direction, very little of which went to economic assistance after deduction for the civil and military services exacted of its recipients.

At an early date, the industrial world must begin to get along on its own. The market process will settle on a new cost of energy, closer to its value in its essential uses. So long as the liquid fuels last, they will probably find their principal use in transportation at a price that may weaken the commitment to personal transportation. A wiser disposition of resources, if one could be devised, would save those molecules for better uses than combustion; they are the starting materials for the huge volume and diversity of industrial organic chemicals and plastics that serve so many useful (and some essential) purposes.

Alternatives to petroleum and natural gas, even for the supply of liquid fuel, are to be had from abundant supplies of other fossil fuels. There is even, without doubt, more petroleum to be had at much higher cost and risk to the environment in unproved deposits in the fragile ecosystems of the Arctic or the outer, deeper slopes of the continental shelves. They might stretch the petroleum age to the length of a full human lifetime.

There are also the Athabasca tar sands in northern Alberta and the oil shales of Colorado, together containing hydrocarbons in quantities comparable to the initial supply of petroleum. Considerable expense must attend the recovery of usable fuels from these materials. Their excavation might amount to ecological calamity. Disturbance of the vast tar-sand deposits, in the upstream reach of the northward-tilted watershed of the Mackenzie River, could have consequences reaching all the way to the Arctic Ocean. The ash from the retorting of the oil shale, it has been estimated, would fill all the canyons in Colorado. Before the price of energy rises high enough to bring these on stream, it will finance already demonstrated technologies for the liquefaction and gasification of coal, which is more accessibly available in still greater abundance.

The Hubbert plot for the production and consumption of the initial supply of coal shows the age of that fossil fuel extending over 1300 years [see illustration on page 176]. The mining and burning of the middle 80 percent falls in the 300-year period that starts with the year 2000. Peak consumption comes at somewhat less than 25 billion tons a year after 2100. If the world had to depend exclusively upon coal for its energy, output at that tonnage would be required as early

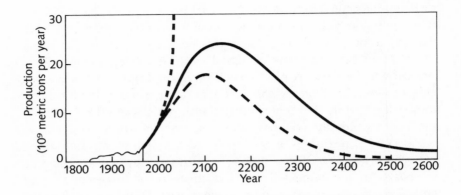

THE "COAL AGE" *is plotted in accordance with two estimates of original reserves (8000 and 4000 billion tons) and rates of consumption. Difference in the two estimates makes but a small difference in duration of the "age": 80 percent of the coal will be consumed between A.D. 2000 and A.D. 2300.*

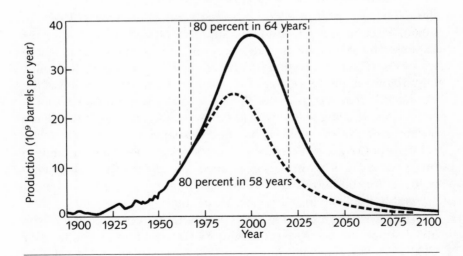

THE "PETROLEUM AGE" *is also plotted in accordance with two estimates of original reserves (1350 and 2100 billion barrels) and rates of consumption. The period in which 80 percent of all the petroleum will be consumed began in the 1960s and lasts, in either case, not longer than a human life.*

as 2050. The coal is there, however, and the requirement would be no more than eight times the present output.

The world faces no shortage of fossil fuels. The increasingly urgent concern is the rising cost to the biosphere of the rising consumption of coal and of the remaining petroleum and natural gas. In the long run, the biosphere cannot be expected to tolerate the consumption of these fuels in the quantities necessary to extend industrial revolution to the preindustrial countries and bring the right of a human lifetime to each member of the growing world population.

Of nearly equal concern in any reckoning of the rising energy needs of the preindustrial countries is the inverse relation between the distribution of coal deposits and of world population. In the preindustrial world, only China and India possess significant reserves, but not much more than enough to carry them into the first decades of full industrialization. The principal fossil-fuel resources of the postpetroleum age are in the industrial countries, not in the preindustrial countries that supplied the petroleum.

Even with more efficient use of energy and a fairer sharing of the world supply of fuel, it is evident that a doubling or tripling, at least, of the primary energy requirement of humankind impends and must be met in the next century. Apart from environmental considerations, people must begin immediately to develop alternatives to coal.

Coal remains, nonetheless, the first alternative to the liquid fuels. Consumption of coal is already increasing faster than the increase in the total consumption of energy. The doubling of the energy supply by the combustion of coal in any combination with the other fossil fuels must more than double the industrial injection of carbon dioxide into the atmosphere. Continuation of that perturbation of the mixture of gases in the planet's atmosphere must heighten the peril to civilization with every increase in the rate of injection. Coal, in addition, makes the principal contribution to the now regional, prospectively global, fallout of acid rain. At the present rate of coal combustion, the vegetation downwind from the world's industrial centers is showing injury. The evidence that will tie those symptoms to acid rain must certainly advertise itself upon further increase in the consumption of coal. At that time, the injury may prove to be irreversible.

Fortunately, the technologies that make it possible for coal mines to replace oil wells also make it possible to reduce the contribution to acid rain. Processes for the gasification and liquefaction of the hydrocarbons in coal have been demonstrated in use, as in Germany during World War II. Middle- and low-tech as these processes are, they can surely be brought back on stream at higher efficiency under high-tech process-control systems.

The same controls, plus familiar technology, can divert the oxides of sulfur and nitrogen into side streams from the process flow. In the huge capital investment that impends, environmental protection can be figured as a minor cost. Moreover, the concentration at processing centers of the preliminary combustion that liquefies or gasifies the coal presents fewer points for the venting of polluting gases and so for investment in pollution-control technology. No investment in pollution control can reduce, however, the release of carbon dioxide to the atmosphere.

Reliance on coal has other environmental consequences of a more local kind, evident in the forlorn landscapes of the older coal-mining centers—in the United States, in Appalachia and in the strip-mined prairie north of the Ohio River. Environmental-protection legislation came on too late to forestall windrows of spoil in southern Illinois and streams running with poisons leached from the coal beds in West Virginia and Kentucky. Without considerable vigilance, worse consequences must attend development of the country's principal coal reserves along the eastern slopes of the Rocky Mountains. The strip mining of the coal seams there, which lie as much as 300 feet thick, will not leave sites that can be restored to any semblance of their prior state; the effects of this disturbance on surface and ground waters can make it more than local. The distance of these mines from their markets presents, however, opportunities for concentration of measures for the control of acid rain; the products of beneficiation will travel by pipeline to the market more cheaply than coal.

Environmental considerations aside, coal can cover the immediate energy requirements of industrial civilization. It can mitigate the political and economic paroxysms that must inevitably attend the waning of the liquid fuels. Coal cannot meet, however, the ultimate demand for energy. In the interim, its continued combustion presents grave risks. Along with petroleum and natural gas, it should be conserved for better uses than burning. Government, industry, and the engineering and scientific professions should aim to develop, at the earliest date, substantial alternative sources of primary energy that do not generate carbon dioxide.

It is difficult now to recall, much less to credit, the promise of free energy that was heard at the time in the explosion of the first nuclear weapons. The fission of a gram of uranium does, indeed (in accordance with the celebrated equation from Einstein's special relativity) liberate 22,500 kilowatt-hours of energy. That is equal to the energy content of about one ton of coal or a half ton of petroleum. In the fission reaction, a measurable portion of the gram—0.0009 gram, not the entire gram—transmutes to energy. Mass losses (or gains) also attend chemical reactions, the boiling or cooling of water, or the stretching and relaxation of a spring; these losses or gains lie, however, at or beyond the boundary of measurement. Transmutation of the total gram of uranium would yield the energy contained in 3000 tons of coal, or 20 million kilowatt-hours. This was the notion that inspired the writings of H. G. Wells long before its ultimate popularization at Hiroshima and Nagasaki.

The first steps toward realization of the promise of this source of energy for peaceful uses stumbled into calamity. In the fever of the arms race, the most readily engineered nuclear fuel cycle was packaged for the propulsion of submarines. That same package was scaled up for installation in central power stations. To keep this particular cycle running safely requires the same vigilance in a power station as in a submarine. Accidents in Britain, the United States, and the Soviet Union show that this was too much to expect of civilian morale. Since the Soviet industry took the same path of least investment in scaling up its submarine reactors, the error in the United States and Britain cannot be charged exclusively to the profit motive. It must be noted also that the French adopted the same fuel cycle. They get nearly all their electricity from their nuclear reactors and have some left over for export, and they have not yet had a Windscale, a Three Mile Island, or a Chernobyl to explain to their citizens.

Apart from accidents at the reactor, the burning of the fuel produces radioactive "garbage." The half-lives of some elements—the half-life is the time required for a gram of an element to reduce its radioactivity by half—are measured in the tens of thousands of years. Since the institutions of civilization exhibit considerably shorter half-lives, the devising of secure methods for disposal of this lethal garbage presents an unsolved and quite prohibitive obstacle to the commitment of any large part of the world's energy requirement to fission reactors. Against the huge investment in conceivable disposal technologies stands another obstacle. The fuel cycle on which present reactors operate requires enrichment of the uranium fuel with its fissionable isotope—uranium-235—and puts the charge through a single cycle in the reactor. That gives the world's recoverable uranium a time horizon nearer than that of petroleum.

ENERGY WITHOUT CARBON DIOXIDE

Other fission cycles, using other fissionable elements as well as uranium, are inherently safe—a failure of the cooling system shuts down the reaction. Breeding and recycling of fuel to produce more fuel can extend the resource horizon. The unsolved garbage disposal remains, however, even though the output of a 10,000 megawatt plant can fit under a desk. The carbon dioxide from an equivalent fossil-fuel plant, of course, fills cubic miles of sky. In the present context, that is the best argument for fission power: it generates energy without venting carbon dioxide.

A quite different kind of hazard makes fission power the last-resort alternative to fossil fuels. This plowshare was first a sword. The virgin fuel can be made into bombs. The daughter product that awaits recovery from tons of radioactive garbage around the world for use as fuel is plutonium; this daughter can be made into bombs as well. The spread of nuclear-power technology must inevitably permit and promote the silent proliferation of bomb-making capability. Civilization lives in peril of the nuclear powers and the known protonuclear powers. These are all nation-states. Nuclear-power technology could put the capability in reach of private conspiracies.

Political instability in the Soviet Union now puts in doubt the military discipline that keeps about half of the world's 60,000 ready nuclear bombs and warheads under some control. A significant portion of the U.S. nuclear arsenal is deployed outside the country's borders, where it is exposed to the frailty of political alliance. Nuclear power would multiply by many times the hazard posed by these putatively well-protected stockpiles of weapons of mass destruction.

No such hazard clouds the prospect of nuclear fusion, though a fusion reaction powers the even more frightful thermonuclear weapon known as the hydrogen bomb. The energy in this reaction comes from the loss of mass that attends the fusion of two atomic nuclei. Research into the slow and continuous, instead of instantaneous, ignition of the fusion reaction continues, as it has for 40 years, in the undiscouraged expectation that it can be made to work in about 20 years. That possibility overrides all discouragement. The hydrogen atoms that are to be fused are the most abundant atoms of all; they are in effectively infinite supply. The problem is that the fusion requires temperatures and pressures so far generated reliably on Earth only in a fission bomb.

To get there without a bomb, two procedures have been under investigation. One calls for containment of the reacting atoms in a magnetic "bottle" in which they would be heated and squeezed to the temperature and pressure at which they fuse in the interior of a star. The other procedure calls for containing, crushing, and heating the atoms in converging beams of laser light. Both procedures require tremendous inputs of energy, a substantial multiple of the net energy that is expected to come out. The energy to drive one or the other kind of reactor will be bled from the enormous output. The apparently absurd cost is acceptable because the fraction of the total flux of energy netted from the reaction for useful purposes will be enough. The grail is the energy that lights the stars.

Hydrogen is the simplest atom; it has but a single nuclear particle—a proton—in its nucleus. The fusion of hydrogen to hydrogen (proton to proton) is, however, a quite improbable reaction. It requires the immense gravitational forces in the mass (principally hydrogen) of a star to bring the hydrogen deep inside to the necessary temperature, and it requires billions of years to transmute a significant portion of the mass to energy. Less resistant to fusion are the two isotopes of hydrogen—deuterium, with two particles in its nucleus (a proton and a neutron) and tritium, with three (a proton and two neutrons).

The fusion of deuterium and tritium can be induced—and has been, in experimental apparatus—at lower temperatures and pressures. From the reaction issues helium (two protons and a neutron) plus two free neutrons. The limitation on this reaction as a source of energy is set by the availability of tritium. This short-lived radioactive isotope is obtained by the transmutation of the light metal lithium by exposure to the particle radiation from a fission reactor. With the reaction working, the abundance of lithium would endow civilization with a source of energy equal to the initial supply of the fossil fuels.

Deuterium, a stable isotope, is available in the minuscule heavy-water fraction of the ocean waters. If—a gigantic if— deuterium–deuterium or deuterium–hydrogen fusion could be managed, and if 1 percent of the deuterium in the ocean were some day consumed in the reaction, it would yield 500,000 times the energy contained in the initial supply of fossil fuels.

Fusion is not without its hazards from radioactivity. The two free neutrons from the deuterium–tritium fusion reaction will thoroughly irradiate the structures that contain the reaction, and they will have to be continuously rebuilt. The shorter half-lives of the isotopes in this contamination will make it easier to dispose of them. Whatever problem that presents, however, the fusion reactions yield no carbon dioxide.

As tantalizing as the energy of fusion, but everywhere at hand, is the light of the Sun. Its capture causes no release of carbon dioxide and, what may someday be important, no addition to the Earth's heat flux (and so no increase in the planet's temperature). Fossil-fuel plants do make such an addition, quite independent of the greenhouse effect. They are heating 10 percent of the surface waters of the United States with the energy of sunlight captured millions of years ago.

At the ground, to adopt a round-number working figure, sunlight has a power of 1 kilowatt per square meter. There being 250 trillion square meters on the sunny side of the Earth, that is a great many kilowatts of power. Light from the Sun develops its full 1 kilowatt of power at the ground, however, only during the five or six hours when it shines from high in the sky. But what makes it really difficult to harness this power is that it is spread so thin.

The Sun offers what in thermodynamics is called low-potential energy. The plants of the biomass capture it one quantum at a time and capture no more than 1 percent of the total flux. They accumulate a good deal of energy in the course of the day and year, however, and this is available at higher potential in the form, say, of fuel wood. Present solar-energy technology can actually capture a higher percentage of the 1 kilowatt per square meter than plants do, but not enough to compete with the high-potential energy stored in the fossil fuels. A metric ton (roughly, a cubic meter) of petroleum has the power, in effect, of nearly 60 kilowatts per square meter, for it contains 3325 kilowatt-hours of energy at the present heat-to-electricity conversion efficiency of central power stations.

To get sunlight up to the high potential of petroleum requires collection of the sunlight from a great many square meters. That is, after all, what the organisms that made the petroleum did, over many square kilometers and many years of collecting solar energy.

Sunlight can be brought to high potential instantly and on the spot by focusing it with a simple lens. A larger quantity of sunlight can be gathered and focused with a parabolic mirror. An installation of parabolic mirrors in the Pyrenees, in southern France, has rendered impressive pilot-plant demonstrations of the use of sunlight as a chemically pure source of heat in metallurgy.

On the same basic principle, the collection and focusing of sunlight at temperatures high enough to boil water and spin a turbine is generating electricity in a pilot plant in southern California. The physics of such capture and conversion of solar energy presents no research problem. It is the economics of the solar power plant, at present fossil-fuel prices, that challenges the engineer.

One response to the challenge will take advantage of the higher heat capacity of molten salt compared with that of water vapor. An experimental plant designed on this principle and with the considerable power of 10 megawatts is under construction on the Mojave Desert. Molten salt will store the primary energy of sunlight in larger quantities per unit mass than steam can and will convey it to a heat exchanger that will thereupon deliver steam in larger quantities or at higher temperatures to the turbogenerator set.

At its low potential on a flat surface, sunlight captured in heat collectors supplies hot water to many urban households in sunny climates. Solar heat collectors even appear on rooftops in higher latitudes, as auxiliary contributors to the economy of household heating. These installations are expensive, however, and they do not pay for themselves at present fossil-fuel prices. If they did, there would be more of them on rooftops. This, in itself, demonstrates what is meant by the low potential of solar energy. With continued marginal improvement in efficiency and the inevitable increase in fuel costs, however, these dispersed, small-scale systems may yet give solar energy a large role in reducing the consumption of fossil fuels.

In the middle latitudes, sunlight is available most of the time. There it could displace fuel wood and contribute a valuable supplement to the biological energy of people and their working animals. In villages on the Deccan Plateau of India, the simple reflector oven that temperate-zone campers sometimes use would serve better than the dung fire that scarcely brings water to a boil. Community development programs have pushed such use of sunlight. There is some resistance to the use of solar reflectors, but it is cultural, not technical (for example, some people like to eat at times when the sun is not shining or in places where the sunlight does not reach).

A quite different approach to the capture of sunlight seeks to transform it directly to electrical energy. That is what a photographer's light meter does, and even lamplight is now commonly harnessed to activate hand-held calculators. Photovoltaic "sails" are spread by Earth satellites to capture energy from the sun. For the less romantic purposes of everyday life, the question is again how to do it on a grand scale but economically.

If that can be done, the world will be indebted again to Albert Einstein. He anchored a curiosity—the observation that light generates an electric current in certain metals—securely in the Planck constant, which related the energy of light to its wavelength rather than its amplitude, with shorter wavelengths carrying higher energy. Einstein thereby established the quantum—the photon or corpuscle—of light that transfers its energy to an electron (the "photoelectric effect"), many such events generating an electrical current. Max Planck, persuaded to the wave nature of light, resisted the quantum and this evidence of the dual ("wavicle") nature of light. The quantum remains, nonetheless, Planck's quantum.

The economic test to be met is the cost per square meter of the photovoltaic energy collector and the percentage of the peak solar wattage it captures at that cost. A collector that costs $100 per square meter and captures 20 percent of the solar kilowatt has an output of 200 watts and therefore a cost of 50 cents per peak watt. To that cost must be added the cost of mounting and arraying the collector to the sunlight, including the cost of the considerable real estate to be occupied. On top of all that comes the cost of converting the direct current from the collector into alternating current for delivery to an electric power grid or, alternatively, the cost of storing the energy.

The competition to be met is the $1.10 per watt capital cost of a fossil-fuel central power station. Energy from the central power station must carry the additional cost of the fuel that goes into its boilers. Sunlight enters the photovoltaic collector without cost, but it does so at peak wattage only one-fifth of the time. Over the past 15 years, improvement in the efficiency and cost of photovoltaic collectors has brought the estimated cost of a photovoltaic central power station down from $75 to $1.50 per peak watt.

Whether captured in steam or directly in electrical energy, solar power must exact its environmental cost. At 20 percent efficiency, a 10,000-megawatt plant would spread its collectors over 170 square kilometers. To attach the entire power grid of the United States to the sun would require the dedication of 30,000 square kilometers, about 0.4 percent of the country's land area, to solar collectors. As small as that figure looks, it presents a forbidding piece of landscape.

In the vicinity of the cities, where the energy would be consumed, there is not likely to be land open on the scale required. Location in the desert wilderness of the Southwest seems to be indicated, and on expanses of flat land to minimize the cost to array. There this manmade desert would occupy a much larger percentage of a fragile ecosystem and might put the entire ecosystem in jeopardy. Solar power, whether in big or small installations, is bound to raise environmental and political siting controversies.

Who gets the pollution and who gets the power is not a new question. The laws of thermodynamics have always said that something cannot be had for nothing.

Photovoltaic Hydrogen

Loss of electrical energy on the long transmission lines between the solar power station and its markets—along with the diurnal shutdown of the power station—compels consideration of ways to store and deliver the energy. One way is to store it in the form of hydrogen, produced by electrolytic decomposition of water at the power plant. From the hydrogen, the energy is released at the time of use by the reverse process of combustion of hydrogen with oxygen, which reunites these atoms to form water molecules again. Combustion with air, rather than with pure oxygen, will produce oxides of nitrogen as well as water vapor. The production of those pollutants depends upon the temperature of combustion; where that is a problem, it is subject to control by catalytic converters of the sort now in use in automobile exhaust systems.

Fueling a conventional steam turbine generator set at the modest efficiency of 30 percent, the chemical energy of hydrogen is transformed to electricity for a net yield of 6 percent on the primary solar energy. At this overall efficiency, the annual output of a square meter of photovoltaic surface in the latitudes of the United States will come to about 100 kilowatt-hours. The closed cycle of energy storage and delivery in hydrogen will work as well with any primary energy source—in particular, a nuclear power plant, which faces much the same siting problems as a solar plant.

Photovoltaic hydrogen as a central power station fuel is at the center of interest in Japan, where Project Sunshine is to begin the liberation of the Japanese energy economy from dependence upon fossil fuels by the end of the century. In Germany, a 500-kilowatt photovoltaic pilot plant will soon be capturing solar energy in hydrogen. With Saudi Arabia, the Germans are building its counterpart at Riyadh.

For uses in the chemical industry and in the fueling of booster rockets, electrolysis of water is an established technology, producing hydrogen in huge quantities at the rate of 1000 cubic feet per 150 kilowatt-hours. By pipeline, energy can move from the solar power plant in the form of gas more cheaply than on transmission lines and through the same 400,000-kilometer network that today delivers natural gas. Under standard operating pressure, a pipeline 36 inches in diameter will convey hydrogen at the power equivalent of 11,000 megawatts, 10 times the performance of a 500-kilovolt transmission line.

At the market, the hydrogen will regenerate the electrical energy that freed it from water or will itself be delivered to the ultimate consumer. In industrial boilers, it will take the place of natural gas. In the home, apart from the kitchen, it offers an attractive heating fuel, heating room by room instead of from a central heating plant and humidifying the air with its combustion product.

The transportation power plant can burn hydrogen in its internal-combustion engines. In automobiles, trucks, and buses, hydrogen might promote replacement of those engines with electric motors. The motors would be powered by the cooler combustion of hydrogen with oxygen in fuel cells, the exact reverse of hydrolysis, to generate electricity.

To longer memories, hydrogen recalls the flaming catastrophe of the airship *Hindenburg* at the mooring tower in Lakehurst, New Jersey. In pipelines, however, hydrogen presents no hazard not already managed in piping natural gas. A 200-kilometer pipeline in Germany has been moving 4000 billion cubic feet of hydrogen per year since the 1930s without mishap. At the kitchen range, the usual local utility's "producer" gas, now largely displaced by natural gas, was a mixture containing 50 percent hydrogen, 40 percent carbon dioxide, and 10 percent carbon monoxide. The full domestication of hydrogen, nonetheless, requires more engineering.

For use in automobiles, the problem is one of the volume as well as the safety of hydrogen. Liquefaction reduces the volume, but it requires a massive tank to hold the pressure. With less weight for containment, hydrogen can be safely stored in a metal hydride compound. For cold combustion in the fuel cell or hot combustion in the engine, it is released simply by warming the container—for example, with exhaust steam from the engine. Hydrogen-fueled internal combustion engines and fuel cells have both been demonstrated in automobiles and buses.

As the volume of liquid hydrogen to be contained increases, the relative weight committed to containment decreases. This makes liquid hydrogen the prospectively ideal fuel for large vehicles—trucks, buses, and even airliners. At the same cruising range, according to Carl-Jochen Winter, director of the Solar and Hydrogen Research Center at Stuttgart, a hydrogen-fueled aircraft will have 30 percent less takeoff weight than a fossil-fueled one. Its engines will be smaller and quieter as well. A Soviet airliner made the first hydrogen-powered flight in 1988.

Short of providing answers on the grand scale to the energy requirements of the industrial economies, photovoltaic solar power commends itself for use at many different scales in the preindustrial countries. Those countries have more hours of sunlight at peak wattage. In place of central station power grids, smaller plants at dispersed sites can bring electric power to the villages, eventually at modest capital cost. Hydrogen from the same plants can stop the burning of fuel wood.

Another way to capture solar energy is to extract it from the relatively warm water in the upper levels of the ocean. Under the 1-kilowatt-per-square-meter power of the sun, the energy is absorbed in the sea water at the standard rate of 1 calorie for each increase in temperature of 1 degree Celsius per cubic centimeter. In the interchange of energy between the ocean and the atmosphere, however, by no means is all of the sunlight absorbed; but solar energy is available in the water at a potential within reach of extraction.

To make "ocean temperature energy conversion" (OTEC, for short) work, there must be a difference of at least 20 degrees Celsius between the temperature of the sun-warmed surface water and cold bottom water nearby. At that difference in temperature, the warm sea water holds 8 kilowatt-hours of energy per cubic meter (or metric ton) at present central-power-station efficiency, just enough to justify the trouble it takes to get it out. In an OTEC power plant, steam is boiled from the warm sea water (or from a refrigerant, such as ammonia, warmed by the warm sea water) in an evaporator under pressure equivalent to that in the atmosphere at altitudes of 27 to 30 kilometers—a pretty good vacuum. The low-pressure, rarefied steam thus boiled from a ton of warm sea water rushes like a Martian hurricane through the helicopter-sized blades of the OTEC turbine and yields 8 kilowatt-hours of energy to the spinning turbine; it loses the last of the 20-degrees-Celsius difference in temperature upon its precipitation on the condenser cooled by the bottom water. By contrast, a ton of high-temperature, high-pressure steam, dropping 300 degrees Celsius between the inlet and the outlet of a conventional power-plant turbine, yields more than 100 kilowatt-hours of energy.

Extraction of any appreciable amount of energy from the low-potential sea water requires the pumping of many cubic meters of it through the OTEC plant every hour. Pumps to bring in the warm and the cold water and to maintain the vacuum in the evaporator consume a necessarily large percentage of the energy generated by the plant; in one reasonably efficient pilot plant, it was 65 kilowatts out of the gross output of 100 kilowatts. An efficiency of 35 percent, however, is quite acceptable in fossil-fuel steam plants.

Improbable as this approach to the generation of energy appears, the United States, France, and Japan have all had OTEC pilot plants in operation. The attraction is the abundance of energy available. At the difference in temperature of 20 degrees Celsius, a cubic kilometer of sea water contains 8 trillion kilowatt-hours of energy. A 100-megawatt OTEC plant needs to extract but a tiny percentage of it. For research and development, the tasks are to shave mils from the operating costs of evaporators, turbines, and condensers and to develop materials from which to fashion the huge pipes for deployment to the cold abyss. The distance between the abyss and the market for the captured energy will require storage and packaging of the energy again—perhaps in the form of hydrogen for shipment by tanker.

In some parts of the world, the condensed steam has value, as desalted water, equal to that of the energy generated. Moreover, the nutrient-rich bottom water pumped through the condensers could be used to sustain aquaculture in ponds or in enriched open surface waters. If OTEC technology ever goes on stream, it could make a significant contribution to the world supply of protein.

On that scale, however, OTEC technology will surely be pumping a great deal more bottom water than can be used for protein production. Care will have to be taken in disposal of the large balance. Since the abyss goes undisturbed for ages on end, there has been no experience with any substantial redistribution of the nutrients it takes out of circulation. This time, the inevitable environmental cost of energy resides in the prospect of monstrous algae blooms or the measures that must be taken to avert them.

The biomass—strictly speaking, the phytomass—comes high on the list of environmentalists who are concerned with finding a nonpolluting primary energy source. Its combustion, from the products of current and recent fixation of carbon by photosynthesis, does not increase the input of carbon dioxide to the atmosphere as much as the combustion of the fossil fuels, which draws upon carbon stored in the Earth over many years tens of millions of years ago. Brazil has relieved its dependence upon imported petroleum by a vast expansion of its sugarcane plantation. Ethanol from the sugarcane fuels the country's internal-combustion engines, either alone or in a "gasohol" mixture with gasoline.

Any large input to the world's energy economy from cultivated land must come, however, by subtraction from food production. As for the forest biomass, it is already yielding more than it is growing in a year.

The plant life of the desert, on the other hand, holds the possibility of a net addition from the biomass to the fuel supply. All around the world, members of the spurge or euphorbia family thrive unattended in the desert. The hydrocarbons in their sap have a higher energy content than the carbohydrates the make the bulk of the tissue in most plants. Geneticists are looking into these plants for ways to improve their productivity. Another desert plant, the guayule, a member of the sunflower family, has been harvested for production of rubber; it is now thought of as a potential producer of motor fuel.

It is on the biomass, unfortunately, that the preindustrial village economies must presently depend. Their households burn more than 40 percent of the 3 billion cubic meters of wood cut from the world's forests each year. In the vicinity of most villages, people are burning the wood faster than it grows. Enlarging rings of deforestation surround villages in the dry-land farming regions of Africa south and west of the Sahara. The burning of cow dung in the household fires on the Deccan Plateau in India consumes 400 million tons each year of material that ought to be returned to the impoverished soil. Much illness in those households is attributed to the low heat content of this fuel, which brings milk to a temperature at which contaminating microorganisms thrive and not much higher. In India and more widely in China, villagers are learning to use dung and human excrement together with other organic wastes in "biogas" tanks that generate methane for fuel and yield a clean sludge for fertilizer.

The oil-pricing shocks to the world economy excited interest in other sources of primary energy. The hydroelectric power resources of most preindustrial countries remain still largely unexploited. In industrial countries, where they are more fully developed, the proposal of a new dam site brings out the pickets. More acceptable to amateur ecologists are the wind, the tides, and the waves of the ocean and the heat welling up from the Earth's hot interior. They all share the virtue of relative perpetuality, if not renewability. They are inconstant or inaccessible, however, and much of their original energy is lost in the mechanical contraptions and boilers set up to harness them. Wind farms, with forests of sleek, aerodynamically efficient windmills, have actully put energy into the California electric-power grid. The few fjords and tidal raceways where the tides might be harnessed remain undeveloped; the prospective capital cost of the harnessing continues to inflate faster than fossil fuel prices.

Energy has been extracted from the heat of the Earth's interior by taking opportunistic advantage of hot springs that bring the heat to the surface. Few such springs are located, however, in the markets for their energy, and the hot water tends to be loaded with elements and compounds dissolved from the rock that foul pumps and pipes. Nonetheless, geothermal energy from such sources moves into the electric-power grid of California and is exploited successfully elsewhere in the world. At sufficient depth, on the other hand, geothermal energy is available everywhere in the planet's crust. Rock at 150 degrees Celsius underlies 10 million square kilometers of U.S. territory at a depth of 10 kilometers; in the Rocky Mountains, rock at that temperature can be reached at 5 kilometers under 180,000 square kilometers of territory; at a few places, rock at a depth of 5 kilometers has a temperature of 300 degrees Celsius. Development of hot dry rock as a source of energy—already referred to as HDR energy—awaits development of its own technology. Such depths in hard and increasingly hot rock challenge the art of drilling. The rock in the hot depths must be fractured to permit inflow of the water that is to bring up the heat. It will take energy to force water into the rock in a closed loop with the returning steam.

Development of HDR technology is proceeding actively in many countries. In the United States, the work is centered in the National Laboratory at Los Alamos, famous for fashioning the first nuclear bombs. The "plant cost" of drilling to sufficient depth and fracturing an adequately large mass of hard rock plus the operating cost of injecting the water and capturing the steam pose, at present, significant economic hurdles.

An inexhaustible reservoir of energy exists in the active imagination of the astrophysicist Thomas Gold, at Cornell University. He starts from the knowledge that hydrogen is the most abundant element in the lithosphere and that carbon is also relatively abundant. Since no compounds are immortal, and chemical bonds are broken and remade in the churning of the interior lithosphere, hydrogen and carbon must find their way out of bonding with other elements and very likely into embrace with one another in methane gas (CH_4). Somewhere under enormous pressure in the depths of the Earth, Gold concludes, the gas must accumulate in vast quantities.

Gold cites mysterious and otherwise unexplained eruptions and exhalations of methane from the ocean bottom, where the crust is thinner, in support of his hypothesis. A deep well drilled in the continental bedrock in Sweden a few years ago released methane that could not have had biogenic origin. The Swedes were impressed enough to be drilling now another well.

Combustion of methane yields, of course, carbon dioxide. If Gold's hypothesis is ever sustained, abiogenic methane might still find use—joining the fossil fuels as a starting material for the petrochemical industry, methane being the product of pure petrochemistry unassisted by the biosphere.

More Energy from Efficiency

Since 1973, the most fruitful source of new usable energy in the U.S. economy has been improvement in the efficiency of the use of energy or, put the other way around, reduction in the waste encouraged by the low price of the imported liquid fuels—items (c) and (d) in the Amuzegar agenda cited earlier (page 172). The United States achieved a 10-mile improvement in the miles-per-gallon average of its motor vehicles, even as its greater reliance on personal transportation increased the consumption of energy for this purpose by more than 10 percent. Industry reduced its energy consumption by more than 25 percent; households and commercial and office space, by 20 percent. Most of the economizing on primary energy consumption went into the increased production of electricity. The increase of 72 percent in kilowatt-hours was secured, however, with efficiency that held the increase in the consumption of primary energy for this purpose to 68 percent. For the economy as a whole, the consumption of energy per dollar of GNP declined by more than 25 percent.

With still more gains to be made, efficiency in use remains the most economical way to increase the effective energy supply in the United States and the rest of the industrial world. The high cost of money and of plant and machinery have brought the public utilities to the financing of (and even the sharing of investment with their customers in) energy-saving measures. One such investment is in "cogeneration." This is the use of the steam downstream from the turbine generator for indoor heating and other uses of lower-potential energy. New and old cities of the Soviet Union are thus centrally heated—in one successful demonstration of the uses of central planning—by the power plants that supply their electric energy.

In the United States, large commercial and industrial concerns are setting up their own power plants to take advantage of the economy of cogeneration and are selling their off-hours energy to the local public utility. The rate-making regulatory agencies are encouraging the utilities to share such investment, although some people fear that taking big customers off line may jeopardize the power network and its performance for the public.

After a ninefold increase, from 1950 to 1980, U.S. central-station capacity rose by little more than 25 percent in the 1980s. This is a measure, in part, of the degree to which big industrial plants have undertaken the generation of their own electrical energy. In larger part, it testifies to economies and improvements in the efficiency of energy consumption secured by U.S. industry in response to the rising cost of energy. By comparison, the U.S. household has a longer way to go in achieving the energy savings that are possible.

The party walls of the "townhouse" that has replaced the single-family house in new construction in the suburbs save heating energy. At its affordable price, unfortunately, not much else is built into the townhouse to save more of that energy. Development of lamps that put out more lumens per watt is coming, along with studies that show that the U.S. household can be just as happy with less indoor light. The Clean Air Act amendments of 1990 set, as an antipollution target, another improvement in miles per gallon for the automobile of A.D. 2000.

Similar economy measures in other industrial countries continue to bring decrease in the consumption of energy per unit of GNP. All told, the major industrial countries reduced their energy consumption per capita by about 5 percent from 1973 to 1985, even as they increased their GNP by more than 30 percent.

Responsible students and developers of energy-conservation technology go so far as to argue that the world economy can achieve its necessary threefold or fourfold economic growth without increase in primary energy consumption. Amory Lovins and his colleagues, the best-known proponents of energy efficiency, have buttressed their case with economies demonstrated in every use of energy from indoor heating to transportation. Without doubt, these measures will come into wider use as the price of energy finances and induces their introduction. In the industrial countries, gross national product will go on increasing faster than the consumption of energy.

When and as the preindustrial countries resume economic growth and industrialization, however, they are bound to increase their consumption of energy ahead of any increase in their GNP. Increased output and consumption of electrical energy is to them one of the first benefits for which they look to industrialization; such industrial plant as they have installed is less efficient and more energy-intensive in operation. Their agriculture has, as its first need, a huge increase in nitrogen fertilizer, a highly energy-intensive commodity.

India and China will continue to rely upon their coal resources for industrial growth at great cost to their landscapes and to the planetary atmosphere. Few other preindustrial countries, except the oil exporters, are self-sufficient in energy. At the higher prices to which fuels will move from now on in international commerce, their dependence upon imported fuels will be a decisive factor compelling radical reconstitution of their debt to the industrial world.

The present average energy consumption of the preindustrial countries, stated in its coal-equivalent, comes to something less than one ton per capita. Like many averages on the distribution side of economics, this one stands high above the mean. The average itself is inflated by the higher energy consumption, at 1500 kilograms, of the countries of South America, with their large urban populations. Not much of that energy reaches the half of the population that lives in the shantytowns and considerably less of it reaches the 30 percent of the continent's population that is rural.

In China, as one measure of the country's progress in industrialization, energy consumption approaches the coal equivalent of 800 kilograms per capita. On the Indian subcontinent, where economic development has had relatively less impact upon traditional village existence, energy consumption averages 200 kilograms. In Africa, the average is 34 kilograms. Since these averages do not include fuel wood, they might be tripled by conversion of fuel-wood consumption to coal-equivalent energy. The meager rations would still contrast with the consumption of 14 tons per capita in the United States and 5 tons per capita in the rest of the industrial countries.

Any attempt to estimate the ultimate future energy demand of humankind must reckon with a world population of not less than 10 billion. That population, it is hoped, will enjoy a level of physical well-being at which fertility control will have halted population growth, as it has in the industrial countries. If it has not, then population growth must continue to some larger number beyond.

By the U.S. standard, arithmetic shows, that level of well-being would be the energy equivalent to 140 billion tons of coal; at the standard of the rest of the industrial world, 50 billion tons. Neither of these figures lies beyond the resources now available to humankind. Nonetheless, if there could be a standard less burdensome to the planetary ecosystem, it would be well to aim for it. Calculation of a minimum standard may establish a range for the demand that the human population is about to lay upon the Earth.

It is a hopeful augur for the prospect of a stable world population that China has experienced a decline in its rate of population growth from 2.5 percent in 1965 to 1.2 percent at present. This has come at a level of well-being sustained by the burning of 800 kilograms of coal-equivalent energy per capita. That is less than 10 percent of the consumption per capita of the United States and 20 percent that of the other industrial countries. Here may be an indication that passage of the world population through the demographic transition need not come at levels of physical well-being that lay such heavy demand upon Earth's resources.

For the rest of the preindustrial population, if it is to follow China's example, energy consumption equivalent to 800 kilograms of coal per capita might be regarded as the minimum target. Revolutionary morale and economic democracy as well as increasing well-being have motivated the people of China in the practice of fertility control and in their acceptance of compulsion in the matter. Elsewhere, and even prospectively in China, the availability of energy must allow for inequity in its distribution.

To begin with, it is not likely that the people of the industrial nations will accede to reduction of their level of well-being, although they will likely be compelled to secure it at less energy cost. This population, growing to 1.5 billion by the middle of the next century, may well be able to make do comfortably at the present average energy consumption, equivalent to 5 tons of coal per capita, enjoyed by the industrial nations other than the United States.

For the 6 or 7 billion population of the present preindustrial countries by the middle of the next century, it is not unreasonable to hope that progress in industrialization will have brought their energy consumption to the equivalence of 2 tons of coal per capita, the present world average. As in China, approach to that level of consumption and its associated level of well-being should secure to the population the survival of its infants and hasten its passage through the second phase of the demographic transition. Rounding the indicated total upward sets a goal for development and a burden for the planetary ecosystem of up to 25 billion tons of coal-equivalent energy by the middle of the twenty-first century. By the end of that century, a stabilized world population of 10 billion might see its energy demands leveling off at about 5 tons per capita.

It is unthinkable that such increase in the flow of energy should be sought from the burning of coal or any other fossil fuels. At 4 tons per capita, the injection of carbon dioxide into the atmosphere would equal the annual turnover of the biosphere, if that had not already been perturbed by smaller and earlier increase above the present rate of input from the consumption of fossil fuel. Some increase, counting only the increasing coal consumption (from their own resources) of China and India, must be accepted as inevitable. The urgency that must be accorded to the development of alternative sources of primary energy is plainly stated.

In the preparatory conferences that are setting the agenda for the UN Conference on Environment and Development, the Scandinavian countries have taken the lead in calling for action to reduce the input of carbon dioxide into the atmosphere from human activity.

They propose that the conference at Rio de Janeiro produce an international convention setting specific targets and specific dates for reduction in the consumption of fossil fuels.

The alternative technology readiest for expansion is, unfortunately, nuclear power. As market forces compel revival of the technology in the industrial countries, inherently safe reactor cycles will be there to take over from the submarine cycle. Technology to manage the disposal of spent nuclear fuel must be developed on an accelerated schedule, however, and the nonproliferation treaty must be given new iron teeth to prevent the diversion of fuel to weaponry.

The price of energy will mightily encourage conservation, meaning reduction of the waste of energy. The price will also, doubtless, motivate development of small-scale, dispersed ways to capture the energy of the sun and of the wind it sets in motion. Thus, the rooftop solar heat collector that has disappointed so many well-meaning householders will find its way back into the market, especially in new construction. A sufficiently large market for this apparatus will reduce costs and stabilize quality.

Meanwhile, the development of renewable or perpetual sources of energy will at last get under way in earnest. For the long term and on the grand scale, the most promising technology is the photovoltaic harnessing of solar energy. Improvement in the efficiency of the primary collector surface and increase in the price of energy from other sources will surely intersect in the near future. At that point, it may be expected, development and installation of the technology will accelerate.

At full power, solar-photovoltaic energy may reverse again the energy balance between the present industrial and preindustrial worlds. Sunlight could make the Arabian Peninsula the source of hydrogen that it is now of petroleum. With 1 percent of its barren surface—25,000 square kilometers—under photovoltaic arrays, it could produce hydrogen in volume each year equivalent to 5 billion barrels of oil, the entire world's present entire production. The same percentage of the land area of the planet under photovoltaic arrays would more than meet the entire world energy requirement equivalent to the 25 to 50 billion tons of coal projected on page 195.

Short of fusion power, there appears to be one way, now in reach, to supply the human population with all the energy it needs and may desire without imperilling the biosphere in which its existence is embedded. The enormous investment in this reconstruction of the energy economy will lend corresponding stimulus to revival of the world economy. During the several decades required thus to secure the supply of energy, humankind may find time to sort out its values and secure equitable distribution of this primary good.

In reserve is the energy of the ocean to be extracted by OTEC technology or the energy of the Earth's interior to be extracted by HDR technology. It appears that the human species is not fated to perish by the fouling of its nest.

5

AGRICULTURAL REVOLUTION

The world's farmlands are producing food enough to keep everyone well fed and in good health. Yet, at all times, 400 million people are wasted by starvation, and another 600 million do not get enough to eat. This contradiction finds its resolution, of course, in the way food is distributed around the world. Another 500 million people suffer malnutrition from eating too much. In the poor countries, people—children especially—die of kwashiorkor, from not enough protein, and of marasmus, from not enough calories of any kind. In the rich countries—in the United States, for example—nearly 20 percent of the people over the age of 45 are more than 30 percent overweight, and more than half have heart and circulatory troubles associated with a diet rich in sugar and animal fat.

The maldistribution of food is thus international. Over the past 150 years, the application of new understanding from the life sciences and the injection of increasing flows of energy have been raising the productivity of agriculture in the industrial countries. These countries produce nearly half of the world's food, much more than enough for their one-quarter of the world's population. In the preindustrial countries, meanwhile, population growth has overrun the technology and institutions of traditional agriculture.

The maldistribution of food is also national. Poor people go hungry in the rich countries. Some people in the poor countries suffer obesity and other afflictions caused by eating too much of the wrong kinds of food.

The food anxiety that periodically seizes the public in the industrial countries nonetheless puts the production, rather than the distribution, of food at the center of concern. The people of the United States had one such seizure at midcentury when the world population was beginning to double to its present size. A small library of best sellers remains to testify to the despair of—and the disdain for—the people of the poor countries, which the authors shared with so many of their readers.

The "spawning millions" of India and China, in the judgment of the demographer William Vogt, could not escape "Malthusian forces" and achieve "any considerable industrial development for decades to come." The conservationist Fairfield Osborn saw a world population of 3.6 million, projected for the year 2000, encroaching on the limits of the Earth. In their book *Famine—1975!* William and Paul Packard, one a foreign-service officer, the other an agronomist, prescribed triage for the nations that were to be afflicted by that famine.

The poor nations, the Packards said, should be sorted into three classes: (1) those "in which the imbalance between food and population is great but the degree is manageable"; (2) those "which have the necessary agricultural resources . . . to cope with their population growth"; and (3) the "can't-be-saved" nations "in which the population growth trend has already passed the agricultural potential. . . . To send food to them is to throw sand in the ocean."

According to the "lifeboat ethic" of the biologist Garrett Hardin, writing some years later, triage is not morally compelled. When surrounded and outnumbered by people drowning in the water, he advised his readers, those in the boat need take none aboard and should stand by to repel boarders.

If apparently qualified authorities can be so prostrated by anxiety about the supply of food, then any doubt about that question ought to be set at rest. The increase in food production since 1950 that outran the concurrent doubling of the population does not of itself prove that the supply can be doubled again. How that was managed must be comprehended, if one is to be confident that it can be done again and, if necessary, yet again. The way may thereupon be cleared to consider the truly intractable question of distribution.

European subsistence farmers were still practicing forest-fallow or slash-and-burn agriculture when irrigated paddy fields were supporting high civilization in Asia—albeit with recurrent famine that carried off some percentage of the peasantry. The European farmers increased their output to sustain the growing population and the arrival of high civilization in Europe by perfecting temperate-zone, rain-fed agriculture and extending it to ever wider acreage. The long rotation of forest-fallow—a few years of cultivation with 15 to 20 years of fallow—gave way to the shorter rotations of crop with pasture and of nitrogen-consuming with nitrogen-restoring crops. In England, early in the eighteenth century, the "horse-hoeing husbandry" of Jethro Tull (who was educated at Oxford, trained for the bar at the Inns of Court, and drawn to farming by inheritance of land) established the planting of crops in rows for readier cultivation and weed control.

On-the-farm development of agricultural technology culminated in the English "high farming" and "new husbandry" of the middle of the nineteenth century. This is agriculture self-sustained by "internal inputs" of animal manure and green-manure crops that is so warmly publicized today by the advocates of "organic" farming and gardening. The increase in productivity and in output had meanwhile helped to support the accumulation of capital for industrial revolution and had permitted diversion of the labor force to employment in the cities.

Progress in agricultural technology now began to come from off the farm. In North America, the flat expanses of deep-sodded prairie invited the invention, over the half century from 1830 to 1880, of the reaper, the harvester, the binder, and the combine in turn. With each advance, the ratio of acres per day per man increased from the acre a man could reap in a day with the cradled scythe to the 2 acres, the 4 acres, the 8 acres, and then the 18 acres that could be brought in with the harvester, the two- and then the four-horse binder, and then the combine. For all its increase in output per man-hour, however, the mechanized extensive cultivation of the prairie produced lower and even declining output per acre, as compared to the classical intensive cultivation of the land in Europe.

The manufacture of agricultural machinery was for a while the biggest manufacturing industry in the United States, especially upon the roll-out of the tractor early in this century. The tractor brought not only further increase in the size and capacity of the reapers and combines but an increase in farm productivity of a more decisive kind. It freed up the millions of acres and billions of man-hours required to maintain the horse power-plant. Corn and feed grains became available in new abundance as food to be consumed directly by people or indirectly as feed for cattle and fowl.

For the industrial populations, cattle ceased in part to perform the function of making the indigestible cellulose of plant tissue a source of human nutrition. Cattle digest cellulose with the help of the symbiotic bacteria that inhabit their rumen or "second stomach." Now, in their "finishing" for slaughter, they are fed more grain than the people they are soon to feed.

To the Japanese, in the confines of their volcanic islands, economics dictated land-saving rather than labor-saving technology. The Japanese were the first to show, early in this century, how genetics and fertilizer could raise output per hectare—or, for a given output, reduce the land required. Availability of nitrogen fertilizers in the form of herring meal from Hokkaido and soybean cakes from Manchuria brought development of "fertilizer-consuming rice culture."

Strains were selected, principally by the farmers, for the vigor of their response to nitrogen. They had to be shorter of stem, as well, to hold up their heavier heads and not topple or "lodge" and be lost to the harvest. By the 1920s, half the rice land in Japan was planted with these strains, and this tryout of the green revolution to come was flourishing in Japan's colonies, Formosa and Korea.

In the United States, at the turn of the century, the most decisive off-the-farm contributions to agricultural technology began to come from the university and the laboratory. This was the country's reward for its commitment to science and higher learning. The Morrill Act, enacted during the Civil War, had offered endowment from the public domain to encourage the new states on the Western prairies to establish the "land-grant" colleges for cultivation of the arts of "agriculture and mechanics."

At Michigan State College of Agriculture and Applied Science (later to become Michigan State University), William Beal applied a discovery of Charles Darwin's to the breeding of corn (maize). Darwin had noted that the mating of distant strains in a species produced offspring endowed with "hybrid vigor." Beal planted two strains of corn side by side, emasculating one of them by removing its tassels. The seeds from that strain, sired by the tasseled corn in the next row, did exhibit hybrid vigor. To establish the strain reliably in the field required, however, contributions from other investigators. George H. Shull, at the Carnegie Institution of Washington, and Edward M. East and Donald Jones, at the Connecticut Agricultural Experiment Station, uncovered the missing genetic principles.

The experiments that produced the first hybrid corns in the laboratory seed plots are reenacted every season by the technologists of the hybrid-corn seed industry. Within a decade of the first release of the seeds to cultivation in the early 1930s, the yield in the U.S. Corn Belt increased from 22 bushels to 33 bushels per acre. In that brief time, 90 percent of the land came to be planted with the new seed. In the U.S. Corn Belt today, yields of 120 bushels per acre are attained, and 300 bushels per acre are not unheard of. The now worldwide hybrid-corn seed industry raises the productivity of land planted to corn on every continent and has made this gift of the New World to human nutrition second only to wheat in tonnage harvested.

Beal, Shull, East, and Jones had created not only hybrid corn but a method for raising the productivity of every field and garden crop-plant. Their method differs in a fundamental way from the artificial selection practiced by primitive and traditional farmers that brought agriculture through history to the end of the nineteenth century. While the modern breeder chooses, as early farmers did, a plant (or an animal) for a desirable trait, the breeder establishes that trait in the offspring by increased control over the genetic mechanism that conveys it, based on objective understanding of that mechanism.

From such understanding, seed growers are alert to the hazards as well as the gains to be had from manipulating the genetic mechanism. The traits incorporated in a hybrid corn represent a small fraction of the genetic capacity of the older land races of corn from which they are selected. As early as 1956, one-fifth of the U.S. corn crop was lost to a fungus. Resistance to the fungus was incorporated, from the genetic inventory of the land races, in the next year's seed. Thus, for every field-crop species, the seed industry conducts the constant matching of genetic capacity to the cyclic changes in the pressures of the environment.

Agricultural genetics is now the technology of an industry not often in the sights of stock-market traders. As of 1980, this industry had $12 billion in sales worldwide, about one-third in the United States. The industry is dominated by 50 transnational corporations that have been buying up smaller companies, especially successful developers of seed for single species. In Europe and the United

States, these enterprises have come to enjoy patent protection on their house seed varieties. The concentration of market power in this corner of the world economy is "even more significant at the crop level," according to the UN Centre on Transnational Corporations, "with three firms holding 80 percent of the patents on beans and four firms holding 45 percent of the patents on cotton, 60 percent on lettuce, 48 percent on soybeans and 36 percent on wheat."

Hybrid seeds are of particular interest to these enterprises, because the plants they produce either have infertile seed or, if it is fertile, the seed fails to transmit the qualities for which it was patented. Success for a given variety means reorders for the next year. Farmers in the industrial countries have come to put the purchase of seed on their annual profit and loss statements. In the preindustrial countries, farmers are discovering that dependence on purchased seed brings them into reckoning with all of the new technology that comes with it and with the world economy.

GENETIC DIVERSITY AND THE FOOD SUPPLY

Success in the selection of seeds for particular characteristics to the exclusion of others has seriously narrowed the genetic base of the major field-crop plants. The U.S. Department of Agriculture and the state universities are engaged in the systematic building and maintenance of gene banks for each of them. On protected plots, they regenerate the seeds not only of the broader-based land races but, in the case of corn, of the ancestral wild grasses from which Amerindian farmers long ago bred this remarkable plant.

The argument from genetic diversity in favor of establishing protected refuges for entire ecosystems finds here a life-or-death argument in its favor. Gene banks are being established for every crop plant in every country with the resources to do so. A valuable contribution to the U.S. corn gene bank came not long ago from the state of Jammu and Kashmir in India: seeds of a land race of corn that had been cultivated there ever since its introduction from the United States in the early nineteenth century. On the grasslands of Eurasia and North America, the still more ancient wild ancestors of wheat and corn may be found growing.

In the laboratory, control of the genetic mechanism now reaches to its molecular apparatus. Desirable traits will be conveyed in time across species barriers by the technique of recombinant DNA.

The section of the DNA chain encoding a desired trait may be snipped out of a chromosome in one plant and recombined in the chromosome of an entirely different one.

By this technique, it may be possible to endow other crop plants, such as wheat and rice, with the photosynthetic efficiency exhibited by maize, sorghum, and sugarcane. Photosynthesis in the latter plants fixes four, instead of only three, atoms of carbon (from carbon dioxide in the atmosphere) in the primary organic compound it produces. The transfer of this so-called C_4 trait to plants that have the C_3 trait has high priority, to be sure, on the agenda of genetic engineers.

It may be possible to transplant genes across even more distant evolutionary barriers. Nitrogen, the necessary element in proteins, is fixed from the atmosphere by bacteria symbiotically incorporated in the root tissues of clover, alfalfa, and other legumes. That trait may someday be transferred from the bacteria to the genetic apparatus of wheat, corn, and rice plants, thereby reducing the need for, if not obviating the use of, nitrogen fertilizer. Beyond are the genes for tolerance of salt, for resistance to the stress of drought, for repelling or surviving insect predation, and for accommodation to a wider range of photoperiods—of seasonal changes in the duration of daylight—permitting the seed to be planted at latitudes higher or lower than those of its native habitat.

This endless frontier has opened in time for the closing of the Earth's land frontier. The engine of industrial revolution—the seeking and the application of objective knowledge—has set in motion the second agricultural revolution. Increase in the world's food supply to answer the increase in population has already come, for the first time, from an increase in the output of the land rather than from an increase in the extent of land under cultivation.

In the industrial countries, the second agricultural revolution has tightly integrated the farm into the industrial system. Often remarked upon is the decline in U.S. agricultural employment—from more than 12 percent of the labor force in 1950 to less than 3 percent in 1985. Often celebrated is the increase in the number of people fed by one U.S. farmer—from 7 people in 1900, to 16 in 1950, and then to 75 in 1985. The astonishment and the numbers belie the true and more significant state of affairs. In fact, a much larger number of people are employed in feeding the nation. About 75 cents of each consumer dollar at the store goes to pay the farmer's many helpers.

They make their contribution in a division of labor that starts before the farmer goes to work and carries on long after he is done.

There are the hybrid-seed growers and, before them, supported by the consumer's taxes, the faculty in colleges and universities, including research scientists working on fundamental questions that, to their own surprise, will turn out to be relevant to agriculture. The external inputs of farm machinery and fuel, electric energy, fertilizers, pesticides, and animal pharmaceuticals employ as many people off the farm as there are farmers. On the output side, the transport, storage and refrigeration, the processing and packaging, and, finally, the distribution and delivery of the product employ a still larger number of people. All told, the feeding of the U.S. population employs one out of five persons in the labor force and remains the country's largest industry.

The inputs to the modern farm, and its outputs as well, may be reduced to the common denominator of energy. A study of the energy budget of a typical German 25-hectare farm showed a doubling of the energy input over the century from 1880 to 1979 [see tables on page 207]. In 1880, human and animal labor constituted 65 percent of the total expenditure of energy. Most of that energy, plus the 32 percent of the energy carried over in seed from the previous year's crop, may be reckoned as generated by the nearly self-sufficient farm from the food and feed it produced. In contrast, the 1979 farm draws less than 1 percent of its operating energy from human biology and none from any animal. It draws all the rest of the twice as much energy it requires from the economy around it. Even after deduction of that energy cost, it yields twice as much nutritional energy to the economy as the farm of 1879.

A similar input–output computation may be performed for U.S. farms, thanks to the work of David Pimentel at Cornell University and others who have studied the increasing input of energy into the increasing output of agriculture. The exercise shows how completely the country's agriculture has been incorporated in its industrial system. With the standard conversion factors and judicious rounding of numbers, the inputs as well as the outputs can be expressed in the "calories" (strictly speaking, kilocalories) by which people keep track of their nutrition.

In 1987, not the biggest year in U.S. agricultural history, the farms produced 330 million tons of wheat, corn, sorghum, soybeans, and rice, the basic field crops that engage the principal acreage. At 3.6

Energy Input to a German Farm

ENERGY SOURCE	ENERGY INPUT (%)	
	1880	1979
Human labor	13	0.4
Animal labor	52	–
Seeds	32	10
Fertilizers	1	49
Equipment	2	2
Fuel	–	23
Electricity	–	6
Plant-protection chemicals	–	1
Machines	–	8
Totals:	100 (= 60 million kilocalories)	100 (= 120 million kilocalories)

Output of Energy in Crops

CROP	AREA (HECTARES)		YIELD (TONS/HECTARE)		ENERGY OUTPUT (MILLIONS OF KILOCALORIES)	
	1880	1979	1880	1979	1880	1979
Cereals	15	16.7	1.4	5.0	82	325
Potato	4	–	1.4	46.7	41	361
Clover, pasture	6	–	3.2	–	70	–
Totals:	25	25			193	686

ENERGY PROFIT *from farm in Germany quadrupled with the displacement of biological energy inputs by fossil-fuel energy inputs between 1880 and 1979 and a doubling of the total input. Almost all the inputs to the 25-hectare farm were generated on the farm in 1880; almost all came from off the farm in 1979.*

million kilocalories per ton, that harvest held a total nutritional energy of 1,200,000 billion kilocalories. That unwieldy number can be more compactly stated as 1200 petacalories (peta = 10^{15}) in the numeration now adopted in scientific literature. It is, of course, more easily visualized as 1.3 tons of grain per capita.

Though short of protein and of certain essential amino acids, the 1987 crop held fully three times the individual year-long caloric requirement of the country's population, even at the U.S. average intake of 3600 kilocalories per day. In fact, U.S. consumers get not much more than 10 percent of their calories directly from grain. They get much more than half of their calories, however, from grain indirectly in the products of the abattoir, the dairy, and the hen house. To supply those calories, the cattle and poultry consume more than half the grain harvest. The yield to human nutrition is about 15 percent of the original calories in the grain. That is better than the standard shrinkage to 10 percent from step to step in the ecosystem food chain because the yield includes milk and eggs from living animals as well as meat from slaughtered ones.

After all this eating by animals and people, there is left the surplus of grain for export—28 percent of the 1987 harvest. The export of that food establishes the principal presence in international trade of the world's foremost industrial country.

In all the other crops—the hay, alfalfa, and other fodder harvested for the cattle and the vegetables, fruit, and sugar that supply the remaining scant half of the population's nutrition—the farms yield perhaps an additional 800 petacalories to human nutrition, for a total output of about 2000 petacalories. On the common denominator of energy, the grand total corresponds to about 500 million tons of grain. That comes to about 2 tons of grain-equivalent per capita. After exports, about 1.5 tons of primary plant tissue goes to feeding the individual U.S. consumer, nearly twice the average individual ration in the industrial world.

On the input side, the farms draw from the rest of the industrial system about 1000 petacalories in various forms, ultimately derived, of course, from the burning of fossil fuels. Most of this energy goes to reduce the expenditure of biological energy by the farm labor force. The 2.9 million man-years employed on the farms constitutes the smallest of the energy inputs, at most 4 petacalories, a negligible percentage of the total input of energy to agriculture. Moreover, it is the only one reckoned here that is generated even in part on the farm. It is reduced to its small size, first of all, by the input of motor fuel.

With the British thermal units (Btu) ordinarily invoked to measure the energy content of gasoline converted to calories (in the ratio of 4 Btu per kilocalorie) 300 petacalories, one-third of the total external energy input, drives the cultivating and harvesting machines. The barns, the indoor machines, and the farmhouse consume an additional 100 petacalories of electrical energy, calculated by the appropriate interconversion of energy units. These inanimate calories also hold down the input of human energy. So do the 100 to 200 petacalories that supply pesticides and related inputs from the chemical industry.

The most productive of all the external energy inputs is the 400 petacalories that make the fertilizer. This is the input that increases the yield per unit of land. Conversely, this energy may be thought of as land-saving, just as the rest of the external energy input is labor-saving. The biggest part of it is expended in the artificial fixation of nitrogen from the atmosphere. It is this energy that realizes the genetic potential of the high-yielding varieties of seed that have more than doubled the yield from U.S. farmland during the past 50 years. If all of the fertilizer is charged to the field crops alone, it still returns four times its energy to the rest of the economy.

In the balance of this round number accounting of the total energy budget of the U.S. farm, there is a generous allowance for the energy embodied in machinery and equipment, amortized at the usual rate. This input serves to replace manpower, as inanimate energy does in other industries. Farming in the United States, for all but a very small number of farmers, has ceased to be a way of life. It is a business that gives them time to live like the rest of their fellow citizens.

The 200-petacalorie output of the farm, of course, incarnates calories captured from sunlight and none, except for the calories in the fertilizer, of those accounted for here. Under typical practice on rain-fed land, the field crops—the grains, hay, and fodder—return three and more times as many calories as go into planting, cultivating, and harvesting them. The other crops return but a fraction of the energy invested, a fraction so small as to bring the total yield down to no more than twice the expended calories. To deliver food at last to the kitchen—to refrigerate, process, package, and distribute it—requires more than twice again as much energy from fossil fuels as that expended on the farm; all told, 17 percent of U.S. fossil fuel consumption goes to feeding the population and laying down food on the dock for export. The input of fossil solar energy, thus totalled, comes to 1.5 times the current input from the sun that is harvested in crops.

The second agricultural revolution is now worldwide. The high-yielding varieties of the field-crop plants and the fertilizer that stokes the filling of their seed have proved surprisingly portable. That is because the village farmer, disciplined by chance-taking every day, has proved to be the model economic man, ready to act rationally in his self-interest. Few developments in the history of technology have spread so fast and so widely. The average output per unit of land in preindustrial countries still runs at no more than half that of the land in the industrial countries. It runs at less than a quarter of the output of the land under cultivation by the best practice. Yet, largely by increase in output per hectare, the preindustrial countries in which most of the world's poor people live succeeded in keeping the increase in food output ahead of the increase in their populations over the past four decades.

Extension to the preindustrial countries of the average practice of the new agriculture will answer the next doubling of the population; the established best practice is ready, if necessary, to answer the increase after that. This much may be projected from the recorded numbers. Realization of the promise will engage the will and the labor of billions of men, women, and children in the poor countries. It will require, as well, generous assistance from the rich countries in the transfer of the technologies that supply the external inputs (especially fertilizer) and secure the higher yields per hectare. The increase in output from the farms must outrun the increase in population if the number of human beings is to double for the last time in the next century.

THE GREEN REVOLUTION

The green revolution that has carried the second agricultural revolution to the traditional agricultural countries had a quiet beginning a half century ago. The Rockefeller Foundation, in the persons of George Harrar, Sterling Wortman, and Warren Weaver, arranged with the government of Mexico for the establishment of the Oficina de Estudios Especiales in that country's department of agriculture. In its laboratory at Chapingo, Mexican scientists and graduate students, with the counsel of U.S. agronomists (including Norman Borlaug, who was later to receive the Nobel Peace Prize that celebrated the green revolution) went to work first on wheat.

High-yielding varieties of wheat were already under cultivation in the United States. Their development had proved more difficult than that of high-yielding varieties of maize. The male and female organs of wheat are united in the same flower, as they are in most plants; such plants, in contrast with maize, cannot be so easily "detasseled." Hybrid wheats are not as strictly hybridized as the corn strains; they are selected from the many varieties that turn up in the second generation from the first-generation hybrid and then inbred. The task at Chapingo was to develop strains adapted to Mexican soils and climates.

Within five years, Chapingo was releasing the first new wheat to Mexican farmers. Yield per hectare increased abruptly from 750 to 3200 kilograms. Soon enormous territory was planted to high-yielding wheat strains by agribusiness enterprises in the northwestern state of Sonora.

For the small farmers of Mexico, Chapingo selected second-generation offspring of hybrid corn adapted to their circumstances. With the help of 100 kilograms of nitrogen fertilizer per hectare, these strains multiplied the output per hectare four times to 4000 kilograms. The caloric energy contained in the additional 3000 kilograms of corn is 13 times that contained in the fertilizer. With the farmer's own metabolism supplying the rest of the energy that raises the corn, this energy gain goes straight to the bottom line.

By 1956, Mexico—hitherto, like the other Latin American countries, dependent upon imported food—had become a food-exporting country. That Mexico is now once again a food-importing country relates more to distribution than to production questions, starting with the distribution of land.

On the Chapingo precedent, the Ford Foundation joined with the Rockefeller Foundation in the creation of the International Rice Research Institute (IRRI) in the college of agriculture at the University of the Philippines in Manila in 1963. From the basic crossing of high-yielding Japonica strains of rice with hardy Indica strains, the IRRI laboratory released its first strains for cultivation in 1966. By 1969, they were being harvested from 10,000 hectares in South Asia and probably from an equal territory in China. Today they are growing on half the irrigated rice lands of South Asia, on more than half of those in China, and on substantially all the rice lands in the Philippines and Indonesia.

Typically, the high-yielding strains of rice double the output per hectare. They carry other equally significant traits. The most widely cultivated strain, IR-8, is insensitive to photoperiod and so grows over a wide range of latitude; it resists blight and insects, and it matures in 120 days (compared with the 160 days of native strains), permitting the growing of two crops per year. The IR-36 strain bears traits of 13 different native varieties from six nations; it too is resistant to blight and insects, and it matures in 110 days, allowing three plantings a year in the right latitudes; it is grown on 10 million hectares in Asia. For protection of the high-yielding strains, IRRI maintains a gene bank of 30,000 native varieties that embraces much of the genetic capacity of the species and reflects the ingenuity of rice breeders over 10,000 years of traditional cultivation.

The basic understanding from which these developments flow is, of course, universal. The technology that applies it is locality-specific. A high-yielding variety must be adapted to the soil, the amount and timing of moisture, and the seasonal photoperiod, among other things, of the place where it is to be grown. One development laboratory cannot serve the whole world. Under the auspices of a consortium of UN technical agencies, national governments, and philanthropic foundations known as CGIAR, the Consultative Group on International Agricultural Research, plant geneticists and agronomists are now at work in nine international research institutes in Asia, Africa, and Latin America. IRRI is, of course, one of these institutes, and it continues its work on rice. Chapingo has become CIMMYT, the Spanish initials for International Maize and Wheat Improvement Center, and it is working also on barley and triticale, the promising hybrid of wheat (*Triticum*) and rye (*Secale*).

CIAT, the International Center of Tropical Agriculture in Colombia, has encouraged the spread of rice culture in Latin America by boosting yields there from 3 tons to 5.4 tons per hectare. Already of immense consequence is its work on cassava. This root crop is native to Latin America; it long ago found its way into cultivation throughout the middle latitudes of the world, especially in Africa and the Southwest Pacific Archipelago. Like the potato, it offers a large return on little labor; unimproved varieties will yield as much as 10 tons per hectare. From CIAT have come strains that yield 50 tons per hectare.

Cassava may be taken as symbolic of the opportunities open and of the work that waits to be done in agricultural research. For the major field crops—wheat, corn and rice—the gains in sight have been accomplished. The "harvest index"—the distribution (by weight) of dry matter between the edible seed and the remainder of the plant—has been pushed in these plants from 20 or 30 percent to somewhat more than 50 percent. That appears to be the limit. Further increase in yield from the field crops awaits results from molecular biology, such as transfer of the C_4 trait from another crop plant or, perhaps, a roadside weed.

On the other hand, improvement in the output of the protein-rich legumes, the white potato, the sweet potato, sorghum, and millet have not kept pace with population growth. On these plants, on livestock health and improvement, and on the problems of agriculture in the arid and semiarid lands, the other six institutes of the CGIAR network have been put to work. At the same time, the preindustrial countries are establishing their own national laboratories and cadres of native agronomists, thus far most successfully in India and China.

Output of the basic cereals has increased in the preindustrial countries enough to permit diversion of an increasing percentage to animal feed and a measurable increase in the protein fraction of the diet. In the two most populous countries, the extension of aquaculture with the encouragement of the UN Food and Agriculture Organization (FAO) has brought in a source of protein that does not require subtraction from the supply of primary edible plant tissue. Fish ponds yield 4 million or more tons of protein in China and 2 million tons in India. The total world yield from aquaculture, at around 10 million tons, now comes to 10 percent of that from the fisheries. The sea-ranching of salmon, fated to return to their natal water even if it is the hatchery pond alongside a cannery, has enriched the diet of the industrial world.

The annual production of food in the preindustrial countries has more than doubled since 1950. Part of this increase must be credited to extension of the land under cultivation. China has made an addition of 10 percent to its cultivated land; India extended its cultivated land by 40 percent, with perilous invasion of marginal soils. In the preindustrial world as a whole, the increase came to 20 percent. With credit for a second crop on the 50 million new hectares of irrigated land, the contribution to the increase in food production by extension of the land under cultivation may be raised to 25 percent. The rest of the increase in food supply in the preindustrial world must be credited to increases in output per hectare.

For the next doubling of the food supply, the preindustrial world must look to such an increase in output again. Subject to environmental considerations, Africa and South America have arable land not yet brought under cultivation. Still more land can effectively be made available there and in the Mediterranean countries by increases in cropping intensity—increases in the percentage of arable land harvested each year—by crop rotation and fertilizer. To feed the growing population on those continents, even with extension of cultivated land, the increase in food supply must be secured primarily by extension of the second agricultural revolution. With no land frontier, the growing population of Asia must look to the revolution for substantially all of the necessary increase in its food supply. The technology is in hand. It is being put to work on more land on all the continents. The question then is whether the Earth can sustain this additional demand upon its resources.

The question can be put more precisely. The human species already diverts to its needs and uses, as shown in Chapter 2, a substantial percentage of the annual turnover of energy and matter in the biosphere. Human activity has begun to perturb some of the cycles in that vital turnover. The question is how to sustain the biosphere through—and beyond—this next huge increase in the human claim on its energy and substance. The thin margins compel the human species to learn soon to live within, and not outside, the natural order.

As compared with the planetary consequences of the rise in the combustion of fossil fuels, the environmental impact of agriculture is local. People have brought more than one-tenth of the Earth's land area, however, under cultivation. They have brought more than half of this large total territory under cultivation since the middle of the last century. On the geological time scale, that is sudden enough to be reckoned as an event. Local impacts can be seen now to converge in regional consequences with no less than global implications.

Erosion comes forward as the most visible and consequential of these impacts. The formation of soil on the land and its washing into the ocean is a geological process that joins the lithosphere, atmosphere, hydrosphere, and biosphere in concerted interaction. Through freeze and thaw, the hydrosphere and the atmosphere split and spall the continental rock, especially rock exposed in the mountains. Carried by wind and water to the lowlands, the grains of lithosphere in time become incorporated in the biosphere. In their range of sizes from sand to fine powder, they present a large aggregate surface in the soil to which organic matter adheres and, in this intimate contact, dissolves those elements from the lithosphere that are essential to life processes. Even from under the forest primeval, the soil eventually finds its way by erosion to the stream, the river, and, at last, the ocean. From the sod of the savannas, it erodes twice or three times as fast. Under natural circumstances, the formation of new soil, uphill and upstream, more or less balances the loss by erosion downstream on a cycle of about 500 to 1000 years, depending upon geology and climate.

Unavoidably and understandably, the clearing of the forest and the breaking of the sod for cultivation speeds up erosion. The rate of erosion now becomes a function of human behavior, of the forestry and husbandry practiced on the land. Over the 10,000 years since the first agricultural revolution, it is estimated, people have cleared more than half the world's forest land. They now have 1.5 billion hectares (about 10 percent of the planet's land area) under cultivation and 3 billion hectares in pasture.

Monitoring of the deltas of the world's rivers shows that 90 billion tons of silt washes into the ocean each year. If all that erosion had to be charged to cultivated land, it would amount to 60 tons of soil per hectare, a layer 4 millimeters thick. The topsoil, averaging about 25 centimeters in depth around the world, would be gone in little more than 60 years, at 30 to 200 times the rate at which it forms. Not all the silt comes, however, from cultivated land. Some comes, as it all does in the special case of the Yellow River, straight from the deforested uplands. In the natural cycle, that material would migrate over thousands of years down the upland slopes into the alluvial soils of the river valleys and only thence to the sea. The 90 billion tons of silt indicates erosion at three or more times the natural rate from the total planetary land area.

Where it occurs, erosion at the rate of 60 tons per hectare from cultivated land can be seen plainly to be too much. In the basin of the Irawaddy River in Burma, on the Deccan Plateau in India, on the high central plateau of Madagascar, in the basin of the Acelhuate River in El Salvador, erosion proceeds at that rate and higher on many millions of hectares. In those places, thousands of hectares are going out of cultivation every year, and desertification is on the march. Erosion, proceeding at the rate of 20 to 40 tons per hectare, scours a layer 2 millimeters thick from the soil of the United States each year and carries it away at 20 times the rate of natural soil formation.

The reduction and prevention of erosion requires no high technology. Land on slopes steeper than 30 degrees is terraced or left to pasture or forest. At all grades above zero, ploughing on the contour conserves energy as well as soil. Such measures prevent, halt, and repair gullying. Between plantings, stubble and litter or the planting of a green-manure crop protect the soil from sheet erosion: wind-driven raindrops hitting bare ground at a slant splash soil particles into the wind, to be carried many feet.

Yet, over most of the United States, the concerned air traveller can be depressed to see how little of the land has been brought under soil-conservation practice. Contour plowing distinguishes family farms in the Eastern states, but it is rarely seen elsewhere. For miles on end, the prairies west of the Mississippi River are streaked by sheet erosion. The problem is again one of distribution, in this case, the distribution of economic incentive.

THE IRRIGATION FRONTIER

For the world's most crowded lands, in Asia, irrigation holds open the principal land frontier. It effectively doubles or triples the land under cultivation because it permits double- and triple-cropping. It is expected that the irrigated land, presently 220 million hectares and more than double that irrigated in 1950, will double early in the next century.

In accordance with that first law, however, irrigation has its cost as well as its benefit, its hazard as well as its promise. The lands first brought under irrigation, in the Tigris and Euphrates valleys, testify today to one hazard—that of salination. The soil there remains barren and economically irreclaimable. The salt comes from the same source as the salt in the ocean; all fresh water on the continents contains some salt, dissolved from the lithosphere. Alternatively, depending upon the geology of the water source, the soil may be poisoned by alkali. The salt or alkali accumulates in the soil as the residue either from evaporation of irrigation water spread on it above ground or from evaporation below ground from a water table that is too close to the surface.

A water table too close to the surface may also prevent the drainage of irrigation water from the soil, which is necessary to carry the salt away. This is associated with the third hazard of irrigation: waterlogging of the soil.

Studies conducted by FAO show as much as half of the world's irrigated land suffering salinization, alkalization, or waterlogging. About 10 million hectares go out of cultivation each year. Some of the worst irrigation calamities have happened in rain-fed, temperate-zone countries, where the investment was not necessary but was thought to be profitable. Once the damage is done, it presents an economically forbidding cost of repair. The ruined land becomes a regional hazard, its runoff spreading the blight to fauna as well as flora. In the tropics and semitropics, irrigation water can also harbor the vectors, such as mosquitoes and snails, of parasitic diseases, such as malaria and schistosomiasis.

The need for land is nonetheless large enough in some countries and the short-term promise sufficient in others to assure that irrigation will continue to be extended to new land. According to Istvan Szabolcs, a principal soil scientist of Hungary, whose own country is suffering the aftermath of some ambitious irrigation projects, it will be wiser to invest money in preventative engineering on new sites than to attempt to reclaim the old ones there.

None of the untoward outcomes are inherent in the technology. They can be avoided by paying attention to geology, by sufficient investment (principally in capacious drainage systems), and by careful management of the flow of water into and through the soil. Irrigated land in China has been cultivated for thousands of years and remains as productive as ever, and more so in response to the second agricultural revolution.

The fertilizers and the pesticides that contribute so much to the increase in yield per hectare also endanger or damage the environment in their own ways. The law propounded by Justus von Liebig early in the nineteenth century explains the need for fertilizer: it is the essential element in least supply that limits biological production. In cultivated soils, nitrogen is most likely to be that element.

A nearly "noble" element, nitrogen resists compounding with other elements and must be forced into it by an expenditure of energy. (From nitroglycerin and other nitrate explosives, it readily lets go of that energy upon detonation.) All multicelled organisms depend upon the few families of bacteria that fix nitrogen from the atmosphere for incorporation in protein molecules. In nature, the nitrogen cycle is completed by denitrifying bacteria that return nitrogen to the atmosphere.

Artificial fixation of nitrogen, which is now conducted in a volume equal to that fixed naturally by bacteria, first became economically feasible early in this century. It came in time to appease a seizure of anxiety about the food supply then widely bruited as the threat of "nitrogen starvation." The same abundance that makes nitrogen fertilizers the principal active ingredient in the second agricultural revolution also makes nitrogen a major environmental pollutant.

In compounds agreeable to life processes, the abundance of nitrogen has speeded up the production of biomass in inland and inshore waters. The result is the loss of oxygen from the water to the rotting of the efflorescing algae and other vegetation, the process called eutrophication. Under natural conditions, eutrophication degrades an aquatic ecosystem over long periods of time with slow accumulation of the detritus of the local biomass. Lakes become ponds; ponds become marshes, and the marsh becomes a meadow or a forest floor. With the new abundance of nitrogen, the blooming and then the rotting of nitrogen-fixing algae reduces the availability of oxygen for higher forms of life and abruptly degrades the aquatic ecosystem, suffering also from an overgrowth of weeds. Game fish give way to rough fish, and aquatic plants entangle swimmers.

Much nitrogen fertilizer, on the other hand, forms nitrates, saltlike compounds with metals that are not assimilated by the denitrifying bacteria. Disagreeable to other forms of life as well, these nitrate compounds poison soil bacteria, disrupting the soil ecosystem. They also poison higher organisms as pollutants of ground and surface waters.

Less wasteful use of nitrogen fertilizers can do most of what can be done to reduce nitrogen pollution. The use of fertilizers that break down into compounds more readily assimilated by plant tissue and denitrifying bacteria can help as well.

It is all very well to prescribe such remedy. The familiar economic advantage of internalizing the profit and externalizing the cost exerts its customary stubborn resistance. One energetic center of economic initiative makes a profit; the cost to the environment remains to be paid by the public, organized to repair the damage only after it has been done. The remedy may be supplied in the end by molecular biologists. When they have learned to transfer the nitrogen-fixing genes from bacteria to plants, they will secure substantial reduction in the use of artificially fixed nitrogen.

With nitrogen supplied, phosphorus usually takes its place as the limiting element. In contrast to nitrogen, this is a highly reactive element, forming energetic compounds with many others. It is essential to life as the energy carrier and transfer agent in the living cell. While relatively an abundant element, phosphorus is widely dispersed and hard to come by in concentration. A field full of nitrogen-responsive plants will be hungry for it. To supply the rising demand, the fertilizer industry has begun to dredge phosphorus from offshore deposits. There, unfortunately, it tends to be associated with heavy metals from the continental rock. While the association can be dissolved at some expense, phosphorus is being used as it comes, for the present—perhaps until the hazard becomes damage done.

The pesticides, especially the insecticides, present the most immediate and significant pollution problems because they so directly affect animal and human health. In the United States, the persistence of DDT and its concentration in the food chain nearly extinguished the raptors at the end of that chain. Public outcry at this and other untoward consequences of the accumulation of DDT in the environment taught the industry a lesson. Insecticide chemists proceeded to introduce a weak link or two into the molecular structure of compounds designed to replace DDT. Contamination of the soil and ground water by their breakdown products has now become apparent in regions of heavy and prolonged use.

Often the hazard is the still more direct one of immediate toxicity or cumulative injury to the crop duster and the farmer on the ground. A corresponding range of hazards attends the use of the herbicides. There is no getting away from the fact that pesticides, directed as poisons to particular forms of life, tend to be poisonous to others.

Less extravagant and less wasteful use of these materials can, again, much mitigate their side effects. Plants can be bred for resistance to insects and even to crowd the growth of weeds. The timing of planting and the rotation of crops can avoid and suppress the enemy. As principally labor-saving inputs, the pesticides confront the industrial countries, rather than the preindustrial countries, with problems. Their work is often done equally well in the preindustrial countries by human labor applied intensively to wielding hoes and rakes and picking off the bugs, one by one.

Having enjoyed the benefits of the new agricultural technology, farmers in the industrial countries are beginning to recognize its costs. The U.S. Department of Agriculture has ratified the advice of organic farmers that greater reliance be placed upon the regenerative power of the soil, regarded as a live ecosystem.

It is possible, with the external inputs of fertilizer and pesticides, to grow the same crop year after year on the same field; this is the only way it can be done. With crop rotation, however, the yields from the new technology can be raised by 10 to 15 percent. The plowing in of animal manure or the "green manure" of a crop of alfalfa or of crop residues improves the soil's fertility, water-storage capacity, and tilth (or structure) and maintains its natural population of microbes, earthworms, ants, and other soil-turning insects.

In the Corn Belt of the United States, unfortunately, a tenth or more of the country's total livestock output of 1.7 billion tons of manure is produced in the feeding pens, at a considerable distance from the cornfields. Most of it goes to cause eutrophication of the Mississippi watershed. If pollution control and enhancement of the soil could somehow be harnessed to finance the collection and transportation cost, that manure could significantly reduce the use of fertilizer and enhance the soil of 100 million acres of crop land. No microeconomic interest, however, supports this obvious remedial action.

As the second agricultural revolution realizes its promise in the poor countries, it is likely to do so at smaller cost to the environment than has been experienced in the rich countries. That is because fertilizer as well as pesticides will, of necessity, be more frugally employed. Most of the blunders in their use reported from those countries have been committed by public agencies conducting large-scale pesticide projects under counsel from well-meaning advisors from the outside. Of necessity, even as farmers in the poor countries call in the new technology, they will try to maintain their traditional self-sufficiency.

Traditional farmers in most poor countries are already making full use of the natural resources within their reach. The only way they can increase their output is by adopting the new technology and adapting it to their circumstances. In China, where farmers are said to practice traditional agriculture best, 50 percent of the output is now attributed to high-yielding seed, nitrogen fertilizer, and a 100-fold increase in the input of energy. Still a much smaller input than that in the United States and embodied principally in fertilizer, the fossil-fuel energy goes to multiply the yield from human biological energy, rather than to displace it.

If the second agricultural revolution realizes its promise, the demand for food as well as the output of food, increasing with population increase, will reach a peak and begin to level off in the last quarter of the next century. Most of the increase in need and demand will have been met in the first half of the century, in the next 50 or 60 years. It will have been met, that is, providing increase in food production has been made to outrace population growth and so to establish the security of individual existence that brings population growth to zero.

The goal for food production, therefore, is finite. It is within the bounty of nature and the reach of technology.

THE QUESTION OF DISTRIBUTION

That conclusion brings this discussion to the question of distribution. To accomplish the next doubling of the world output of food on time will require early redistribution, at least in some small part, of the knowledge, wealth and power that divide the world between rich and poor nations and divide nations between rich and poor people. As might be expected, these divisions turn, first of all, on agriculture. Farmers in the rich nations stand in the same relation to the economic systems of those nations as the poor nations stand in relation to the world economy.

Agriculture in the rich nations remains the last production sector subject to market forces. Prices for its output still respond to supply and demand. That is in contrast to the highly centralized industrial sectors, where not more than three producers dominate each industry; prices for their output move continuously upward, secured by strong ratchets against fallback. Farmers accordingly face perpetual inflation in the prices they pay for the inputs they purchase from industry, which add up to nearly half of their total costs. The imparity in economic power between agriculture and industry brings, in every industrial country at one time or another, such imparity in income as to provoke the organization of farmers in protest. To this "farm crisis," the political process invariably responds, in violation of free-enterprise shibboleths, with the provision of subsidies in one form or another.

Every industrial country has its farm lobby, and no political question is more vexed than that of the design of subsidies to try to adjust farm output to effective domestic demand and to narrow the gap between farm and other incomes. The purchase by the U.S. government of price-depressing surpluses from the country's farmers took tons of wheat, butter, and other commodities out of the domestic market during the late 1950s and through the 1960s. Under Public Law 480, the surpluses were shipped as food aid to preindustrial coutries, answering desperate need there, especially in India. Alternatively, the government paid surplus-suppressing bounties to the farmers to take land out of production. They were offset at first by rise in yields per acre but now have significantly reduced the harvested acreage and the grain harvest.

Tariff and nontariff barriers to competitive agricultural imports surround every rich country. They occasioned rancorous argument in the organization of the European Economic Community. They now surround that community against the world and brought the "Uruguay round" of negotiations under the General Agreement on Tariffs and Trade (GATT) to an equally rancourous impasse between the United States and the European community in 1990. Negotiations broke off before they reached the defenses the United States maintains around its agricultural economy.

In every country, even as the number of farmers declines, their political effectiveness in defense of their subsidies and tariff protections seems invariably to rise. According to the agricultural economist Vernon Ruttan, when a nation stops taxing and starts subsidizing its farmers, that nation has completed its industrialization.

As farmers to the rich nations, the poor nations have neither the political nor the economic power to claim parity. Food and agricultural raw materials made up more than half their exports to the rich countries at the beginning of this half century. For Latin American countries that have no oil to export, their plantations and ranches continue to supply nearly 50 percent of total exports, and for such countries in Africa, the farms produce nearly 60 percent. To the rich nations that import these goods, they represent less than 10 percent of total consumption; except for the protests of coffee and tea drinkers, their absence would scarcely be noted.

The imparity that governs this trade has widened since 1950. Decline in agricultural prices is a long-term trend in the world economy [see illustration on facing page]. It is punctuated now and

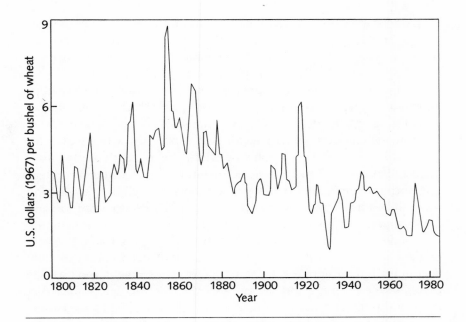

THE PRICE OF WHEAT *has declined since 1800 despite periods of sharp increase attending shortages owing to harvest failure or crises in human affairs. The decline, observed in most agricultural prices, reflects increase in efficiency of production and in relative value of products of manufacture and of services.*

then, as it was in the early 1950s, by price increases that set off the recurring food anxiety of the industrial world. The world may be frightened by another price rise in the 1990s. The success of the Reagan farm policies in reducing the size of the U.S. carry-over of food grains has left little cushion against failed monsoons in South Asia and renewed drought in Central Africa.

From any price rise, whether caused by crop failure or crop control, the price trend returns to its former downward slope. As economic development proceeds, it brings an increasing variety of goods and services to the market. Consumer expenditure for food becomes a declining percentage of the household budget; food production, increasing so long as the population increases, makes a declining percentage contribution to the gross national product. In the export of agricultural products to the industrial world, the terms of trade for the poor countries have declined 15 percent over the past decade and 25 percent over the past 15 years. The terms factor in not only the decline in prices for their exports but the relentless increase in the prices of the industrial goods they buy in exchange.

In the preindustrial countries, except the Arab oil exporters, agriculture remains the largest economic sector. Much as their former colonial suzerains did, their governments look to agriculture to support the "modern" urban sector and supply the wherewithal for economic development. Upon liberation, the plantations that supplied the principal exports before liberation received the first attention and investment of the new governments, though they employ no more than a tiny fraction of the population. Their output of food and raw-material exports expanded ahead of the rest of the agricultural economy in the first decades after the war. Upon finding export markets for such products as peanuts, some African countries have encouraged their farmers to raise them; government monopolies purchase the output at prices well below market to sell it abroad at the world price in order to cadge thereby precious foreign exchange.

Subsistence farmers were, in general, left to continue fending for themselves. Food prices, held low in favor of urban consumers, gave the farmers small motive to produce any surplus above their own needs for sale to the domestic market. Without the incentive to employ new technology, productivity on the food-producing farms increased much more slowly than on the plantations and farms producing export products. In consequence, the city economies or modern urban sectors of the preindustrial countries became dependent upon imported food. Most of them are so dependent today, and food imports by the preindustrial countries increased from $4 billion in 1970 to $22 billion in 1985. Necessarily, food imports have higher political priority than the import of the technology and equipment necessary for the nation's economic development.

By outside counsellors, the preindustrial nations continue, even now, to be advised that their situation is as it should be. The free-market law of comparative advantage brings in view a rational planetary division of labor. If the Corn Belt of the United States produces the cheapest grain and could, at full throttle, feed the world, it should do so. That would free the preindustrial countries to find the contributions they might make most efficiently to the world economy. With the encouragement of such counsel, financing by loans and grants from abroad, and pressure from growing urban populations, political leaders in many preindustrial countries turned their first attention in the early years to "programs" of industrialization featuring visible (if not practical) "projects," to the neglect of the rural hinterland.

Beginning perhaps two decades ago, continued population growth and increase in the relative as well as the absolute numbers of impoverished people in the preindustrial countries compelled revision of the received doctrine of economic development. It was recognized again that agriculture in all but a few preindustrial countries continues to engage 70 percent and more of the population and produces most of the GNP—if that term can be stretched to include product that does not move far from the villages where it is produced and, therefore, scarcely enters the national economy. The traditional agricultural village is also the locus of the world's deepest poverty. International financial institutions and the bilateral aid agencies, as well as progressive leaders in the preindustrial nations, have joined the UN technical agencies in the new consensus: industrial development cannot proceed without concurrent development of agriculture.

The meeting of food needs from domestic resources, in the new consensus about economic development, makes its first contribution by substituting for food imports. It generates demand for the products and services of the supporting input and output industries of modern agricultural technology. For investment in these industries, it frees the foreign exchange that pays for imported food. Domestic markets for other industries come into being. Some of these begin to produce for export. Not only economic growth but economic development—the entraining of the countryside as well as the cities in the cultural revolution of industrialization—has got under way.

The countryside, once entrained in development, generates powerful demand to sustain continued development. In the language of economics, the markets of preindustrial countries show high elasticity of demand for food. An income increase of 1 percent generates an increase of 0.8 percent in expenditure for food. That contrasts to the average propensity in the populations of industrial countries to spend 0.4 percent or less of a 1 percent increase in income on food. In those countries, moreover, the expenditure goes to processing, packaging, and advertising—to "gourmet" satisfactions—rather than to food itself. In the population of Japan, not all of which participates in that country's economic success, the elasticity of demand for food is 0.6 percent. For cereals from grain a Japanese household will lay out 0.2 percent of a 1 percent increase in income; for meat from grain, it will spend the whole extra 1 percent. In the United States, the elasticity of demand for cereals is 0.0; in effect, families will not increase their consumption of cereals even if they can get them free—in which case, they might even reduce their consumption of cereal.

The plain word for the high elasticity of demand for food in the preindustrial countries is hunger. In contrast to the 1.5 tons of grain-equivalent that sate the U.S. consumer, the population of the preindustrial world gets by on the consumption of somewhat less than 400 kilograms of grain-equivalent per annum. More than half of that is consumed as grain directly, in cereals and breads. In the daily average intake of 2400 kilocalories, only 200 kilocalories is in animal protein.

These averages are adequate to sustain a relatively inactive person, and they represent an improvement on the situation of 50 years ago, when average intake in these countries was under 2000 kilocalories. They conceal, however, the inequality of distribution and the inadequate daily rations not only of the estimated 400 million starving people but the additional 600 million men, women, and—especially—children who never have enough to eat.

THE BACKWARD-SLOPING SUPPLY CURVE

Much of that quotient of misery is suffered in the villages by the small farmers and their families and by the increasing numbers of the landless. Their hunger asserts itself in the peculiar behavior of the village market. If the value of the food the family produces for itself is figured in the largely nonmonetary income of the small farm, that income exhibits the same elasticity as incomes in town. When rising prices increase the farmer's income, the family eats more and sells less to the market [see illustration on the facing page].

This "backward-sloping supply curve" confounds the law of supply and demand. With not much to say about distribution, however, economics does not distinguish one consumer from another; the supply curve slopes the wrong way because the hungry consumer is at the same time the producer. When prices fall, the supply curve slopes the wrong way again. The family eats less in order to put enough food on the market to cover essential expenses, starting with rent to the landlord and interest to the village moneylender.

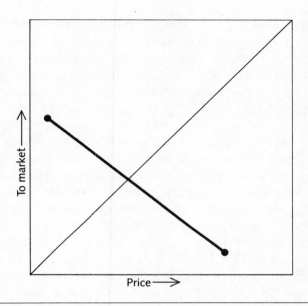

"BACKWARD-SLOPING SUPPLY CURVE" *(thick line) characterizes subsistence farmer's response to increase in price. Confounding the law of supply and demand (thin line), the farmer sends less to market as price increases. Consumer as well as producer, the farmer can afford to eat more when price is high.*

Agricultural development—the introduction of the new technology—faces, accordingly, forbidding obstacles. A national government can make direct investments, as in irrigation works. It can conduct research; it can sponsor extension services assigned, perhaps first of all, to reduce the loss of as much as 200 kilograms per capita of grain-equivalent to vermin and weather. In sum, it can invoke many tangible measures to increase production. When the government attempts to do something about distribution, on the other hand, it takes on a different order of problems.

Thus, attempt to supply economic incentive to the farmer, the measure sure to bring increase in production in every poor country, collides immediately with the existing order of distribution. There is, to begin with, the distribution of land. The subsistence farmer's holding is likely to be too small or too insecure in tenure to motivate the risk even of labor to improve productivity. The marketing system accords the farmer, on the average, the same junior interest in the harvest as in the industrial countries; most of the senior interest has to go, however, to the landlord and the moneylender, not to the merchant who sells fertilizer and implements. The 60 to 70 percent markup to the urban consumer in preindustrial countries vanishes, correspondingly, in the deterioration of product and the claims of middlemen, not in processing, refrigeration, and packaging.

Through this thicket, a well-intentioned national government finds it difficult to frame policies or to take such action as price or market manipulation that will reach and motivate the small farmer. Even the benefit of direct action by the government, such as investment in irrigation, is engrossed first by larger landholders who spare little for their tenant farmers and less for the independent small farmer. The government must reckon the return on such investment, in any case, against the long term and the risk of weather and crop. That is why, in most countries, the capital flow has proceeded in the other direction, by taxation of the largest economic sector in support of "more urgent" nonagricultural projects and by pricing food low for the urban population. To attempt a change in the institutional arrangements of traditional agriculture—as by land reform—is to invite the political opposition of local economic powers, who are, in most countries, the principal political backers of the government, to begin with.

Against such steep gradients, the second agricultural revolution has made its way into the agriculture of all the continents. It has had its greatest impact in Asia, where the scarcity of land places highest priority on increases in yield per hectare. Success of the revolution is attributable to two distinguishing features: the high portability of the technology and the indifference of its results to the scale of operation.

Within five years of the release of the first rice and wheat strains from IRRI, they were planted on 50 million acres. In China, high-yielding varieties of rice and wheat plus fertilizer brought a threefold increase in total output and yield per hectare. In India, the output and yield per hectare doubled and increased the supply of grain per capita from the country's own soil for the first time. From Mexico, where it started, the new technology percolated into every Latin American country, with small farmers as well as big landholders planting more than half the land to the new varieties of wheat and corn in almost all countries. In sub-Saharan Africa, which has seen an actual decline in the total output of food as well as in the supply of food per capita during the last 15 years, the few countries under more progressive leadership, such as Kenya and Tanzania, brought in the green revolution to keep the increase in food production more nearly even with their high rate of population growth.

Inevitably, the larger farmers caught the trend first and profited most. In Punjab, straddling the India–Pakistani frontier, mechanization accompanied the green revolution in wheat farming; 700,000 tenant farmers were tractored from the land. Elsewhere, however, small farmers have proved as successful as large in increasing the yield from their land by planting the higher-yielding seed and applying fertilizer with their own hands. These same farmers are distinguished also for the care they give their land. For many, the green revolution was the saving of what small property and independence they could claim.

For future increases in production and productivity in the preindustrial countries, the second agricultural revolution has a long course to run. In India, half of the hectares planted to rice, one quarter of the hectares planted to wheat, and 35 percent of the hectares planted to corn await planting to the new varieties. While the application of fertilizer has multiplied eightfold since 1965, the present 50 kilograms per hectare is less than one-third that used in China. Japan employs four workers per hectare, twice as many as India or China, to achieve a yield per hectare four times that of India and twice as high as that of China. The land-maximizing technology of the green revolution yields generously to intensification by labor. Adoption of Japanese methods, it has been estimated, would reduce underemployment and unemployment in rural India by half. The attainment of Japanese productivity would make the country's present misery a part of the memory of the painful past.

Moving against the institutional resistance and rigidity of the traditional order in the preindustrial world, the second agricultural revolution has set in motion the breakdown of that order. It has raised the average nutritional status of the population everywhere but in Africa. It has accelerated the incorporation of the villages in the national economies. In the villages, it has turned subsistence farmers into producers for the market. Some preindustrial countries are arriving at the level of self-sustaining food production from which the industrial countries moved on into their industrial revolutions.

The second agricultural revolution sets up its own demand for industrialization. Fertilizer is the first requirement on the input side; the larger preindustrial countries are producing their own fertilizer at close to self-sufficiency. To deliver the output to markets beyond the village requires transportation, refrigeration, processing, and packaging industries for which the considerable losses of product in existing primitive marketing systems can help supply financing. To deliver its full benefit to the people in each country, the second agricultural revolution must be attended by industrial revolution.

China, from the most highly developed base in traditional agriculture, has made the most effective use of the new technology. Since 1950, it has more than tripled its output of grains. With no more than a 25 percent increase in land under cultivation (of that 25 percent, 15 percentiles represents credit for the second crop on the 15 million acres brought under irrigation), it secured substantially all of that increase in output by tripling the yield per hectare. That was accomplished by rapid introduction of high-yielding varieties of rice and wheat and by crowding their response to nitrogen with a sevenfold increase in the use of fertilizer to nearly 200 kilograms per hectare. Against a doubling of the population, the increase in output secured a 75 percent increase in the supply of grain per capita, from 200 to 350 kilograms per year. On the consequent huge expansion of its human capital, China's centralized government has pressed forward the most rapid industrial revolution in history.

At the root of this success was the peasant revolution. Collective and cooperative village organization, with allocation of incentives to the household, supplanted exploitation by landlord and money-lender. With the new agricultural technology brought to the villages by the center, Chinese farmers increased the productivity of their land ahead of the rest of the preindustrial world. Distributed through the narrow spread of incomes in the urban population, the increasing output went straight to increase in human capital. The reward to the villagers has been the extension to them of the first relaxation of central controls and the installation of market-economy arrangements that have produced peasant millionaires.

At liberation in 1947, India had a population of 400 million, nearly as large as China's. The Indian villagers were poorer than the Chinese by at least the difference between the amounts of grain produced per capita in the two countries, less than 150 kilograms a year in India compared with 200 kilograms in China. India's democratically elected government addressed the people's poverty as it first priority, with noblesse oblige in place of revolutionary ardor. It mobilized the urban population for industrial revolution that was to improve the villager's lot. On behalf of the small farmers, it organized and subsidized credit and marketing societies (6000 of them by 1959) that took the crop, not the land, in security; it guaranteed minimum prices and purchased buffer stocks to stabilize prices, set up fertilizer-supply depots, and sent extension agents to the villages to teach the new technology.

The village oligarchy, left carefully intact, was not easily circumvented. A report of the Indian Reserve Bank from the late 1950s declared: "When the local cooperation society gets into the charge of the village moneylender, and more especially the landlord-money-lender, he becomes the society, the depositor and the borrower, all of them together or each in turn, with the ease with which the one Godhead becomes Brahma, Vishnu and Siva—Creator, Preserver and Destroyer. . . ." Shipments of the U.S. harvest surplus under Public Law 480, worth $3.3 billion dollars by 1968, saw India through the first desperate years of the slow start-up.

Triaged by the Packards as a 'can't be saved' nation, India secured its first increases in food production by increasing the land under cultivation from 140 million to 160 million hectares. With its own Rice Research Institute in operation at Cuttack, in the state of Bihar, before the establishment of IRRI in Manila, the country's agronomists went early to work on the task of increasing the output per hectare. The 85 percent increase in total output achieved by 1973 (over the pitiful starting output of 55 million tons) could be attributed to the increase in cultivated hectares but, more promisingly, to a cumulative increase in output per hectare of more than 40 percent.

Major national effort went to begin the impounding of the average 660 million cubic meters of rainwater delivered so erratically and torrentially by the annual monsoons. The average flow of the Ganges River is 2800 cubic meters per second, but it fluctuates between 1700 cubic meters per second in the dry season and 56,000 cubic meters per second in the monsoon. On unirrigated land, the crop must be grown and harvested during the weeks through which the land holds moisture from the rains that it absorbed and that did not run off into the rivers. Supplied with water the year around, much of India's land could produce two and even three crops per year. From less than 100 million cubic meters in 1950, impoundment now exceeds 300 million cubic meters and approaches half the average annual delivery by the monsoon. The land under irrigation has doubled, from 20 to 40 million hectares.

The tripling of India's total output of grain to 166 million tons in 1985 is owed principally to the doubling of the output per hectare. This achievement has brought increase in the population's daily average intake of calories from a wasting 1700 kilocalories to a still inadequate 2500 kilocalories. To provide adequate nutrition to its prospective 1.2 billion population, India possesses the necessary resources and the technology to work them. It is a question for sociology, economics, and politics.

The people of sub-Saharan Africa have secured an increase of the output of food since 1950 almost entirely by increasing the number of hectares under cultivation. In effect, each additional family in the fast-growing population has got its food by opening up new land. Following such primitive practices as slash-and-burn and bush-fallow, they plant and harvest less than half their cropland from year to year. Barred from the best 10 million hectares of river-valley land by insect vectors of parasitic diseases, they overwork the poorest land. In consequence, they lose millions of hectares each year to desert that advances at the rate of 5 kilometers per year into the Sahel region on the southern perimeter of the Sahara. The nomadic peoples, who have so successfully employed cattle to secure their nourishment from plant life inedible by man, are being compelled by the increasing density of their population to abandon their technology and way of life for "sedentarization" on the barren land. For more than a decade, the nutrition of 400 million out of the 500 million Africans has been in decline.

What the Africans want most are the professional cadres trained in the agricultural sciences that have led the Chinese and the Indians into the second agricultural revolution. The first generation of Africans taught by qualified African scientists is graduating from universities in Nigeria, Kenya, and Tanzania. These centers and the three CGIAR laboratories at Ibadan, Nairobi, and Addis Ababa will begin the deflection of African history in the next century. Occupation and development of the 10 million hectares of river-valley land may be facilitated by the control of the insect disease-vectors issuing from the work of the International Centre of Insect Physiology and Ecology at Nairobi. Persons outside Africa who deplore the prospect of 2.5 billion Africans in the year 2100 will want to help these people and institutions.

The population of Latin America has more than doubled in the present half century to more than 400 million. The populations of the 21 nations in South and Central America continue to grow at rates exceeding 2 percent in almost all of them and closer to 3 percent in the most populous. That is the measure of the inequality in distribution of wealth and income that holds the overwhelming percentage of the Latin Americans in poverty.

The 70 percent of the poor who live in the shantytowns around all the cities cannot themelves do much about food production. Neither can the 60 to 90 percent of the rural poor who work holdings of less than 5 hectares and hold, in most countries, much less than 10 percent of the land. The 5 to 10 percent of the landholders, the *latifundistas,* who own 90 percent of the land, appear, on the other hand, to have little incentive to increase the output from their holdings. Except in Argentina, where they produce grain and wheat for export, and in Mexico, where the big grain farmers now produce for the domestic market, they have made indifferent use of the new agricultural technology. Even in Argentina and Mexico, the yield of grain per hectare runs at half that of the United States. To feed their urban populations, all of the Latin American countries, except Argentina, have been importing food in increasing volume.

For production of the food to feed its prospective 700 to 800 million population, Latin America holds one of the world's great land frontiers in the 140 million hectares—compare China's 110 million hectares—grossly underutilized by its *latifundistas.*

For the world, as for Latin America, the economic problem, defined as the getting of three square meals a day, has been solved. That other economic problem, the distribution of the bounty of nature and technology, must find its solution in the next century.

6

INDUSTRIAL
REVOLUTION

In addition to food, people have other necessities. They enjoy luxuries as well. When luxuries have been enjoyed long enough, they become necessities. Somewhere between want and surfeit, people arrive at that level of well-being at which, consciously or unconsciously, they make an arithmetic calculation; for the sake of their first children, they restrain their fertility.

Until the most recent times, the occasion to consider such a decision was reserved to the very few at the top of society. In that moral tale from ancient Rome, Cornelia, daughter of Scipio Africanus and wife of Tiberius Sempronius Gracchus, had but two "jewels" to exhibit: Tiberius Junior and Caius. Only within the present half century have whole national populations arrived at the level of well-being that motivates restraint of fertility. Those populations, having made the passage through industrial revolution, have arrived at, or are all approaching, zero growth.

If the same opportunity is to be extended to the rest of humankind, industrial revolution must soon proceed worldwide. If industrial revolution is to proceed fast enough in the preindustrial countries to stabilize the world population at a size at which the Earth's resources can sustain the motivating well-being, those countries must have substantial help from the industrial countries.

That obligation has been known for 50 years. At the end of World War II, the industrial countries promised to render the economic and technical assistance—to make their contribution to the accumulation of capital and to transfer the technology—necessary to advance the development of the preindustrial countries. Division of the industrial world by the intervening Cold War has kept the preindustrial countries and their people waiting.

There is now reason to hope that the industrial nations, upon the abrupt termination of that hostility, may find it in their best interest to make good on their promises. Such assistance as they claim to have supplied in the interim went principally to Cold War objectives and against economic development. The two sides have still more to regret. The nations of the poor shed most of the blood drawn by the Cold War; in want and political disorder, two-thirds of them live under military dictatorship.

At this turning point, it is useful to reexamine the models of industrial revolution that the contending parties pressed upon their preindustrial clients. Part ideology and part precipitate of experience, and argued as they were from ulterior motives, the models may not help leaders of the next industrial revolutions to face new realities.

The foremost model derives from the first industrial revolution. At this stage of human evolution, it finds in individual pursuit of self-interest the energy that drives the economy. It entrusts decision-making to the market. There, the rational pursuit of self-interest by free and equal contenders finds resolution in the price that brings supply and demand into equilibrium. Value is thereby objectified and the direction of economic progress is chosen.

In accordance with strict derivations from this model now in vogue, the preindustrial countries are being advised to prosper with trade rather than aid. In the world market, they are to offer their goods competitively priced in reflection of their comparative advantage in resources, technology, and human skills. That is the fairest price. At that price, free trade engenders more trade. From rising exports of primary goods, the preindustrial countries may expect to develop domestic demand for imported consumer goods. Their expanding internal markets will thereafter sustain domestic production of those goods, and savings for investment will generate demand for primary and intermediate goods and then capital goods to produce them. Through trade, the market process will bring the preindustrial countries into the industrial world.

When that world was at its dawn, Adam Smith set down this epitome of industrial revolution by the market system: "It is the object of that system to enrich a great nation rather by trade and manufacture than by the improvement of the cultivation of the land, rather by industry of the towns than by that of the country."

The second model embodies the Russian–Soviet industrial revolution. It finds the source of economic energy in the aspirations of the people, placed in temporary custody of the state. By will and plan, ahead of any market demand, the state secures the extraction of primary goods and the building, in turn, of industries for the production of capital goods. During this period of capital accumulation, consumer goods are available to each only according to his means. Then this straight-line development proceeds to the production of consumer goods in such abundance that they can be had by each according to his needs. Comparative advantage does not rule in the planning of production for use as against profit. Other purposes may be served by deployment of capital, such as decentralization of the economy, the build-up of backward regions, and such heroic engineering enterprises as the dream "Project of the Century"—the reversing of the northward flow of the great rivers of Siberia.

The real world has, of course, seen neither competing model in pure form. There are more approximations of the first than of the second among the preindustrial countries. The People's Republic of China, however, holds a fifth of the world population.

CIRCULAR AND CUMULATIVE CAUSATION

In the real world, social and economic processes rarely reach equilibrium or move in a straight line. The vicious circle is the rule, more precisely formulated by the Swedish economist Gunnar Myrdal as the "principle of circular and cumulative causation." From his work on the problems of race in American society, reported in his book *An American Dilemma,* Myrdal drew this illustration of the principle: ". . . the Negroes' low plane of living is kept down by discrimination from the whites while, on the other side, the Negroes' poverty, slum dwellings, health deficiencies, unstable family relations, and criminality stimulate and feed the antipathy of the whites for Negroes."

It was the turning of like circles of cumulative causation, up to the middle of this century, that brought the congregation of industrial enterprises in the U.S. Northeast and the confinement of the South and West to the supplying of its raw materials. The circles ground so fine as to set up discriminatory freight rates that discouraged the location of industry in those internal colonies [see illustration on facing page].

Against social unrest stirring in Britain and Germany, in consequence of the rich becoming richer and the poor becoming poorer, conservative governments in those countries established the first welfare states before the end of the nineteenth century. In all industrial market economies today, with 30 percent or more of the gross national product (GNP) turning over in their public sectors, every government conducts, to a greater or lesser degree, regulatory interferences with the market process that, in Myrdal's words, "have the common purpose of counteracting the blind law of cumulative social change and hindering it from causing inequalities between regions, industries and social groups."

Thus, in the United States, the New Deal undertook to brake the "back-setting" of the South and the West and did so by large public-works expenditures in the two regions. More Federal expenditure in World War II located aircraft factories and shipyards there. From high-tech industrialization ignited by military procurement, there grew what came to be known as the Sun Belt. Closing the circle of circular and cumulative causation, economic interests of the Sun Belt had their part in the commitment of the Federal budget in the 1980s to "rearmament" and the high endless frontier of the Strategic Defense Initiative. By a complementary back-setting effect, the formerly dominant Northeast industrial region has evolved into the Rust Belt of today.

The corresponding process of circular and cumulative causation under centralized state planning was summarily described by the Soviet economist Wassily L. Selyunin: "This kind of economy . . . cannot work for man; it can only work for itself. It produces more and more means of production—that is, machines, equipment, electricity, fuel, metals—in order to again use all this in the next cycle for still more production of nonconsumable goods—that is, things that people cannot eat."

The industrial ministries in Moscow proved incompetent to ascertain the aspiration of the people in the absence of a market. It being easier to produce for one customer, the Soviet economy came under domination of the same sort of military–industrial complex as that against which Dwight D. Eisenhower warned his fellow citizens in his farewell address.

TERRITORIAL FREIGHT RATES *priced rail shipment of manufactures from the U.S. Northeast lower than same shipments originating in rest of country during the 1930s. In this diagrammatic map, discriminatory rates present uphill contour cliffs discouraging to the location of industry ouside the "official" territory.*

    The era of *glasnost* and *perestroika* began in the spring of 1985, when the Central Committee of the Communist Party of the Soviet Union called off the Project of the Century. The citation of "public opinion" in that decree stands also as the Party's first concession to the proposition that the people's aspirations are best ascertained by the people themselves.

    Plainly, the social order equal to the task of securing to all its members the benefits of industrial technology remains to be invented. The market is imperfect. The state is incompetent. The vicious circle is ineluctable. People will, of course, persist in the effort to secure those benefits for themselves; not all will do so with consideration for the wants and needs of others.

THE UN AND ECONOMIC DEVELOPMENT

In the brief interim between the end of World War II and the onset of the Cold War, the still allied industrial nations organized the United Nations. Near the top of the agenda for the new concert of nations was the economic development of the colonies that were to be liberated under its trusteeship. The necessary assistance to their development was to come through the international economic and technical agencies undergoing organization in those hopeful first hours of the return to peace. To establish the round-number dimensions of the required assistance, the General Assembly of the United Nations in 1949 convened the Group of Experts for the study of "Measures to Promote the Economic Development of the Under-developed Countries."

The group was well chosen for its assignment. All of its members were economists—A. B. Cortez of Chile, D. R. Gadgil of India, George Hakim of Lebanon, W. Arthur Lewis of Jamaica, and T. W. Schultz of the United States; they were experienced in the applied economics of public policy, and they represented both sides of the transaction in assistance and more than one school of economics.

They defined the required assistance as that which would move the surplus manpower of the underdeveloped countries from agriculture to industry. Food production in those countries could be made to increase at the rate of 2.5 percent per year. That would exceed population growth and make it possible, they calculated, to release 1.0 percent of a country's manpower each year for employment in industry. To transfer the technology and to get people employed in industry, investment at the rate of $2500 per person would be required. From such calculation, they arrived at an annual capital requirement of $19 billion. Trade (in accordance with the prescription of Adam Smith) and domestic savings in the under-developed countries were to generate $5 billion a year and perhaps as much as $9 billion. The difference between the capital generated internally by the underdeveloped countries and their capital requirement was to be supplied by the industrial countries at the rate of $10 billion to $14 billion per year.

The group of experts cannot be faulted for making small plans. At that time, scarcely $1 billion was moving from the industrial countries to the preindustrial countries, and 70 percent of that was going to develop new oil fields. Moreover, $10 billion to $14 billion was on the order of 2 to 3 percent of what was then the gross product of the industrial countries.

To attract private investment, the experts recognized, there had to be massive prior investment in "improving basic facilities. . . . The bigger the public investment is, the bigger will be the private investment." That was "in part the job which the International Bank for Reconstruction and Development was set up to do." To lending by the Bank on the scale required there was, however, an "obstacle." This was that "the amount which can profitably be invested at a 4 percent rate of interest depends on the amount which is being spent at the same time on improving social capital; and especially on public health, on education and on roads and communications."

For such non-interest-bearing investment, they called for "inter-governmental grants." They calculated that grants at the rate of $3 billion a year, administered by an International Development Authority, might prime the pump for the rest of the required flow of capital.

Implicit in their proposal of such outright gifts of capital was a simple arithmetic calculation. It showed that the transfer of $3 billion per year from the gross product of the rich countries ($600 billion, or about $600 per capita in 1950) could be "comparatively unpainful," whereas the saving of that crucial sum from the gross product of the poor countries ($100 billion, or about $60 per capita) might be "very painful," to invoke J. K. Galbraith's definition of economic assistance.

Over the four decades since the report was filed, the so-called "official development assistance" that has flowed from the industrial nations on both sides of the Cold War has never come up to the percentage (0.5 percent) of their gross product commended by the group of experts. The preponderance of it came from the market economies and went to the preindustrial countries they had incorporated in the world market economy; that is, the world economy minus the "centrally planned" economies, meaning principally China. How much of the total can be credited as contributions to development requires closer examination, because so much of that official assistance came with Cold War objectives.

At the pure economic-assistance end of the scale can be placed the flow through the multilateral channels of the United Nations technical agencies. Here can be counted also the capital contributions to the World Bank and related international banking institutions, though they were boycotted by the other party to the Cold War. The flows to support these institutions in doing "the job . . . [they were] set up to do" fluctuated between 15 and 30 percent of the total "official development assistance" for all purposes.

COLD WAR AND ECONOMIC DEVELOPMENT

The preponderance of that assistance moved bilaterally from donor to chosen donee. The motivation for official assistance and its contribution to development may be judged from the distribution of the funds disbursed in bilateral agreements by the United States. Over the 40 years, the total laid out to "developing countries" under those agreements mounted to $220 billion in current dollars (that is, in the current value of the dollar from year to year). This total comes to a minuscule fraction (less than 0.1 percent) of the recommended 0.5 percent of the GNP of the country over those years. It includes more than $60 billion in military assistance. Most of the military outlay went to fewer than 10 "strategic" countries that received more than half of the total disbursement.

Thus, more than $30 billion went to Indochinese clients for military and other assistance in the course of the Vietnam War. Another $20 billion went to Taiwan and South Korea, principally in the course of that episode, but starting with the Korean War. Another $60 billion was spent to shore up the front at the eastern end of the Mediterranean, beginning with the retrieval of Greece from the Soviet penumbra in the late 1940s and counting the $30 billion accumulated on the Israeli account over the years.

The motivation for the bulk of the outlay is clear. Except in the cases of Israel, Taiwan, and South Korea, it is difficult to detect any by-product stimulus to economic development from its expenditure. The shambles of Indochina says that kind of money buys the opposite outcome. The daunting face that Africa turns to the world says much the same for U.S. support of the machinations of South Africa in Angola and Southwest Africa (now Namibia) and the arming and supplying of first this side and then that side in the border wars and civil strife in Sudan, Somalia, and Ethiopia—all to counter the complementary enterprises of the Soviet Union in those places.

Considering, on the other hand, the small return to U.S. policy from nonaligned India, the cumulative $10 billion outlay to that country can be reckoned as pure economic assistance. India received more than half of this assistance before 1965, in stronger dollars and in much-wanted wheat.

An audit of the official development assistance accounts of the other industrial nations on both sides of the twilight struggle would doubtless find a similar concordance between size of outlay and perceived national interest in the donee. Assessing the flow of official development assistance most generously, perhaps 30 percent of it can be credited to development. That is about 0.3 percent of what the group of experts prescribed.

It cannot be said that economic assistance to economic development failed. It never had a trial.

During the 1960s, the primary economic energy generated by self-interest began to move private investment funds and commercial credit from the industrial to the preindustrial world in a dollar volume equal to that of official development assistance. Swollen by the bank loans that recycled the petrodollars, private funds moved at twice that rate in the early 1980s. This real money was evoked by the economic growth set going in the preindustrial countries by the huge appetite for their resources that was developing in the industrial countries.

The prolonged boom started by the postwar recovery of the industrial world and sustained by the low price of petroleum launched what must now be recognized as the second colonial conquest of the preindustrial world. In the words of Barbara Ward, one of the first economists to understand the connection between environment and development, these four decades have seen "the most widespread and sudden intervention of man's works in pretechnical societies ever experienced in history."

Measured in bales, barrels, and tons—not in the world's inflating currencies—the exports of the preindustrial countries have multiplied four times since 1950. The growth that their economies have seen has not come from economic and technical assistance. It is the consequence of their incorporation in the expanding industrial market economy of the world.

The international bookkeepers show world trade growing faster than the world economy. In the standard accounting, world trade increased from 7 or 8 percent of the total output of the world economy in 1950 to 14 or 15 percent of it in 1985. Free trade is celebrated in the literature of development as leading the world's economic growth. It is the natural beneficence of trade, not intervention with aid, that has brought the preindustrial countries into the world economy.

Those figures exaggerate the movement of trade, however, and in the wrong direction. The postwar recovery and growth of the

European economy inflates the world-trade figure. Intra-European trade has grown with that recovery; the reckoning of U.S. interstate commerce in the world-trade total would inflate world trade some more. Subtraction of the trade among the countries that will pool their economies in the European Economic Community in 1992 reduces world trade in 1985 to 10 percent of world output in 1985. A second correction makes the current world-trade figure still more comparable with that of 1950: subtraction of the OPEC override on the price of oil brings 1985 world trade down closer to 8 percent of world output.

These corrections also produce a more accurate measure of the contribution exacted of the preindustrial economies over the four decades to the growth of the industrial economies. Their share of world exports increases from 23 percent to 33 percent of the world total recorded in 1970 and from 31 to 44 percent of the 1985 total—39 percent of that year's world trade with the OPEC price adjustment. What increase there has been in world trade relative to world product has come from the rising demand of the industrial nations for the agricultural output and primary resources, especially petroleum, of the preindustrial countries.

The preindustrial economies thereby incorporated in the world market economy proceeded to grow at a fast rate. Their exports increased to 20 percent and more of their GNP, compared with the 5 to 10 percent exported by most industrial economies. In the economies of the preindustrial countries that supplied the oil to the industrial countries, of course, exports came to a much higher percentage of their GNP, above 75 percent of the GNP of Saudia Arabia when the oil moved at the peak OPEC price. From 1960 into the 1970s, the preindustrial countries, led by the big exporters, grew at a faster rate—7 percent and above—than the industrial market economies, which grew at less than 5 percent.

The growth of the preindustrial economies recorded, first of all, the increasing volume of their exports. Growth received further stimulus from investment by their customers, principally large corporations now classified as "transnational," in their export-producing extractive industries. From the governments of the industrial countries, in bilateral and in multilateral public loans and grants, came investment in the building of the infrastructure, the transportation, communication, and electric-utility networks and the cities and harbors of the preindustrial countries—all to facilitate movement of their exports. More recently, where growth has advanced sufficiently, the preindustrial economies have seen investment from overseas in consumer goods and service industries in response to rising market demand in their cities created by incomes from their export activities.

After 40 years, the world map shows substantial change in the location of industry. The preindustrial countries were credited with less than 5 percent of the world's "manufacturing value added" (MVA or "value-added") in 1950; by the early 1980s, their share had climbed to nearly 15 percent [see illustration on page 33]. In a new international division of labor, the people of the preindustrial countries have taken over the labor-intensive functions in industries reaching across the technological spectrum from textiles to solid-state electronics. In principle, in accordance with the dominant model of industrial revolution, the preindustrial countries have each been finding their place in the world economy corresponding to their comparative advantage—that is, their comparative advantage with respect to the possession of resources and the cost of labor.

Demonstration of the second model has been limited, of course, to a few preindustrial countries: China, the centrally planned economies of North Korea and Indochina; after 1960, Cuba and, more recently, Myanmar (Burma). Through most of the postwar period, these countries isolated themselves from, or were excluded from, the world economy. In isolation from the Soviet Union as well, China improved upon the Soviet model with respect to agriculture; it kept essential village institutions intact and secured increases in the output of food from the start. With abundant human capital thereby made available, China entered into its industrial revolution according to centrally directed plan, the means of production coming first. In the 15 percent of industrial activity now located in the preindustrial countries, China's industrial establishment constitutes a substantial 20 percent. By the early 1970s, China felt secure enough to open its economy to investment from the market economies and, sooner than the Soviet model, to market forces.

When the colonies of the prewar empires entered the world economy as independent nations, they found that independence to bargain does not necessarily get a better price. Competitors just as poor as they are there to cut it. The market itself can be lost to old substitutes and new synthetics. The new contenders in the market encounter, as well, the inevitable "imperfections" that qualify the working of the market system in the real world.

Especially in the first postwar years, the market most readily and almost exclusively accessible to each of the new countries was that of its former imperial "home" country. The old bill of exports remained the first source of income. The familiar market imparity of extractive to manufactured goods remained as well. Tariff and non-tariff barriers in the industrial countries continue to shelter more costly producers in those countries of the export commodities of the preindustrial countries and await any attempt by a preindustrial country to add value by manufacture to its exports. Sugar-beet growers in the United States and other industrial countries (the beets return half the calories expended to grow them) could not otherwise compete with cane-cutters in the preindustrial countries (the cane returns double and more the calories expended). Cotton farmers in the United States enjoy the same protection; textile manufacturers, even more of the same.

TRANSNATIONAL CORPORATIONS AND DEVELOPMENT

To their "home" countries or to the world market, from year to year, the preindustrial countries have found their access and connection being made by an ever smaller number of ever larger transnational corporations. These corporations are the winners in the world market contest; they have been getting bigger as their competitors have been getting smaller. The 350 largest (about half of them domiciled in the United States) had a combined annual turnover of $2700 billion in 1985. That was 30 percent of the entire GNP of the world market economy and larger by several hundreds of billions of dollars than the combined GNP of all the preindustrial economies, China included. Conducting a corresponding percentage of world trade, these corporations conduct an increasing percentage of that as intracorporate transactions; the U.S. corporations carry 45 percent of their lion's share of the country's trade on their own books.

Whatever their country of domicile, the transnational corporations tend to do an increasing percentage of their business outside that country. Some make more of their sales, more even of their product, and most of their profit in other countries. This is true, in one or more respects, of General Motors (in 1985 the largest of all), Ford, Dow Chemical, and IBM; of Daimler-Benz, Siemens, and Hoechst; of British Petroleum, B.A.T. Industries, and Imperial Chemicals; of Elf Aquitaine, Peugeot, and St. Gobain; of Sony and Honda, of course; and of Philips Gloeilampenfabrieken, Ciba-Geigy, and

Preindustrial Countries with Twenty Largest GNPs Compared with Transnational Corporations with Twenty Largest Sales Totals, 1985

COUNTRY	POPU-LATION (MILLIONS)	GNP PER CAPITA ($)	GNP ($ BILLIONS)	TOTAL SALES ($ BILLIONS)	TRANSNATIONAL CORP.
China	1,124	255	265	96	General Motors Corp.
Brazil	135	1,673	225	87	Exxon Corp.
India	759	255	195	82	Royal Dutch-Shell Group
Mexico	79	2,247	175	56	Mobil Corp.
Saudi Arabia	12	8,145	95	53	British Petroleum
South Korea	41	2,104	87	50	Ford Motor Co.
Indonesia	166	500	85	46	IBM
Nigeria	95	806	75	44	Texaco Inc.
Argentina	30	2,157	65	29	Chevron
Algeria	22	2,648	57	29	E. I. du Pont de Nemours & Co.
Egypt	47	1,154	54	28	General Electric
Turkey	49	1,071	53	28	Toyota Motor Co.
Venezuela	17	2,865	50	27	Nippon Oil Co. Ltd.
Thailand	51	746	38	24	Amoco
Colombia	29	1,191	34	22	ENI
Philippines	54	601	33	21	Unilever
Malaysia	15	2,000	31	21	Atlantic Richfield Co.
Pakistan	100	309	31	21	Chrysler Corp.
Libya	4	7,484	27	20	Matsushita Electrical Ind'l Co.
Syria	10	1,929	20	21	Hitachi Ltd.

COMPARATIVE LISTING *of the preindustrial countries with the largest gross national products and the transnational corporations with largest sales shows entities of much the same order of magnitude. The corporations are able, as sovereignties in their own right, to exact concessions from governments.*

Electrolux. The last three might be classified as obligatory transnationals, being domiciled in the Netherlands, Switzerland, and Sweden, respectively—economies too small to contain them.

Technology knows no national boundaries. Recruiting management from their overseas subsidiaries and finding shareholders around the world, the transnational corporations have been losing, some deliberately shedding, their national identities. As increasingly stateless entities, they burke the sovereignty of nation-states, large ones as well as small. These corporations recognize national sovereignties for purposes of their own choosing. They buy raw materials, locate plants, make sales, charge costs and report profits, submit to jurisdiction and pay taxes in and among nations in accordance with comparative advantage. Practices and products banned in some states can find markets in others. Thus, DDT and other pesticides that have been banned in most industrial countries continue in manufacture, on sale, and in use in preindustrial countries.

Competition of the transnationals in the world market turns on their relative control of market forces and their choice of global strategy. They may opt for profit or for growth in this market or that. They may choose as well not to compete but to divide the world market by explicit or implicit understanding.

The transnational corporations are the organizers of the new world economy that is integrating in an interdependent whole the economies of nation-states. Their managements are the technocracy of that economy, making most of the decisions about the deployment of new and old technologies around the world. With a common culture and community of interest, they are as much in command of the world market as they are subject to it. Their 25 million employees hold the best jobs in their home countries as well as in their host countries, and they are leading members of the local elite wherever they are.

Disquiet at their ascendant power in countries of their domicile as well as in the preindustrial countries has excited efforts to write codes of conduct for the transnational corporations. Labor unions in the industrial countries enlisted the International Labor Office to do so on their behalf. Pediatricians sought the writing by the World Health Assembly in 1981 of the International Code on the Marketing [especially in the cities of the preindustrial countries] of Breast-Milk Substitutes. Even the Organization for Economic Cooperation and Development (OECD), the consortium of the principal industrial market economies, has issued guidelines to its members for coordination of their attempts to regulate the transnational corporations and for the protection of individual privacy in "transborder data flows of personal data."

In 1977, an intergovernmental working group convened by the UN Economic and Social Council began negotiation of a comprehensive Code of Conduct on Transnational Corporations. Some delegations sought emphasis on "full respect for national sovereignty; the permanent sovereignty of States over their natural resources, wealth and economic activities; noninterference in internal and intergovernmental affairs; and the right of States to regulate and control the activities of transnational corporations." Others insisted that invocation of such principles be balanced by reference to "international law, the protection of legitimate activities and the principle of fair treatment." Unsettled was the question whether the code was to have the force of law, with signatory nations obliged to enforce it, or the weight of a set of guidelines. A draft code submitted in 1982, with disputed issues reflected in bracketed alternative formulations, remains still to be settled and promulgated by the Council.

For the preindustrial countries, the transnational corporations constitute the world market, supplying their closest linkage to the industrial world. The corporations are in those countries, it goes without saying, for their own purposes, not to promote the economic development of their hosts. It is to them, not to the unseen hand of the market, that the preindustrial countries must look for the return on the export of primary commodities from farm, forest, and mine that is their source of capital for future growth.

The export of foodstuffs and industrial raw materials from their cultivated land and their forests yields the primary income from the world economy to some 55 nations, habitations of 600 million people, including 300 million of the very poorest. Food exporters go into the world market with the comparative advantage in latitude, climate, and soil that admits the cultivation of coffee, tea, sugar, spices, and fruits that cannot be grown so well or at all in the temperate latitudes of the industrial world.

Within those countries, the cultivation, harvesting, and shipping of food grown for export employs a small percentage, not more than 5 percent, of the labor force. The considerable postwar investment in yield improvement from these plantation crops came ahead of the improvement of the cereal and root crops that feed the populations. The plantations are frequently owned, legally or effectively, by the customers that take away the product. In some countries, "para-statal" enterprises organize production of the crop by small farmers and manage its marketing. In either case, a junior percentage even of the export price stays in the country of origin. Over the past four decades, after a brief postwar rise, the prices of these commodities have trended downward, despite the swelling of the markets for almost all of them.

The price declines must be attributed in part to the oligopolies that distort the market for each commodity. Some 15 transnational corporations control more than half the food trade. Fewer companies control higher percentages of the shipment of each of the more lucrative commodities. United Brands (formerly United Fruit), Castle and Cook, and Del Monte, for example, control half the banana market. Eight corporations control 60 percent of the coffee market; two of them, Nestlé (the world's biggest food company) and General Foods (now Philip Morris) control 20 percent of it between them. Four tobacco companies (B.A.T., Rothman's, Philip Morris, and R. J. Reynolds) control 75 percent of that market. In every case, the sellers outnumber the buyers, making it a buyer's market.

Prices come under further pressure from tariff and nontariff barriers that shelter uneconomic production of some products, sugar notoriously, in the industrial countries. Attempts by the food-exporting countries to add value to their exports by processing and packaging encounter still other tariff and nontariff barriers. In the market on the other side of those barriers, they meet "defensive responses" from the controlling transnational corporations.

One branch of the food industry, luxury or "gourmet" foods, has prospered largely free of such inhibitions to trade. While demand for staple foods levels off above the incomes that purchase sufficiency, the demand for luxury foods has risen as consumer affluence has increased in the industrial countries. With their sales organizations, sensitive sensory organs, probing every market, the transnational food corporations were alert to this novel consumer response as soon as it made its appearance in the late 1960s.

On their own or in joint ventures with partners in the preindusrial countries, transnational food corporations have organized vertically integrated enterprises—from plantation, through processing plants, to dockside, and then to market—in off-season and exotic fruits, in prepared poultry and other meats, processed seafood, and the like. With labor cost a significant factor, Mexico, the Philippines, and Thailand became major centers of the new industry. The Dole company displaced its natal, but unionized, Hawaii as tropical-fruit capital in favor of the Philippines. A major new food company is ITT (formerly International Telephone and Telegraph), attracted to luxury foods by way of diversification. The integrated production and marketing of these products by a single company gets them tariff treatment as being more "domestic" than imported, like the electronic circuits that go through offshore assembly on their way to market. This still unsated market now absorbs nearly one-third of the food exports from the preindustrial countries.

Raw materials for industry from plantation and forest support the poorest countries in the world market: jute from Bangladesh, rubber from Liberia, cotton from Mali. These exports encounter the same imperfections in the market as does food. The marketers, usually para-statal agencies, must contend first with oligopoly. Combinations of three to seven of the 15 transnational corporations that dominate the market form up for each commodity. At their destinations, rubber competes with synthetics, jute competes with other natural fibers and polyethylene filaments, and cotton competes with natural and synthetic fibers.

Cotton goes into a world market organized by the Multifibre Arrangement among the industrial market economies. Worked out in 1973, it limited the growth of textile imports from the preindustrial countries, at first to 6 percent per year and then to lower percentages in succeeding rounds of negotiation. Those lowering ceilings may be further reduced under the Arrangement by bilateral agreement between the industrial importing country and the preindustrial exporter, where the industrial country claims "market disruption"; at one point, the United States had 21 such agreements in force. The cotton market has been shrunk as well by the long-term decline in the weight of fiber per unit garment, affecting all fibers.

Some of the transnational corporate customers for industrial raw materials are competitors, as is Cargill (the family-owned, world's largest enterprise in the production and distribution of agricultural output, headquartered in Minneapolis, Minnesota) with its own plantations in various preindustrial countries. At the ports, high tariff and nontariff barriers protect competitors in the market, petrochemical producers of synthetic fibers as well as cotton farmers. On the other side of these barriers, the same transnational corporations control the downstream commodity exchanges and other channels of sale and await as final customers. Except for a momentary hardening of prices in the 1970s, the producers of these commodities have been shipping them in ever greater tonnage for less real return since the early 1960s.

Minerals are the primary export of a dozen preindustrial countries—most of them better off than the agricultural exporters—

whose populations total 150 million. The comparative advantage of these countries, principally on the continents of Africa and South America, is the possession of ores with higher content of the desired metal than the worked-out mines and lower-grade deposits in the industrial countries.

Preindustrial countries supply more than 60 percent of the copper ore and metal, 85 percent of the tin, nearly 70 percent of the bauxite (the principal ore of aluminum), and nearly half the iron ore in world trade. The ores and their metals returned $14 billion in export revenue in 1985, about 6 percent of the total export income of the preindustrial world. By 1980, chronic decline in world prices, contention with oligopoly in the market for each mineral, and the example of the oil producers had provoked nationalization of the mines and forward processing of the ores in all of the exporting countries.

The great transnational nonferrous-metal corporations remain, nontheless, the market. Thus, seven copper companies dominate the price-setting on the London Metal Exchange and the New York Commodity Exchange. Tariff barriers favor ores and ore concentrates over metal, and the metal is recycled in the industrial markets with high efficiency. The four transnational tin corporations (two of them—Patino in Bolivia and the Overseas Chinese Banking Group in Singapore—domiciled in preindustrial countries) manage the tin market. The six aluminum companies consume three-quarters of the world's bauxite and produce more than 80 percent of the alumina and aluminum, operating some of the alumina and aluminum plants in and for their bauxite-supplier countries.

As the exporters gained value-added on their ores by forward processing (for example, smelting copper ore to copper), they lost comparative advantage. The transnational nonferrous-metal companies withdrew their investment capital for deployment at home—in the United States, to work lower-grade ore with higher technology. Whatever stratagem the mineral-exporting countries have attempted, their return on their resources has declined per unit export almost continuously through the four decades.

Petroleum, for the reasons considered in Chapter 4, is the one mineral that endowed its producers to meet their customers on equal footing. Yet OPEC could not for long keep its members in line as non-OPEC producers eroded its price; by 1985, the inflation-discounted price had fallen below the first price set by OPEC in 1973.

Consumers, if not industries, in the industrial world resumed their bad habits, and oil importers are even more dependent than a decade ago on the oil resources of the preindustrial countries. The United States was importing half of the petroleum it consumed in 1990, compared with 40 percent in the oil-crisis year 1980. The country's dependence on offshore refineries has increased as well, as the producing countries have compelled the oil companies to concede the value-added to their crude by refineries located within their borders and often operated for them by the companies.

From the huge flow of funds brought to them over the past decade and a half by the increase in the world oil price, the oil-producing countries, and some of the oil companies as well, are investing in the mining and processing of nonferrous metals. Bahrain and Dubai are operating aluminum smelters. The oil exporters are beginning to consider how they will make their living after the oil is gone. This broadening of the market for ores and concentrates may also improve the outlook for the nonfuel mineral exporters.

THE COMPARATIVE ADVANTAGE OF POVERTY

All the preindustrial countries share a comparative advantage in the possession of abundant man-, woman-, and child-power available for work at low wages. This is not a natural endowment, of course, comparable to climate and soil or an oil pool. It is the outcome of the recent history that has divided humankind between rich and poor nations. The industrial revolution to which the preindustrial countries aspire promises to erase it. The exploitation of this advantage commended itself nonetheless to the most conscientious leaders in the preindustrial world as a first step up the ladder of manufacturing value-added. After the example of the Japanese, their labor force might move up from the making of shoddy goods to skilled employment at higher wages in high technology. On the other side of the transaction, entrepreneurs were eager to concede, and to make good use of, this advantage. The transnational corporations, with their increasing sophistication in geography, had work ready for those idle hands.

The big textile companies had made immense investment in the physics of pulling filaments and in the intricate mechanics of spinning, knitting, and weaving. Yet handwork still took a major percentage of their product to market. In the United States, the economic development of the South had narrowed and eliminated the comparative advantage that had brought the industry down from New England. Despite successful lobbying for higher tariffs by unions as well as by employers, the United States was the world's major importer of clothing. Burlington, Levi Strauss, and the other big U.S. companies accordingly adopted the strategy of "outward processing."

They now send their capital-intensive woven cloth, often mechanically precut, abroad to the Far East, Latin America, and the Caribbean for the labor-intensive work that makes the finished product. Upon return of their cloth in finished products, the tariffs go only against the work done, at low wages, abroad.

The Japanese have pursued the same strategy. They have made textiles, however, the first tutorial step in a division of labor between their home islands and Korea, Taiwan, Malaysia, Indonesia, and Thailand that may some day include less labor-intensive manufacturing.

As one of the basic-needs goods, along with food and shelter, textiles is established in all preindustrial countries as a village craft and a nascent urban industry. It employs 25 percent of the non-agricultural labor force and appears on the export bill of virtually all preindustrial countries. From 25 percent of world exports of clothing in 1970, the share of the preindustrial countries has increased to more than 50 percent. Industrial development is coming along with this growth. The capital-intensive branches of the textile industry have begun to grow in the preindustrial world, expecially in India and in the Japanese economic sphere.

Now, associated with textile exports, the related clothing-accessory and shoe industries are significant and growing earners of export income. Related also in technology and marketing channels are shoddy goods—toys, clothing accessories, trinkets, and the like—and the production of these is devolving to the preindustrial countries in the new international division of labor. These are the industries that notoriously get their work done in sweatshops and employ child labor, comparative advantages difficult to secure in most industrial countries.

At the top side of the sociotechnical hierarchy, the new high technology of solid-state electronics hired out its labor-intensive work to the preindustrial labor force from the very beginning. Fiercely competitive in capital-intensive innovation, the U.S. and now the Japanese contenders in this arena have kept the price of a unit of circuitry on the semiconductor chip descending on the same steep slope throughout the 40-year history of the industry. No leader of innovation in the industry has sheltered earnings behind prices set by laggards. Competitors of this mettle could not afford to keep at home the handwork of attaching the chips to each other and to the world outside. In Korea, Taiwan, Hong Kong, and Singapore most notably, they found dextrous workers with the requisite education and teachability and the need to accept low wages. This contracting out and branch-planting of the work bought almost equally significant economies in the salaries of middle management and in general overhead.

There has been no high technology transferred in this traffic. The chips and other piece-parts are shipped in; the assemblies and subassemblies are shipped out. From the middle management of the assembly shops, however, have emerged entrepreneurs who import chips and export assembled final products of their own design. The economics of this niche in the solid-state electronics industry is not unlike that of niches to be found in textiles: low capital investment and high premium on bright ideas.

To make their low-priced labor force more accessible to employers from overseas, preindustrial countries have established "export processing zones." Manufacturers ship into these zones, tariff-free, their raw materials, intermediate products, and component parts for the handwork that takes them to the next or final stage of production. The labor incorporated in the products shipped out constitutes a significant percentage of the exports of a number of countries, particularly those celebrated as "newly industrializing," including South Korea, Hong Kong, Singapore, Brazil, and Mexico. Upon opening its shores to the world economy in the 1970s, China established several such zones, suppressing any acknowledgment of their resemblance to the humiliating foreign concessions of colonial times. In 1980, there were more than 50 of these zones in preindustrial countries, employing more than a million workers, a high percentage of them female.

In the Mexican zones—along the Texas, New Mexico, Arizona, and California border—U.S. corporations have come to employ 500,000 Mexican workers over the past decade. They pay them less than $1.00 per hour. The Mexican workers do the labor-intensive assembly of the products for which Xerox, Eastman Kodak, RCA, IBM, General Electric, Chrysler, Kimberly-Clark, and other companies not long ago employed U.S. workers at much higher wages in Rochester, N.Y., Detroit, Mich., Pittsfield, Mass., and other cities. The Mexicans are able to accept their low wages because they live without sanitation and the usual amenities in shantytowns they built with their own hands around the border cities. The companies are able to make wage savings estimated at $8 billion with the acquiescence of Mexico in this employment of its citizens and special tariffs—applied only to the low-wage value-added—arranged by the U.S. Congress.

The nearly 2000 factories owned by U.S. companies along the northern border of Mexico are called *maquilas,* after the mill to which a farmer takes his corn for grinding. In this transaction, there is no technology transfer. The *maquiladora* arrangement is a measure of the poverty of Mexico and its people. It is equally a measure of breakdown of social arrangements and the decline of factory jobs in the United States.

Some preindustrial countries have been exporting their labor in person. *Gastarbeiters* from Turkey filled jobs at the bottom of the expanding German economy as Germans moved upward in employment and income. Algerians and Francophone black Africans are at home in France. Pakistanis, Indians, and Anglophone black Africans have changed the color of the slums in Britain. From Kuwait, the Iraqi army dispersed a population of nearly a million Lebanese, Palestinians, Egyptians, Pakistanis, Indians, and Bangladeshis who were supplying the intelligentsia as well as the skilled and unskilled work force for the 600,000 native Kuwaitis.

The big cities of the United States, Florida, and the states that were once part of Mexico are being compelled to recognize Spanish as a second language. Amnesty did not bring all the illegal immigrants forward; cities all over the country are losing representation in the House of Representatives to undercounting of the transient poor in the 1990 Census. With the quotas of all nations and continents filled by legal immigrants, the founding Anglo-Saxon is the new U.S. "minority" person.

URBAN ENCLAVES OF DEVELOPMENT

The economic growth brought to the preindustrial countries by the export of food and agricultural raw materials, of their mineral resources, and of the labor of their people is in evidence in their cities. In what is most often the capital of the country, official buildings (most often built by the departed colonial power) declare the presence of the state, and new office and apartment blocks house the hybrid community of people employed by the country's export enterprise. On the one hand are the native bureaucrats and entrepreneurs; on the other, the expatriate executives and staff persons employed by the transnational corporations interested in the country's exports and the accessory financial, legal, and accounting concerns they bring with them.

The incomes of these people, far above the average and still farther above the median income of the country, support an economy of consumer goods and services and its community of mostly native shopkeepers, tradesmen, and artisans. From the combined communities, consumer demand excites enterprises in light industries. Food processing and beverage bottling, printing and publishing, radio and television, building materials, textiles, furniture, and housewares are the liveliest native industries in the preindustrial countries. The demand also brings imports of luxury and fashion goods, pharmaceuticals, consumer electronics, automobiles, and household appliances. In the cities of the more advanced and larger preindustrial countries, transnational manufacturers have established branch plants or local affiliate factories to produce those products there.

Companies of that size are able to decide when it is more profitable for them to export to a market or to manufacture in it. The output of the transnational manufacturers makes up a large percentage of the total industrial output of some preindustrial countries, including the newly industrializing countries (Argentina, 33 percent; Brazil, 44 percent; Mexico, 39 percent), and like percentages of their manufactured exports. These plants function very much as *maquilas,* importing their raw materials and components through their parent's purchasing departments. Purchasing little from local suppliers, they do not significantly promote technology transfer.

Successful indigenous manufacturing enterprises do not escape the notice of the transnational corporations in their line of business. The purchase of local enterprises in textiles, food processing, beverages, pharmaceuticals, and the like is an economically attractive alternative to starting up a subsidiary. The purchase moreover eliminates a competitor. The six Mexican pharmaceutical companies in the business of confecting physiologically powerful hormones from steroids extracted from the tissues of plants native to

Mexico were all bought up by transnational corporations that now control 85 percent of the pharmaceutical industry in that country.

The export transaction with the outside world brings into the preindustrial country not only income, investment capital, and the manufactured products of the industrial world but the sociocultural pressures and influences of the world from which they come. The relatively high compensation of people in the expatriate community gives visibility and force to their spending and living habits, felt most strongly by those who work most closely with them. Together, as the elite of the community, the expatriates and the native official, executive, professional, and white-collar people live and set the example of a way of life at a distance from that of the country and its people. Their example is amplified by the communications media, which are dominated by the advertising and marketing culture of the industrial world. As compared with the 5 or 6 percent of air time given to commercials on television and radio channels in the industrial countries, the television and radio stations in the preindustrial countries give commercials between 12 and 20 percent of the time.

The consumer preferences and style of behavior pressed on the indigenous people is not always fitting for their circumstances and income. This was the gravamen of the international controversy about the promotion by transnational corporations of breast-milk substitutes to new mothers in the preindustrial countries. The smoking habit now so vigorously promoted in preindustrial countries by the four tobacco transnationals is held to be inappropriate in many quarters in the industrial world. The summary complaint from the preindustrial intelligentsia is that more wants are created than satisfied. That is condoned by some as instilling ardor for economic development; it is denounced by others as cultural imperialism.

It is the cities, rather than the countrysides, of the preindustrial countries that have been incorporated in the world economy. Culturally as well as economically, they are radically reconstituted as enclaves of the outside world in countries not nearly as much changed from their old ways during the last four decades. More specifically, the cities have become enclaves of the industrial country that is most involved in their country's economy. In Africa and Asia, that is most often the former colonial home country; in Latin America and the Philippines, it is the United States; in East Asia and Southeast Asia, it is increasingly Japan.

The correspondence can be seen in the percentage of trade between the preindustrial country and the industrial, in the concentration of investment by the transnational corporations domiciled in the industrial country, and in the percentage of the preindustrial country's debt held by the banks in the industrial country. Thus, Latin America exchanges nearly one-third of its exports for one-third of its imports with the United States, much more than with any other country; more than 60 percent of the transnational affiliates doing business in the region belong to parent companies domiciled in the United States, and 80 percent of the region's bank debt is held by U.S. banks.

By the process of circular and cumulative causation, the economic growth of the past 40 years has locked the countries of the preindustrial world in deepened dependence upon the industrial countries, often the countries that held them in hegemony before World War II. Political independence has not brought economic independence. In their dependence, to whichever industrial power (or group of transnational corporations) it runs, the preindustrial countries have not made the effort and progress that they should have made in the urgency of their need to get on with industrial revolution.

The new urban governmental and business communities typically display no strong will to take on that task. The affluence they already enjoy is a novel and sufficiently heady experience. Among the merchants and landowners in possession of the relatively modest indigenous capital, there is a strong preference for liquidity and a greater propensity to seek havens for their capital abroad than to make a fixed investment at home.

DEVELOPMENT IN THEORY AND PRACTICE

The governments universally avow commitment to the encouragement and planning of the economic development of their countries. They first did so with the encouragement of the industrial powers, the United States foremost. John F. Kennedy put the acceleration of development by national planning at the center of his address to the UN General Assembly in 1961, when he moved the proclamation of the First Development Decade. He made the existence of a national plan a condition for the receipt by any country of its share from his pledge to commit 1 percent of the GNP of the United States in support of the development effort.

In that pledge, the industrial countries unanimously joined. Confronted a decade later with their failure to make good on the pledge, they reduced it to a "more realistic" 0.7 percent of their GNP. Only Canada (under the leadership of Lester Pearson—Prime Minister and bearer of the Nobel Peace Prize—and of Maurice F. Strong), Sweden (at the prompting of Gunnar and Alva Myrdal), and one or two other countries—but none of the major industrial powers—have ever met even the reduced pledge.

Virtually all of the preindustrial countries have been publishing five-year plans. Relying on the promise of economic assistance, the plans at first invariably filled the projected gap between domestic resources and the plan's capital requirement with a round number for external capital input. Failing such assistance, few have succeeded in mobilizing the internal resources, human and material, required to carry their plans forward. Most remain "soft states," as Myrdal called them. None command as high a percentage of the GNP of their country as the government of the United States, which now professes so strongly the impropriety of governmental intervention in the private affairs of the economy.

The five-year plans set brave goals for industrial development. Such development would employ the surplus manpower from the countryside, as the group of experts had visualized. Its benefits would trickle back and down to the villages. Economic growth would eventually lift everyone out of poverty.

Economic policy, as framed by the preindustrial countries (with well-meaning counsel from the industrial countries), for a long time gave little consideration to agriculture. It remains almost everywhere biased in favor of the city as against the country. Food prices are kept low. The city people are politically the more visible and audible. As displaced persons from the countryside implode into the shantytowns, city populations have become unruly. Economic policy is sometimes compelled by the imminence of civil disorder. The farmer is further disadvantaged by overvaluation of the currency for negotiation of prices on imports. That, plus inflation, raises the price of everything the farmer has to buy.

For tax revenues, the governments naturally look to village agriculture, the largest sector of the economy. The disincentives thus set for the farmers increased the dependence of the urban populations on food imports in many preindustrial countries, as noted on page 224, especially in Africa and Latin America.

With the encouragement of counsellors from the industrial market economies, most five-year plans sought economic development by the route of import substitution. The bill of urban consumer-goods imports supplied the agenda for these plans. This was the right strategy, according to the counsellors, because it fit the model of the classical first revolution, which began with the manufacture of consumer goods and thereafter moved upstream, propelled by market forces, to the building of heavy industry. It was right, moreover, because it ran opposite to the Marxist–Soviet model, which prescribed the building of heavy industry first. These considerations made it possible, despite the offense to the principle of free trade, to condone the invocation of tariffs to protect the "infant industries" that were to make the import substitutions. In the 1970s, Indonesia set tariffs above 50 percent on the value of consumer goods, at less than 25 percent on intermediate goods, and at less than 20 percent on capital goods.

The establishment of a successful consumer-product manufacturer behind a tariff barrier moved the demand for imports upstream to the producer's goods that go to make consumer product, as planned. At this point, however, any measure to encourage indigenous production of the producer's goods invited the strenuous opposition of the downstream manufacturer of the consumer product: indigenous competitors in the manufacture of the product might also be supplied from that source. Opposition of this kind to domestic production of the producer's goods was just as strenuous and more effective when it came from a transnational corporation that had bought out the successful indigenous manufacturer of the consumer product and had a larger profit sheltered by the tariff barrier.

Counsellors from the industrial countries now began to advise their clients that import substitution was the wrong strategy. Import substitution, it was said, tended to set up interests that stifled whatever impulse to development it evoked. The policy nonetheless saw South Korea through the first 75 percent of the expansion of its industrial capacity.

South Korea, along with the other "newly industrializing countries" of East Asia, is more celebrated as a model of the strategy of export-based development now being urged on the preindustrial countries. That strategy turns, in most countries, on the regrettable comparative advantage of low labor costs. Singapore gets 90 percent of its export income from its export processing zones. The export of labor has fostered growing but not necessarily developing economies.

PUBLIC INDUSTRIAL ENTERPRISES

Whether by import substitution, by export promotion, or by both strategies, the countries that have come furthest in economic development, even into the circle of the "newly industrializing," have done so under strong governmental leadership. The governments have employed the complete battery of tariffs, price controls, preferential credit allocation, tax concessions, and outright subsidies to steer and encourage development under private enterprise. They have invariably also acted as entrepreneurs themselves, assembling the capital and building, owning, and operating heavy-industrial enterprises.

The government of South Korea owned and operated 12 of that country's 16 largest industrial enterprises in 1972, setting the foundations in steel and energy for the manufacture of durable consumer goods by private industry. In Mexico, state-owned enterprises did 30 percent of the manufacturing in the 1970s and absorbed 60 percent of the manufacturing investment. The ten largest industrial enterprises in Brazil and the nine largest in Indonesia were state-owned. India puts more than half of its investment each year into the capital-intensive, state-owned, heavy-industrial enterprises that generate 15 percent of its manufacturing value-added.

The publicly owned industrial enterprises of the preindustrial countries now have an established presence in the world economy. A half-dozen of them appear in the list of the 350 largest transnational corporations. They are big enough to negotiate with those corporations at eye level. In joint ventures with their privately owned counterparts, they have become significant channels for technology transfer. They are playing a strategic role in hastening industrial revolution in an important group of countries, as will be seen.

Even as the new international division of labor has increased the share of the preindustrial countries in the world's industrial output, the gulf between their estate and that of the industrial countries has been widening. That division of labor was, after all, a function of the low wages it maintained in the preindustrial world. In

Public Manufacturing Enterprise in Preindustrial Countries

COUNTRY	PUBLIC SECTOR'S SHARE IN TOTAL (%)			
	INVESTMENT	VALUE-ADDED	OUTPUT	EMPLOYMENT
Iraq	96	40	–	–
Egypt	81	65	65	70
Bangladesh	80	70	–	–
Pakistan	70	85	40	22
India	60	–	19	–
Mexico	65	30	–	15
Venezuela	60	–	–	–
Sri Lanka	55	65	60	6
Turkey	50	50	–	35
Brazil	33	20	–	–

GOVERNMENT INTERVENTION *plays a significant role in effort to industrialize preindustrial market economies. Public investment goes largely to capital-intensive enterprise. Brazil and Mexico are ranked as "newly industrializing"; India is third largest preindustrial economy; Bangladesh is the poorest big country.*

round numbers, stated in constant 1950 dollars, the combined GNP of the industrial countries increased from $600 billion to $3000 billion in the 40 years from 1950 to 1990; the preindustrial economies in that time grew from $100 billion to $900 billion. As can be seen, the fivefold increase in the GNP of the industrial countries brought a huge $2400 billion absolute growth of product, which was distributed to relatively stable populations. The nearly tenfold increase in the GNP of the preindustrial countries gave them an absolute increase only one-third as big, which was to be shared by growing populations. While the GNP per capita (the common, if coarse, denominator of material well-being) increased by about the same percentage in the two worlds, the absolute difference in product per capita increased fourfold.

In the preindustrial countries, most of the increase went to the urban populations, sharpening national as well as international inequities in the distribution of incomes. The conditions of existence in the villages remained much as before, except in sub-Saharan Africa, where more people have less than in 1950.

THE "NEW INTERNATIONAL ECONOMIC ORDER"

From the widening gulf between the two worlds, there came, in the early 1970s, cries for a "new international economic order." In 1974, in the midst of the first "oil shock," a caucus of 77 preindustrial countries secured a proclamation of the new order by the UN General Assembly. The old order, characterized by "inequity, domination, dependence, narrow self-interest and segmentation," was to be replaced by an order based upon "equity, equality of sovereign nations, interdependence, common interest and cooperation." The industrial countries were enjoined to cooperate in translating these protestations into "negotiable issues."

The resolution drew no interest from the industrial countries. The United Nations returned briefly to the front pages of the U.S. press with accounts of the scornful rejection of the new international economic order by the country's UN ambassador. GATT, by now known in the preindustrial countries as the "rich man's club," continued to ignore the internationalization of inequity imposed by tariff and nontariff barriers even as it failed to resolve differences within its own membership. The United Nations Conference on Trade and Development (UNCTAD), the "poor man's club" organized in 1964 at the behest of the preindustrial countries, remained the monitor of the facts and figures of that inequity with no power to redress it.

On their own, preindustrial countries undertook to frame an agenda of negotiable issues at a conference of the UN Industrial Development Organization at Lima, Peru, in 1975. Toward the narrowing or filling of the gulf, they set a target: by the year 2000, they should be producing 25 percent of the world's industrial ouput. That required an annual increase of their manufacturing value-added by 4.5 percent above that forecast for the industrial countries. To that end, the industrial countries were to meet their commitment to devote 0.7 percent of their GNP to economic assistance. More important, they were to open their markets to the manufactured exports of the preindustrial countries. An improvement in export income that can be earned every year is worth more to a preindustrial country than a generous grant-in-aid. It may be said to be their due under the free-trade doctrine propounded by spokesmen for the industrial market economies.

A UN study of the world economy, already under way and published in 1977, made it possible to put numbers on visions of such magnitude. The method of input–output analysis, for which the Nobel Prize in economics had been conferred on Wassily W. Leontief in 1973, offered refinement on the estimates of the 1949 group of experts. The method anchors macroeconomic projections in the matrix of interindustry exchanges of goods and services that produces the product of an economy. Since those microeconomic transactions are technologically determined, the input–output table presents a working model of a country's industrial system for projecting and estimating and for testing hypotheses at the macroeconomic level that is anchored in microeconomic data. From input–output tables for 60 countries, the study, conducted by Leontief himself and his colleague Faye Duchin, projected three scenarios for the world economy to the year 2000.

The first scenario had the old order doing business as usual. For an upper tier of "resource rich" preindustrial countries, mostly the petroleum producers with 10 percent of the world population, the gulf as measured by the difference between the average income per capita in the industrial world and in their own was reduced from a multiple of nine in 1970 to three in 2000. For the rest of the preindustrial countries, with 59 percent of the world population, this scenario widened the gulf between incomes in the two worlds from 14 times to 19 times.

An alternative scenario calculated the cost of reducing by 50 percent the difference in output between the industrial world and countries with 59 percent of the world population, a measure that would more than double the income per capita of those people. Operating on this scenario, the input–output model of the world economy showed that the industrial countries would have to allocate 3.1 percent of their combined GNP to the effort and accept some diminution of their income per capita. For those countries, then putting more than 6 percent of their GNP into armaments, this scenario was conceded to be politically infeasible.

The third scenario tested a "peace dividend." From a one-third reduction in arms expenditure, it diverted 15 percent and then 25 percent of the released resources to economic assistance. This modest increase in economic assistance—ranging from 0.25 percent to 0.5 percent of the GNP of the industrial countries—promised to keep the gap between the industrial and the preindustrial countries from widening. The estimate of the Group of Experts, who made the 1950 UN study of the capital requirement for the economic development of the underdeveloped countries, was, evidently, not far from the mark.

By 1975, however, the repricing of oil by OPEC had terminated that subsidy of the postwar boom in the industrial nations and pushed them, especially the United States, deeper into the slough of stagflation in which they were already caught. They were setting full employment aside as a goal of economic policy and retrenching their welfare states. The recycling of petrodollars in what are now acknowledged to be improvident bank loans helped keep a few of the preindustrial economies moving ahead until the second "oil shock," that of 1979.

The world economy has been becalmed ever since, with only a momentary recovery in the late 1980s, terminated by the Iraqi invasion of Kuwait. The industrial countries have not only reduced their imports from, and their new investments in, the preindustrial countries but cut their official development assistance as well. Economic growth has terminated in all but a few preindustrial countries.

In 1960, Egon Glesinger, chief forester of the Food and Agriculture Organization, whose career as an international civil servant began under the League of Nations, wrote:

> Adequate foreign aid can upset the unwelcome conclusion, advanced by one school of economists, that coercive power is necessary to the process of capital accumulation, all the more so when the margin of squeezable resources is narrowest. . . . But the need for coercion . . . has now been obviated by the enormous surplus capacity of the industrially advanced nations. The economic function of the dictator can be neutralized by foreign aid.

In the absence of aid that would obviate the need for coercion, dictatorships govern two-thirds of the preindustrial countries. Now the governments and the banks of the industrial countries and the international banking institutions are attempting to negotiate a reverse flow of aid from the poor to the rich countries—that is, payment of the $1200 billion debt that burdens the preindustrial countries. In exchange for the rescheduling of interest and amortization payments, the creditors urge and compel their debtors to adopt "stabilization" and "structural adjustment" measures designed to improve their credit ratings and to make them more attractive to private investors.

The Old International Economic Order

"At the root of the poor performance and debt problems of developing countries," the World Bank explained in its 1986 World Development Report,

> lies their failure to adjust to the external developments that have taken place since the early 1970s, coupled with the magnitude of the external shocks. Many developing countries tried to offset the effects of external shocks, higher inflation and lower growth by borrowing more, mostly at short-term maturities and floating rates. The shift in favor of commercial bank lending at floating rates in the 1970s left developing countries vulnerable to an increase in interest rates and to reductions in the volume of private lending. The 1979 oil price increases and the recession of the early 1980s exposed these weaknesses.

The external developments to which the debtor countries failed to adjust consisted, of course, in the decline of their trade with the industrial countries and the deterioration of its terms. This applies especially to the poorest countries of sub-Saharan Africa; they lost their livelihood. That is why they necessarily exhausted "their access to short term capital and depleted their foreign exchange reserves."

About one-quarter of the debt is owed by the newly industrializing countries of Latin America. It is they that went so improvidently into the private credit market at floating interest rates. They did so at the invitation of the U.S. banks, burdened with petrodollars, that are now sharing their embarrassment. If this debt is ever repaid, it will not be repaid by the people who negated the inflow of the borrowed money by sending their capital out of the country. It will be repaid by people who can least afford to repay it—and at interest rates that have floated upward on the mounting national debt incurred by the same U.S. government that presses deflationary austerity on their countries.

The economist A. O. Hirschman has spoken of the prospective cancellation of part or most of the debt burden of the preindustrial countries as "inadvertent economic assistance." The assistance would have served its recipients better had it been rendered earlier on the scale proposed by the group of experts in 1950. It would have come, moreover, with the more expansionary counsel that accompanied the earlier, inadequate flows of official development assistance, not the bleak deflationary counsel issued today.

NEWLY INDUSTRIALIZING COUNTRIES

Despite the failure of the industrial world to meet its obligation and promise to render the assistance that would reduce the stress of capital accumulation, some preindustrial countries have managed the task, not without its human cost. There are seven such countries, and they may be said to be approaching the verge of industrial revolution. What distinguishes the seven countries is their possession now of a strong base in heavy industry. One of them, of course, is China. The others are market economies. Mexico and Venezuela are oil exporters; South Korea is buoyed by exports of manufactured goods. (There are exporters of oil and manufactures, however, that have not acquired comparable industrial capacity.) The other three countries are India, Brazil, and Argentina; they built their heavy industries in support of the development of their own domestic markets. In all of these countries, it was aggressive government policy, not market demand, that brought the building of their heavy industrial plants. The governments of the market economies in this group of countries operate those plants under public ownership.

Such corporations had their role in the first industrial revolution. The East India Company, chartered by Parliament and placed under control by the Cabinet, conducted colonial conquests that opened markets to the Lancashire mills. Industrial revolution got a head start in Germany from state-owned blast furnaces in Silesia, Prussia, Hanover, and Bavaria. In the industrial revolution of Japan, it is hard to think of the *zaibatsu*—the great banking, trading, and manufacturing conglomerates financed by the baronial fortunes of the old order—as not serving as agents of the state. They did so as effectively as their successor *keiretsu*, some under the control of the same feudal families, do today.

Governmental intervention in the economies of the industrially most advanced preindustrial countries must also have found precedent in the second, Soviet–Russian model of economic development. Besides China, however, India is the only country that has avowed any ideological motive.

All of the governments had compelling pragmatic reasons for intervening in the market and taking action that was almost always against near-term comparative advantage. There was no private capital ready for lumpy investment in heavy industry, none able to accept the high risk and wait a long time for low return. With room for only one enterprise in the industry, there was no private capital to finance even a private monopoly and no disposition to see it operated by a transnational corporation. There were also strong positive motives for governmental initiative: to develop the hinterland, to increase manufacturing value-added on the country's export commodity, to encourage enterprise in industries downstream, and, above all, to reverse the cycle of cumulative causation and start it turning in the direction of economic autonomy.

The public industrial enterprises come under scorn in the international financial press as unprofitable burdens on their national economies. They are nonetheless prizes sought after by entrepreneurs and competing transnational corporations in the debt-for-equity swaps that have become the fashion in negotiation of the rescheduling of debt and interest payments conducted by public as well as private creditors of the preindustrial economies.

Due largely to progress in the seven countries that verge on self-sustained industrialization, the preindustrial world is now consuming 24 percent of the world's steel and producing more than 15 percent of it. There is steelmaking in 50 countries, most of them recycling local or imported scrap through electric furnaces to make concrete reinforcing bar and light structural shapes. Integrated steel plants make steel starting from iron ore in 20 countries, and capacity exceeds 1 million tons in 17 of them. Capacity exceeds 5 million tons in the seven countries: China, 52 million tons; Brazil, 25 million tons; India, 20 million tons; Mexico, 13 million tons; South Korea, 12 million tons; Argentina and Venezuela, 7 million tons each.

The steel these countries produce—75 percent of the steel in the preindustrial world—supplies indigenous machine-building and heavy chemical industries that support their growing consumer-goods manufacturing industries. These countries account, all told, for 85 percent of the manufacturing value added in the preindustrial countries and 53 percent of their manufactured exports. It is among these nations that one must look for the earliest next industrial revolutions. With India and China in the company, these nations bring more than half the population of the preindustrial world to the verge of industrial revolution.

This is not the "official" list of newly industrializing countries. For admission to that list, the threshold appears to be a relatively high income per capita as well as a relatively high degree of industrialization. Argentina, Brazil, Mexico, and South Korea qualify for the usual list,

Steelmaking Capacity of Industrial and Preindustrial Countries

	CAPACITY (MILLIONS OF TONS)
Industrial countries	
EEC countries	206
United States	170
Japan	170
Other market economies	87
USSR	200
Other centrally planned economies	97
Total (industrial countries)	940
Preindustrial countries	
China	52
Brazil	25
India	20
Mexico	13
South Korea	12
Argentina	7
Venezuela	7
Other preindustrial countries	50
Total (preindustrial countries)	186
Total (both)	1,126

START ON INDUSTRIALIZATION *in seven key preindustrial countries is measured by steelmaking capacity. China and India hold nearly half the population of preindustrial world; Brazil, Mexico, Argentina, and Venezuela, two-thirds of the Latin American population. Steel sets foundation for other heavy industries.*

along with Hong Kong and Singapore. The latter are excluded here as being entrepots for low-wage intermediate processing of the products of transnational corporations, not nations on the way to economic autonomy. Venezuela, with the highest income per capita in Latin America and not the most unequal distribution of that income, has been overlooked in the compilation of such lists. China, with the largest industrial establishment in the preindustrial world, and India, with the third largest, are excluded perhaps by their low income per capita.

CHINA

For China, during the civil war in that country, the Soviet Union conducted an imperfect demonstration of its model of economic development by dismantling and carrying off the industrial plant built by Japan in Manchuria during the 1930s. On the Soviet model, nonetheless, China built its industrial plant starting from the heavy end first. The regime of Nikita S. Khrushchev opened universities in the USSR to aspiring engineers and scientists from China during the 1950s and started a modest flow of economic and technical assistance that terminated in a renewal of ideological contention in the early 1960s. Otherwise, China found its way on the course of industrialization on its own. Deprivation of the consumer economy provided the "savings" for accumulation of the necessary capital. Because it takes a million tons or more of steel to build a million tons of steel-making capacity, the first million tons of capacity was the hardest to build. At 52 million tons capacity today, it takes only 2 percent of the annual output to build the next plant.

China's own steel built the country's industrial infrastructure, the railroads that tie the country together, the first bridges across the two great rivers, and the communications and electric power systems. Soon China had its own heavy machinery and heavy chemicals industries, equipping and supplying its mines and factories. By 1990, at 52 million tons capacity, China was the world's fourth largest steel producer. It ranked first in the production of cement, second in the production of coal, third in the production of chemical fertilizer, and fifth in the production of oil, synthetic fibers, and electrical energy. Only its huge population—and the tiny output per capita of all these commodities—keeps China in the category of preindustrial countries.

While the Soviet Union attempted to operate its industries from ministries in Moscow, the Chinese delegated much of this responsibility to the managers of the enterprises, many of which were set up as free-standing corporations. The increase in industrial output, now 43 percent of the GNP, began to exceed the output of agriculture, now 36 percent, in the 1970s.

In 1973, secure in basic industrial capacity, China opened its economy to the world economy to acquire the high technologies not in the command of its engineers in consequence of their country's economic isolation. For all the stops and starts in its new relations with the world, China is big enough and its market attractive enough to the transnational corporations to give China a buyer's market. Its engineers and entrepreneurs pick and choose, from among the transnationals, the corporation best equipped to help on a given salient, and they are able to insist that the proffered technology be "truly advanced by international standards."

From about 2 percent in 1949, the rate of China's population growth increased to 2.6 percent in 1965. That reflected decline in the death rate. Then, by 1985, decline in the birth rate brought the rate of population growth down by 1.5 percentiles to just above 1 percent. Much is made of the rationing of pregnancies in the communes and the "one-child family" campaign and its harsh enforcement. These measures would be unthinkable, however, if the incomes of the Chinese had not ascended above the Kuznets threshold of $150 in real income (see page 108). Nor would they be in any way effective without the motivation supplied by the reduction in the infant-mortality rate. That was secured by good nutrition and the country's unique health-care system. Moreover, egalitarian income distribution and the revolutionary ardor it supports helped people put up with the compulsions to which they submitted.

Whether the privatization of agriculture and the introduction of market incentives will reduce these restraints on fertility remains to be seen. There are reports of breakdown of the health-care system and of waning revolutionary morale. The trend has hitherto indicated a rate of population growth below 1 percent at the year 2000.

INDIA

At its liberation in 1947, India had a steel capacity of 2 million tons in the ownership of two private industrial dynasties. That was adequate to the effective demand of the domestic market. It was not nearly enough for the need of 500 million of the world's most needful people, not all of whom could summon effective demand for food. It was their need that made Jawarhalal Nehru embrace the country's economic development as the transcendent obligation of the government. To keep the industrial dynasties and the rest of the business community working with the government, he set aside the revolutionary socialism of the liberation movement and propounded his own "socialist pattern" of development in 1950. In that pattern, private enterprise was to be there to satisfy effective new demands as the country's development generated them.

The central government reserved to itself—and, where appropriate, to the state governments—the building (from the ground up, in large part) and the operation of India's transportation, communication, and electric-power systems. For the development of the country's resources and the building and operation of its heavy industries, the central government created publicly owned, free-standing, tax-paying corporations. Thus holding the "commanding heights" of the economy, it conducted development by plan. To himself, Nehru reserved the chairmanship of the planning commission.

Nehru did not need Gunnar Myrdal to tell him that India was a soft state. For the first five-year plan, starting from 1947, the government commanded less than half the country's capacity for capital formation. The present plan deploys 75 percent of it, secured to the government by a highly progressive income tax and a virtual governmental monopoly on foreign trade. The second plan, drawn by the renowned statistician P. C. Mahalanobis, started the building of India's heavy industrial system. It was an import-substitution plan directed at producers' and capital goods.

The plan set ambitious goals from year to year beyond the reach of India's indigenous capital. From the holders of that capital, who recognized no need for such stretching of the country's resources, the government of India experienced opposition and sometimes sabotage. Over and above what it could extract by taxation of its wealthy citizens and accumulate from the foreign trade surplus it carefully protected, the government sought the required capital in the promise of economic assistance. That expectation was largely disappointed, except for the food aid from the United States that made hungry men and women into human capital. The shortfall in the second and following plans corresponded closely to the shortfall in economic assistance. By the mid-1960s, the plans were self-reliant, and India was insulating (if not isolating) itself from the world economy.

Today, India's public manufacturing enterprises produce its steel, its central-station electrical machinery, its heavy mechanical machinery (such as rolling mills), its railroad rolling stock, and its earth-moving and mining machines. They build and operate its shipyards, oil refineries, and petrochemical plants.

Many of these enterprises have joint ventures with transnational corporations. Like China, and unlike smaller preindustrial countries, India is able to persuade these joint-venture corporations to buy their raw materials and component parts from India's own public and private industrial establishments and, where appropriate, to sell their intermediate products to Indian private manufacturers for final processing. India sets the same terms on the licenses it issues to transnational corporations to set up affiliates in the country; those corporations produce 14 percent of the country's gross national product. These arrangements secure technology transfer and keep manufacturing value-added in the economy.

India's publicly owned industrial system has built the largest railroad network in Asia (and the fourth largest in the world), a highway system of 1.5 million kilometers, a pipeline net, and an electric-power system. For the country's agriculture, public enterprises built the major waterworks and canals that doubled the hectares under irrigation. They produce seed and fertilizer, and the publicly owned food corporation operates the warehouses, elevators, and refrigeration plants to meet the need as well as the demand for food. To businesses in the private sector, the public industrial enterprises are supplying basic and intermediate materials and component parts, and they are devolving a lengthening list of products to the private sector for manufacture.

While these enterprises are often called upon to take action for nonbusiness purposes, such as the location of a plant in a backward region, they pay taxes and generate half the capital for their continued expansion. They employ two-thirds of the industrial work force and earn 15 percent of the country's export income. The Steel Authority of India is one of the 350 largest transnational corporations, engaged in joint ventures in other preindustrial countries. Bharat Heavy Electricals Ltd. exports turbine-generator sets and boilers and has built complete electric power systems for Libya and Saudi Arabia. Hindustan Machine Tools Ltd. exports its machines, with General Electric computer controls, to the United States.

India's industrialization exerts a powerful centripetal force upon its diverse and centrifugal population. It has made the country self-sufficient and relatively solvent, compared with other preindustrial countries. It has begun to bring technology to the villages and to bring the villages into the nation. A stationary satellite and television sets centrally installed in almost every village—broadcasting and receiving news, weather forecasts, instruction in nonagricultural technology, lessons in hygiene, and entertainment—for the first time give the country something approaching a common consciousness. The summary measure of the country's progress is the decline of its population growth rate from 2.3 to 1.7 percent.

In the Indian population, however, there are now more of the world's poorest people than there were at liberation. Industrial revolution proceeds slowly in the world's largest parliamentary democracy; too slowly, perhaps.

Pakistan and Bangladesh have followed India's example and are building their industrial plant in the public sector. At its founding in 1948, Pakistan asserted its identity as a market economy, declaring that "assignment to public agencies of tasks which can be successfully accomplished by private enterprise will restrict the pace of development." By the mid-1960s, at the termination of the Ayub Khan military dictatorship, the Pakistani government was ready to take stronger initiative, now declaring that "private enterprise is not attracted to some industries because of their technical complexity, high capital requirements or relatively low profitability. . . ." To command the necessary capital, the new government of Zufikar Ali Bhutto nationalized the country's banks and insurance companies.

In 1972, East Pakistan became Bangladesh in a more revolutionary mood and nationalized the financial and industrial institutions at the outset. With steel as the index and with capacities of 1.5 and 0.5 million tons respectively, Pakistan and Bangladesh have barely started their industrialization.

EAST AND SOUTHEAST ASIA AND JAPAN

South Korea made abrupt entry into the world market; from less than $1 billion in 1970, it pushed its export income to $35 billion in 1985. A declared market economy, in opposition to communist North Korea, South Korea has been under authoritarian government from its beginnings. The government has never shrunk from initiatives that could move the country's growth and development ahead. It literally pushed exports with subsidies of more than 10 percent of their value-added. It placed the building and operation of capital-goods and producer's-goods industries, as the economy's "leading sector," under publicly owned corporations. By public ownership, the market imperfections that might be introduced by private monopoly in that sector were to be avoided. Making market imperfections work the other way, these public enterprises supplied raw materials at low prices to the private enterprises that produced the exports. To its large textile and other soft goods exports, South Korea was able to add $11 billion worth of automotive and industrial machinery exports in 1985.

The industrializing of South Korea, and of Taiwan as well, has been supported strongly by the productive agricultural systems they inherited from their days of occupation by Japan. As an occupying power, Japan had no compunction about land reform; getting rid of the landowner class in both countries facilitated occupation. The South Korean government took care to see that the country's farms kept the work force of its new industries fueled with food, supplying fertilizer priced by the country's planning board.

The classification of South Korea and Taiwan as newly industrializing countries testifies to the success of the strategy followed by Japan in its own climb up the value-added-by-manufacture ladder since the end of World War II. As early as the mid-1960s, the rising income per capita of the Japanese labor force was putting the country's labor-intensive industries at a disadvantage. With government subsidy, the *keiretsu* conglomerates proceeded to resettle these industries in South Korea and Taiwan and, more recently, in Indonesia, Malaysia, and Thailand. Those countries have emerged among the world's important exporters of the labor-intensive manufactures formerly associated with Japan, and South Korea has become an exporter of automobiles. Japan remains the principal trading partner of Taiwan and South Korea, except that more of South Korea's exports go to the United States. Much of what South Korea exports to the United States incorporates imports from Japan.

Japanese corporations and financial institutions make two-thirds or more of their overseas investments in preindustrial countries. They make more then half of these investments in the preindustrial countries of East Asia and Southeast Asia. Private investment is preceded and strongly supported by the flow of funds from the Japanese government. The Japanese Export-Import Bank issues buyer's credits to buyers of Japanese goods, seller's credits to Japanese exporters, and overseas investment credits to Japanese investors. The bank also makes direct loans to governments for resource-development projects, developing energy and mineral resources that are later to be of interest to Japanese industry. The follow-up development phase brings in the Overseas Economic Cooperation Fund, the Investment Cooperation Agency, the Petroleum Development Corporation, the Metal Mining Agency, and the Overseas Development Corporation. To its preindustrial clients, Japan offers a complete economic-development service.

With such encouragement from Japan, taking steel again as the index, industrialization has proceeded to the point where Indonesia and Thailand each have 2 million tons of installed capacity and Malaysia has 0.5 million tons. These countries are employing the vehicle of public industrial corporations to hasten development. Public enterprises in food processing and distribution in Indonesia and Thailand ensure that need is met as well as demand. Indonesia supplies public financing to such labor-intensive industries as textiles, building materials for low-cost housing, and small-scale manufacturing in the villages.

Thailand, further along, puts public financing and management into development of forest and mineral resources and oil and oil refining. Enjoying annual economic growth at the rate of 10 percent, it is likely to be the next country in the Japanese economic sphere to enter the category of the newly industrializing. Japan has replaced the United States as the largest investor. At $4 billion a year, it is supplying half the foreign direct investment and is employing 10 percent of the country's labor force. For the Thai market, a Japanese auto assembly plant is producing 300,000 pickup trucks, made popular in the country by its earlier close association with the United States. The plant will be producing more units for export to the United States. Coming from Thailand, they will not count against the Japanese import quota.

The accelerating progress of industrialization in the preindustrial countries of East and Southeast Asia promises to bring their population growth rates down close to 1 percent early in the next century.

THE ARAB NATION

The oil-exporting countries of the Arab nation, princely or radical, Islamic or secular, are employing public corporations to conduct the investment of oil revenues in industrial development. Oil production in all these countries is conducted under state ownership. They seek value added to their petroleum exports with state-owned refineries and petrochemical plants. These enterprises have now set up demand for steelmaking capacity: nearly 5 million tons in Iran; 3 million tons in Algeria; 2 million tons in Iraq; 1 million tons each in Syria and Libya. Demand for the large-diameter pipe employed in oil wells and pipelines has installed sophisticated rolling-mill technology in some of this plant. The princely states lag, with capacities under 1 million tons.

The political turmoil among these states, the extreme income disparities within them, the subordination of women, and Islamic evangelism in many of them reduce the prospect that economic progress will bring early reduction in their population growth rates. Those rates will doubtless remain above 2 percent beyond the year 2000.

SUB-SAHARAN AFRICA

The spread of industrial revolution within the preindustrial world has largely by-passed the countries of sub-Saharan Africa. Between them and the other preindustrial countries there has opened a gap of the kind that separates them all from the industrial countries. In 1963, the African countries could be credited with perhaps 10 percent of the manufacturing value-added in the preindustrial world; by 1980, their share had fallen to no more than 5 percent. The decline in relative output conceals, of course, some absolute increase in output, which is substantial in a few countries. Zaire and Zambia, for example, captured value-added when they began smelting their ores and exporting copper in the late 1970s. In the attempt to move forward despite declining and even reversing exchange balances, all of the sub-Saharan countries went deeply into debt, their burdens now ranging from half to more than double their GNPs.

The official status of their debt—it being owed to public rather than to private creditors—has not spared the African countries the deflationary counsel to balance budgets, reduce consumption, devalue currencies, and the rest of the agenda of austerity. In their state of poverty, this counsel reduces not only their present but their future growth. That is true especially of cuts in expenditures for health, nutrition, and education, which subtract from tomorrow's human capital. The effect must be to widen the gap that has opened on the far side of the world's gap.

Population growth continues above 2 percent throughout sub-Saharan Africa. Some people have been heard to speculate that this high rate of growth may be contained by the epidemic of the acquired immune deficiency syndrome, called AIDS, in the region. That outcome is unlikely, of course, without consequences going far outside the region—to the regret of everyone, including people given to such speculation. Containment of the high rate of population growth in sub-Saharan Africa requires a cure for the prior affliction of poverty, which makes AIDS widespread in Africa and in comparably impoverished populations even in the industrial countries.

LATIN AMERICA

The four Latin American countries that have set foundations in heavy industry for self-sustained industrial revolution contain two-thirds of the 360 million population of the region. Their continued progress, it might be hoped, will bring the rest of Latin America along with them. For them and for the region as a whole, that prospect is clouded by the extreme inequities in the distribution of income and wealth that prevail in all of the countries. Such inequity means fewer consumers qualified with effective demand for the products of industry, on the one hand, and, on the other, a high preference for liquidity over fixed investment in industry among the possessors of wealth.

Argentina was the first of the countries to start, before World War I, on the track to industrialization. The exports of beef and wheat from the pampas established Argentina strongly in the world market. The great wealth of the *latifundistas* brought them into circles of wealth in Europe. While the Argentineans preferred to invest abroad, their country attracted a flow of European capital during the first decades of the century. With the Great Depression of the 1930s, the first round of investment from overseas died away. The country now had a business community and an urban working class with economic interests at odds with the holders of its primary wealth. Out of their conflict came the dictatorship of Juan Perón.

The end of Perón brought a new wave of investment from overseas in the early 1960s. Deficits on the balance of payments and political instability brought that wave to a halt in military dictatorship. Today an overseas debt that is 60 percent of GNP, a debt-service burden that is 60 percent of export earnings, and hemorrhagic inflation threaten the restored civilian government. A Peronist president, who acceded to the full agenda of deflationary measures pressed by the country's creditors and to the swapping of debt for equity in the public industrial enterprises, has been losing his popular following and has had to face military mutiny.

Brazil's subcontinental territory, its wealth of resources, and its big population together engender aspiration and pressure for economic growth against the most extreme inequality in the distribution of wealth and income in Latin America. The government has been the seat of such aspiration when it has not been in the keep of military dictatorship. The holders of great wealth have been happy to have their government assume the large risk and low return on investment in the infrastructure of industrial revolution. On more than one occasion, the government has pulled their chestnuts out of the fire by taking over troubled enterprises and assuming their obligations in joint ventures with transnational corporations.

Of the total investment in Brazil's 200 largest industrial enterprises, the public corporations deploy 80 percent. One of these, and one of the 350 largest transnational corporations, is Petrobras, which controls 96 percent of the petroleum refining and petrochemical industry. Of the steel capacity of 25 million tons, 20 million is in public ownership. In 1980, 75 percent of the capital formation was in the public domain.

A new class of managers calling themselves the "bourgeois of the state" conduct the public and the private enterprises as well, untroubled by the distinction in ownership. The scale of their operations and their demonstrated abilities put them on equal footing with their counterparts in the transnational corporations. The terms they negotiate in the establishment of joint ventures bring substantial technology transfer to Brazil's industries.

In the slowdown of the world economy, the vigorous growth of Brazil came to a stop in double-digit inflation, capital flight, and a debt equal to half its GNP. A new president is applying the standard deflationary corrections at the prompting of the country's creditors and coping with rising discontent among the people.

For Mexico and Venezuela, nationalized oil provided the capital for the building of heavy industry. In Mexico, 65 percent of industrial investment is in public industrial enterprises. Pemex, the state-owned oil-production, oil-refining and petrochemical company, is one of the 350 transnationals. Other public enterprises operate the steel, heavy chemicals, and fertilizer industries.

The harsh division of the rich and poor in Mexico went unhealed in the first oil boom in the 1920s and 1930s. Mexico's second chance, with the discovery of vast new oil pools in the 1970s, in time to ride the OPEC price rise, appears to be dissipating in the same way.

Upon the breaking of the 1980 OPEC price and the relative as well as absolute decline in the price of oil, Mexico went heavily into petrodollar debt with U.S. banks and thereby postponed the "adjustments" now prescribed by its creditors. In the deepening economic distress, the Institutional Revolutionary Party faced serious popular opposition for the first time in the 1989 presidential election. Upon his dubious victory, the new president, Carlos Salinas de Gotarí, was able to threaten the United States with his possible displacement by the radical if not revolutionary opposition. He secured thereby a rescheduling of the debt, standing at more than 50 percent of the country's GNP.

The Salinas government has proceeded faithfully to administer the full prescription of deflationary adjustments, including the swap of equity in public manufacturing enterprises for debt. It has now acceded to the Bush administration's invitation to put its low-wage labor force at the full disposal of U.S. industry in a free-trade union of their countries' economies. Apparently, such union has popular support in Mexico; a public-opinion poll showed 59 percent of the respondents in favor of forming one country with the United States if that would improve their circumstances.

Whether the free-trade union will find ratification in the U.S. Congress remains to be seen. It is strongly opposed by organized labor, who are beginning to understand that their jobs constitute the principal contribution their country has made in recent years to economic development in the preindustrial world. A free-trade union with Mexico is almost the ultimate sacrifice they could make to that end. Some 30 or 40 million Mexicans are counted among the world's poorest people, and their increase in numbers proceeds at 3 percent.

Venezuela's public industrial enterprises conduct all of its oil production, refining, and shipping and 50 to 75 percent of the operations of the various branches of its petrochemical industry. They built and operate essentially all of the steel industry and 25 to 50 percent of the various machine-building industries. These public enterprises have close linkages to downstream manufacturing and stimulate new ventures in the private sector. To noneconomic social objectives—leading ultimately to income redistribution—the government deploys substantial portions of its investment capital. In the interior, it has been building the well-planned Ciudad Guayana as a steel and industrial center close to the country's resources. For "social equity," it operates 24 food-processing centers, produces fertilizer priced to subsidize agriculture, and manufactures materials for prefabricated low-cost housing. The relatively strong internal market completely engrosses the growing private industrial sector, leaving to the public enterprises the generation of export income.

With petrodollars so freely available into the early 1980s, Venezuela built its foreign debt to a towering 60 percent of its GNP. Service on the debt came to a bearable 15 percent of export income, however, as long as the country's oil went to market at the OPEC price. Since the collapse of that price, Venezuela has been acceding to its creditors' agenda of deflationary measures and putting public industrial enterprises on the block.

The abrupt ending of the Cold War has left one model of economic development in the field. Counsel issuing from it ought to reflect the reality as well as the theory of the market. The state had its role in the first industrial revolutions; the governments of the preindustrial countries have theirs to play in the worldwide industrial revolution. The incompetent state must be put in harness with the imperfect market to brake the vicious circles of cumulative causation.

7

HUMAN DEVELOPMENT

Through the 40 years of the Cold War, each of the contending parties claimed custody of human hope and aspiration. One was the champion of freedom; the other, the keeper of the peace. The exhaustion of the two parties and the collapse of their contention has now cleared the air to bring into sight the true end of human striving.

"The massive habits of physical nature, its iron laws, determine the scene for the sufferings of men," Alfred North Whitehead wrote.

> Birth and death, heat, cold, hunger, separation, disease, the general impracticability of purpose all bring their quota to imprison the souls of women and men. . . . The essence of freedom is the practicability of purpose. . . . Prometheus did not bring to mankind the freedom of the press. He procured fire.

In increasing numbers, the people of the industrial nations have come to experience practicability of purpose. Their experience—of a human existence—is open now to all of humankind.

Command of the iron laws resides in people, not in machines. The liberation of human capacity secured by industrial revolution is thus a precondition to its progress. People in the preindustrial countries must share in the material benefit of the present round of industrial revolution even as they carry it forward. The world population is growing too fast to keep them waiting two and three generations.

If they must wait, as the people of the industrial countries did, there will be too many grandchildren in the already populous nations of the poor for any to enjoy the meals the present generation goes without. In 1963, in *The Making of the English Working Class,* E. P. Thompson declared the hope that "causes which were lost in England may, in Asia and Africa, yet be won."

The causes were lost not alone in England but in the coercion and privation that accumulated capital in all the industrial revolutions that have followed. To be won in Asia and Africa, the causes must soon enlist people of the industrial world whose grandparents endured the earlier revolutions. To their credit, those people have promised the transfers of capital and technology that can neutralize the economic function of dictators. The promise has been outstanding, however, for nearly half a century. An early start on its fulfillment is required if a human existence is to be open to the world population on a habitable Earth.

INDUSTRIAL REVOLUTION=ENVIRONMENTAL PROTECTION

Industrial revolution is the ultimate population-control measure. It has been accompanied so invariably by the slowing and then halting of the growth of the population engaged that there can be no doubt about this prescription. Industrial revolution has to be recognized also, therefore, as the ultimate environmental-protection measure. Hazards to the environment laid by industrial technology, it has been shown, are subject to cure by technology. Concern for the environment is now compelling redistribution of the incentives and reform of the institutions that put technology to work in the industrial countries. The same concern must now be turned to accelerating industrial revolution in the preindustrial countries.

From a peak just above 2 percent per year around 1970, the rate of world population growth has fallen close to 1.5 percent. This is the summary expression of many more indexes of improvement in the human condition that measure the progress of the now worldwide industrial revolution in the present half century. The increase in the rate of population growth between 1950 and 1970 was itself the favorable sign of lengthening life expectancy among all the peoples of the world. That signified the entry of the population of the poor nations into the first phase of the demographic transition, in which death rates decline. The fall in the rate of growth since 1970 indicates the entry of the population of many (including the largest) poor nations into the second phase of the transition, in which birth rates decline. It took many more than 20 years to see the populations of the industrial nations through the corresponding passage from the first to the second phase of the demographic transition during the nineteenth and early twentieth centuries.

There could have been no decline in birth rates without significant improvement in the most vital of the associated statistics. Along with the familiar indicators of economic health and growth—GNP per capita, employment in industry, foreign-trade balance, and the like—the UN Development Program (UNDP) has begun to track indicators of "human development." One crucial indicator is the "under-5" mortality rate (the number of deaths of children under five years of age each year per 1000 live births). In Human Development Report 1990, the first in what is to be an annual series, UNDP recorded the reduction of the under-5 mortality rate in the preindustrial world from nearly 250 per thousand in 1960 to less than 125 per thousand in 1988. Countries that showed the largest declines in this mortality rate showed correlative declines in fertility.

Medicine, on which the industrial world stints no expense, had little to do with this reduction in child mortality. It is the outcome of concurrent improvement in nutrition, in access to safe potable water, in sanitation, and in the more familiar economic indicators as well [see tables on pages 304 and 305].

Of particular relevance also to fertility control are the indicators of school enrollment and literacy, especially in the female population. The adult literacy rate in the preindustrial world increased from 43 percent in 1970 to 60 percent in 1985. The school-enrollment indicators showed 87 percent of the boys and 79 percent of the girls enrolled in primary school, 45 percent and 33 percent in secondary school, and 9 percent and 5 percent in higher education.

The most portable technologies of industrial revolution—sanitation, medicine, popular education—have reached the preindustrial world first. They have shown their impact in positive change in human-development indicators everywhere, in some countries outrunning the economic indicators. Country by country, of course, these indicators vary widely. Thus, enrollment in primary schools ranges from 100 percent in countries further along in industrial revolution—or in countries that make a policy of investment in human capital, such as Zimbabwe, Cuba, and Sri Lanka—down to 50 percent and less among the lagging countries.

Female literacy and enrollment indicators correlate closely with the "contraceptive prevalance" rate found in surveys now conducted regularly throughout the preindustrial world. In general, all of these indicators move together. Family-planning campaigns have proved largely fruitless where the indicators for infant survival, nutrition, sanitation, and literacy do not support them. On the other hand, where those indicators are supportive, recent experience has shown that contraception can be successfully promoted in populations living at levels far below those at which it became a general practice in the industrial countries.

The expansion of adult literacy and of school enrollments stand as supreme success stories in the development enterprise of many preindustrial countries, happily including the largest and by no means the richest of them. It is remarkable that adult literacy in China—where illiteracy was nearly total in the countryside as recently as 1950—now stands at 70 percent of that huge population and that 99 and 91 percent of Chinese boys and girls of primary school age—in number equal to the entire population of the United States—are in school.

On thinner resources, India succeeded in lifting adult literacy in its heterogeneous population from 34 to 43 percent between 1970 and 1985 and has close to 80 percent of its children—but a lower percentage of its female children—in primary schools. Indonesia, the third most populous preindustrial country, started later and has now surpassed its bigger neighbors, lifting adult literacy from 54 to 74 percent and getting 99 and 97 percent of its boys and girls enrolled in school. Again, progress of this magnitude was made over much longer time periods by the industrial nations at corresponding stages in their economic development.

For all the successes of these recent decades, the poorest people remain as poor and as numerous as before. The indicators of human development cited here describe change in the averages of human existence in the preindustrial world. They average out large differences in the conditions of existence within this 75 percent of the world population. A steady-state 1 billion people in the population have experienced little of the improvement shown by the indicators. Their circumstances remain closer to those of the 1 billion most deprived people in the population of 1970 than to those of their contemporaries today.

Progress must be celebrated, accordingly, in percentages. The 1 billion, in round numbers, was 25 percent of the world population in 1970; it is 20 percent of the present world population.

Against hope and expectation for the future, the 1 billion population continues to increase its numbers at an average rate exceeding 2 percent. It does so by maintaining its fertility at a high rate against an under-5 mortality rate in excess of 250 per thousand live births. The associated indicators describe the appropriate setting. These people live without adequate sanitation, exposed to bacterial infection and parasitic infestation; 750 million are without access to safe water, and their daily caloric intake falls 10 percent short of the minimum requirement. Half of the children under five years of age are underweight, and their adult stature will be stunted by two to five years of growth forgone. Among the 1 billion are most of the world's nearly 1 billion adult illiterates.

Of the world's 1 billion poorest people, 500 million live north and south of the Himalayas and in East Asia. China has brought its share of this population down to 200 million, 20 percent of its own population. India is home still to 250 million of the world's poorest; it can be said, however, that they constitute a declining percentage of the country's population. In Africa south and east of the Sahara, the world's poorest are close to half of the 500 million population, a percentage that is growing. Some 60 million are in the Arab nations, and nearly 100 million are in Latin America and the Caribbean. In those countries, the desperately poor are a much smaller minority of the population, living far below the average income of their fellow nationals. This is the condition also of some millions of people in the industrial countries, whose numbers have been growing in the decade of economic stagnation.

ECONOMIC DOWNTURN HALTS DEVELOPMENT

In the course of that decade, the favorable trends in human development in the preindustrial world have slowed, leveled, and even reversed. The prospects of the most deprived people there have darkened. These ominous developments have followed on the dampening and stagnation of growth and activity in the world economy dating back to the mid-1970s.

The situation cannot be explained by any accident or malevolence of nature beyond human control—except, perhaps, the location of the planet's last major oil reserves outside the territories of the industrial market economies. In 1973, the sellers of the oil found it in their power to set its price. The response of the industrial market economies terminated the prolonged postwar economic boom. Frightened by the prospect of inflation upon repercussion of the oil-price increase elsewhere in their systems, they put deflationary brakes on their economic growth. Especially for conservative governments in the United Kingdom and the Federal Republic of Germany, such policies comported with ideology; they tightened the money supply, reduced social expenditure, and gave freer rein to private enterprise.

The Reagan administration in the United States similarly committed the economy to management by laissez-faire. It continued the operation of the Federal government, however, in the deficits into which the military intervention in Indochina had taken it. On one side of the ledger, the administration reduced the government's revenue by cutting corporate and personal income taxes, arguing that this would free money for investment and stimulate the economy from the "supply side." On the other side of the ledger, it increased the government's expenditures. To the "uncontrollable" outlays for social security and welfare mandated by the New Deal and the Great Society, the administration added increasing outlays to purchase high-technology military hardware. The combined subtraction and addition tripled the accumulated Federal deficit over the course of the past decade and made interest payment the second biggest item in the budget.

At the high interest rates at which the U.S. Treasury had to cover the deficits, there was little incentive for long-term investment of any of the high incomes freed by the tax cuts. At the bargain prices afforded by the interest-inflated exchange value of the dollar, the same freed-up incomes developed an appetite for manufactured imports. Domestic inflation was thereby averted, but the country's foreign-exchange balance went deeply into deficit as well. With both the government and the affluent citizenry borrowing from abroad, the world's biggest creditor became the world's biggest debtor. The U.S. economy was becalmed with the economies of the rest of the industrial world in the doldrums of no growth.

To the preindustrial nations, the forces thus exerted on the world economy brought deepening distress. Decline in their exports and in the terms of trade for what they did export put one nation after another into current-account deficit. Growth of the "newly industrializing" economies was sustained for a while by the recycling of the petrodollars in loans, especially by the U.S. banks. Interest payments on debt swollen by these easy-money loans at rates inflated by the U.S. Treasury soon increased to punishing percentages even of the big export earnings of the newly industrializing countries. In 1983, the flow of funds between the industrial and preindustrial worlds went into reverse; by 1990, the preindustrial countries had, in effect, extended $200 billion in aid to the recovery of the industrial countries.

The weak and tentative recovery of the industrial market economies in the late 1980s—by which time inflation had discounted the price of oil in current dollars back to its pre-OPEC level—brought no corresponding increase in their imports from the preindustrial world. Especially to the distress of sub-Saharan Africa, the rich nations had learned to live without certain agricultural raw materials and were recycling copper and other metals above ground more efficiently. Food exports from some African countries were displaced by competitive cultivation of their products in Southeast Asia and the Caribbean under sponsorship of the transnational marketers of luxury foods.

Meanwhile, the centrally planned industrial economies had been brought down by the limitations of central planning. The collapse of the Communist regimes in the USSR and Eastern Europe freed the German Democratic Republic for reunification with the Federal Republic of Germany. The industrial world had deep problems and stirring events to keep it self-engrossed. Few people outside the UN agencies concerned took note that the Fourth Development Decade—the first one having been called by the UN General Assembly on motion by John F. Kennedy in 1961—had begun in 1990.

The industrial nations had acquired, nonetheless, a tangible stake in the resumption of development. As early as 1985, James A. Baker, then Secretary of the Treasury of the United States, conceded for the industrial creditors that the preindustrial countries could not service, much less ever pay, their then $800 billion debt without economic growth. Their growth, he acknowledged moreover, would require continued financing by their creditors. The "Baker Plan" made such financing contingent on adjustment of national policies to make the debtor country more attractive to investment from overseas and to indigenous capital so often prone to flight. In negotiations with debtor nations, the World Bank and the International Monetary Fund, as well as other bilateral lenders, were already pressing such policies on debtor governments.

The adjustment measures urged and effected reflect not only the ideology of the creditors but the priorities of the debtor governments. In most countries, balancing of the national budget seriously reduced expenditures and programs that had channeled economic growth into human development. Budget cuts in the low-income countries, most of them in Africa, reduced expenditures on health by 50 percent between 1972 and 1988; the middle-income countries cut their health expenditures by 30 percent. The low-income countries made equal cuts in their education budgets, from 20.5 to 9 percent of their governmental expenditures, during the same period. Under counsel from their creditors and under the burden of their debts, the newly industrializing countries in Latin America cut their health and education budgets as well: Argentina, by 65 percent; Brazil, by 42 percent; Mexico, by 43 percent. Venezuela managed to keep health and education outlays at a constant percentage of the national budget through this decade and a half. Indonesia, alone among the heavily indebted countries, managed to increase that percentage.

Everywhere, the budget cutting uncovered a feature of the social order emerging in the preindustrial countries. One budget line held its own. With reductions going to other lines, the percentage of total government expenditure reserved for "public administration" invariably increased. The government payroll identifies the elite of these new societies and furnishes the living and the social security of the higher-income, more highly educated people. Overloading of that payroll often leaves inadequate funds for office equipment and supplies. Thus, in Kenya, budget cutting increased the percentage of the public administration budget allocated to salaries from 60 percent to 90 percent.

Investment in human development fared better in countries less integrated in the world economy and so not strapped by debt. Foremost among them are the two largest countries, India and China. The policies that have secured improvement in the health and literacy of nearly half the population of the preindustrial world continued in force. Largely unaffected by the world recession, these countries also maintained increases in GNP growth per capita through the early 1980s, China at 5 percent per year and India at more than 2 percent per year. The economies of East Asia, despite entrainment in the recession of the world economy, maintained their rates of investment in human development as well.

The most serious untoward human consequences of the recession relate, of course, to the halting of economic growth and the consequent decline in GNP per capita in so many other preindustrial countries. Many African countries had been experiencing decline in available calories per capita in the 1970s, with population growth outrunning increases in agricultural production. In the 1980s, these countries saw decreases in production, exacerbated by the 1984–1985 drought. The number of malnourished people in Africa is estimated to have increased from 60 million in 1970 to 100 million in 1985. Statistical reporting from these countries tends to be belated and uncertain. Since women and children suffer first and worst in reversal of national fortunes, there must have been a leveling, if not a reversal, of the decline in the rates of infant and under-5 mortality.

The economic downturn in the Latin American countries worked its principal harm on the poorest people there. According to the UN Children's Fund (UNICEF), 32,000 more infants died in Brazil in 1984 than in 1982, indicating a pronounced increase in the infant-mortality rate. The reported infant-mortality rates increased in Uruguay, Guyana, and Guatemala and stopped decreasing in Costa Rica and Panama. Region-wide statistics that show sharp declines in real wages and in food consumption suggest that other Latin American countries have the same increase in human deprivation to report.

THE URBANIZATION OF POVERTY

For the present and for some time to come, however, it appears that poor people will manage to survive on their own, even against rising casualty rates. They do not count on their governments for much help. It would not occur to them that people in the rich countries should, or even might, have an interest in their existence. At this very time, under pressures exerted by the hugest increase in population in history, they are engaged, worldwide, in the most vaulting leap of adaptation ever undertaken by members of the human species. From the villages, dispossessed and without livelihood, they are moving into the cities.

Until about two decades ago, the cities in the middle latitudes were growing principally from within, by the survival and fertility of their residents. Now everywhere, even in the metropolitan countries of Latin America, they are growing by immigration of people from the countryside. At the present rate of resettlement, half of the world population will be living in cities in the first decade of the next century. More than half of the present urban population of the world inhabits the cities of the preindustrial countries; by the year 2000, twice as many people will be living in those cities as in the cities of the industrial countries. Of the 10 urban agglomerations of 10 million or more population in 1990, five were in the preindustrial countries; of the 23 such agglomerations forecast for 2000, 17 will be in those countries [see table on facing page]. Half of the urban population of the preindustrial world will be living in some 500 cities with populations of 1 million or more.

The urban immigrants, the overwhelming majority of them young adults, come in search of a living. To the new cities of Africa, they come straight from the village. On other continents, much migration proceeds from village to town to city in the networks of kinship. The migration is often temporary. Single males come to the city for a season or two of work to send or bring income home before they move their families to the city. They succeed, most of the time, in finding work for at least part of the time; they surely find more alternative ways to make a living than at home in the village. In the mass, they make no inconsiderable contribution to the economic growth of their countries, which their substandard earnings go to subsidize.

The cities of the preindustrial world are ill prepared to receive their expanding populations. A dwelling is most often one room; its average occupancy is 2.23 persons in Africa, 2.17 in Asia, and 1.76 in Latin America. Families and workers at times take turns, occupying rooms and beds in shifts. Islamic countries have their mosque-dwellers; Calcutta and Bombay, their sidewalk-sleepers.

The earlier and more fortunate settlers occupy the slums, older buildings in and around the central cities. The abandonment of Old Delhi for new subdivisions beyond its boundaries left mansions for occupancy at a much higher density. New Delhi, in its outward growth, has engulfed ancient villages; some surviving residences of village landlords do service as urban slum dwellings. In Bombay, early in the century, slumlords and the municipality built *chawls*— three- and four-story tenements without water or sanitation—that still house poor families. New tenements in Hong Kong—15 stories high,

Megacities

25 LARGEST CITIES IN 1980	POPULATION (MILLIONS)	25 LARGEST CITIES IN 2000	PROJECTED POPULATION (MILLIONS)
*Tokyo–Yokohama	17.7	Mexico	25.8
*New York	15.6	São Paolo	24.0
Mexico	14.5	*Tokyo–Yokohama	20.2
São Paolo	12.8	Calcutta	16.5
Shanghai	11.8	Bombay	16.0
*London	10.3	*New York	15.8
Buenos Aires	10.1	Seoul	13.8
Calcutta	9.5	Teheran	13.3
*Los Angeles	9.5	Shanghai	13.3
*Rhein–Ruhr	9.5	Rio de Janeiro	13.3
Rio de Janeiro	9.2	Delhi	13.3
Beijing	9.1	Jakarta	13.2
*Paris	8.7	Buenos Aires	13.0
*Osaka–Kobe	8.7	Karachi	12.0
Bombay	8.5	Dhaka	11.2
Seoul	8.5	Cairo–Giza	11.1
*Moscow	8.2	Manila	11.1
Tianjin	7.7	*Los Angeles	11.0
Cairo–Giza	6.9	Bangkok	10.7
*Chicago	6.8	*Osaka–Kobe	10.5
*Milan	6.7	Beijing	10.4
Jakarta	6.7	*Moscow	10.4
Manila	6.0	*London	10.0
Delhi	5.9	Tianjin	9.1
Baghdad	3.9	*Paris	8.7

*In industrial countries

URBANIZATION OF POVERTY *is already well under way: 15 of the largest cities in the world are in the preindustrial countries. By A.D. 2000, 17 cities of more then 10 million population will be in those countries. The cities are ill-prepared for their populations, about half of which will live in shantytowns.*

supplied with water, sanitation, and electricity and festooned with their denizens' laundry on poles projecting from the balconies— dominate the city's skyline at its waterfront.

The more recent migrants occupy the shantytowns that burgeon alongside all preindustrial cities. Of the 20 million population of Mexico City, 8 million live in its illegal subdivisions, and the *favelas, citas miserias, barriadas,* and *calampas* around other Latin American cities hold like percentages of their populations. More than 65 percent of the population of the fast-growing cities of Africa live in their shantytowns, and the percentage is growing. The inhabitants of these settlements have had to build them most often on the least desirable land, on steep hillsides or in wet lowlands not otherwise regarded as fit for dwelling places. At times they succeed in taking over more desirable open land that is hoarded around the preindustrial cities, often by government agencies for purposes that go for years unfulfilled.

At the first appearance of these unsightly and unseemly communities at the edge of city after city, they have excited the authorities and the better-off townspeople to take action against them. They have been burned and bulldozed, at times with the counsel of well-meaning advisors from some industrial country. They have always been rebuilt, however, either on the site or elsewhere, and new shantytowns have burgeoned alongside them. Augusto Pinochet did succeed in driving the shantytowns of Santiago, Chile, outside the city limits, forcing their resolute inhabitants to accept a two-hour daily round trip to work.

The shantytowns, impermanent as they appear and vulnerable as they are, have persisted to become part of the cityscape in the preindustrial world. They are there to stay for some long time on the periphery of the fastest-growing cities in the world. Whatever the plans of the formal city, they are shaping the growth of many of those cities. Springing up along new highways, overrunning and incorporating existing villages, shantytowns are connecting city to city in new urban agglomerations.

From the Indonesian words *cota,* for "city," and *desa,* for "country," the geographer T. G. McGee has coined the term *cotadesasi* for this extension of the diversity of urban economic activity into the countryside of the preindustrial countries. This mode of urbanization is familiar to the industrial world as urban sprawl. In these exurban settlements, people are able to hedge the insecurity of urban employment by raising pigs and chickens and cultivating truck gardens for the city market. Their time is thus available at lower pay to entrepreneurs who follow them out of the central city to set up light manufacturing plants and consumer-service establishments. The growth of the central cities, notably including Calcutta, has begun to slacken in favor of this occupation of exurbia.

It has proved impossible, except in the centrally planned economies, to stop the implosion of people from the villages into the cities. China has stemmed and diverted the pressure of its growing population by locating industries in the villages, by building new industrial cities, and by rigorous policing of internal passports. In Latin America, Cuba reduced the pressure on Havana by land reforms that settled much of the population on lands formerly tied up in *latifundia,* by decentralizing its modest industrial development, and by the rigorously egalitarian distribution of its average $2000 GNP per capita, which has helped to bring the rate of population growth down to 1 percent. The continuing growth, at 1.2 percent, of China's one-fifth of the world population has compelled the country to permit its bigger and older cities to grow. Shanghai is already one of the more-than-10-million agglomerations; Beijing is projected to join it in A.D. 2000. China has succeeded, however, in housing its urban populations in buildings that meet its minimal standards, at least, by massive building campaigns.

Such campaigns in the market economies of the preindustrial world have not fared as well. In a slum-clearance drive, authorities in Seoul, South Korea, displaced 100,000 households to "replace" them with 16,000 dwellings. Nigeria, in a $3.5 billion campaign that the country could ill afford, built 100,000 new dwellings, which were promptly occupied by the better-off. In Karachi, the Pakistani government sponsored a drive that was to build 30,000 to 40,000 housing units; the drive ended after eight years with 800 units built. The housing campaign undertaken by Tanzania in that country's first five-year plan built no more units than it demolished. The saying in those countries goes: the money was spent, so the project was completed.

Housing, most authorities have now been forced to concede, is not the problem. The shanties embody the self-sufficient ingenuity of village dwellers who have always built their own shelters. At no cost to the economy, they use materials available in the countryside, from demolitions in the formal city and from the city dump. The dwellings are sufficient to the climate. Inside, they are most often spotless, every piece of furniture homemade and, if not, just as cherished and well kept. The problem, in fact, is elsewhere: water and sanitation, to begin with.

In the country as well as in the city, securing a supply of potable water within reasonable walking distance constitutes the most urgent public-health objective of the preindustrial world. It is the water poor people drink that gives them most of their illness. The water most often comes from surface sources that are invariably contaminated; it requires intensive and expensive treatment. Unless other provision is made, it is available in shantytowns only from vendors pushing wheeled tanks. The price people pay is usually much more than enough to finance the delivery of water by pipe. The problem, then, is to mount the sociopolitical enterprise required to install such service.

The attempt to supply potable water confronts authorities in the preindustrial countries with an open-ended demand. Experience has shown that the amount of water consumed is a function of its availability. From a communal tap within a walking distance of 200 meters, a consumer will draw 20 to 40 liters of water per day. A single tap in the yard of a dwelling encourages that consumption to rise to 40 to 60 liters per day. In upper-income dwellings, with kitchen and bathrooms, consumption per capita climbs to 200 liters per day. Potable water, abundantly available in most industrial countries, proves thus to be one of the primary blessings of industrial revolution. Its supply is a sensitive indicator of the progress of the revolution.

What contaminates the water most often—and most consequentially—is human excrement. The esthetics of living with feces in gutters and open sewers is not the first concern of people who are compelled to do so. Even a friendly observer has remarked on "their insensitivity to the quality of their environment." That is their accommodation to the environment imposed by poverty.

The monthly cost per household of municipal sewerage comes to about half the income of a low-income household in a preindustrial country. This mode of disposal, in any case, requires political rather than market decision to mobilize the necessary resources. Evidently, nations as well as households face needs with prior claims on income. Of 3119 towns and cities in India, eight had sewer systems in 1985; 114 cities of more than 50,000 population pollute the Ganges with untreated sewage and street run-off. Worldwide, to furnish sanitation for more than 3 billion new urban inhabitants will require the investment of $1000 billion (in 1978 dollars) before the year 2000.

The metabolism of any city lays considerable burden on the environment. A city of 1 million population in an industrial country draws 625,000 tons of water per day, consumes 2000 tons of food, and burns 9500 tons of fuel. To the near environment, it returns 500,000 tons of waste water, 2000 tons of solid waste, and 950 tons of gaseous and particulate air pollutants. Industrial economies are responding to the environmental consequences of the return flow with increasing outlays for waste treatment and recycling. Until that $1000 billion is invested, the cities of the poor must continue to devastate their environments.

The shantytowns, squatting illegally on the land, their improvised houses in violation of the building codes, do not appear at first on the books of the cities they embarrass. Most often, in consequence, they go without the standard municipal services— without schools, public transportation, waste collection, police protection, and electric power, as well as water and sanitation.

Effort to get one of these services to a shantytown most often misses the people in greatest need of its benefits. Thus, the strategy of providing "site services"—water and sewerage to begin with, instead of attempting to build housing—endows a shantytown plot with value. The value brings an offer that the poorest households cannot refuse.

Access to public services constitutes a major mode of redistribution of wealth and income in the industrial economies. Skewed access to those services in the preindustrial countries increases the real gap between their rich and their poor.

What at last compels attention to the shantytown is the organized agitation of its population. The people organize first in self-defense against the harsh fallout from the meanness of their existence that pits them in intense competition with one another at every income niche. The worst of what is said and thought about life in these communities is, at times and places, true. They are beset by crime, vice, and violence. As in the underclass of the U.S. economy, one-third of the households are headed by a single female. The casualty rate among small children, especially from trauma incurred in unsafe housing and in the streets, is high.

In the *favelas* of Rio de Janeiro, which held one-third of the city's population in the 1960s, the anthropologist Janice E. Perlman found vigorous and effective community organizations. They usually had large memberships, a small core of activists, and an aggressive leader evoked by the hard circumstances. From self-policing, they went on to challenge the city establishment. The older communities did secure services for which they agitated—a community standpipe for water and even the piping of water to some of the households, perhaps a low-cost shallow sewer system, an extension of the city transportation system, police protection, a school.

The new urban population thus, eventually, confronts every city with the fact of its existence. Jorge Hardoy, who has studied the process at close range in Latin America, concludes: "The courage to challenge repression has become a non-conventional resource for the construction and management of cities."

In full expression of the social animal in man, the *favelas* are rife with organization. There are soccer clubs and sewing clubs, church parishes and religious societies, and the musical groups and carnival clubs that supply the brightest color to the Mardi Gras that makes Rio famous. In other cities, the poor thus also make the best of their circumstances.

INFORMAL AND FORMAL ECONOMIES

Relations between the shantytowns and the formal cities remain, however, necessarily at arms length. The shantytowns are the seat of the informal economy, which is defined by its own non-tax-paying illegality. Against their economic competition, the lower-income groups in the formal economy jealously defend their status and monopolize the benefits of what social services they have cadged from the state. The governing elite has the full support of these lesser people for the measures they take to keep the shantytowns and their people at the social and economic margin.

The people of the shantytowns get what little cash income they have in service to the formal economy. In the morning, men and women go out from their homes to the city, there to employment as domestics, to the meanest jobs in shops, laundries, hotels, restaurants, garages, and like consumer-service establishments, to casual labor on construction sites, to running errands, shining shoes, or pedalling pedicabs—in sum, to work in all the forgotten nooks and crannies of the formal economy.

A major industry of the informal economy in every preindustrial country is the collecting and recycling of solid waste. It employs 1 or 2 percent of the informal work force everywhere.

"Waste" is culturally defined; the formal economy's waste is the informal economy's raw material. The waste output of the industrial

economies averages 1 to 2 kilograms per day per capita. In preindustrial countries, the average is half that, but most of the waste there
is generated by the upper-income groups, and their output ap-
proximates that of comparable income earners in the industrial
countries.

Like every other material good, salvageable solid waste is
relatively scarce in preindustrial countries. While paper makes up 37
percent of the solid waste of London, it is only 3 percent of the waste
output of Calcutta. Metals constitute 13 percent of the solid waste of
the borough of Brooklyn but only 4 percent of Jakarta's.

The recycling of paper and metals in the preindustrial
countries starts at the source, at the curbside. The collection as well
as the production of waste is a function of neighborhood income. In
Tunis, the rich quarters are cleaned up two or three times a day—by
the gleaners and scavengers of waste, not by the municipality. In
Cairo, the *wahiya* clan monopolizes the collection of domestic waste,
and the *zabaleen* controls the sorting of the waste and sale of
salvaged materials, starting with 2000 tons of paper per month, to
recyclers.

By such enterprise, half of the waste paper of Mexico City gets
recycled, twice the world average. Since the manufacture of molded
paper products and even some grades of paper from waste paper
requires small investment and since the raw material is so assiduously
collected at such low return to the collectors, the recycling of paper
is well advanced in the preindustrial countries.

In contrast with the waste of the formal economy, the waste
from the shantytowns is mostly putrescible food leavings. In Calcutta,
"garbage farms" compost this material, from the formal as well as the
informal economy, for sale to truck gardens close to the city.

To the formal economy, the informal thus contributes wealth,
and its people render services that the better-off could not otherwise
afford. The abundance of domestic servants makes life grand and
easy for upper-income households in every preindustrial country. In
Bombay, as a child boards the suburban train for school in the city, a
"bearer" sets out from home on the run with her lunch for delivery at
midday; in Amedhabad, a servant sleeps on the marble floor at the
guest-room door. Homes in the shantytown are often sweatshops,
employing the women and children of the household in the sewing
of textiles for the country's export trade. In Manila, the "paratransit"
service of the battered "jeepneys" provides 64 percent of public

transport; in Kanpur, the numerous pedicabs bear 88 percent of it. Rio de Janeiro is endowed by the builders of its shantytowns with $100 million worth of housing. The GNP of the poorest countries in sub-Saharan Africa is equaled, it is estimated, by the activity of their informal economies.

Some of the most important economic activity of the informal economy goes on inside the shantytown. Much of this is non-monetary. Services are bartered for services: a house repair for a truck repair; a washing done in exchange for a yard cleanup. The shantytown is largely self-sustaining. Its current balance with the formal economy runs, therefore, strongly positive, from the services its inhabitants render to the formal economy at low cost.

The fragile formal economies of many preindustrial countries depend upon this crucial subsidy from their poor. If its value could be calculated, it would be a large multiple of the economic assistance they receive from the industrial countries. For some time to come, the formal economies will maintain their distance from the informal.

The leap to urbanization that is the experience of rising numbers of people clears for them the path of human development. City people, even the shantytown dwellers, enjoy better health than villagers. The rates of infant, under-5, and maternal mortality are lower in the city. Adult literacy is higher, and a higher percentage of the children go to school. Some have gone to the university. Upon migration to the city, these people find themselves entrained in industrial revolution.

People enjoying better circumstances in the industrial countries may find it difficult to recognize this translation of existence from country to city as human development. For the new urban residents in the preindustrial countries, there is no doubt that they have experienced progress. With Lord Kelvin, designer of heat (that is, Promethean) engines, they will declare: "I found a better way!" They have begun to know practicability of purpose.

THE HUMAN DEVELOPMENT INDEX

Necessarily, and on the whole, the indicators of human development correlate and move positively with the economic indicators. As the preindustrial countries progress in their industrial revolutions, that $1000 billion investment, already under way, is beginning to bring potable water and sanitation to the shantytowns. Value added by manufacture will generate thousands of billions of dollars more for investment, which will bring the shantytowns into the cities and the informal economies into the formal.

In the *Human Development Report 1990,* the statisticians of the UN Development Program propose a new kind of index of progress. It is to stand alongside GNP per capita and to counter the "narrow and misleading attention to only one dimension of human life" that is fixed by that familiar index number. The "human development index number" is the summary expression of three indicators: life expectancy, literacy, and "income for a decent living standard." Life expectancy serves as the comprehensive surrogate for the indicators of biological development and health. Literacy is, of course, the threshold for enrollment in the industrial revolution; the literacy rate summarizes other indicators of the state of a country's educational system.

The personal-income indicator in the human development index is a richer number than GNP per capita. The International Price Comparison Project, in which a half dozen international agencies are collaborating, provides income numbers adjusted to "purchasing-power parity" that indicate what standard of living the average income in each country will buy. In addition to relative exchange values of currencies and price levels, the adjustment reckons with the value of nonmonetized goods and services in the village economy and the value of the social goods and services not purchased by personal incomes in centrally planned economies and in market economies as well. Since "there are diminishing returns in the conversion of income into the fulfillment of human needs," these numbers in the human-development index are transformed to their logarithms. This operation narrows the gap between the top and bottom incomes stated in GNP per capita.

Thus, the GNP-per-capita scale, by which national economies are most often compared, suggests that the Swiss, at $21,330 per capita in 1987, were 142 times better off than the people of Zaire, at $150 per capita. After adjustment by purchasing power parity and transformation to the logarithm, that difference shrinks to about 20 times. While it would take teams of anthropologists, social psychologists, and, perhaps, psychoanalysts to prove it, the smaller figure seems more plausible. The gap of 20 times is wide enough.

Averaged together, the three chosen indicators of human development produce a composite index number. A concededly first experiment in the fashioning of such an index, it tells a great deal more about how people fare in a given country than does the GNP per capita. The human development index ranks Japan at the top and Niger at the bottom. On the GNP-per-capita scale, Japan's $15,760 places it fourth, behind Switzerland's $21,330. The life-expectancy component of the index, as summary surrogate for other health indicators, puts Japan in first place, however, and Switzerland in third place on the human development scale. Niger similarly exchanges places with Zaire on the two scales. In twentieth place on the GNP per capita scale, Niger goes to the bottom of the human development scale with a life expectancy of only 45 years and an adult literacy rate of 14 percent, while a life expectancy of 53 years and an adult literacy of 62 percent lift Zaire, with the lowest GNP per capita, to twentieth place on the human-development scale [see table on page 307].

In second place on the GNP-per-capita scale, at $18,530, the United States drops to nineteenth place on the human-development scale—behind Ireland and Spain, among others. Its life expectancy of 76 years is significantly reduced by the experience of the country's poor, especially the black poor, and by its infant-mortality rate of 10 per thousand. Its adult literacy rate of 96 percent compares to Japan's 100 percent and reflects the degraded state of the country's urban educational systems.

The order in which the human-development index ranks a country among the 130 countries in the world of more than 1 million population thus directs attention to what the people of that country have made of their economic growth or lack of it. Review of the more specific social indicators, prompted by the summary index number, invariably yields insights into a country's social policies and arrangements. In general, as will be seen, those that rank higher on the index are those that have taken measures to that end by redistribution of income and investment in human capital.

At the top of the list and credited with "high human development" appear, of course, all of the 31 industrial nations. The average GNP per capita there is high enough to lift all but a minority of the population in each country out of poverty, even with the bottom 20 percent receiving but a tenth of the share in the national income that goes to the top 20 percent. Counted in that bottom share in the incomes of the market economies are the income transfers that, in all those countries, redress imperfections in the distribution of income by the market. Not counted in personal incomes in either the market or the (formerly) centrally planned economies, however, are the large expenditures on public services, human capital, and income transfers that absorb 20 percent and more of their GNP. These expenditures raise the qualitative indicators of human development throughout industrial civilization.

Human Development Report 1990 also places 15 preindustrial nations in this top rank. It is no surprise to find among them the "newly industrializing countries" of East Asia and Latin America, given the high GNP-per-capita figures for each of them. However, this group of preindustrial countries also includes four countries—Chile, Costa Rica, Cuba, and Jamaica—whose GNP-per-capita figures are smaller than those of countries that rank well below them on the human-development scale.

Chile jumps 34 places from its rank on the GNP-per-capita scale to its rank on the human-development scale; Costa Rica, 26 places; and Cuba and Jamaica, 25 places. All through the Pinochet dictatorship, the world recession, and the "adjustment" compelled by its creditors, Chile has maintained expenditures on education and medical care, including long-standing maternal-care and infant-care programs targeted at lower-income groups. In the decade beginning in 1975, the country's life expectancy increased from 65 to 72 years; infant mortality declined from 58 to 22 per thousand live births, and adult literacy increased from 89 to 98 percent. In Chile, and in Jamaica as well, such policies compensated for disparities in the distribution of income that are typical of Latin America. In Costa Rica and in Cuba, especially, yield from social expenditures was amplified by more equitable distribution of their small GNP per capita.

The ranking of the oil-exporting countries of the Arabian Peninsula and North Africa moves from one scale to the other in precisely the opposite direction. On the human-development index, Kuwait, Saudi Arabia, the United Arab Emirates, Oman, Libya, and Algeria fall 34 to 50 places out of their ranking on the GNP-per-capita scale. They land among the 40 countries credited with "medium human development," but they are lifted there by their high average GNP per capita; on the other components of the index and the indicators that underlie them, the oil countries compare with some of the poorest countries in the "low human development" category. In the well-being of their relatively small populations, a little of the enormous tide of oil revenue could have gone a long way.

China ranks nineteenth among the 40 "medium human

Ranking of Nations on Human Development Index

COUNTRY	HDI	HDI – GNP	e(0)	<5MR	H%	E%	Litcy	TFR	20% T/B	GNP/cap
Human development index >.800										
Japan	130	4	78	8	4.9	5.0	100	1.7	4.3	15,760
France	123	4	76	10	6.6	5.3	100	1.8	7.7	15,830
United Kingdom	121	8	76	11	5.3	5.3	100	1.8	5.7	10,420
Germany (FRG)	119	−1	75	10	6.3	4.5	100	1.4	5.0	14,400
Ireland	114	8	74	9	7.8	6.9	99	2.5	5.5	6,120
United States	112	−17	76	13	4.5	5.3	96	1.8	7.5	18,530
Israel	111	3	76	14	2.1	7.3	95	2.9	6.7	6,800
Chile	107	34	72	26	2.1	5.2	98	2.7		1,310
Czechoslovakia	106	4	72	15	4.2	5.2	98	2.0		5,820
USSR	105	4	70	32	3.5	5.2	100	2.4		4,550
Costa Rica	103	26	75	22	5.4	4.7	93	3.2		1,610
Hungary	101	14	71	19	3.2	3.8	98	1.7	5.2	2,240
Argentina	99	10	71	37	1.6	3.3	96	2.9	11.3	2,390
Poland	98	15	72	18	4.0	4.5	98	2.2		2,070
South Korea	97	5	70	33	0.3	4.9	94	2.0	6.8	2,690
Cuba	92	26	74	18	3.2	6.2	96	1.7		1,600
Mexico	91	10	69	68	1.7	2.8	90	3.5	19.6	1,830
Venezuela	89	−6	70	44	2.7	6.6	87	3.7	18.2	3,320
Kuwait	88	−34	73	22	2.9	4.6	70	4.8		14,610
Malaysia	85	5	70	32	1.8	7.9	74	3.5	14.4	3,850

HDI: Human development index ranking (HDI)
HDI – GNP: HDI minus gross national product (GNP) ranking
e(0): Life expectancy at birth
< 5MR: Under-5 mortality rate
H%: Health expenditures as a percentage of GNP
E%: Education expenditures as a percentage of GNP
Litcy: Literate adults as a percentage of population
TFR: Total fertility rate
20% T/B: Income distribution: Share in GNP of top 20 percent income group as a
multiple of share of bottom 20 percent income group.

development" nations, lifted by its revolutionary enterprise 44 places
from its rank among the nations at the bottom of the GNP-per-capita
scale. Sri Lanka ranks second among that group, lifted 45 places by
less revolutionary interventions of the state sanctioned by tradition

COUNTRY	HDI	HDI – GNP	e(0)	<5MR	H%	E%	Litcy	TFR	20% T/B	GNP/cap
Human development index > .500										
Sri Lanka	83	45	71	43	2.1	5.2	87	2.6	8.3	400
Brazil	81	–5	65	85	1.3	3.4	78	3.4	33.7	2,020
Thailand	78	23	66	49	1.3	4.1	91	2.5	8.8	850
U. Arab Emirates	77	–50	71	32	1.0	2.2	20	4.8		15,830
Iraq	76	–20	65	94	0.8	3.7	89	6.3		3,020
Libya	67	–36	62	119	3.0	10.1	66	6.8		5,460
China	66	44	70	43	1.4	2.7	69	2.4		290
Philippines	65	19	64	73	0.7	1.7	86	4.3	10.3	590
Saudi Arabia	64	–43	64	98	4.0	10.6	50	7.2		6,200
Indonesia	54	18	57	119	0.7	3.5	74	3.2	7.3	450
Myanmar	50	39	61	95	1.0	2.1	79	4.0		200
Human development index < .500										
Kenya	42	12	59	113	1.1	5.0	60	8.1	25.0	790
Cameroon	41	–23	52	153	0.7	2.8	61	5.7		970
India	37	12	59	149	0.9	3.4	43	4.3	7.0	300
Pakistan	36	3	58	166	0.2	2.2	30	6.4		350
Tanzania	35	23	54	176	1.2	4.2	75	7.1		180
Cote d'Ivoire	32	–20	53	142	1.1	5.0	42	7.4	25.6	740
Nigeria	24	–12	52	174	0.4	1.4	43	5.5		370
Bangladesh	23	6	52	188	0.6	2.2	33	6.4	7.2	470
Zaire	20	15	53	138	0.8	0.4	62	6.1		150
Niger	1	–19	45	228	0.8	4.0	14	7.1		260

INVESTMENT IN HUMAN CAPITAL *and equity in income distribution correlate with marked contrasts among nations in other indicators of human development. Thus, Brazil, with extreme disparity in income distribution and relatively low expenditures on health and education, shows high under-5 mortality rate and low level of literacy compared to Venezuela and Sri Lanka. Favorable indicators in those columns correlate inversely with total fertility rates, as in South Korea and Cuba, TFR of 2.0 is close to replacement fertility rate. The indicators for China, with GNP per capita at $290, compare favorably with those of richer countries.*

from its colonial past. The people have enjoyed free medical care and free education to the university level since 1945. Until 1979, the state subsidized 70 percent of the rice they consumed; such subsidy now supports a much smaller percentage of consumption, but it is targeted to those who need it most. In this group, Vietnam, Laos, and Myanmar (Burma) show comparable jumps—40, 37, and 39 places, respectively—from their rank on the GNP scale; all are classified as "centrally planned economies."

In reflection of the substantial social expenditures of Thailand and Indonesia, these two market economies gain 23 and 13 places, respectively, on the human-development scale. The third of the economies of Southeast Asia spurred to fast growth by Japanese investment, Malaysia already appears in the "high human development" category.

Among the 44 countries in the "low human development" group, four climb a significant number of places from their rank on the GNP-per-capita scale. Kampuchea (Cambodia), despite civil disintegration in the 1970s under the spillover of the war in Vietnam and civil war ever since, climbs 38 places. In sub-Saharan Africa, expenditure on health and education lift Zambia and Madagascar 24 places, and Tanzania 23 places, above their GNP ranking among the 20 poorest nations. Most of the other 40 countries in the "low human development" category, the poorest in the world, lose places. The human condition in those countries is, by comparison with others on the human-development scale, worse than is suggested even by their low GNP per capita. In contrast, India manages, with sustained social expenditure by the central government and the more progressive states, to lift its 800 million population, larger than the combined populations of the other countries in the "low human development" group, 12 places higher on the scale.

THE END OF POPULATION GROWTH

The ranking of countries on the human-development scale corresponds remarkably well with projections of world population

---

(Facing page) RANKING OF NATIONS *by GNP per capita and on human development index (HDI) gives insight into income distribution and social expenditures. The oil-producing nations Kuwait and Saudi Arabia fall 30 or more places from rank on GNP to rank on HDI scale; Chile, Sri Lanka, and China rise 30 places.*

Comparison of GNP Rank and HDI Rank
of Various Countries, 1990

GNP rank			HDI rank
129	United States	Japan	130
127	U. Arab Emirates	France	123
126	Japan	United Kingdom	121
122	Kuwait	Germany (FRG)	119
120	Germany (FRG)	Ireland	114
119	France	United States	112
113	United Kingdom	Israel	111
108	Israel	Chile	107
107	Saudi Arabia	Czechoslovakia	106
106	Ireland	USSR	105
103	Libya	Costa Rica	103
102	Czechoslovakia	Hungary	101
101	USSR	Argentina	99
96	Iraq	Poland	98
95	Venezuela	South Korea	97
92	South Korea	Cuba	92
89	Argentina	Mexico	91
		Venezuela	89
87	Hungary	Kuwait	88
85	Brazil	Malaysia	85
83	Poland		
81	Mexico	Sri Lanka	83
80	Malaysia	Brazil	81
77	Costa Rica	Thailand	78
73	Chile	U. Arab Emirates	77
66	Cuba	Iraq	76
64	Cameroon	Libya	67
55	Thailand	China	66
52	Cote d'Ivoire	Philippines	65
46	Philippines	Saudi Arabia	64
		Indonesia	54
41	Indonesia	Myanmar	50
38	Sri Lanka		
36	Nigeria	Kenya	42
33	Pakistan	Cameroon	41
30	Kenya	India	37
25	India	Pakistan	36
22	China	Tanzania	35
20	Niger	Cote d'Ivoire	32
12	Tanzania	Nigeria	24
11	Myanmar	Bangladesh	23
6	Bangladesh	Zaire	20
5	Zaire	Niger	1

growth made by the variously responsible UN agencies and the World Bank. These projections are anchored in fine-grained demographic data which the international civil service assembles from national records. For all but the poorest nations, the continuous updating of data on the age–sex structure and on fertility and mortality rates makes it possible to construct live computer models of populations. Together they make a model of the world population that responds realistically to questions put to it. It is this model and the computer exercise of it that underpin current projections of the arrival of the world population at an ultimate stable total of 10 or 11 billion early in the twenty-second century.

Recent projections show the world population increasing to a total of somewhat more than 6 billion in the year 2000. Significantly, they show fertility in countries with a total population 3.3 billion in 2000 reaching the "replacement" rate [see page 104] during the following decade. That portion of the world population continues to grow, from lengthened life expectancies, for about a generation thereafter to a projected stable total of 4.4 billion.

The 3.3 billion is the population in 2000, first of all, of the countries classified as having attained "high human development." These are the industrial countries, many of them already at the replacement fertility rate, plus most of the newly industrializing countries that are now trending toward that rate. To the 3.3 billion total, however, a significant group of other countries, ranked on the human development scale in the "medium" category, also add their populations.

The largest addition to the total is the population of China, with its population projected at 1.2 billion in A.D. 2000. To see that country arriving at the replacement fertility rate before 2010, it must be assumed that the present trend in fertility, fostered by the country's equitable income distribution and its heavy investment in the formation of human capital, will persist. The 212 million population of Indonesia projected for 2000 makes the next largest contribution, joined by Thailand, with 66 million, and Malaysia, with 11 million. The smaller populations of Chile, Costa Rica, Cuba, and Jamaica will also have arrived at the replacement fertility rate.

The projections show India bringing the next hugest national population, 994 million in 2000, to the replacement fertility rate early in the following decade. The growth momentum in the Indian population, owing to the presence of a large number of young people with their childbearing years ahead of them, carries the country to a projected ultimate stationary population of 1.7 billion. That is 100 million larger than the ultimate 1.6 billion population projected for China.

The addition of India's 1.7 billion to the 4.4 billion accounts for about 6 billion of the world's projected stable population of 10 to 11 billion. To that ultimate world population, the last population explosion will add the balance of 4 to 5 billion.

The explosion that will produce nearly half of the projected ultimate world population presently engages the populations of the countries recognized as the poorest and most backward. Among these are Pakistan and Bangladesh in South Asia; Iran and the Arab countries of Asia Minor and North Africa, including the richest oil exporters; most of the countries in sub-Saharan Africa, and the lagging Latin American economies. They have a present combined population of 1 billion. Fully half of this population is increasing at 3 percent or more each year; the rest, at more than 2.5 percent per year. By A.D. 2000 their numbers will have nearly doubled to 1.7 billion.

As the high crude growth rate indicates, these people are only now entering the first phase of the demographic transition. It is not anticipated that they will complete the second phase, with arrival at the replacement fertility rate, much before the middle of the next century. The large numbers of people then under age 15 will give this population a strong growth momentum that will level off at the estimated ultimate 4 to 5 billion at the end of the century.

The UN demographers are the first to insist that their projections are not predictions. The data and the variables incorporated in the models are purely demographic, with "stylized" assumptions supplying the independent variables. Thus, for sub-Saharan Africa, "total fertility rates are assumed to remain constant for some time and then to decline until the replacement rate is reached." The economic conditions and social policies that underlie the initial demographic conditions in various regions of the world, and those that might bring the scheduled decline in fertility in sub-Saharan Africa, are not specified. Nonetheless, implicit in the projections must be the assumption that the generalized trends of recent decades in these external circumstances—the stylized "exogenous variables" in the demographic equations—will continue and that they are going to improve, somehow, in sub-Saharan Africa.

The huge contribution to the projected ultimate world population from the 1 billion people in the poorest and most backward nations could be huger still. The further out the computer projections run, the more uncertain they become. What can be predicted is that postponement of the arrival of those nations (so many of them in sub-Saharan Africa) at the replacement fertility rate will carry them to a still larger population base from which their growth might then be hoped to level off. The assumed timing of the decline in their fertility must be sustained by the necessary antecedent improvement in their economic and social circumstances.

The circumstances that established present trends in the population of China and India are equally crucial to setting the date when those countries reach the replacement fertility rate. The contribution the two countries are projected to make to the portion of the population that first halts its growth is very likely the minimum. It could be much larger if their arrival at the replacement fertility rate is postponed by unfavorable change in their economic life and social policies.

On other sets of assumptions, computer runs incorporating the same demographic data have projected world populations as large as 18 to 20 billion in the twenty-second century.

That possibility ought to fortify the resolution of institutions and of people in possession of the power to encourage the industrial revolution of the preindustrial countries. It gives compelling ratification to policies that secure the benefits of that revolution to human development. A less crowded world is surely, at least from the point of view of the earlier generation, a happier one for everyone's grandchildren.

Continued stagnation of the world economy could reverse the near-term slackening in the rate of population growth in the preindustial world and compel projection of an ultimate population much larger than 10 billion. On the other hand, concerted action taken now to hasten industrial revolution there, especially to restart the economic growth of the sub-Saharan countries, could reduce the projected 10 to 11 billion world population by a billion or more.

At this fork in the road, old Adam keeps his grip firm on the wheel. Self-interest, as always, makes the worst-case analysis: there will never be enough to go around. All must continue, therefore, the war against all.

Thus, in the dawn of the day after the Cold War, the dictator of

Iraq extended his oil claims by occupying Kuwait. (Failing this opportunity to rouse the Arab nation, Saddam Hussein dispersed the Kuwaiti population of workers and intellectuals from other Arab countries, who lost all they had.) Operation Desert Storm rescued the supply of oil to the industrial countries and secured it at prices that permit the continued wasteful consumption of this diminishing resource and discourage development of alternative sources of primary energy. Incidental to this ugly episode, perhaps a tenth of the rescued oil pool went to foul the sea and sky. That cost is unregretted by most Arabs; it is not their oil.

They and the other peoples of the preindustrial world remain duly impressed, however, by the overnight dismantling of the electric power, communication, transportation, and municipal service systems in Iraq, that represented a relatively superior level of development among Arab countries. The remounting of the technology of mass destruction for rapid deployment on the periphery of the industrial world has conveyed a plain message. In the words of Crown Prince Hassan of Jordan: "If the oil wars have begun, the water wars may not be far behind—and then conflicts stemming from the consequences of soil loss, forest loss, high global temperatures and rising sea levels."

While the familiar old future holds the foreground, it can be seen that people yearn to see another. The United States celebrated its military triumph alone. Persisting economic doldrums pre-empted attention in the politics of the industrial nations that joined the United States in the United Nations police action. Overriding U.S. reluctance and objection, the European community is seeking the integration of Eastern Europe, including the republics of the former Soviet Union, in the world economy. (Just as Japan has been building its Greater East Asia Co-Prosperity Sphere, so Germany's *Drang nach Osten* may now win in peace objectives sought by violence in World War II.)

Among the leaders of the European community are those, notably Richard von Weizsaecker and Gro Harlem Brundtland, who recognize that the reunification of the industrial world makes it possible now to render the assistance necessary to accelerate industrial revolution in the countries of the poor. There are signs even that the U.S. electorate has had its fill of adventure abroad and looks to Washington for action on the decay of the domestic economy that has begun to threaten public order.

To Accelerate Economic Development

The first thing the industrial nations must do to improve the world's prospects is to get their own economies back to work. One way to do that is to put them to work on the worldwide industrial revolution. The market economies tolerate the presence of unused capacity and unmet need—of unemployment and poverty—in their populations. The (formerly) centrally planned economies, which never began to meet consumer demand, have idle capacity to produce capital goods. Revival of the industrial economies will renew their demand for all of the commodities, in addition to oil, that the preindustrial countries want to export. Their exports can begin, at last, to finance their industrialization. Without growth in the world economy that has made them its dependents, those countries will see growth only in their populations.

Not much can be done, however, until something is done about the debt that overhangs the richest and the poorest of the preindustrial countries. The debt must be compromised at the earliest date to permit their governments and business communities to extend the time horizon of the planning and investment they must do. Some large portion of the total will be recognized as never to be paid. To amortize and pay the interest on the debt of $1200 billion would consume in its entirety the earnings on a half century of exports from the poor to the rich countries at the 1980s annual average of $300 billion. Some of the debt should be credited as paid in the reverse flow of funds from the poor to the rich over that decade. The excess interest paid in that flow of funds was set by the profligate mismanagement of the U.S. economy.

Reality has already been conceded by the "Baker plan" and by the later "Brady plan," which defer payment of principal and even of interest and proffer new loans in return for the institution of economic "discipline" in governmental policies. The imperiled U.S. financial system is in no position to insist upon repayment of its share of the $1200 billion debt. With the largest banks in the United States on the "troubled" list of the Federal regulators, the taxpayers are already being prepared to assume the risk of a major part of the petrodollar debt owed by the newly industrializing countries. Erasure of the debt of the poorest countries seems easier to manage politically. It is "official" debt, already owing to governments. The money can be loaned again in the form of economic-development funds, on the precedent of the funding of the grain shipments to India under Public Law 480. The countries in sub-Saharan Africa, the world's poorest, owe $270 billion in official debt. As a start on the funding of the still huger capital requirement needed to reignite their economic development, former UN Secretary General Xavier Pérez de Cuellar has proposed that the existing debt be cancelled.

For best return on the renewed financing of the worldwide industrial revolution, the bilateral and multilateral bankers of the world economy will extend financing in the pragmatic spirit that is the real genius of the market. Loans to governments will credit public expenditure on health and education as investment in human capital, not "consumption expenditures" charged to the current budget. Lenders will more usefully address the more uncomfortable questions of overmanning and corruption in national budgets. Some imbalance in a national budget and a degree of inflation will be discounted as stimuli and symptoms of economic growth, not unheard of in industrial countries. Overvaluation of a currency will be offset against unfairness in the terms of trade. The performance of a public industrial enterprise will not be assessed exclusively by its bottom line; it will be valued also for the patriation of value-added and the transfer of technology it secures, for the pioneering of a backward region, for the downstream enterprises it supplies, and for the economic and human development it excites.

To supply lasting stimulus to the growth of the world economy, the industrial countries will practice what they preach about free trade. They insist upon, and compel where they can, the lowering of tariff barriers around infant industries in the preindustrial countries, and, at the same moment, they yield to protectionist pressures arising in their own economies. Political calculus determines which imported product they allow to incorporate cheap labor from the poor countries. Farmers swing more influence than textile workers; textile workers, more influence than workers in the solid-state electronics industry. The tariff fence set up for the farmer, however, goes into the profit of the luxury-food transnationals, and textile tariffs yield windfall profits to the vertically integrated manufacturers that import cheap labor in value added to their own cloth.

"Freedom for the pike," the economic historian R. H. Tawney said, "is death for the minnows." Consumers in the rich countries have common cause with producers in the poor countries. They have an equal interest in correcting arrangements that inhibit the growth and cheat the future of both rich and poor countries.

To answer the urgent and immediate need to restart industrial revolution in the preindustrial world, it will be necessary for the industrial countries to reenact the Decade of Development resolution adopted by the UN General Assembly in 1961. Economic development requires investments that cannot meet the terms of debt financing. They cannot compete with abounding opportunities in industrial countries that set those terms. Time, as one of the terms, is out of scale with the time required for an investment in infrastructure or in heavy industry to pay its way.

The industrial countries will accordingly reinstate their original promise to contribute 1 percent of their GNP each year to the economic assistance—in free gifts or loans on the softest terms—of the developing countries. For 1992, that promise is for $175 billion; for year after year thereafter, if all goes well, it is for still larger sums. Reflecting, as such figures do, the widening gap between the rich and the poor, the funds for economic assistance begin to be big enough to ensure that the preindustrial countries reach the replacement fertility rate on schedule. They will excite, on the scale required, the follow-on private investments for interest and profit that are necessary to sustain and accelerate industrial revolution in the preindustrial world.

The governments of the industrial countries will be moved by their citizenries to make this commitment. In the aftermath of the UN Conference on Environment and Development in June 1992, people will comprehend the fusion of these two concerns in the definition and resolution of the human predicament. Already aroused by degradation of the environment, they will begin to devote equal fervor to the cause of development. They will see poverty as the ultimate threat to the environment, laid by the abuse and mismanagement of industrial technology that keeps the poor in thrall to the rich. They will join the worldwide industrial revolution to end poverty, understanding that the continued growth of the human population lays the ultimate threat to the environment, both natural and human.

The Uses of Economic Assistance

In the allocation of the 1 percent of GNP freely given, it will be right, as well as within the power of the donor, to invoke moral criteria. Thus, in the words of its minister of economic cooperation, the

German government will be "looking closely at the level of spending for arms and such factors as human rights and economic freedoms in the various countries." Taxpayers can insist that aid go first to governments that will use it best. They can require that it be used for investment in human development. That is the best use for it because no other investment yields higher returns. It is the best use for a free gift because those returns can be paid to no one.

The health of the people of the preindustrial countries offers the readiest return on investment from the 1 percent. A substantial call on assistance funds can be laid by the faltering campaign to bring safe water within the reach of the half of the world population that dwells in the traditional village. A study conducted by WHO in Africa concluded that infants lie in greater danger from water stirred into a breast-milk substitute than from nursing at the breast of a mother infected with AIDS. The WHO campaign to bring potable water within a kilometer of every household by the year 2000 has less than a decade and more than half the distance to run.

WHO deploys less than 5 percent of the present annual flow of $30 billion in aid and soft loan money that runs from the rich countries to the poor. (The United States has been chronically a year and a half in arrears on its WHO dues.) Yet 1976 saw the last death from smallpox; an immunization campaign instituted by WHO soon after its founding has eliminated that historic scourge from the world population. In 1974, WHO launched a second campaign: to secure the immunization of all the children in the world against polio, diphtheria, whooping cough, and tetanus. Less than 5 percent of them were then being immunized. Now more than 60 percent of the world's children are receiving the required three doses of vaccine before age 1, and measles has been added to the list. The cost is estimated at $1.20 per child.

That campaign played its part in the 50 percent reduction of the under-5 mortality rate achieved since 1960. Of the 14 million under-5 deaths still recorded each year, 90 percent are caused by those infections in the unimmunized and by dehydration caused by diarrheal diseases. Field workers for WHO and UNICEF are reducing the under-5 deaths from dehydration, 35 percent of the total, by teaching mothers a simple oral rehydration procedure, using a sachet of salt and sugar supplied to a family's larder at a cost of 10 cents or less.

Similar primary-health-care stratagems are being fielded at the same low cost against other mass afflictions of poverty. The addition of iodine to salt in the Andes, the Himalayas, and other highland regions is averting the risk of goiter and cretinism, to which more than 500 million people are exposed. Iron in the salt is preventing the iron-deficiency anaemia that afflicts half of the women in the poorest countries. An essential drug kit assembled by WHO physicians costs less than $100 and meets most of the medical crises that are likely to arise in a poor community. As demonstrated by the Chinese, a member of the community can be trained to administer these drugs and to do the triage that identifies those cases requiring management by people with more advanced training.

Primary health care, however, is as novel to the medical economies of the poor countries as it is to the rich. WHO economists have found that 75 percent of the pitifully scarce funds available for medical care—less than 1 percent of GNP in the poorest countries—goes to "provide expensive medical care for a relatively small urban minority." A World Bank study found that larger expenditure from the national health insurance system in Brazil went to finance renal dialysis, coronary bypass surgery, and like procedures for 12,000 people than was allocated to the preventive and primary care of the 41 million desperately poor inhabitants of the northern and north-eastern states. Effective demand, as distinguished from need, and the differentials in incentive offered to pediatricians as compared to radiologists have similarly warped the expenditure of public funds for medical care in the United States—and for medical education and research in this country as well.

The model primary-health-care enterprise is presented, of course, by China [see page 131]. Costa Rica, Cuba, and Sri Lanka have developed their own systems, with comparable effect upon their demographic trends. Yet, the same money that would train 1 million primary-health-care workers went to the education of 50,000 physicians in Latin America between 1985 and 1990. There and in sub-Saharan Africa, economic stagnation has cut into funding for primary care and left increasing numbers of children unvaccinated. A modest allocation from the promised more than $100 billion per annum could reverse this untoward trend and vastly amplify the reach of the programs demonstrated by WHO and the other technical agencies of the United Nations.

Education is the next investment in human capital that invites allocation from economic assistance. The heroic effort of the preindustrial countries that raised their primary-school enrollments from 310 million to 444 million between 1970 and 1985 went largely unaided. Most of the aid, peaking at $5 billion in 1986, was spent on "tertiary" education. The recession in the world economy has compelled reduction of educational expenditure in many countries, even when it was not negotiated by creditors, halting their progress toward universal primary education. As of 1985, an estimated 100 million children were out of school, 60 percent of them female. Before A.D. 2000, school systems must find places for them and for another 100 million in countries where the under-15 population is still expanding. (China and India, their under-15 populations in decline, have classrooms in excess.)

The status of women in the preindustrial countries, especially in Asia and the Arab nations, should lend a strong motivation to external aid for education. Girls are in the minority—as small as one-third—in primary-school enrollments, and they drop away to small fractions of the entering classes of universities. For the priority accorded to boys, aid can neutralize what economic rationale there is and can weigh against other rationales as well. Education is the way to the liberation of young women for the roles they will be called upon to play in their changing societies. Their liberation turns ultimately on their ability to decide whether and when to bear a child; without literacy, they have neither the choice nor the power.

External assistance to education could well go to the estimated minimum $20 billion required to build schools for 200 million additional children. It could go to increase the 67 cents spent by the poorest countries to supply each child with learning materials to the $4 per child spent by the middle-income countries. A significant objective for educational assistance could be reduction in the size of classes. Cuba reports positive returns, including measurable reduction in the number of years a child takes to complete primary schooling and in the number of children not completing their schooling, from shrinking classes down from the usual 30 or 40 children per class to the standard, established by the American educator John Dewey, of 18 children per class. Since teacher salaries constitute as much as 95 percent of the school budget in the poorest countries, this is an expensive option. For the quality of education, there is no better prescription.

The Return on Human Development

The students of human capital investment have computed the social as well as the private rate of return from expenditures on education. A World Bank report shows a 24 percent social rate of return on primary education and a 31 percent private rate of return—meaning the return to society and to the individual, respectively—for 43 preindustrial countries surveyed. That is surely competitive with investment in plant and machinery and must precede them. The rates of return on expenditure for secondary and tertiary education fall below those high figures, the private rate somewhat less than the social. To the goverments of preindustrial countries, the lesson is to emphasize and improve upon primary education, especially in the early stages of industrial revolution.

The same lesson applies to economic assistance to education. In sub-Saharan Africa during the 1980s, the priorities were reversed; per student, aid was parcelled at $1.10 to primary education, $11 to secondary education, and $575 to higher education. Ultimately, of course, the preindustrial world must internalize industrial technology, with advances in fundamental knowledge and its applications originating in its own universities and industrial laboratories. The foundations of these institutions must be laid first in the primary and secondary school systems.

The $1000 billion required to deliver potable water and to supply sanitation to 3 billion new city dwellers before A.D. 2000 presents another crucial and fruitful investment in human development. External funding can ensure the meeting of that deadline for the elimination of water-borne diseases from those cities. That could equal 500 million less population in the ultimate census; the return will be the larger, the earlier the investment is made. More immediately, it will stop the devastation that the cities of the poor are wreaking on their near and regional environment.

While the giver of aid has the right and certainly the power to tie strings to it, the wise giver will restrain impulses from ideology. External intervention in economic development has been blighted by ideology from its beginnings. Back then it was state-planned investment in import substitution to achieve independence from imports by indigenous production under the protection, if necessary, of tariff barriers to competitive imports. Now the dogma is the free market.

Without doubt, the market is the natural organization of economic activity. It arises spontaneously in every shantytown; the informal economy subsidizes the frail formal economy and fills the interstices created by its protective restraints. The black market confounds the centrally planned economy and circumvents monopoly in open economies. Imposed by dogma, on the other hand, "the market" has amplified the damage done by the world recession to one preindustrial economy after another. In the name of credit-worthiness, it has disrupted vulnerable enterprises in human development and laid cruel costs on the poorest elements in those societies.

The governments of the preindustrial countries command a far smaller percentage of the turnover of their economies than the governments of the industrial countries. They are, in that sense, less "socialistic," even though they may avow such heresy. A pragmatic giver will concur in the dictum of the Mexican economists Rocio and René de Villarréal: "Very often in these countries, before regulating the market, the State first has to create it." The newly industrializing economies—especially the four "tigers of the Pacific rim," South Korea, Taiwan, Hong Kong, and Singapore—celebrated as exhibits of free-market development, trace their success to vigorous government intervention at the outset and at crucial turning points since.

Events cannot wait for preindustrial markets to muster demand for industrial capacity on their spontaneous own. Time is of the essence in the race to increase production ahead of increase in population. The apparatus of industrial technology is in hand. The appetite for risk and the resources for heavy investment are not there in the private sector of most preindustrial countries. Against the turning of the cycle of cumulative causation that locks the country in neocolonial dependency, the state is the only institution that stands. When it sets up a public manufacturing enterprise, it is with a political as well as an economic motive. No natural law requires that such an enterprise, which may have a monopoly in a small economy, be placed under private ownership or in the custody of some transnational corporation. The issues at stake transcend economic doctrines.

With economics, that enterprise must, of course, ultimately come to terms. Public manufacturing enterprises have been known to do so. Some have found places in the transnational corporate community. To the benefit of the world economy, their presence promotes diffusion of power and initiative within it.

EQUITY AND ECONOMIC DEVELOPMENT

At its most refined, advice issuing from free-market dogma echoes Sir Humphry Davy's exultation in the "unequal division of property and labor." It speaks reverently of the upper-income propensity to save; anxiously, about the blunting of incentive by marginal tax rates, and frugally, on the necessity for social expenditure. Contrarily, the human-development index, most sensitively expressed in the fertility rate, argues for equity in the distribution of income. The record shows that little upper income has gone into domestic investment in preindustrial countries except by the route of taxation.

Among preindustial countries, those with the most extreme differences between their top and bottom income groups—notoriously the high-income oil-exporting countries and the middle-income countries of Latin America, but including also the poorest countries in sub-Saharan Africa—have the higher fertility rates. The possessors of their wealth make their investments in the industrial countries, not in their own. The countries with narrower spread in income distribution—most notably China, but also the other centrally planned economies, the newly industrializing economies of South Korea and Taiwan, and a few other market economies, such as Costa Rica—are already approaching the replacement rate. These countries promote human development in other ways, of course, but in the same spirit of equity. They have, moreover, mobilized the small savings of lower income groups for community development and like enterprises.

The counsel of equity has special relevance to the long-range future of the human species. China and India give promise of stabilizing their numbers at a much lower GNP per capita than the industrial nations that preceded them through the demographic transition. The two populations together will constitute about half of that portion of the world population that first arrives at the replacement fertility rate. They will impose, for some time at least, much less than half of the burden that population lays upon the environment.

Environment and development, taken together, signify the desirability of early accommodation of the human species to the finite bounty of the biosphere. Wider public understanding of the relationship has already excited public opinion in the rich countries to set boundaries on ordinary real estate development schemes as well as the location of landscape-blighting industrial installations. The same understanding is bound to generate increasing political support for economic assistance by the rich industrial economies to the economic development of the preindustrial world. People are recognizing that the poor, with their more modest demand on the bounty of the biosphere, have needs that must be met if the human species expects to be here to stay. The scale and rate of the required effort, however, requires some deeper, more "natural" compulsion, arising from the internal dynamics of those economies.

THE COMPULSIONS FOR ECONOMIC ASSISTANCE

In the market economies, that may well be their compulsion to grow. Growth in these economies—by what J. M. Keynes called "the subterfuge of investment"—offsets inequity in the distribution of wealth and income in their populations. Without change in relative shares, growth increases, or promises to increase, the incomes of people at the bottom as well as at the top. The media of mass communication advertise the gap between the extremes. That serves, most of the time, to excite economic incentive in the receivers of middle-level incomes, at least. There are thresholds of disappointment and frustration in each economy, however, at which political stability is threatened. Even the U.S. economy, the most apolitically stable of them all, must have its upset point. It may not be much above the 6 percent unemployment now 'accepted' by the house economists as the level that permits economic growth to be managed without inflation.

The stagnation of the world economy puts all of the market economies under rising political compulsion to get growth restarted. The (formerly) centrally planned industrial economies, stalled on dead center by the collapse of their political systems, are driven by the same compulsion. For the idled work forces and factories of both systems, the preindustrial countries provide, if not a market ready and able to pay for imports, an inventory of human needs that can keep them at work for at least two generations.

The economic compulsions and necessities at the three corners of the world economy might find their mutually productive resolution in the comparative advantage that distinguishes each of them. The complementary fit of their respective advantages suggests the start-up of a new triangular trading system that would restart economic growth at all three corners. The triangular trade in slaves, cotton and molasses, and textiles and rum, which financed the first industrial revolution, supplies a working precedent. Seeking markets for their facility in the invention and production of consumer goods, the market economies could meet, overnight, the destabilizing demand for those goods in the former centrally planned economies. Those economies, with their idle overcapacity for the production of capital goods, could manufacture those goods for the preindustrial countries, while they learn to serve demand for consumer goods within their own economies. The preindustrial countries, closing the triangle, would supply the revived markets for their primary commodities.

Once trade begins to move around the triangle, it will excite enterprise to put idle resources to work on all sides. In the U.S. economy, the threat of competition from the (formerly) centrally planned economies for the new capital goods markets in the preindustrial countries will surely bring the business community to consider the economic stimulus to be had from government expenditure on the transfer of technology to those countries.

The Federal government has been the biggest customer of U.S. industry since 1941. The Cold War made it possible to substitute government purchase of armaments for the investment not forthcoming from the private sector. When the Kennedy administration took office in 1961, investment and the demand for capital goods were not sustaining growth in the U.S. economy. The Kennedy tax cut did not produce the desired surge of investment in the domestic economy. Arms procurement, it turned out, could also serve to stimulate economic growth, or at least to keep the economy going.

Both capital goods and armaments create employment without putting products into the market to absorb the wages they pay. Those wages generate additional demand and, therefore, additional jobs in consumer-goods industries and, by this "multiplier" effect, keep the system growing or at least running in place. Military procurement has kept the system running by taking a sufficient percentage of its output off the market and—in plain language—burying it in the ground.

Government purchase of capital goods and consumer products in support of industrial revolution in the preindustrial countries would have the same effect. Instead of burying these more useful products in the ground, however, it would ship them abroad. There, before long, economic growth would create markets for U.S. exports purchased without intermediation by the government.

In the Soviet Union, of course, armaments were the subterfuge for incapacity to manufacture and market consumer goods. With no armaments to produce, the two kinds of industrial system can now be turned to supplying the consumer goods and capital equipment for the abolition of poverty.

THE LOW COST OF ECONOMIC ASSISTANCE

Paul Hoffman, the U.S. automobile manufacturer who headed the UN Special Fund for economic development in the 1950s, urged his fellow taxpayers to consider how little technical assistance actually cost the United States or any other donor economy—and how much that little bought. Out of the average $1.00 spent on technical assistance, an average of 80 cents laid out for hardware stayed inside the country. The wages paid for the hardware excited additional economic activity worth at least $1.00. In the recipient country, the 20 cent net cost of the economic assistance triggered additional investment of $5.00 in plant and infrastructure to put the technology to work. The "savings" for that larger investment were already there in abundance—in underemployed manpower and underutilized resources.

The installation of U.S. technology in a country that is to be jump-started into economic development by such technical assistance will make that country, as the Japanese for their part are demonstrating in East and Southeast Asia, a market for the purchase thereafter of U.S. technology and manufactures. To the growth of the U.S. economy, the switch from unusable weapons to productive goods will thus lend a new thrust. With Canada, the country's principal trading partner, the United States does 1.5 times the business that it does with Latin America. The Canadian population is 6 percent the size of the Latin American population. At the Canadian level of development and present market share, the Latin American market for U.S. goods would multiply 24 times. Given economic catatonia in the countries of South and Central America, and in sub-Saharan Africa as well, those countries hold little interest for the U.S. business community.

The massive transfer of technology required to carry industrial revolution worldwide will be much facilitated by the yielding of national sovereignty to new multilateral authorities that is under way around the world. The European Economic Community (EEC) after 1992 can be seen as better organized for the transfer than the economies that now pursue postimperial ends in their separate spheres of interest. For the emergency-assistance measures that ought to be instituted to restart the development of sub-Saharan Africa, for example, the European economies will be the readier to make their contribution alongside the United States and Japan.

The EEC constitutes, as well, a supranational authority to which transnational corporations may be held responsible. Those sovereignties may even be induced by such authority to reckon the acceleration of economic development in their preindustrial host countries as a consideration in the deployment of their investment capital.

Multilateral economic unions in the preindustrial world correspondingly present more rationally organized recipients of assistance and, later, units of production and trade in the world economy. What is more, such emerging entities as the Central American Common Market, the Caribbean Community, the West African Economic Community, and the Association of Southeast Asia Nations are drawn together by the logic of ecology as well as economic interest. In sub-Saharan Africa, the many economically subcritical countries will find their comparative advantage in the pooled resources of continental and subcontinental unions.

Considerations of ecology are likely to organize a number of significant economic unions around the development and conservation of major river valleys. No more than 35 great watersheds contain the habitations of two-thirds of the world population. Not more than a dozen of these systems are contained within the borders of a single country [see back endpapers].

The fragility of the Jordan River watershed has compelled Syria, Jordan, Lebanon, and Israel, despite their fulminating mutual hostilities, to abide tacitly by the plan for the sharing of its waters developed in the late 1940s by the U.S. agronomist Walter C. Lowdermilk. With peace coming to Indochina, the four nations on the peninsula may join in executing the Mekong Valley Plan to harness the 50-fold flooding of that great river for electrical power and irrigation to see their nearly 150 million population through the demographic transition. All through the war, the Mekong Valley Plan consortium, including the Indochinese states, laid the foundations for this effort. The security of the Amazon watershed engages the interests of Colombia, Ecuador, Peru, and Bolivia as well as Brazil; degradation of the rain forest has begun to organize their concerted attention.

The evolution of political and economic institutions toward the organization of an ultimate world polity appears to be under way.

As the industrial revolution goes worldwide, the technologies to renew and sustain the biosphere are coming on stream. Of first concern, of course, is the impending multiplication by four or five of world energy consumption. The capture of solar energy in hydrogen is at the pilot-plant stage—either directly, by photovoltaic arrays, or from storage in sea water by OTEC technology. Hydrogen can also store and transport energy welling up from the Earth's hot interior. By the end of this century, the combustion of hydrogen will begin to displace the combustion of fossil fuels. The energy requirements of civilization will then be met by the Sun, scheduled to continue shining for 5 billion years, and by the most abundant element in the universe. And the consumption of energy will then no longer perturb the energy equilibrium and temperature of the planet.

While the perfection of agriculture need never cease, it already knows, in the words of the farmer, "how to farm twice as good as I do now!" In fact, the best yields per hectare of every major field crop come at four or more times the average. Only the failure to make the best technology perform at its best will require the extension of arable land in the next century. The inevitability of local crop failures, even as the green revolution makes its way into the preindustrial world, and the year-to-year vagaries of the climatic system lay special obligation on the industrial agricultural systems. They must maintain surpluses in readiness to meet food emergency and even famine, especially in Africa.

By the time the demand for food reaches its peak, in the last half of the next century, the increasing productivity of agriculture will begin to reduce the area under cultivation. Meanwhile, institutional and behavioral failings, not lack of knowledge, continue to deplete the productivity of the precious soil resource. As it becomes impossible to accept declining yield, bad practices and habits will have to give way to the application of sustained-yield technology, and they are already doing so. In time, with half of the world population living in cities, the composting of urban waste will be recognized as an economic necessity, and the compost will be available for return to the soil whence it came.

Good design is continuing to reduce the weight in use of every raw material per dollar of GNP. In the automobile, the reduction of steel since 1950 exceeds 25 percent. Steel scrap has long since charged the furnaces. The recycling of other metals meets increasing percentages of demand for them in new products, even as design reduces the amount required.

Of no less relevance to the conservation of resources, higher-order, scarcer elements are yielding uses to the humbler and more abundant ones. Silicon is the emblematic element of this development in technology. In compound with oxygen in clay, it was the material of the first manufacturers, the potters whose pots stored the first harvests. In the semiconductor chip and the light-transmitting fiber, silicon is the material now of the extended human nervous system. In this function, it displaces copper and has carried the extension and externalizing of the nervous system far beyond the reach of copper. As the most promising photovoltaic element, it may supply industrial civilization with electrical energy. In lower technologies, this second most abundant (after oxygen) of the elements in the Earth's crust will continue to serve human purposes in greater tonnage, as in building materials, than any other. There can be no worry about the supply of carbon, nitrogen, oxygen, hydrogen, and silicon. The first four of these elements constitute the raw materials of biotechnology; the last two serve the inexhaustible technologies of physics.

Industrial civilization has more to be concerned about when it comes to the disposal of the materials it has used. Even after the most frugal salvaging and recycling, material remains to be disposed of. Every stratagem, from land-filling to incineration, defaces and endangers the near and distant environment. Here is a true frontier of technology.

What may at last prove to be the best solution is suggested by the hydrologic cycle. The rains and their runoff carry everything on the land, and ultimately the land itself, into the ocean. The addition of the wastes of industrial civilization to that flow has been poisoning the estuaries and inshore waters for decades. Now it has begun to pollute the continental shelves. These are the most productive waters and esthetically the most intimate.

A generation ago, oceanographers proposed that civilization improve upon the hydrologic cycle: Let the waste be transported from the land straight to the abyss of the ocean. Further research will identify the trenches where the bottom water lies most remote from the life of the planet. They are at subduction boundaries, where the plunging ocean floor will someday return the stuff to the continental rock whence it came and may come again some day [see the illustration on page 73]. Multilateral conventions, institutions and disposal operations will be required to accumulate the material, to decide where to put it, and to move it there.

Of more immediate hazard are the toxic wastes. Chemical and metallurgical technology will go on generating these in greater quantity and variety for a long time to come. As contaminants of the sewage of most big cities, they make that rich material unusable. There is no technological frontier to be crossed here. From painful and costly experience, the implicated industries are learning to contain production wastes by recycling in the process stream. Environmental consciousness will subject the disposal of many consumer products—for example, dry-cell batteries and alpha-particle smoke detectors—to incentives or penalties, refunds or fines. On the precedent of the Montreal convention that banned CFCs, multilateral agencies will monitor and license the introduction and disposal of new compounds in the processes and products of manufacture. Composting of the bulk of urban waste will thereupon become feasible.

THE STATIONARY STATE

The next 50 years will see the world population through its last surge of growth. In that time, industrial revolution must accommodate the hugest surge of human want. For another century, unmet demands and entirely new demands will drive the continued expansion of industrial output. It will require a century and a half, therefore, to carry the expansion of production up and across the top of the S curve of growth to meet the needs of the world population as it increases and at last levels off at 10 or 11 billion. That will give people time to sort out their values and reconstitute their institutions. In the not so distant past, those values and institutions served the creation of high civilizations by distributing want. They have failed, however, to secure the benefit of industrial revolution to the growing world population, and they imperil the planetary environment. The revolution has come too abruptly on the time scale of social evolution to permit the framing of values for the distribution of plenty.

The economy of growth, it is now clear, must give way at last to the economy of equity. The moral questions implicit in this ultimate transition have been lurking in the subconscious of economics ever since Adam Smith delegated them to the invisible hand. In undertaking the necessary revision of the values governing the production and distribution of goods, people will do well to consult, for example, John Stuart Mill.

A century and a half ago, Mill wrote:

> It must always have been seen, more or less distinctly, by political economists that the increase of wealth is not boundless: that at the end of what they term the progressive state lies the stationary state, that all progress in wealth is but a postponement of this. It is scarcely necessary to remark that a stationary condition of capital and population implies no stationary state in human improvement. There would be as much scope as ever for all kinds of mental culture, and moral and social progress; as much room for improving the Art of Living, and much more likelihood of its being improved, when minds ceased to be engrossed with the art of getting on. . . .

As the present doubling of the world population proceeds, people must accomplish the necessary reconstruction of their values and institutions. We have not much more than a century to find our way to the steady-state adjustment of our appetites, as well as our numbers, to the finite dimensions of the planet and the vulnerable cycles of its biosphere. This only one world is our own to make and to keep.

BIBLIOGRAPHY

Suggestions for further reading are set out here in the order in which they are prompted by topics raised and encountered from page to page. The suggestions do duty, also, as annotated references to sources and authorities I have consulted.

As I have entered the references to the numerous articles from *Scientific American* listed here, I have realized how long I have been at work on this book. One entry is the lead article in the May 1948 issue; that was the first issue of a new magazine of science launched under the then 102-year-old name of *Scientific American*. To show the relevance to history of the work of science was as much my motivation in the start-up of the new *Scientific American* as to bring the work itself to the wider audience the magazine now reaches in nine languages around the world.

CHAPTER 1

Page 1   Population growth and population explosion: *The Human Population,* a single-topic issue of *Scientific American,* September 1974.

Demographic transition: Frank W. Notestein, "Population," *Scientific American,* September 1950; Kingsley Davis, "Population," *Scientific American,* September 1963; Tomas Frejka, "Prospects for a Stationary World Population," *Scientific American,* March 1973.

Page 8   The U.S. Domesday book is *Statistical Abstracts of the United States,* issued annually by the Bureau of the Census, Department of

Commerce. *Historical Statistics of the United States, Colonial Times to 1970,* takes some of the principal series as far back as 1610.

Iron and steel: These estimates require no digging in archaeological middens. The historical record shows world production of iron did not exceed 100,000 tons per year until well into the seventeenth century. Production at that rate for 10,000 years, from the very beginning of the agricultural-urban revolution, would have brought no more than a billion tons above ground. Exceeding a million tons per year for the first time in the early nineteenth century, 10 million tons at middle of the nineteenth century, and 100 million tons only in time for World War I, cumulative production could not have exceeded 5 billion tons by 1950. Since then, steel production climbing past 750 million tons per year, has brought more than 10 billion tons of iron above ground. World capacity now exceeds 1 billion ingot tons. (The teaching of arithmetic fixes attention on the last digit in a number. In vital statistics and national bookkeeping, the significant digit is the first one; it derives its significance from its place to the left of the decimal point. The last digit, especially to the right of the decimal point, is not to be credited.)

Fossil fuels: See the graph on page 176 and M. King Hubbert, "The Energy Resources of the Earth," *Scientific American,* September 1971.

Electrical energy: World output was less than 1000 billion kilowatt-hours in 1950, rising to more than 2000 billion in 1960, nearly 5000 billion in 1970, and more than 10,000 billion by 1990.

Page 9   The reach of human perception, extended by the instruments of science: Charles Eames, et al., *Powers of Ten,* Scientific American Books, New York, 1981.

Philosophy of science: Percy Bridgman, *Reflections of a Physicist,* Philosophical Library, New York, 1955.

Page 11   *The Mechanization of Work,* a single-topic issue of *Scientific American,* September 1982.

Page 12   Demographic transition: See note for page 1.

The Malthusian equation: Thomas Malthus, *An Essay on the Principle of Population,* 2 vols., Patricia James, ed., Cambridge University Press, Cambridge, 1990. Malthus carried his two series out to 8 and 12 doublings of the population, at which "population would be to the means of subsistence as 256 to 9 [and] as 4096 to 13."

Page 13   Termination of population growth: *World Population Prospects: Estimates and Projections as Assessed in 1984,* Population Division, United Nations, New York, 1986.

Page 15   Deforestation: Robert Repetto, "Deforestation in the Tropics,"

Scientific American, April 1990; Peter van Dresser, "The Future of the Amazon," *Scientific American,* May 1948.

Abuse of resources: Arthur E. Goldschmidt, "Resources and Resourcefulness," *Bulletin,* American Academy of Arts and Sciences, Boston, February 1949.

Page 16   The propensity for toolmaking: Sherwood Washburn "Tools and Human Evolution," *Scientific American,* January 1949: L. S. B. Leakey, "Olduvai Gorge," *Scientific American,* January 1954.

Page 17   On how many ever lived: Edward S. Deevey, "The Human Crop," *Scientific American,* April 1956.

Page 18   Agricultural revolution: Robert J. Braidwood, "The Agricultural Revolution," *Scientific American,* September 1960 and Richard S. Mac-Neish, "The Origins of the New World Civilization," *Scientific American,* November 1964.

Page 19   Industrial revolution, a pioneering enquiry into its onset: John U. Nef, *The Conquest of the Material World,* University of Chicago Press, Chicago, 1964.

The conquest of the ocean: J. H. Parry, *The Discovery of the Sea,* The Dial Press, New York, 1974.

Page 20   The Lunar Society: Lord Ritchie-Calder, "The Lunar Society of Birmingham," *Scientific American,* June 1982.

Page 21   Carboniferous capitalism: Asa Briggs, "Technology and Economic Development," *Scientific American,* September 1963.

Involuntary saving: B. S. Keirstead, *Capital, Interest and Profits,* John Wiley & Sons, New York, 1959.

Secret history: E. P. Thompson, *The Making of the English Working Class,* Victor Gollancz. London, 1963; Eric Williams, *Slavery and Capitalism,* University of North Carolina Press, Chapel Hill, 1944.

Page 23   Infanticide: William L. Langer, "Checks on Population Growth, 1750–1850," *Scientific American,* February 1972.

Page 24   The world polity of Bretton Woods was hopefully envisioned in Alvin H. Hansen, *America's Role in the World Economy,* W. W. Norton, New York, 1945.

Page 25   Economic assistance: Report by a Group of Experts, *Measures for the Economic Development of Under-Developed Countries,* United Nations, Lake Success, 1951; Stringfellow Barr, *Let's Join the Human Race,* University of Chicago Press, Chicago, 1950; *Technology and Economic Development,* a single-topic issue of *Scientific American,* September 1963.

Economic assistance defined: J. K. Galbraith, *Economic Development,* Harvard University Press, Cambridge, Mass., 1962; Ragnar Nurske, *Problems of Capital Formation in Underdeveloped Countries,* Oxford University Press, New York, 1960.

Page 25   The two cultures and the response from the "other" culture: C. P. Snow, *The Two Cultures and a Second Look,* Cambridge University Press, Cambridge, 1964.

Page 28   Transnational corporations: Centre on Transnational Corporations, *Transnational Corporations in World Development, Third Survey 1983,* and *Fourth Survey 1988,* United Nations, New York; United Nations Secretariat Department of Economic and Social Affairs, *Multinational Corporations in World Development,* United Nations, New York, 1973.

Page 29   Capital flight: Donald R. Lessard, *International Financing for Developing Countries: The Unfulfilled Promise,* The World Bank, Washington, D.C., 1986.

Page 31   The World Commission on Environment and Development [WCED] report to UN General Assembly is most accessibily available in WCED, *Our Common Future,* Oxford University Press, New York, 1987.

Page 32   Comparative shares of economic groupings in world manufacturing output: United Nations Industrial Development Organization [UNIDO], *Industry in a Changing World,* United Nations, New York, 1983.

   Economic growth in the Soviet Union: Raymond B. Powell, "Economic Growth of the U.S.S.R.," *Scientific American,* December 1968; statistical series maintained by UN agencies (see note for Chapter 3, page 121).

Page 34   "Lousy jobs": Eli Ginzberg, "Youth Employment," *Scientific American,* May 1980.

Page 35   Income distribution by quintiles: tables 636 and 724 in *Statistical Abstract of the United States* for 1975 and 1990, respectively.

Page 37   The food supply: Roger Revelle, "Soil Dynamics and Sustainable Carrying Capacity of the Earth," in *Global Change,* T. F. Malone and J. S. Roederer, Eds. Cambridge University Press, New York, 1985. In his round number calculations, Revelle evidently rounded the conventional 3.6 million kilocalories per ton of grain (see page 37, chapter 1) up to 4 million. Conforming his calculation to the conventional raises his estimate of the ultimate food requirement by about 10 percent.

Page 39   Energy consumption in United States and other countries: tables 930 and 1433, respectively, *Statistical Abstract of the United States,* 1989.

page 40   Sustainable development of the biosphere: W. C. Clark, and R. E. Munn, editors, *Sustainable Development of the Biosphere.* Cambridge University Press, Cambridge, 1986.

   Biosphere and noosphere: Vernadsky, V. I., *The Biosphere,* Synergetic Press, London, 1986.

CHAPTER 2

Page 45   *The Biosphere,* a single-topic issue of *Scientific American,* September 1970; Harold Zirin, "Hot Spots in the Atmosphere of the Sun," *Scientific American,* August 1958; David I. Groves, "An Early Habitat of Life," *Scientific American,* October 1981.

Page 47   *The Dynamic Earth,* a single-topic issue of *Scientific American,* September 1983.

Page 48   Evolution of the atmosphere: Helmut E. Landsberg, "Origin of the Atmosphere," *Scientific American,* August 1953; Von R.Eshelman, "The Atmospheres of Mars and Venus," *Scientific American,* March 1959; James F. Kasting, Owen B. Toon, and James B. Pollack, "How Climate Evolved on the Terrestrial Planets," *Scientific American,* February 1988.

Page 49   Origin of life: George Wald, "The Origin of Life," *Scientific American,* August 1954.

Chemical evolution: Richard E. Dickerson "Chemical Evolution and the Origin of Life," *Scientific American,* September 1978.

Clay and the origin of life: A. G. Cairns-Smith, "The First Organisms," *Scientific American,* June 1985.

Page 50   Life and light: George Wald, "Light and Life," *Scientific American,* October 1959; Max Delbrueck and Roderick K. Clayton, "Purple Bacteria," *Scientific American,* November 1951.

Cellular evolution: J. William Schopf, "The Evolution of the Earliest Cells," *Scientific American,* September 1978; Albert L. Lehninger, "How Cells Transform Energy," *Scientific American,* September 1961.

Page 55   The ozone layer: Richard S. Stolarski, "The Antarctic Ozone Hole," *Scientific American,* January 1988.

Page 56   Symbiosis and evolution: Lynn Margulis, "Symbiosis and Evolution," *Scientific American,* August 1971.

Burgess Shale fossils: Simon Conway Morris and J. B. Whittington, "The Animals of the Burgess Shale," *Scientific American,* July 1979.

Page 57   Continental drift: J. Tuzo Wilson, "Continental Drift," *Scientific American,* April 1963; Robert S. Dietz and J. J. Holden, "The Breakup of Pangaea," *Scientific American,* October 1970.

Page 58   Mesozoic extinctions: Dale A. Russell "The Mass Extinctions of the Late Mesozoic," *Scientific American,* January 1982.

Page 60   The biomass as phytomass: George Woodwell, "On the Limits of Nature," in Robert Repetto, ed., *The Global Possible,* Yale University Press, New Haven, 1985.

Page 64   Photosynthesis: Govindjee and Rajni Govindjee, "The Absorption of Light in Photosynthesis," *Scientific American,* December 1974.

Page 66   The Gaia hypothesis: J. E. Lovelock, *A New Look at Life on Earth,* Oxford University Press, Oxford, 1987.

The task of ecology: Warren Weaver, *Science and Imagination,* Basic Books, New York, 1967.

Page 68   Human demand on the biosphere: Gene E. Likens, and Robert H. Whittaker, "The Biosphere and Man" in H. Leith, ed., *Primary Productivity of the Biosphere,* Springer Verlag, New York, 1975; J. Olson, J. A. Watts, and L. J. Allison, *Carbon in the Live Vegetation of Major World Ecosystems,* U. S. Department of Energy (TR004 DOE NRB 0037), Washington D.C., 1983.

Page 69   Extinction and conservation: O. H. Frankel and M. E. Soule, *Conservation and Evolution,* Cambridge University Press, Cambridge, 1981.

Page 75   Human occupation of the biosphere: J. F. Richards, "World Environmental History and Economic Development," in *Sustainable Development of the Biosphere* [see Chapter 1 page 40].

Page 78   Slash and burn: W. B. Banage, "Policies for the Maintenance of Biological Diversity," paper for WCED, 1985.

Page 80   The European landscape: René Dubos, *The Wooing of the Earth,* Charles Scribners & Sons, New York, 1980.

Page 85   CFCs: J. R. Simon, "Fluorocarbons," *Scientific American,* November 1949.

Page 89   Acid rain: Volker A. Mohnen, "The Challenge of Acid Rain," *Scientific American,* August 1988.

Page 93   Transnational corporations: Centre on Transnational Corporations, *Environmental Aspects of the Activities of Transnational Corporations,* United Nations, New York, 1985.

CHAPTER 3

Page 99   Population growth, the demographic transition, and prospects for a stationary world population: see notes for Chapter 1, pages 1 and 13.

Page 105   Alexander Herzen, *From the Other Shore,* Oxford University Press, New York, 1979.

Page 108   Economic and population growth of the industrial countries: Simon Kuznets, *Growth, Population and Income Distribution,* W. W. Norton, New York 1979; Surhendra Patel, "World Economy in Transition, 1850–2060," in R. Feinstein, ed., *Capitalism, Socialism and Economic Growth,* Cambridge University Press, Cambridge, 1967. In some contradiction with his view of population growth as the "dynamics of political economy," J. S. Mill may have been the first to recognize evidence of the deceleration of population growth that so invariably attends faster increase in production; writing a half century after Malthus, he observed: "Subsistence and employment in England have never increased more rapidly than in the last 40 years, but every census since 1821 showed a smaller proportional increase of population than that of the period preceding..." (page 159, *Principles of Political Economy,* see note page 470, Chapter 7).

Page 110   The implications of the studies conducted by the Bureau of Home Economics of the Department of Agriculture were developed in companion volumes: Edwin G. Nourse, et al., *America's Capacity to Produce* and Harold G. Moulton, et al., *America's Capacity to Consume,* the Brookings Institution, Washington, D. C. 1934. The latter established $2500 as the "minimum" family income: the income that would purchase adequate nutrition as well as meet other necessities. This is the "poverty" income in today's terminology. In 1936, that income was 80 percent of the country's average income. By 1959, the poverty threshhold was 50 percent of the average; since 1970, it it has stood at about 30 percent of the average. In 1989, by this definition, 13 percent of U.S. families were in poverty.

Pages 111   Technological disemployment: Wassily Leontief and Faye Duchin, *The Future Impacts of Automation on Workers,* Oxford University Press, New York, 1986.

Page 113   The societal "nervous breakdown": J. M. Keynes, "Economic Possibilities for Our Grandchildren," in *Essays in Persuasion,* W. W. Norton, New York, 1963.

Page 114   Park Avenue and the Bronx: Robert Heilbroner, *The Economic Problem,* Prentice-Hall, Englewood Cliffs, N.J., 1968.

Page 116   Income distribution: A. B. Atkinson, *The Economics of Inequity,* Clarendon Press, Oxford, 1975.

Children in poverty: tables 71 and 736, *Statistical Abstract of the United States,* 1989.

The ecology of child development in the United States: Urie Bronfenbrenner, "The Origins of Alienation," *Scientific American,* August 1974.

Page 117   Soviet steel and electrical energy figures: (UNIDO), *Industry and Development,* Global Report 1988/89, UNIDO, Vienna, 1988.

Page 118   Domestic life in the Soviet Union: Basile Kerblay, *Modern Soviet Society,* Pantheon, New York, 1977.

Page 119   Public opinion in Poland: Stefan Nowak, "Values and Attitudes of the Polish People," *Scientific American,* July 1981.

Page 121   The international civil service, first assembled by the League of

Nations in the 1920s and now functioning in the Secretariat and the technical and financial agencies of the United Nations, conducts the global bookkeeping that underpins generalization about the human condition on this and the following pages. Primary nodes in the network are the Statistical Office of the Department of International Economic and Social Affairs and the Population Division in the office of the UN Secretariat; the secretariat of the UN Conference on Trade and Development [UNCTAD]; the World Bank and the International Monetary Fund [IMF]; the Food and Agriculture Organization [FAO], the Industrial Development Organization [UNIDO] and the World Health Organization [WHO]. The mounting flood of data is accessible in such annuals as the *World Economic Survey,* the *National Accounts Statistics,* and the *World Population Prospects* from the statistical and policy divisions of the UN Secretariat, the annual *Global Report* of UNIDO, the annual *State of Food and Agriculture* from FAO, the periodic *Handbook of International Trade and Development Statistics* from UNCTAD, the annual *World Development Report* of the World Bank, the quarterly *World Economic Outlook* of IMF.

Page 123   From 1946 to 1985, 'foreign grants and credits' to Taiwan and South Korea from the United States accumulated to $6 billion and $15 billion, respectively [Table 1399, *Statistical Abstract of the United States,* 1990]. In 1990 dollars, the flow of funds during the first two decades came to $17 and $26 billion dollars, respectively.

Page 128   Industrial revolution in China: Chen Ding "The Economic Development of China", *Scientific American,* September 1980; Fox Butterfield, *China, Alive in the Bitter Sea,* Random House, New York, 1990; William Hinton, *Fanshen, A Documentary of Revolution in a Chinese Village,* Monthly Review Press, New York and London, 1966.

Page 131   Child development in China: Institute of Pediatrics—Chinese Academy of Medical Sciences," Studies on the Physical Development of Children," *Chinese Medical Journal,* English edition, new series, vol. 3, no. 6, 1977.

Page 135   India and South Asia: Gunnar Myrdal, *Asian Drama, An Enquiry into the Poverty of Nations,* The Twentieth Century Fund, New York, 1968; John P. Lewis, *A Quiet Crisis in India,* The Brookings Institution, Washington, D.C., 1962; Lawrence Veit, *India's Second Revolution,* McGraw-Hill, New York, 1976.

Page 138   Food as capital: V. M. Dandekar, *Use of Food Surpluses for Economic Development,* Gokhale Institute for Politics and Economics, Poona, 1956.

Page 139   World Bank fertilizer-plant loan: P. C. Mahalanobis, *Talks on Planning,* Indian Statistical Institute, Calcutta, 1961; Lawrence Veit, see note for page 135.

Page 139 Industrial revolution in India: Raj Krishna, "The Economic Development of India," *Scientific American,* September 1980; Pitambar Pant, "The Development of India," *Scientific American,* September 1963.

Page 140 "Non-factory" industry in India: M. C. Shetty, *Small Scale and Household Industry in India,* Asia Publishing House, Bombay, 1963.

Page 142 Poverty in India: Pranab K. Bardhan and T. N. Srinivasan, *Poverty and Income Distribution in India,* Indian Statistical Institute, Calcutta, 1974.

Page 144 Southeast Asia: Peter N. Nemetz, ed., *The Pacific Rim, Investment, Development and Trade,* University of British Columbia Press, Vancouver, 1990.

Page 146 The Arab Nation: Mohammed Almana, *Arabia Unified, a Portrait of Ibn Saud,* Hutchinson and Benham, London 1980; Keith Stanley MacLachlan, *Economic Development of the Middle East Oil-Exporting Countries,* London Economist Intelligence Unit, London, 1978.

Page 148 Israeli agriculture: Walter C. Lowdermilk, "The Reclamation of a Man-Made Desert," *Scientific American,* March 1960; G. Stanhill, "Irrigation in Israel," *Proceedings, Israel-China Workshop on Agricultural Water Use Efficiency,* Beijing, April 1991.

Israeli desalination technology: P. Glueckstern, "Cost Estimates of Large Reverse Osmosis Systems," *Desalination,* no. 81, Elsevier Science Publishers, Amsterdam, 1991.

Page 149 Stagnation in Africa: Jennifer F. Whitaker, *How Can Africa Survive?* Council on Foreign Relations, New York, 1976; Edward S. Ayensu, "The African Crisis," background paper for WCED, 1985; Organization for African Unity, *Lagos Plan of Action for the Economic Development of Africa 1980–2000,* International Institute for Labour Studies, Geneva, 1982; Olusola Akinrunade and J. Kurt Barling, *Economic Development in Africa,* Pinter, London, 1987.

The political setting of the mysterious death of Dag Hammarskjold is explored in Conor Cruise O'Brien, *Murderous Angels,* Little Brown, Boston, 1968.

Page 151 Poverty and the African environment: W. Banage, "Policies for the Maintenance of Biological Diversity," paper for WCED, 1985.

Page 155 Industrial revolution in Latin America: Raul Prebisch, *Latin America, A Problem in Development,* University of Texas, Institute of Latin American Studies, 1971; Raul Prebisch, *Toward a Dynamic of Latin American Development,* Economic Commission for Latin America (ECLA), Mar el Plata, 1983; Celso Furtado, *Economic Development of Latin America,* 2d ed., Cambridge University Press, New York, 1976; Celso Furtado, "The Development of Brazil," *Scientific American,* September 1963; Pablo Gonzalez Casanova, "The Economic Development of Mexico," *Scientific American,* September 1980; *Income Distribution in Latin America,* ECLA E.71 II.G.2.

CHAPTER 4

Page 161   *Energy and Power,* a single-topic issue of *Scientific American,* September 1971; *Energy for Planet Earth,* a single-topic issue of *Scientific American,* September 1990.

Page 163   Inanislaves: R. Buckminster Fuller, *Nine Chains to the Moon,* J. B. Lippincott, Philadelphia, 1938.

Page 166   Conurbation: *Cities,* a single-topic issue of *Scientific American,* September 1965.

Page 172   The price of oil: Jihangir Amuzegar, "The Oil Story," *Foreign Affairs,* vol. 51, no. 4, 1973.

Page 174   Fossil fuel reserves: M. King Hubbert, "The Energy Resources of the Earth," *Scientific American,* September 1971.

Page 175   Oil shales and tar sands: Eugene Ayres, "The Fuel Situation," *Scientific American,* October 1956.

Page 178   Gasification of coal: Arthur M. Squires, "Clean Power from Dirty Fuels," *Scientific American,* October 1972; Harry Perry, "The Gasification of Coal," *Scientific American,* March 1974; Neal P. Cochran, "Oil and Gas from Coal," *Scientific American,* May 1976.

Page 179   Alternative nuclear fuel cycles: Alvin M. Weinberg, "Power Reactors," *Scientific American,* December 1954; Hugh C. McIntyre, "Natural-Uranium Heavy-Water Reactors," *Scientific American,* October 1975.

Nuclear garbage disposal considered: Hans Bethe, "The Necessity of Fission Power," *Scientific American,* January 1976.

Page 180   Nuclear power and proliferation: David Rose and Richard K. Lester, "Nuclear Power, Nuclear Weapons and International Stability," *Scientific American,* April 1978.

Page 181   Fusion reactors: Bruno Coppi and Jan Rem, "The Tokomak Approach in Fusion Research," *Scientific American,* July 1972; John L. Emmett, John Nuckolls, and Lowell Wood, "Fusion Power by Laser Implosion," *Scientific American,* June 1974.

Page 183   Low-potential solar energy: Eugene Ayres, "Windows," *Scientific American,* February 1951; Arthur H. Rosenfeld and David Hafemeister, "Energy-Efficient Buildings," *Scientific American,* April 1988.

Page 184   Photovoltaic capture of sunlight: Eugene Ayres, "Power from the Sun," *Scientific American,* August 1950; Bruce Chalmers, "The Photovoltaic Generation of Electricity," *Scientific American,* October

1976; Julie L. Schnapf and Dennis A. Baylor, "How Photorecptor Cells Respond to Light," *Scientific American,* April 1987.

Page 185   Hydrogen storage and transmission of solar energy: Derek P. Gregory, "The Hydrogen Economy," *Scientific American,* January 1973.

Page 186   Hydrogen as fuel: J. J. Reilly and Gary D. Sandrock, "Hydrogen Storage in Metal Hydrides," *Scientific American,* February 1980; Carl-Jochen Winter, "Canned Heat," *The Sciences,* March-April 1991.

Page 187   OTEC: Terry R. Penney, and Desikan Bharathan, "Power from the Sea," *Scientific American,* January 1987.

Page 189   Energy from the biomass: David Pimentel, et al., "Biomass Energy from Crop and Forest Residues," *Science,* vol. 212, 5 June 1981.

Page 190   Geothermal energy: Donald W. Brown et al., "Hot Dry Rock Geothermal Energy," in *Energy and the Environment in the 21st Century,* Jefferson Tester, ed., MIT Press, Cambridge, 1990.

Other sources of energy: Peter M. Moretti, and Louis V. Divone, "Modern Windmills," *Scientific American,* June 1986; Joseph Barnea, "Geothermal Power," *Scientific American,* January 1972.

Page 192   Energy conservation: Amory B. Lovins, Arnold P. Fickett, and Clark W. Gellings, "Efficient Use of Energy," *Scientific American,* September 1990.

Page 193   Miles per gallon: John R. Pierce, "The Fuel Consumption of Automobiles," *Scientific American,* January 1975.

Energy for the villages: Amulya Reddy and Jose Goldemberg, "Energy for the Developing World," *Scientific American,* September 1990.

CHAPTER 5

Page 199   *Food and Agriculture,* a single-topic issue of *Scientific American,* September 1976.

Page 200   Food-production anxiety: William Vogt, *Road to Survival,* Sloane, New York, 1948; Fairfield Osborn, *Limits of the Earth,* Little Brown, Boston, 1953; William Packard and Paul Packard, *Famine—1975!,* Weidenfeld and Nicholson, London, 1968; Garrett Hardin, "The Lifeboat Ethic," *Psychology Today,* September 1974.

Economic history of agriculture: Pierre Crosson, *Agricultural Development and Productivity,* Johns Hopkins University Press, Baltimore, 1976.

Page 203   In metric terms, at 26 kilograms per bushel and 2.47 acres per hectare, these harvests are, respectively: 1.4, 2.1, 7.7, 19.2 metric tons per hectare.

Page 204   The genetics of maize: Paul C. Mangelsdorf, "The Origin of Corn," *Scientific American,* August 1986.

Gene banks: Beadle, George W., "The Ancestry of Corn," *Scientific American,* January 1980.

Page 205   Genetic engineering: *Industrial Microbiology,* a single-topic issue of *Scientific American,* September 1981.

Page 206   Energy in U. S. agriculture: David Pimentel, "Food Production and the Energy Crisis," *Science* vol. 182, 2 November 1973; David Pimentel, ed., *Handbook of Energy Utilization in Agriculture,* CRC Press, Boca Raton, Florida, 1980.

Page 208   Petacalorie: The numeration employing prefixes from Greek for each successive third power of 10 (kilo = 10^3, mega = 10^6, beva = 10^9, tera = 10^{12}, peta = 10^{15}, and so on) was adopted for scientific literature to avert confusion occasioned by national idiosyncrasies in denotation by the Latin "billion," "trillion," etc. Thus billion in U.S. and French usage denotes 10^9, but denotes 10^{12} in British usage; correspondingly, quadrillion denotes 10^{15} (i.e., peta) and 10^{24} in the two usages, respectively.

Page 210   The green revolution: Edwin J. Wellhausen, "The Agriculture of Mexico," *Scientific American,* September 1976; R. Hertford, *Sources of Change in Mexican Agricultural Production, 1940–1965,* U.S. Department of Agriculture, Foreign Agricultural Economics Report #73, 1971.

Page 211   IRRI: M. S. Swaminathan, "Rice," *Scientific American,* January 1984.

Page 212   Technology in agricultural economics: Vernon Ruttan, "Implications of Technical Change for International Relations in Agriculture," at conference on Technology and Agricultural Policy, National Academy of Sciences, December 1986, Washington, D. C.

Page 215   Measurement of soil erosion: Herbert Friedman, "The Science of Global Change," in *Global Change* [see note for Chapter 1, page 37].

Page 216   Hazards of irrigation: Istvan Szabolcz, "Agrarian Change," background paper for WCED, 1985.

Page 217   Nitrogen fixation: C. C. Delwiche, "The NitrogenCycle," *Scientific American,* September 1970.

Page 218   Eutrophication: Edward S. Deevey, Jr., "Bogs," *Scientific American,* October 1958.

Page 219   Phosphorus in life processes: Peter C. Hinkle, and Richard E. McCarthy, "How Cells Make ATP," *Scientific American,* March 1978.

Page 220   Organic farming: Robert Rodale, "Regenerating our Agriculture," paper for Only One Earth Forum 1987, René Dubos Center for Human Environments, New York.

Page 221   Parity: Bruce L. Gardner, *The Economics of Agricultural Policies,* Macmillan, New York, 1987.

Page 222   Subsidization of agriculture: Vernon Ruttan, "Technology and the Environment," *American Journal of Agricultural Economics,* vol. 53, no. 5, December 1971.

Page 224   Plantation exports: G. L. Beckford, *Persistent Poverty: Underdevelopment in Plantation Economies,* Oxford University Press, New York, 1972.

Page 225   Agriculture in the strategy of economic development: Subrata Chatak and Ken Ingersent, *Agriculture and Economic Development,* Johns Hopkins University Press, Baltimore 1984; C. K. Eicher and J. M. Staatz, eds., *Agricultural Development in the Third World,* Johns Hopkins University Press, Baltimore 1984; Pierre Crosson, "Agicultural Development — "Looking to the Future" in *Sustainable Development of the Biosphere,* [see note to Chapter 1, page 40.]; Michael Lipteon, *Why Poor People Stay Poor—Urban Bias in World Development,* Harvard University Press, Cambridge, Mass., 1976.

Page 226   Backward sloping supply curve: Food and Agriculture Organization, *State of Food and Agriculture 1960,* FAO, Rome, 1961.

Page 227   Economics of agricultural development: T. W. Schultz, *Transforming Traditional Agriculture,* Yale University Press, New Haven, 1964.

CHAPTER 6

Page 237   Circular and cumulative causation: Gunnar Myrdal, *Economic Theory and Underdeveloped Nations,* Duckworth, London, 1957.

Page 238   Freight rates: Tennessee Valley Authority, *The Interterritorial Freight Rate Problem of the United States,* G. P. O., Washington, D. C., 1937.

Planning of development: Edward S. Mason, *Economic Planning in Underdeveloped Areas,* Fordham University Press, New York, 1958; Benjamin Higgins, *Economic Development,* W. W. Norton, New York, 1959.

New Deal in the U.S. South: Arthur E. Goldschmidt, "The Development of the U.S. South," *Scientific American,* September 1963.

Page 340   Group of Experts: see note for Chapter 1, page 25.

Page 243   Preindustrial countries in the world economy: Barbara Ward and René Dubos, *Only One Earth,* George J. McLeod Ltd, Toronto, 1972.

Page 246   Transnational corporations in world economy: see note for Chapter 1, page 28.

Page 249   Trade and development: A. Fishlow et al., *Rich Nations and Poor Nations in the World Economy,* Council on Foreign Relations,

New York, 1978; UNCTAD, *Handbook of international trade and development statistics, 1987 Supplement,* United Nations (E/F.87.II.D.10), New York 1988; UNIDO, *Handbook of Industrial Statistics,* 1988, UNIDO (E/F.88.III.E.5), Vienna 1988.

Page 252   World trade and investment in preindustrial countries: R. Ballance, J. Ansari, and H. Singer, *The International Economy and Industrial Development,* Allenheld, Osmun & Co., Totowa, N. J. 1982; A. G. Frank, *On Capitalist Underdevelopment,* Oxford University Press, New York, 1975.

Page 256   *Maquiladora:* Seymour Melman, *Profits Without Production,* University of Pennsylvania Press, Philadelphia, 1986; Sandy Tolan, "The Border Boom", *New York Times Magazine,* 1 July 1990.

Page 259   Development in economic theory: Albert O. Hirschman, *Strategy of Economic Development,* Yale University Press, New Haven, 1958; UNIDO, *Industry in a Changing World,* United Nations (E.83.II.B.6), New York, 1983; C. H. Kirkpatrick, et al., *Industrial Structure and Policy in Less Developed Countries,* George Allen & Unwin. London, 1984; Robert H. Bates, ed., *Toward a Political Economy of Development,* University of California Press, Berkeley, 1988; Paul A. Baran, *The Political Economy of Growth,* Monthly Review Press, New York, 1957.

Page 262   State intervention in industrialization: UNIDO expert group conferences, Vienna, May 1978 and October 1981 — issue papers by Praxy J. Fernandez, ID/WG.298/6 and ID/WG.343/1, Pavel Sicherl ID/WG.298/9 and JavedA. Ansari ID/WG.343/3; "Approach to Evaluating Performance of Public Industrial Enterprises," *Industry and Development Global Report 1988,* UNIDO, Vienna 1989.

South Korea: Leroy Jones, *Public Enterprises and Economic Development,* Korean Development Institute, 1975.

Mexico: Rocio Villarreal and René Villarreal, UNIDO ID/WG.298/5 and ID/WG.343/3.

Brazil: UNIDO/IS.357.

India: A. K. Roychowdhury, et al. UNIDO/IS.367.

Page 264   The new international economic order: J. N. Bhagwati, *The New International Economic Order in the North-South Debate,* M. I. T. Press, Cambridge, 1977.

Page 265   Disarmament and economic assistance: Wassily W. Leontief, *The Future of the World Economy,* Oxford University Press, New York, 1977; Wassily W. Leontief, "The World Economy in the Year 2000," *Scientific American,* September 1980.

Page 266   Economic assistance vs. coercion: Egon Glesinger, "The Mediterranean Project," *Scientific American,* July 1960.

Page 267   Debt and development: The World Bank, *World Development*

Report 1986, Oxford University Press, New York, 1986; G. K. Helleiner, "Balance of Payments Experience and Growth Prospects of Developing Countries" and Tony Killick, "Unsettled Questions about Adjustment," in UNCTAD, *International Monetary and Financial Issues for the Developing Countries,* United Nations (E.87.II.D.3), New York, 1987.

Page 269   Steel capacity in preindustrial countries: UNIDO, *Picture for 1985 of World Iron and Steel Industry* UNIDO ICIS/386, June 1980.

Page 271   World ranking of Chinese industries: calculations by Lin Xizin, former editor, *China Industrial Daily.*

Page 272   Public industrial enterprises in India: "The Emergence of Third World Multinationals," *World Development,* Pergamon, London, 1989.

Bharat Heavy Electricals Ltd: V. Krishnamurthy, UNIDO ID/WG.343/9.

Pakistan: Abid Hussain, UNIDO ID/WG.298/7 and UNIDO ID/WG.343/8 and Reza M. Syed, UNIDO IS/355.

Bangladesh: Muzaffer Ahmad, UNIDO IS/365.

Page 276   Japanese enterprise in the economic development of East and Southeast Asia: Peter N Nemetz, ed., *The Pacific Rim,* University of British Columbia Press, Vancouver 1990; Peter N. Nemetz, "Selected Issues in Pacific Basin Development," *Journal of Business Administration,* vol. 17, nos. 1 & 2, 1987–1988, University of British Columbia, Vancouver, 1989.

Page 281   Venezuela: UNIDO IS.381.

CHAPTER 7

Page 283   The essence of freedom: Alfred N. Whitehead, *Adventures of Ideas,* Free Press, Glencoe, Illinois, 1967.

Page 285   Indicators of human development: United Nations Development Program (UNDP), *Human Development Report 1990,* Oxford University Press, New York, 1990.

Page 287   Poverty: World Bank, *World Development Report 1990,* Oxford University Press, New York, 1990.

Page 291   Urbanization of poverty: *Cities,* a single-topic issue of *Scientific American,* September 1965; UN Centre for Human Settlements (HABITAT), *Global Report 1986,* Oxford University Press, New York 1987; Jorge E. Hardoy and David Satterthwaite, "Urban Change in the Third World," *Habitat International,* vol. 10, no. 3, 1986.

Page 292   Urban implosion in Africa: Tade Akin Aina, "Africa's...Urban Condition," Only One Earth Forum 1987, René Dubos Center for Human Environments, New York.

Page 293   Sociology of the shantytown: Jorge E. Hardoy, and David

Satterthwaite, "Third World Cities and the Environment of Poverty," *Geoforum,* vol. 15, no. 3, 1984.

Page 294   *Cotadesasi:* McGee, T. G., "The Urban Transition in Asia", Only One Earth Forum 1987, René Dubos Center for Human Environments, New York.

Page 295   Comparative necessity in the shantytown: Jorge E. Hardoy and David Satterthwaite "Shelter, Infrastructure and Services in Third World Cities," Habitat International, 1986; Charles Abrams, *Man's Struggle for Shelter,* M.I.T. Press, Cambridge, 1964.

Page 296   Water and sanitation: see note page 291, HABITAT; Ralph Gackenheimer, "Urban Infrastructure," Only One Earth Forum 1987, René Dubos Center for Human Environments, New York.

Cities and their environment: "The Metabolism of Cities," Abel Wolman, *Scientific American,* September 1965.

Page 297   Urban poverty in Rio de Janeiro: Janice E. Perlman, *The Myth of Marginality,* University of California Press, Berkeley, 1976.

Page 298   Waste as resource: Nadia Khouri-Dagher, "Waste Recycling," background paper for WCED, 1985.

Page 303   Equity in economic development: Irma Adelman, *Economic Growth and Social Equity in Developing Countries,* Stanford University Press, Stanford, Calif., 1973; C. R. Frank et al., *Income Distribution and Economic Growth,* Brookings Institution, Washington, D.C., 1977.

Child welfare in Latin America: Oscar Altimir, "Poverty, Income Distribution and Child Welfare...," *World Development,* March 1984.

Page 308   World population projections: The World Bank annual *World Development Report* summarizes the current detailed projections set out in the annual *World Population Prospects* by the Population Division of the UN Secretariat.

Page 315   Investment in human capital: Khadija Haq and Kirdar Uner, *Development for People,* UNDP (E.89.III.B.L.), New York, 1989.

Donor's discretion: Gunnar Myrdal, "Political Factors in Economic Assistance," *Scientific American,* April 1972; in the allocation of economic assistance, the declared policy of the German government is to "look closely at the level of spending for arms and at such factors as human rights and economic freedoms in the various countries." *The New York Times* 3 August 1991.

Page 320   Advice from free-market dogma: The World Bank, "Introduction," *World Development Report 1986,* Oxford University Press, New York, 1986.

Counter counsel: Hollis Chenery, et al., *Redistribution with Growth,* Oxford University Press, Oxford, 1974; Tony Killick, "Twenty-five Years in Development," *Development Review,* June 1986; Georges

Chapelin and Hamid Tabatabai, *Development and Adjustment,* UNDP, New York, 1989.

Income distribution, economic growth and fertility: J. E. Kocher, *Rural Development, Income Distribution and Fertility Decline,* Population Council, New York, 1973; R. E. Looney, *Income Distribution and Economic Growth in Underdeveloped Countries,* Praeger, New York, 1975; W. R. Cline, "The potential effect of income redistribution on economic growth in four Latin American countries," *Development Digest* vol. 9, no. 4, 1971.

Page 324   Multilateralism: Okita Saburo, "The Future of Multilateralism," background paper for WCED, 1985.

River valley development: Maurice A. Garbell, "The Jordan Valley Plan," *Scientific American,* March 1965; Gilbert F. White, "The Mekong River Plan," *Scientific American,* April 1963; United Nations, *Proceedings, Scientific Conference on the Conservation and Utilization of Resources,* vol. 4, "Water Resources," [1950.II.B.5] Lake Success, New York, 1949.

Page 326   Willard Bascom, "The Disposal of Waste in the Ocean," *Scientific American,* August 1974.

Page 328   John Stuart Mill, *Principles of Political Economy,* University of Toronto Press, Toronto, 1965.

NONGOVERNMENTAL ORGANIZATIONS AND PRIVATE VOLUNTARY ORGANIZATIONS

Alexis de Tocqueville, in *Democracy in America,* his account of his visit to the country in 1831–1832 that so uncannily describes the country we know today, observed:

> Americans of all ages, all conditions, and all dispositions constantly form associations. . . . to give entertainments, to found establishments for education, to construct churches, to diffuse books, to send missionaries to the antipodes. . . . If it be proposed to advance some truth or to foster some feeling by the encouragement of a great example, they form a society.

The penchant for voluntary enterprise still grips the citizens of the United States. The "third" or "independent" sector of nonprofit activity in some avowed public interest—not the ballot box—is the site of self-government. In its educational institutions, hospitals, philanthropic foundations, charitable enterprises, community-action corps, movements, causes, and pressure groups, it turns over, by the estimate of the economist Eli Ginsberg, more than 10 percent of the country's GNP. It engages more or less of the lifetime of every active citizen. It commands the policies and programs of the government more directly and decisively than the vote.

For all their vaunting pride in it, the American people hold no monopoly on this kind of activity. Something like their third sector has the same role in the life of every industrial country and is emergent in every preindustrial country touched by industrialization. Immediately upon their release from the suffocating embrace of the Stalin dictatorship, the people of the Soviet Union were organizing movements for every cause and purpose, from the preservation of wooden treasures of medieval church architecture to the rescue of

Lake Baikal from pollution by the paper mills on its shores. Voluntary enterprise in avowed public interests tests, on every front, the practicability of purpose opened up by industrial revolution.

For the United Nations, nongovernmental organizations (NGOs) and private voluntary organizations (PVOs) by-pass national governments in every member country to create a worldwide constituency of individual citizens. It was the volunteer enterprise of individuals, not of government officials, that created the technical agencies of the United Nations, as noted in Chapter 1 (pages 25–26). The newest of those agencies, the United Nations Environment Program, grew out of the agitation of the conservation and environmental movements that convened the UN Conference on Human Environment in Stockholm in 1972. In 141 countries, those movements have compelled the creation of environmental protection agencies.

The concern for human and economic development in the preindustrial countries that must take its place alongside anxiety about the environment in public opinion and policy has recruited its own constituency of individuals and organizations. In the United States, some hundreds of organizations have made this concern theirs. Some, with religious affiliation, now send physicians and agronomists as well as missionaries to the antipodes; some proceed from convictions in economic theory; some mobilize members of the learned professions to bring their competences to bear; some reflect recognition of the claims of economic development by the environmental movement. In the preindustrial countries, these organizations deploy more than $2 billion a year, nearly all of it from private pockets, but including congressional appropriations induced by their activity. A central switchboard reaching nearly 200 of these organizations is **Interaction,** the short name for:

The American Council for Voluntary International Action
Peter J. Davies, Executive Officer
1717 Massachusetts Avenue, NW, 8th floor
Washington, DC 20036
Telephone: (202) 667-8227
Fax: (202) 667-8236

A sampling from its directory, which suggests the broad range of activities in which an individual may become engaged, is given here.

Also included are organizations not listed in the **Interaction** directory.

ACCION International / AITEC
William W. Burrus, Executive Director
130 Prospect Street
Cambridge, MA 02139
Telephone: (617) 492-4930
Fax: (617) 876-9509
Mircroenterprise development; offering consultation, training, and credit to tiny family businesses in Latin America.

African-American Institute (AAI)
Vivian Lowery Derryck, President
833 United Nations Plaza
New York, NY 10017
Telephone: (212) 949-5666
Fax: (212) 682-6174
Promotion of trade with, and investment in, Africa by bringing together African and American business and government leaders; fellowships to African students for graduate study in development-related fields; counsel on development policy to African governments; biweekly U.S. Congressional seminars.

African Medical and Research Foundation (AMREF)
Dr. James R. Sheffield, President
420 Lexington Avenue
New York, NY 10017
Telephone: (212) 986-1835
Fax: (212) 599-5064
In Kenya, Somalia, Sudan, Tanzania, and Uganda, training for village health workers; organization of rural health services linked by radio referral networks and "flying doctor" teams; research in endemic diseases, including AIDS.

Aga Khan Foundation, USA (AKF)
Iqbal Noor Ali, Chief Executive Officer
1901 L Street NW, Suite 700
Washington, DC 20036
Telephone: (202) 293-2537
Fax: (202) 785-1752
Programs in community development centered on early-

childhood education, maternal and child health, and improvement of agricultural productivity by timely delivery of credit, seeds, fertilizer, and new technology, primarily in Africa and South Asia.

Air Serv International
Robert E. Lehnhart, President and Chief Executive Officer
P. O. Box 3041
1902 Orange Tree Lane, Suite 200
Redlands, CA 92373
Telephone: (714) 793-7267
Fax: (714) 793-0226
Air transport service and disaster response in sub-Saharan Africa; international roster of pilots experienced in operation of single- and twin-engine aircraft in difficult environments.

American Friends Service Committee (AFSC)
Corinne B. Johnson, Secretary, International Division
1501 Cherry Street
Philadelphia, PA 19102
Telephone: (215) 241-2750
Fax: (215) 241-7026
Community organization with focus on role of women; well-digging and improvement of water and sanitation systems; school, housing, and clinic construction; new crops and methods in agriculture, horticulture, and animal husbandry.

Amigos de las Americas
Margaret Guerriero, President
5618 Star Lane
Houston, TX 77057
Telephone: (713) 782-5290
Fax: (713) 782-9267
In the Caribbean region and Central America, reforestation projects; well-digging and installation of sanitation systems; school construction; health education, oral rehydration therapy, immunization services, and suppression of rabies by inoculation of local animals.

The Brother's Brother Foundation
Luke L. Hingson, Executive Director
824 Grandview Avenue

Pittsburgh, PA 15211
Telephone: (412) 431-1600
Fax: (412) 431-9116
Supplying pharmaceutical and medical equipment to large medical centers; books and teaching materials to educational systems; vegetable seeds and hand tools to national agricultural-development programs. Long-term commitments in Latin America and sub-Saharan Africa.

Center for International Development and Environment
(World Resources Institute)
    Thomas H. Fox, Director
1709 New York Avenue, NW, 7th floor
Washington, DC 20006
Telephone: (202) 638-6300
Fax: (202) 638-0036
Information and counsel on the connections among economic development, the environment, and human needs to donors in industrial countries and to government agencies, voluntary organizations, and local community groups in preindustrial countries in Latin America, South Asia, and sub-Saharan Africa.

Church World Service (CWS)
    Lani J. Havens, Executive Director
475 Riverside Drive
New York, NY 10115-0050
Telephone: (212) 870-2257
Fax: (212) 870-2055
Programs, throughout the preindustrial world, in community development; organization and financing of cooperatives; promotion of crafts and cottage industries; production, processing, storage, and marketing of agricultural products; sanitation and water supply; primary health care; child nutrition; family planning.

Food for the Hungry, Inc.
    Dr. Tetsunao Yamamori, Chief Executive Officer
7729 East Greenway Road
Scottsdale, AZ 85260
Telephone: 1 (800) 248-6437   (602) 998-3100
Fax: (602) 443-1420
Elimination of causes of hunger by development and introduc-

tion of appropriate and small-scale technologies; construction of irrigation systems; aquaculture, poultry, livestock, and horticulture projects; demonstration and training centers in Mexico, Bolivia, Chad, and Thailand. "Hunger Corps" members volunteer for two-week to three-year stays in poor communities.

Heifer Project International

Thomas H. Hemphill, Executive Director
1015 South Louisiana Street
P.O. Box 808
Little Rock, AR 72203
Telephone: 1 (800) 422-0474   (501) 376-6836
Fax: (501) 376-8906
Increase of protein in food supply of preindustrial countries (in Latin America, East Asia, South Asia, and sub-Saharan Africa) by providing high-quality livestock, equipment, and technical support and by developing livestock-breeding programs.

International Center for Research on Women

Mayra Buvinic, President
1717 Massachusetts Avenue, NW
Washington, DC 20036
Telephone: (202) 797-0007
Fax:(202) 797-0020
Improvement of women's participation in, and benefit from, development programs by research on role of women in preindustrial cultures and countries and dissemination of information to makers of development policy.

Laubach Literacy International

Robert F. Caswell, President
1320 Jamesville Avenue
P.O. Box 131
Syracuse, NY 13210
Telephone: (315) 422-9121
Fax: (315) 422-6369
Instruction for illiterate and newly literate adults in communication skills for their participation in community government and enterprise; emphasis on participation of women.

Osborn Center for Conservation and Development
(World Wildlife Fund—The Conservation Foundation)
    R. Michael Wright, Senior Vice President
1250 Twenty-fourth Street, NW
Washington, DC 20037
Telephone: (202) 293-4800
Fax: (202) 293-9211
Engagement of village people in management of natural resources in connection with grassroots economic-development enterprises in Latin America, Asia, and sub-Saharan Africa.

Oxfam America, Inc.
    Dr. John C. Hammock, Executive Director
115 Broadway
Boston, MA 02116
Telephone: (617) 482-1211   (617) 728-2506—direct
Fax: (617) 556-8925   (617) 338-0187
Self-reliant, participatory development programs in village communities, emphasizing engagement of women; provision of seeds, tools, animals, counsel, and loans to agricultural cooperatives; training of village health workers backed by mobile medical units.

René Dubos Center for Human Environments
    Ruth and William Eblen, Co-Directors
100 East Eighty-first Street
New York, NY 10128
Telephone: (212) 249-7745
Fax: (212) 772-2033
Development of public opinion and policy on questions of environment and economic development; conflict resolution in annual Only One Earth Forum, bringing together independent-sector activists and government and industrial decision-makers; public education through all media.

Rodale Institute
    James O. Morgan, Executive Director
222 Main Street
Emmaus, PA 18098
Telephone: (215) 967-5171
Fax: (215) 967-3044
Promotion of regenerative agricultural technology to planners of

development programs and to village farmers in sub-Saharan Africa, Latin America, and Asia.

Technoserve
Edward P. Bullard IV, President
49 Day Street
Norwalk, CT 06854-3106
Telephone: 1 (800) 999-6757
Fax: (203) 838-6717
Stimulation of enterprise contributing to rural productivity; managerial and technical assistance; supervision of design and construction of plant; selection and installation of technologically appropriate equipment; management in temporary, turn-around situations.

Trickle Up Program
Mildred Robbins Leet and Glen Leet, Co-Directors
54 Riverside Drive
New York, NY 10024-6509
Telephone: (212) 362-7958
Fax: (212) 877-7464
Financing for microenterprise in preindustrial countries: to five-member (at least) partnerships, a first installment of $50 upon submission of business plan; second installment of $50 after 1000 hours of operation and reinvestment of 20 percent of profit (20,000 enterprises financed in nearly 100 countries).

VITA
Henry Norman, President
1600 Wilson Boulevard
Arlington, VA 22201
Telephone: (703) 276-1800
Fax: (703) 243-1865
Consultation services to agricultural, small manufacturing, community-development and resource-development enterprises; data bank on expertise of volunteer engineers and scientists matched to enquiries from preindustrial countries (25,000 enquiries in 1991); provision of financial and managerial assistance to commercial enterprises; VITASAT satellite communications network in sub-Saharan Africa; VITANET electronic work-station access to technical assistance and commodities databases.

INDEX

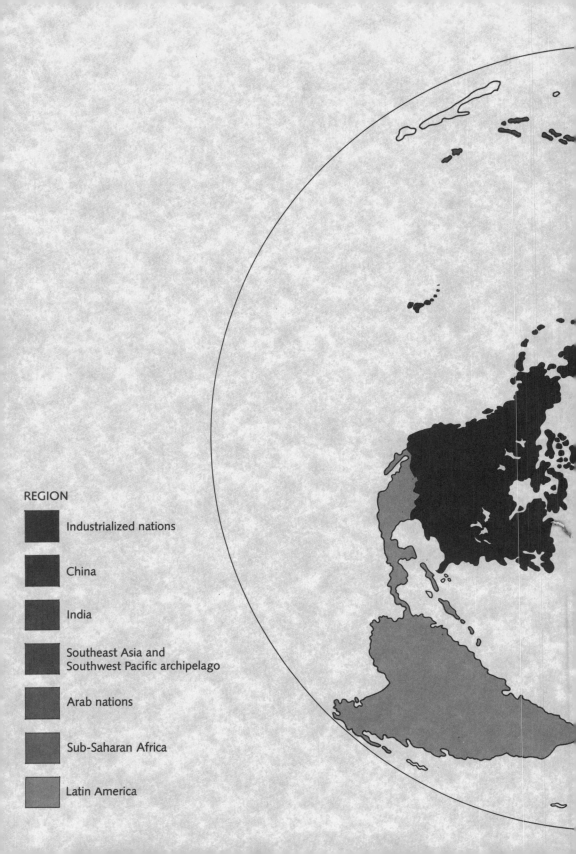

REGION

Industrialized nations

China

India

Southeast Asia and
Southwest Pacific archipelago

Arab nations

Sub-Saharan Africa

Latin America